University of the
West of England

**BOLLAND
LIBRARY**

Please ensure that this book is returned by the end of
the loan period for which it is issued.

13. JAN 2006

11. JAN 2007
12. JAN 2007

FR - Sm

01. JUN 2007

28. APR 2009

Telephone Renewals: 0117 328 2092 (24 hours)
Library Web Address: www.uwe.ac.uk/library

Globalization and Identity: Dialectics of Flow and Closure

Edited by
Birgit Meyer and Peter Geschiere

First published in 1999

Blackwell Publishers
108 Cowley Road, Oxford OX4 1JF, UK

and
350 Main Street
Malden, MA 02148, USA

British Library Cataloguing in Publication Data

A CIP catalogue record for this book is available from the British Library

Library of Congress Cataloguing-in-Publication Data applied for

ISBN 0 631 212388

This text was originally published
as special issue 29:4 of
Development and Change,
Published by Blackwell Publishers
on behalf of the Institute of
Social Studies, The Hague.

Printed in Great Britain by Whitstable Litho, Whitstable, Kent.

Contents

Theoretical Reflections

Globalization and Identity: Dialectics of Flow and Closure

Introduction

Birgit Meyer and Peter Geschiere

The more current the notion of globalization becomes, the more it seems to be beset with vagueness and inconsistencies. The notion as such and the complex reality it attempts to grasp are therefore met with a mixture of uneasiness and fascination by social scientists. This lack of clarity is not exceptional — it seems to be the fate of many fashionable terms and probably also the cause of their popularity — and it is no reason to abandon the notion altogether. Even if globalization amounts to nothing more than a sensitizing notion, rather than an analytical concept, it is important to realize that the ambiguities it calls forth issue urgent challenges, not merely on the level of theory but also with regard to a better understanding of actual global entanglements and the crises to which they give rise.

One of these ambiguities — central to this volume — is that the homogenizing tendencies which appear inherent to globalization as such, seem to imply a continued or even intensified heterogeneity in cultural terms. Economists, political scientists and mass communications experts were the first to explicitly address globalization and attempt to formulate a theory of globality. Their approach was characterized by a strong emphasis on homogenizing effects: through the impact of new technologies of communication and transport, and the intensified circulation of goods and people on a global scale, cultural difference was supposed to disappear. Whether homogenization is seen positively in terms of McLuhan's utopia of the 'global village', or negatively in terms of Western imperialism, both views thrive on the assumption that the world is moving rapidly towards uniformity.[1]

This one-sided emphasis on increasing homogeneity became highly questionable with the more recent attention paid to explicitly cultural

---

With many thanks to Peter Pels, who had to abandon us because he was called to other duties in our programme, but who helped lay the groundwork for this Introduction and for the volume as a whole, and whose editorial fervour set us an example.

1. Seminal examples for this stance are Hamelink (1983); McLuhan (1994/1964); McLuhan and Powers (1989).

aspects of globalization. The shift towards culture certainly does not entail a neglect of processes of cultural uniformization on a global scale, such as the globalization of certain styles of consumption that have struck so many observers (McDonalds and Coca-Cola are the rather tired examples that are usually referred to in this context). Yet it has become increasingly clear that this uniformization generates an emphasis on cultural difference. Often it is the process of globalization itself that appears to lead to a hardening of cultural contrasts or even to engender new oppositions.[2] As the 'global and local are the two faces of the same movement' (Hall, 1991), paradoxically, the culturally homogenizing tendencies of globalization imply continued or even reinforced cultural heterogeneity.

Closely related to this paradox is the precarious balance between 'global flows' and 'cultural closure'. There is much empirical evidence that people's awareness of being involved in open-ended global flows seems to trigger a search for fixed orientation points and action frames, as well as determined efforts to affirm old and construct new boundaries. For students of globalization it is therefore important to develop an understanding of globalization that not only takes into account the rapid increase in mobility of people, goods and images,[3] but also the fact that, in many places, flow goes hand in hand with a closure of identities which often used to be much more fuzzy and permeable.[4] This tension between globalization and identity, between 'flow' and 'closure' — with its violent implications in many parts of the present-day world — is a central focus of the contributions that follow.

Of 'Flux' and 'Fix': Locality as an Issue

A seminal implication of the problem of how to deal with 'flow' *and* 'closure', 'flux' *and* 'fix', is that it highlights the precariousness of locality, not only as a self-evident unit of study for social scientists, but also as a given orientation point for the people being studied. It is this worrying convergence between perspectives of social scientists and of the people concerned that makes recent debates among anthropologists on the issue of locality relevant to a much broader audience. Globalization issues a crucial challenge to 'the mutually constitutive relationship between anthropology and locality', as Appadurai (1996: 178) puts it. Anthropology's emphasis on fieldwork inspires a preference for bounded localities, easy to survey, as the apposite

---

2. Cf. Appadurai (1996); Bayart (1994, 1996); Clifford (1988); Featherstone (1990); Friedman (1994); Hannerz (1987); Jameson (1983); Miller (1995); Robertson (1992).
3. Cf. Appadurai's focus on 'media and migration' as the major 'diacritics of globalization' (1996: 30); on the importance of imagination, see also ibid: 30ff.
4. Cf. Bayart who, in his recent book (a determined effort to pierce *l'illusion identitaire*) emphasizes the paradoxical relation between globalization and *clôture culturelle* (Bayart, 1996: 23).

unit of study. However, globalization directly undermines this search for boundedness, so strong in anthropology but equally present in other branches of social sciences; after all, classification and marking boundaries seem to be basic to scientific research. The 'primitive isolate' may have been exposed as an anthropological myth for some time now; but more recently, other units of study, such as 'the village' or 'the tribe', current in other branches of the social sciences as well, have also turned out to be, to a large extent, products of the scientific imagination.

The inspiring capacity of the notion of globalization is precisely that it forces social scientists to critically reflect upon how they construct their objects, and to search for more appropriate fields of investigation which take into account people's actual entanglement in wider processes. For, whether one likes the term or not, and whenever one deems the process to have begun (since time immemorial or just recently, with the spread of electronic media), debates about globalization have contributed a great deal to the deconstruction of any naïve understanding of locality as given, and have broadened the scope of investigation towards creole cultures, transnational movements and emerging diasporas (Kearney, 1995; see also note 3).

However, the importance of locality as an issue surpasses the field of anthropology or even social science in general. As indicated above, anthropologists' obsession with boundedness is paralleled by the ways in which the people they study try to deal with seemingly open-ended global flows. The search for fixed orientation points and the re-affirmation of boundaries is a common element in people's interpretation of globalization, throughout the world — not only in communalist movements in India or ethnic revivals in Africa, but equally in the propaganda of the new right in Europe. A closer understanding of 'the production of locality' — a theme so strongly emphasized by Appadurai (1996: 178ff.) — is indeed a crucial issue if one wants to understand globalization's paradoxical articulation of flow and closure, flux and fix.

One of the main merits of the notion of globalization might therefore be that it signals the problem of how to 'grasp the flux' (Hannerz, 1992) — both for social scientists and the people involved — without either evoking a deceiving image of globalization processes as free flows for all on a worldwide scale, or stubbornly clinging to bounded units that were, to a large extent, imaginary all along. This is indeed a difficult challenge. As John Kelly argues in this volume, 'to grasp the flux' requires us to dismiss 'the idea that the world is a collection of nameable groups'. In order to develop concepts which are suited to 'grasping the flux', social scientists have to struggle hard to get away from the intellectual habit of 'fixing (. . .) practices, spaces and countries into a map of static differences' (Appadurai, 1996: 18). As Fabian already suggested some time ago, there is a need to 'liquidate' culture, that is, to exchange a static, homogenizing concept of culture in favour of more open, fluid notions which are able to contain the making and unmaking of localities and the shifting of boundaries which these processes entail (Fabian,

1991: Ch. 10).[5] Globalization urges us to focus rather on 'zones of control or of abandonment, of recollection and forgetting, of force or of dependence, of exclusiveness or of sharing, all taking place in the global history that is our element' (Said, 1989: 225). However, this is only possible if we leave behind the classic view — propagated by anthropology, but internalized by social scientists in general *and* by the people concerned — of the world as a conglomerate of separate and internally homogeneous cultures, each with its own essence, so that intercultural contacts are understood in terms of loss of authenticity.

Despite an ongoing and devastating critique, this premise still informs views of globalization in terms of 'Americanization' or 'Westernization' and hence as threatening to erase cultural diversity. The anti-imperialist tenor of such views is certainly to the point, but the problem is that it seems to be intrinsically related to a vision of authentic cultures that have to be protected against the onslaught of cultural imperialism. If we want to take globalization's challenge seriously, we have to surpass such notions — notably by showing how these 'endangered' cultures themselves emerged historically from the colonial enterprise and the ensuing world order. Far from celebrating globalization merely in terms of a creative blending of different, pre-existing cultural traditions, the contributions to this volume try to unravel the politics of the making and unmaking of boundaries, localities and 'cultures' in particular power constellations. Striking examples of this are provided by Seteney Shami's examination of the emergence of a self-conscious Circassian diaspora in different countries of the Middle East and the *bricolages* triggered by the sudden reopening up of their 'homeland' in the former Soviet Empire. Similar concatenations can be studied on a national level, as in Prasenjit Duara's account of the struggle of the Chinese nation-state to domesticate transnational discourses; but also in informal networks at the bottom of

---

5. In anthropology, the notion of 'culture', once taken for granted, is increasingly under siege: see Clifford, who advocates a more ambiguous 'Caribbean' notion of culture, referring to Aimé Césaire and his way of 'reconceiving organic culture ... as inventive process or creolized "interculture"' (Clifford, 1988: 15). Appadurai (1996: 12) wants to avoid 'culture' as a noun since it carries associations of substance, but to retain the adjective 'cultural' since it relates to 'differences, contrasts and comparisons'. Bayart (1996) dedicates a whole chapter to the question *Culture, un mot à jeter?* ('Culture, a word to get rid of?'). In Castoriadis' traces, he proposes abandoning the term 'culture' altogether and replacing it by *l'imaginaire*, since this term has an intrinsic association of ambivalence (*'l'imaginaire a trait à cette zone grise entre le vrai et le faux ... Siège des passions, de l'esthétique, de l'éthique, de l'activité symbolique, l'imaginaire est par définition le domaine de l'ambivalence ...'* ibid: 166). It is striking, however, that elsewhere in the same book, Bayart feels obliged to exercise considerable caution in order to avoid this notion of *l'imaginaire* acquiring the same static and deterministic overtones as 'culture' (ibid: 225). Apparently all notions in this field are threatened by such ossifying tendencies. Instead of abandoning 'culture', one should rather take into account the double-sidedness of this notion and investigate the interplay of its closed, conservative *and* open, creative potentials (de Certeau, 1980: 238–9).

society, as in Norman Long and Magdalena Villarreal's analysis of the different meanings which maize husks achieve after crossing the border between Mexico and the USA.

While transnational flows are the explicit focus of the three contributions just mentioned, the other authors in this volume also start from the premise that there are no absolute boundaries unaffected by global flows. The consequence is that they try to study in detail the local forms which these flows take, since it is especially by following and comparing such different trajectories that we can take up the challenge posed by globalization. The detailed historical, ethnographic, or sociological studies in this volume of particular 'sites', where the blending of global flows with the local becomes visible, can therefore offer an important (and still scarce) supplement to the plethora of studies of globalization from a bird's eye perspective.[6]

As suggested above, however, the necessity to develop theoretical concepts suitable 'to grasp the flux' should not be mistaken for an assertion that globalization would entail mere flow. One of the dangers of this notion is, indeed, that it easily suggests a free flow of people, goods and images throughout the globe. This makes the notion particularly galling for people from more marginalized quarters of the world economy. As Mbembe (forthcoming) so graphically puts it: for the poor in Africa — and probably elsewhere — globalization only seems to mean 'licking at the shop-window' ('*lécher la vitrine*'). A related problem is that the notion can be easily equated with the disappearance of boundaries. Again this is highly misleading. While slogans such as 'There are no borders' characterize the rhetorics of multi-nationals who seek to advertise their products all over the world, global flows actually appear to entice the construction of new boundaries as much as the reaffirmation of old ones. As stated earlier, classical anthropology is not alone in perpetuating the notion of bounded, 'authentic' cultures. In this process of 'cultural closure', notions of 'identity' appear to play a central role. As a lot of recent research (and also a number of contributions to this volume) shows, 'identity' is employed by states in order to create loyal citizens, as much as by groups opposing the state to legitimize claims to alternative forms of allegiance.[7] It looks as if, in a world characterized by flows, a great deal of energy is devoted to controlling and freezing them: grasping the flux often actually entails a politics of 'fixing' — a politics which is, above all, operative in struggles about the construction of identities.

The contrast between these two sides of globalization — global flux versus cultural closure — is highlighted in this volume by the different

---

6. Cf. Jean Comaroff (forthcoming), who notes that 'globalization', 'identity' and other fashionable notions seem to do a kind of vanishing trick with anthropology's familiar topics; this might tempt us 'to situate our studies at levels of generality that fail to capture lived experience, to grasp materialities and meanings as they are produced by ordinary people in ordinary activity'. See also Comaroff and Comaroff (1992).
7. Cf. Baumann (1996); Cohen (1985); Vermeulen and Govers (1994).

tenors of, on the one hand, John Kelly's critical discussion of Ben Anderson's *Imagined Communities*; and, on the other, Wim van Binsbergen's contribution on the 'virtual form' the village has taken in the perceptions of urbanites in Southern Africa, as a continuing orientation point, yet increasingly detached from rural realities. Interestingly, van Binsbergen sees 'virtuality' as a key concept for understanding the forms globalization takes in Africa. It is striking, however, that in his interpretation, this notion of 'virtuality' — in itself a pre-eminently unbounded notion — is related to efforts to reproduce a more or less bounded village space in a new urban setting. This space may be 'virtual' (in the sense of being both related to *and* increasingly 'disconnected' from its formal referent), but it does express a clinging — a 'nostalgic reference' — among urbanites to the village as some sort of primal source of identity. John Kelly, by contrast, criticizes Anderson for his reliance on a similar concept of 'imagined' identity. He tries to surpass these limitations by confronting Anderson's premises with insights from Ruth Benedict and Walter Benjamin. This 'think-piece' does not yet offer clear-cut solutions, but it does highlight, in an original way, the problem of identity-politics in an era of globalization. Kelly argues that Anderson's notion of identity entails its own problems if one wants to understand global flows: it can easily reinforce anthropology's 'intellectual habit of fixing', pointed out by Appadurai (see above); it may serve to revive old notions of bounded spaces and cultures; and it certainly does not meet the challenge 'to grasp the flux'. In this way globalization is reduced to threat and danger, thereby neglecting the creative opportunities it provides, both on the level of actual experiences and social–scientific thinking. Most contributions to this volume address, in one way or another, the tension indicated by the contrasting views of van Binsbergen and Kelly. While on the level of social scientific reflection they refute the view that 'the world is a collection of nameable groups', they investigate processes in the course of which state regimes or socio-political movements try to realize exactly this view by invoking a specific 'identity' as an ultimate reality.

Against the background of such claims it is not surprising that, in recent years, social scientists have shown great interest in the concept of identity. It is also clear that this notion entails its own problems for social scientists who want to take up the challenge raised by globalization processes.

Globalization and Identity

While preparing the conference on which this collection is based and especially while editing this volume, we began to realize that the combination of 'globalization' and 'identity' is a problematic, not to say an explosive one. The full title of the conference, which took place in March 1996 in Amsterdam, was 'Globalization and the Construction of Communal Identities'. This is also the title of the Dutch research programme which organized the conference.[8] A central issue in this programme is the apparent paradox, outlined above, between homogenizing global flows and continued cultural heterogeneity. The Dutch programme focuses particularly on the complex and highly variable processes by which elements of globalization — new images, communication techniques and consumer goods — are used to mark communal, not to say parochial, identities. Examples of such paradoxical articulations will be familiar: in many parts of Africa, accumulation of Western goods is regarded as a sure sign of witchcraft and thus as a way to distinguish between trustworthy and dangerous people; modern technical devices, such as tape recorders, played a crucial role in the spread of Muslim fundamentalism in North Africa and the Middle East, creating a huge market for cassettes of the latest star imam; the recent economic boom of Eastern Asia's newly industrialized countries was accompanied by an equally vibrant boom of spirit cults (see Weller, 1994); Westerners' desire for an encounter with the 'exotic' during their holidays incorporates people all over the world into global relations by requiring them to produce local 'authenticity' as a commodity for global tourism. The precise trajectories of such articulations may differ, yet almost everywhere modern commodities lead to cultural uniformization and, at the same time, to an affirmation of cultural difference.

It is of course not accidental that 'identity' emerges as a central concept in this field of study. As long as globalization is regarded as an overall process of uniformization, there is no need for such a concept, but as soon as this one-sided view is left behind, 'identity' seems to become an inevitable analytical tool in order to grasp how globalization reinforces the production of cultural difference. In the light of the preceding, however, it is also clear that there is good reason to exercise a certain caution. One problem is the double charge of the notion of identity. It refers to people's attempts to 'fix the flow' and mark boundaries in the ongoing flux of globalization processes; but it relates as easily to the nostalgia of social scientists, and notably anthropologists, for the times when it still seemed possible to isolate bounded social formations — when theoretical concepts took the existence

---

8. This programme, initiated and subsidized by NWO/WOTRO (The Hague) brings together more than twenty researchers from the Netherlands and various parts of the South, who study aspects of the central theme in Africa, the Caribbean, and South and Southeast Asia. In 1995, the Dutch programme, together with the departments of anthropology of the University of Chicago and the University of Stockholm, launched the 'Interdisciplinary Network on Globalization'; since then this network has been enriched by the participation of a number of institutes from the South (Centre for Studies in Social Sciences, Calcutta; CEBRAP, Sao Paulo; CODESRIA, Dakar; Middle East Awards, Cairo) and the Faculty of Law and Politics, Rikkyo University, Tokyo. This interdisciplinary network organized a series of conferences (in 1995 in Chicago and Stockholm; in 1996 in Amsterdam; in 1997 in Cairo and Sao Paulo; in 1998 in Calcutta; subsequent conferences are planned for Tokyo and Dakar); one of the aims is to involve institutes from the South more actively in debates on globalization.

of boundaries for granted rather than questioning their, in many cases actually contested, construction. It is precisely this possible confusion between its descriptive and its analytic aspects that can make identity quite dangerous as a notion.[9]

We certainly do not want to advocate a complete rejection of the notion of identity. That might be as chivalrous — or even Don Quixotesque? — as pleas to do away with the concept of culture (see above). Notions such as 'culture' and 'identity' have become so much ingrained in intellectual and, more importantly, in popular jargon that they will still be with us for some time to come. What we do want to suggest is that there are important reasons to question the sudden popularity of the notion of identity which has become, quite imperceptibly, one of the central notions of social science.

Seteney Shami notes with some surprise, in her contribution to this volume, how quickly and completely the notion of identity has eclipsed the notion of class in East European studies, following the collapse of the Soviet empire. Especially in this region, the concept of 'identity' almost inevitably fuses with the idea that present-day tensions are 'only' the re-assertion of old communal feelings, suppressed during the communist regime but apparently 'still the same, after all these years'. There might indeed be good reason to question the 'politics of identity' — not only of the formation of specific identities, but also of the notion as such. Rouse, for instance, has shown how Mexican immigrants learn only in America that they have to have a specific 'identity'. In their home areas, patterns of self-identification are diffuse, permeable and multiple, but in America they are pressurized in all sorts of ways to cultivate and mark their own identity (Rouse, 1995a, 1995b; see also

---

9. See, for instance, Friedman (1994) who, in his explorations on 'Cultural Identity and Global Processes', emphasizes that globalization goes together with 'cultural continuity'; this makes him distrust notions like 'invention of tradition' or 'hybridization'; instead, one of the aims of his collection of articles seems to be to understand the relation between the 'global reordering of social realities' and 'cultural continuity'. This, in itself interesting, programme makes him fall back, in practice, on a highly problematic concept of 'tradition', which — especially in his contributions on Africa — seems to figure as some sort of baseline, just as in the olden days of anthropology. Thus, Friedman characterizes *la politique du ventre* (amazingly enough without any reference to Bayart's use of the term!) as 'the traditional principle' on which African nation states are based (Friedman, 1994: 13). Similarly, he relates the emergence of *les sapeurs*, Brazzaville's colourful dandies, so beautifully described by Justin-Daniel Gandoulou (who again is hardly mentioned), to 'certain fundamental relations' in Congo history which 'were never dissolved'; as an example of such 'fundamental relations' Friedman mentions: 'Life strategies consist in ensuring the flow of life-force. Traditionally this was assured by the social system itself' (ibid: 152). This is the kind of 'convenient' anthropological shorthand which one had hoped to be rid of, certainly in discussions on globalization. Friedman's reversion to such a simplistic use of the notion of tradition as some sort of base line — quite surprising in view of the sophisticated things he has to say about globalization — illustrates how treacherous the triangle of globalization, culture and identity is. Relating postcolonial identities to such a notion of 'tradition' makes anthropology indeed a tricky enterprise.

Long and Villarreal in this volume). Rouse sees this as an inherent part of capitalist discourse with its emphasis on private ownership: one has to 'own' an identity just as the capitalist owns his capital. Therefore, he cautions social scientists not to take the search for identity as a universal, but rather to study it as part and parcel of Western imperialism — strongly promoted, for instance, by the efforts of colonial regimes to fix the identity of their new subjects through the 'identity card'. Chatterjee notes similar processes of fixing identities, which he also relates to the new techniques of domination applied by the modern state — fixing the population by censuses, tax measures, etc., and thus hardening the boundaries of communities that used to be much more diffuse and permeable (Chatterjee, 1993: 221–3). In line with the remarks above, we would add that this fixing not only occurs 'from above', but may also be encouraged by people's own efforts to create clear boundaries and markers in the flux of globalization processes.

Whichever emphasis one favours, it is clear that all this is not mere academic *Spielerei*. For instance, the quite sudden and unexpected eruption of the conceptual opposition between 'autochthons' and 'allochthons' as a crucial political issue in many parts of this globalized world — in Europe and the USA as much as in Malaysia, India or Africa — is worrying. The African examples are particularly striking since one of the hallmarks of African social formations was generally supposed to be their mobility and their inclusive tendencies, which made their boundaries so permeable and shifting that they used to be the despair of social sciences. For some parts of the continent, it even seemed debatable whether one could speak of societies in the sense of clearly demarcated units at all. Yet these same 'open' societies are now deeply marked by debates on who is autochthonous and who is not. A fierce polemic in a recent issue of a Cameroonian newspaper shows the depth of feelings generated by the thorny question of autochthony. A certain Mr Njoh Likumbe, 'Chartered Accountant and politician' in Kumba (in the Southwest Province of Cameroon), proposed the following solution to the problem of identifying the 'real' autochthons: 'Somebody's home is the place where he is buried when he dies'. To which his opponent, Professor Bejanga (who apparently foresaw that, under such conditions, he might not qualify as 'an élite' of Kumba, although he lives there) replied: 'Will I claim home after I am dead and buried? I think my home should not be where I will be buried because I could die in the sea and my corpse never be seen'.[10] Similar altercations lead to violence and bloodshed in many other parts of present-day Africa (and there is a serious risk that they will do so in Cameroon's Southwest Province in the near future). Again, one can cite many parallels from other continents: the sudden emergence of Muslim as an 'ethnic' category in former Yugoslavia or the spectacular re-emergence of Indian

10.   *The Herald* 446 (16–17 April 1997): 6.

nations in North America, raising tricky issues such as the question of who is a 'real' Mashpee and who is not (Clifford, 1988).

Some of the backgrounds to these conflicts are clear. In present-day Africa, for instance, democratization processes reinforce the fear among local groups that they will be dominated by more numerous immigrants. As elsewhere, this combines with worries about increasing pressure on land and other resources and, more generally, with a growing uneasiness about the increasing mobility of people and investments which seems to be an inevitable effect of capitalist development (even, or especially, of its more peripheral forms).

The same opposition between 'autochthons' and 'allochthons' is rapidly emerging as a dominant issue in European politics, under quite different circumstances. Le Pen's formidable success with slogans along these lines in French politics might be as surprising as the emergence of this issue in formerly 'open' African societies. Not that French society was ever marked by a similar degree of openness and mobility, but a fixed adage in the history of French nationalism was that it was not racial but cultural. This was supposed to be its specificity in comparison with other nationalisms. Yet, Le Pen seems to have interpreted this message very differently, and not without success. Again, this can be explained as some sort of rear-guard action, this time from a nation which risks being relegated to a secondary place in capitalism's pecking order and which is, therefore, tempted to invoke nationalism's boundedness as a protection against globalizing influences.

However, such examples also have a more general tenor. In his contribution to this volume, Arjun Appadurai forcefully shows the dangers of such attempts at closure and the deeper reasons why they lead so easily to violence of a particularly murderous kind. He analyses ethnic violence as the ultimate form of identification, which becomes all the more urgent in view of the radical uncertainty which globalization's flux creates about the 'true' identity of people. Typically, such attempts at clarification focus, in particularly gruesome forms, on the body as 'a theatre of deception, of betrayal and of false solidarity'. As Bayart shows, with a wealth of examples along similar lines, identity is always deeply 'polyvalent'. It is precisely by their plasticity and their poly-interpretability that these *significations imaginaires sociales* can be used to try to hold together heterogeneous societies or groups.[11] It is also due to this openness that identities are so resilient and capable of integrating constant change. Yet, the polyvalence of such *significations imaginaires* creates at the same time an obsession with clarification and fixing: precisely because identity is subject to constant reinterpretation and adaptation, it inspires a quest for unequivocal signs and for a purified 'true' identity.

---

11. Bayart (1996: 228); cf. also note 5 above, Bayart's emphasis on the ambiguity of *l'imaginaire*. The central theme of this book is the crucial role of *l'imaginaire* — with its basic ambivalence — in processes of identity formation (and in politics in general).

It is this combination of plasticity and an illusion of purified truthfulness which makes identity such a basically ambiguous and therefore dangerous notion. This dangerous ambiguity is stressed, as Appadurai's clear and therefore all the more unsettling analysis shows, by globalization processes, which reinforce a radical uncertainty about identities and therefore ever more drastic efforts towards clarification and ultimate forms of 'identification.'

* * * * * *

This tension between globalization and identity — between homogenizing trends and reinforced cultural heterogeneity, between flow and closure — is the common focus of this volume, albeit elaborated in different ways in the various contributions. The first eight contributions offer detailed case-studies of how these tensions are acted out in different parts of the world. Until now, the field of globalization studies abounded in generalizing treatises. Complementary case-studies in a comparative framework might now be most conducive to further deepening our understanding of the dazzling variety of the patterns in which cultural boundaries are surpassed *and* reproduced in a globalizing world.

Our first section, 'Nationalism and Transnationalism', brings together four contributions. Seteney Shami shows how, after the breakdown of Soviet state structures, Circassians reconsider their notions of a given, primordial identity and engage in the construction of a new transnational identity connecting Circassians in the homeland and in the various diasporas. She criticizes existing theories concerning the nature of the Soviet state, on the one hand, and nationalism, on the other, which converged in coining such an awkward notion as 'ethno-nationalism', to understand popular movements in this region. Such a perspective imposes a focus on a bounded unit of study, within the confines of the former Soviet empire. Shami focuses instead on the emergence of a self-conscious diaspora whose members try to create links, in all sorts of ways, with people in what they see as their 'homeland'. The opening up of the former Soviet borders gave new dimensions to such efforts.

While Shami's starting point is the breakdown of an empire, Prasenjit Duara concentrates on the construction of an empire, China. He exposes the complex relationship between nationalism and transnationalism in China around the turn of the twentieth century. He shows in particular how the Chinese state, in order to consolidate its power, struggled to incorporate discourses of a dazzling array of transnationalist movements — placing itself not only in the tradition of Confucian and Buddhist universalism, but also integrating discourses of pan-Asianists, glorifying Japan's victories over Western imperialism, and of the emerging overseas diaspora. Duara argues that, as the state's control over a certain territory is an inadequate basis for people's identification with the nation-state, regimes struggle to appropriate long-standing transnational narratives, which potentially run counter to nationalist ideology and threaten to undermine it. His contribution clearly indicates that narratives on the basis of which identities are constructed are constantly in a process of forming and unravelling.

Mamadou Diouf studies a similar intertwinement of transnationalism and nationalism, but in his case 'from below'. He analyses the history of the *quatre communes* of Senegal as an early form of globalization. These four communes, the first French trading posts along the coast, became showpieces of the assimilation ideology after they received full citizenship during the 1848 revolution in France. Diouf focuses on the difficult crystallization of a specific identity among these *assimilés* who emphasized their citizenship in order to demarcate themselves from the *indigènes* in the rest of the colony, but who none the less wanted to retain certain elements of their cultural heritage which marked them off from 'real' French citizens. Islam, especially, became a difficult issue since it made a specific judicial status necessary whilst equality before the law was crucial to the *assimilé* identity.

Jacqueline Bhabha discusses transnationality in a more recent context, focusing on the consequences of European unification for the treatment of 'Third Country Nationals'. She relates this to a central issue in debates on globalization: the question of whether and how globalization leads to a weakening of national states and a surpassing of nationalist frameworks. She shows that, at least in judicial respects, European unity does not unequivocally lead to a weakening of national governments: rather, it seems to provide governments with new opportunities to control the influx of migrants. Although it is still problematic to speak of a new 'European identity', in practice just such an identity, which in principle refers to 'Human Rights', is invoked to justify a closure of the borders to these 'Third Country Nationals'.

Our second section is on 'Commodities and Fantasies'. Norman Long and Magdalena Villarreal address the flows of food and food-related products across national borders in their study of the different meanings which maize husks have for Mexicans in the 'homeland' and in the United States. Rather than taking for granted a universally valid theory of the value and meaning of commodities (as is characteristic for most views of the global economy), they advocate that commodities be viewed as idioms, which are employed by actors in order to constitute particular social relations and which may therefore form matters of severe contention. This view enables them to demonstrate that, while in the sphere of production in Mexico maize husks are associated with 'modern industry', in the sphere of consumption among the Mexican diaspora in the United States they have become associated with 'traditional', 'authentic' Mexicanhood and are regarded as indispensable markers of 'ethnic' identity.

Filip De Boeck, one of the few researchers who has been able to work in the diamond area at the border zone between Zaire/Congo and Angola, shows in dramatic detail how diamond diggers, the *Bana Lunda*, operate in the booming diamond economy. Living under the continuous threat of dispossession and dislocation, they attempt to affirm and even 'fix' their precarious state of self by referring to long-standing notions of personhood and morality. Yet this does not mean that their engagement in the modern diamond sector can be reduced to a return to 'traditional' models of identity construction; it rather entails an effort 'from below' to appropriate and transform modern capitalism as the ultimate source of hegemonic power in the global system.

Birgit Meyer deals with a new and in optima forma 'purified' identity which has made a sweeping appearance throughout post-colonial Africa over the last decades: the 'Born Again' Christians from, especially, the pentecostal churches. Meyer — taking her examples from Ghana where pentecostalism spread fairly early — relates its amazing success throughout present-day Africa to its capacity to provide a solution to people's ambivalence about the new consumer goods. These goods are coveted, but at the same time feared as a threat to one's personal integrity. Pentecostalism takes these fears seriously by connecting seductive global commodities explicitly to the Devil. However, it also provides the ritual means to purify them, so that they can be consumed without danger. In this way, it offers its followers fixed orientation points and a well-delimited moral universe within globalization's unsettling flows.

Peter Geschiere deals with a similar ambivalence between fascination and deep suspicion in the face of the new riches. In many parts of post-colonial Africa these uncertainties are especially expressed in terms of 'witchcraft'. Although this discourse is closely linked to local realities such as the 'house' or the family, it shows a remarkable capacity to incorporate the open-endedness of global flows. Thus, 'witchcraft' became one of the main discourses for people to discuss and 'signify' modernity. Geschiere shows also that Africa is not that special in this respect. For instance, the upsurge of 'spirit cults' in a much extolled NIC like Taiwan betrays basic similarities: in both cases it is the 'overflow of meaning',[12] blurring all boundaries, which seems to make these discourses so eloquent in the face of globalization's fascinating and frightening uncertainties.

The volume closes with three more theoretical contributions which have already been introduced above: John Kelly's critique of the view of the world as 'a collection of nameable groups' through a re-reading of Ben Anderson and a confrontation of the latter's notion of identity with Walter Benjamin's visions; Wim van Binsbergen's piece on the 'virtuality' of the village as an imaginary orientation point for African urbanites in the flux of globalization processes; and Arjun Appadurai's analysis of the 'bodily brutality' of ethnic violence as an ultimate form of identification in order to settle definitively suspicions about one's neighbour's 'true' identity in the face of increasing uncertainty and globalization. Finally, Ulf Hannerz succeeds in bringing

---

12. This notion is very creatively developed by Robert Weller (1994) in his analysis of spirit cults and other movements in East Asia.

together, in his insightful way, some major strands from these contributions in his Epilogue.

Globalization and identity may be a dangerous combination: it is also a challenging one. Its main advantage is that it serves as a reminder that globalization is not only about flows but also entails constant efforts towards closure and fixing at all levels. In combination with the notion of identity, it raises important questions about who creates new boundaries and securities by which to live, why these are created, and against or with whom — in short, how attempts are made to maintain the illusion that the world does indeed consist of 'nameable groups', bound to certain territories from time immemorial. Anthropologists' and other social scientists' 'intellectual habit of fixing' entails the danger of overstressing this aspect so that identity only appears as an antipode to global dynamics, as a means to create closure. In such a perspective, globalization seems to be 'tamed' and deprived of the radical challenge it poses to both the intellectuals who try to understand it and the people who experience it. This makes it all the more important to show that identity has another side: it also has to relate to people's fascination with globalization's open-endedness and the new horizons which it opens up.

REFERENCES

Appadurai, A. (1996) *Modernity at Large, Cultural Dimensions of Globalization*. Minneapolis, MN: University of Minnesota Press.

Bayart, J.-F. (ed.) (1994) *La réinvention du capitalisme*. Paris: Karthala.

Bayart, J.-F. (1996) *L'illusion identitaire*. Paris: Fayard.

Baumann, G. (1996) *Contesting Culture. Discourses of Identity in Multi-ethnic London*. Cambridge: Cambridge University Press.

de Certeau, M. (1980) *La culture au pluriel*. Paris: Christian Bourgois.

Chatterjee, Partha (1993) *The Nation and Its Fragments: Colonial and Postcolonial Histories*. Princeton, NJ: Princeton University Press.

Clifford, J. (1988) *The Predicament of Culture: Twentieth Century Ethnography, Literature and Art*. Cambridge, MA: Harvard University Press.

Cohen, A. P. (1985) *The Symbolic Construction of Community*. London and New York: Tavistock Publications.

Comaroff, Jean (forthcoming) 'Consuming Passions: Child Abuse, Fetishism and "the New World Order" ', *Culture*.

Comaroff, J. and J. Comaroff (1992) *Ethnography and the Historical Imagination*. Boulder, CO: Westview Press.

Fabian, J. (1983) *Time and the Other: How Anthropology Makes Its Object*. New York: Columbia University Press.

Fabian, J. (1991) *Time and the Work of Anthropology. Critical Essays 1971–1991*. Chur, Switzerland: Harwood.

Featherstone, M. (ed.) (1990) *Global Culture: Nationalism, Globalisation and Identity*. London: Sage.

Friedman, J. (1994) *Cultural Identity and Global Process*. London: Sage.

Hall, S. (1991) 'The Local and the Global: Globalization and Ethnicity', in Anthony D. King (ed.) *Culture, Globalization and the World System: Contemporary Conditions for the Representation of Identity*, pp. 19–39. London: Macmillan.

Hamelink, C. (1983) *Cultural Autonomy in Global Communications*. New York: Longman.

Hannerz, U. (1987) 'The World in Creolisation', *Africa* 57: 546–59.

Hannerz, U. (1992) *Cultural Complexity: Studies in the Social Organization of Meaning*. New York: Columbia University Press.

Jameson, F. (1983) 'Postmodernism and Consumer Society', in H. Foster (ed.) *The Anti-Aesthetic: Essays on Postmodern Culture*, pp. 111–25. Port Townsend, WA: Bay Press.

Kearney, M. (1995) 'The Local and the Global: The Anthropology of Globalization and Transnationalism', *Annual Review of Anthropology* 24: 547–65.

Mbembe, A. (forthcoming) *Notes on the Postcolony*. Berkeley, CA: University of California Press.

McLuhan, M. (1994/1964) *Understanding Media: The Extensions of Man*. London: Routledge.

McLuhan, M. and B. R. Powers (1989) *The Global Village*. Oxford: Oxford University Press.

Miller, Daniel (ed.) (1995) *Worlds Apart. Modernity through the Prism of the Local*. London and New York: Routledge.

Robertson, R. (1992) *Globalization. Social Theory and Global Culture*. London: Sage.

Rouse, R. (1995a) 'Questions of Identity. Personhood and Collectivity in Transnational Migration to the United States', *Critique of Anthropology* 15(4): 351–80.

Rouse, R. (1995b) 'Thinking through Transnationalism: Notes on the Cultural Politics of Class Relations in the Contemporary United States', *Public Culture* 7: 353–402.

Said, E. W. (1989) 'Representing the Colonized: Anthropology's Interlocutors', *Critical Inquiry* 15 (Winter): 205–25.

Vermeulen, H. and C. Govers (eds) (1994) *The Anthropology of Ethnicity. Beyond 'Ethnic Groups and Boundaries'*. Amsterdam: Het Spinhuis.

Weller, R. P. (1994) *Resistance, Chaos and Control in China*. London: Macmillan.

Circassian Encounters: The Self as Other and the Production of the Homeland in the North Caucasus

Seteney Shami

INTRODUCTION

Soviet studies today is a field in search of a territory, one whose boundaries have been temporarily designated as the 'post-Soviet space'. This awkward term implies that the societies and states concerned are in a condition of open-ended transition. Yet, it also reveals that, in spite of the reams of analysis concerning the transformation and fragmentation of state, society and economy in the post-Soviet era, the framework of analysis continues to be inward-looking and operating with conceptions of regional blocs, monolithic systems, and bounded territories. This is not to deny that there is much continuity in the relations and structures that characterize the parts of what was once a political entity. This entity, however, never embodied a coherent and seamless system, and the inability to interpret present-day phenomena and to find different terms, spatial and political, to guide such interpretations is as much a reflection of past conceptual inadequacies as of present empirical complications.

One neglected facet of the break-up of the Soviet Union and its accompanying geo-political changes, is the emergence of self-conscious diasporas who locate their historical 'homelands' in this region. Situated in different countries of the globe, members of these diasporas are increasingly involved with their newly-accessible homelands through a variety of social, political and economic relations. One of the lesser-known examples of such diasporas is that of the Circassians who, together with the Chechens, Ossetians, and a myriad others, trace their origins to the North Caucasus which currently encompasses several small republics within the Russian Federation. Since 1992, the independence wars waged by the Abkhasians against the Georgians and the Chechens against the Russians as well as smaller and associated conflicts, point to the volatile politics of nationalism in this region. These politics have galvanized and implicated diaspora populations in various ways.

Concepts of boundary and border, identity and ethnicity, territory and diaspora all need to be re-examined in the new global context. This chapter

---

Various parts of this paper were presented in a number of forums, and benefited from many discussions. I would particularly like to thank Arjun Appadurai, Birgit Meyer, Ayse Oncu, Roger Rouse and Peter Van der Veer for their helpful and perceptive comments.

examines one such diaspora, which traces its origin to the North Caucasus, the Circassians. The break-up of the Soviet Union has enabled some people to journey back to their 'homeland' and even take up residence there once again. Through such journeys and the encounters that accompany them, notions of identity, history, culture and tradition are challenged. This has the dual effect of fragmenting ethnic identity while simultaneously transforming the 'homeland' from an abstract concept to an everyday reality. The ensuing interplay between nation and diaspora is translated by different individuals in different ways. Three narratives of journeys to the homeland are presented here, showing the complex motivations and consequences of such journeys. Globalization, according to scholars engaged in drawing future scenarios, is an accelerating process of disappearing borders, and the free flow of goods, ideas and people. In a world of 'crisscrossed economies, intersecting systems of meaning, and fragmented identities' (Rouse, 1991: 8), nationalism is particularly challenged and national boundaries are increasingly transcended by transnational bonds and identities. Many see in these newly formed linkages, the end of nationalism as a mobilizing sentiment as well of the nation-state as a form of political economy.

It is important to note, however, that it is actually existing nationalisms and states that are threatened, and that what threatens them is not only supra-national solidarities, but also emergent nationalisms, often called 'ethno-nationalisms'. Rather than shelving these 'new' nationalisms as problematic but atavistic symptoms of a 'transition', they should be seen as integral to, and a result of, the production of transnationalism. For example, diasporas, which link populations transnationally, are often produced through a discourse of nationalism. Conversely, nationalism is increasingly being produced by diasporic, or at least by mobile and dispersed, peoples.

In this way, diasporas are interpolated between nationalism (movements which seek to form bounded territorial states as embodiments of nations) and transnationalism (linkages which form solidarities and reciprocities across, and in spite of, national boundaries). Are diasporas then to be seen as a product of globalization? a denial of globalization? or both? Finally, what is the space occupied, from this global perspective, by peoples who have hardly been recognized historically as constituting peoples, as befitting states or as shaping nations? As marginal as they may seem in the arena of shifting global alliances and forces, their lives shed a particular light on processes of globalization and identity construction.

THEORETICAL AND IDEOLOGICAL VACUUMS

'Ethno-nationalism' has emerged as a central explanation for the changing and confusing struggles over statehood, political representation and identity that have marked the post-Soviet era.[1] The guiding assumption behind this term associates the collapse of universalistic ideologies with the rise of particularistic identities (see Laclau, 1994). Ethnic identities are regarded as latent forces somehow kept at bay by hegemonic superstructures. In an ideological vacuum, identities that were submerged, emerge once again. This 'vacuum theory' ignores theoretical reconceptualizations of ethnicity and nationalism which give us, if not a better grasp, then at least a better appreciation, of the unstable and elusive quality of identity and the politics of its construction over time.

Ethnicity and Nationalism

Recent theorizing would appear to have laid to rest representations of nationalism as a mechanistic reflection of a primordial ethnicity which provides the basis of cultural cohesion (for example Smith, 1991). Yet the difficulty of accommodating ethnicity in transnational perspective points to the insufficient problematization of the relationship between nationalism and ethnicity. Benedict Anderson's assertion that 'Communities are to be distinguished, not by their falsity/genuineness, but by the style in which they are imagined' (Anderson, 1991: 6) and his reminder that '. . . nation-ness, as well as nationalism, are cultural artefacts of a particular kind' (ibid: 4) opened up the horizons of research and usefully contested the necessity of nationalism. In general, however, the scholarly rush to study nations tended to focus on the *mode* of representing the nation, on the techniques of the imagination. Theoretically and empirically, this focus neglected the place of ethnicity within the national imaginary, non-national types of communities (religious groupings, dynasties, tribes, classes . . .), and those peoples who had not produced 'successful' post-colonial nationalisms.

Ethnicity and nationalism are intersecting sentiments and ideologies, and both refer to forces of belonging, community, identity and loyalty. Generally, however, they have been analytically situated at different societal levels. Ethnicity was observed through 'minority' cultures while nationalism was interpreted through state ideology. In this way, the former has often been de-politicized while the latter was de-culturalized. Since the creation of any nation is necessarily based on the silencing of competing identities, threats to nation-building and state-building were seen as primarily located in the realm of ethnicity and the varieties of localism expressed through 'the trope of the tribe' (Appadurai, 1996: 159). Ethnicity was relegated to the 'minority' and

---

1. The term is also often used to describe minority politics in contemporary Western Europe. Yet, the potentially interesting comparison in this realm between Western and Eastern Europe is hardly ever made. Rather one finds parallel literatures and an absence of dialogue. See Appadurai (1996) for a wide-angled conceptualization of ethnic violence and the blurring of the distinction between the West and the non-West in this regard.

denied to the 'majority' (Williams, 1989), and therefore ethnicity and nation-ness were seen as diametrically opposed sentiments. One expanded and produced its politics at the expense of the other.

While studies of nationalism tended to displace ethnicity, anthropological approaches, developed within a wider critique of culturalism, have emphasized the constructed nature of ethnic identification, its shifting nature and malleability according to context. However, these studies, in turn, rarely addressed how the wider context is informed, and ethnic categorization determined, by the nationalist ideologies of the encompassing states (Williams, 1989). Ethnic communities and nations, and ethnicity and nation-ness, are both imagined around sets of symbols which differentially emphasize common ancestry, consanguinity, historical immemoriality, linguistic particularity, cultural continuity, and social solidarity. Nationalism and ethnicity are therefore intertwined and also often imbricated with religious adherence and practice. Their imaginative techniques, and the symbols they deploy, however, articulate in different ways with the political expression of community, and with concepts of sovereignty and territory.

For nationalists, the concept of sovereignty holds central place and the state is the primary political expression of community (cf. Anderson, 1991; Conner, 1994). The kind of boundaries created by territory, and more specifically borders, makes possible a discourse that seeks integrity and sovereignty in the translation of an ethnic group into a nation by way of the state. Yet this transformation in the nature of the political community does not erase ethnicity or assimilate it completely. While the nation is conceived of as a fraternity, a horizontal comradeship (Anderson, 1991) that is formed historically, ethnicity continues to be conceived of as an extension of self, perceived as biological and germinal. Being 'natural' rather than historical, ethnicity is seen as 'logically' prior to the nation and its perpetuation is not predicated on statehood. Such a conceptualization allows for the 'group' to exist even if it is de-territorialized, but this should not imply that ethnic identity has no geographical or territorial component. Ethnic identity has a location, and it is constructed in reference to a point of origin, however abstract or unreachable or buried in time that space may be. It is therefore important, in the interpretation of ethnicity and nationalism and their relationship, to problematize the linkage between geography and identity and to investigate the notion of 'territory'.

Nationalism, particularly in non-Western societies, has been mostly addressed in terms of modernization, nation-building and post-colonialism. In these interpretations, the presence of a modernizing state was a given, although the success or failure of these states in mobilizing the loyalties of their populations was seen to vary. What is now troubling to the older paradigms is how to interpret the phenomenon of nationalism *sans* state, or at least in the absence of the political, economic, ideological construct of the nation-state. Locating analysis at either the 'level' of the communal or the national, therefore, obscures possibilities of emergent political configurations and new forms of identity, especially those being produced not in the modern world context of colonial and post-colonial state formation, but in the post-modern global context of transnationality.

Ethno-nationalism and Transnationalism

Suny, a historian of Georgia and Armenia, points out that the prevailing view after the collapse of communism was to see 'current nationalisms as eruptions of long-repressed primordial national consciousnesses, as expressions of denied desires liberated by the kiss of freedom (what might be called the "Sleeping Beauty" view)' (Suny, 1993: 3). It is important to note, however, that the conflicts of the Caucasus, Central Asia and the former Yugoslavia are rarely represented as beautiful awakenings. Rather, the images invoked by primordialism are those of violence, primitivism and revenge.

What, if not these images, does the 'ethno' in 'ethno-nationalism' add to the term? This qualification emerges from an opposition that is drawn between 'ethnic nationalism' and 'civic nationalism' (cf. Ignatieff, 1993; Szporluk, 1994). Through this dichotomy, the former is naturalized and seen as necessarily violent and retrograde and opposed to cosmopolitanism, while the latter is described as being based on territory and not ethnicity, as being democratic and rational and having 'greater claim to sociological realism' (Ignatieff, 1993: 7). Although the pivot of the distinction appears to rest on the form of national identity under construction, the overwhelming pre-occupation is actually with the question of democracy in the post Cold War era and in the post-Soviet successor states. The form that nationalism takes, the dichotomy between 'ethnic' and 'civic' forms, is validated and explained through their differential articulation with democracy, itself portrayed as an ideal form of political representation. Ignatieff (1993), for example, argues for the impossibility of democracy in states based on ethnic nationalism as opposed to civic nationalism. Laclau (1994), on the other hand, asserts that it is possible, if not probable, that a democratic universalism that is cognizant of the rights of particularism may emerge out of the collapse of the older universalizing ideologies.[2]

This type of discussion takes a psychological approach to ethnicity, centring around processes of identification (cf. Laclau, 1994), and relegates the cultural and social construction of identity to a residual process. It empties 'civic' nationalism of its ethnic component and negates the historical and ideological construction of ethnic identity. It therefore evades the question of whether nationalism and ethnicity, as ideologies and practices, can be delinked.

---

2. A more interesting view of the possible articulations of ethnicity, race and democracy, albeit in the very different context of Britain, can be found in Hall (1991). See also Appadurai (1996) for a definitive critique of the 'primordialist thesis'.

Furthermore, such approaches are still informed by conceptions of the necessary congruence of state, territory, polity and political representation.

A further simplification arises out of accepting the self-proclaimed non-national nature of the former socialist states and the laying to rest of the 'national question' through local territorial representation. 'Ethno-nationalism', therefore, is particularly employed to explain instances where the new/old nationalist sentiments do not coincide with recently defunct administrative boundaries. Expressions of communal solidarity are portrayed as reflecting sentiments existing prior to the socialist states and outlasting them. The dimension of religion (particularly Islam) lends added weight to these identities with all its implications of permanence and force (see Singh, 1995).[3]

As a result, the space ('vacuum') created by the disarticulation of borders and sentiments is filled by the concept of 'ethno-nationalism' which is represented as a natural (primitive, anarchic) and hence not cultural (civilized, democratic) project. The coining of the term ethno-nationalism, and its identification as an emergent phenomenon, arises out of the past neglect of how the two types of identity (ethnicity and nation-ness), that represent two different styles of (imagined) community, can be mutually constitutive of one another. The 'vacuum', I would suggest, lies in our theories rather than in the lives of the people who are the subjects of our interpretive authority.

Theories of globalization and transnationalism should alert us that interpretations of 'ethno-nationalism' cannot be situated only in the ideological sphere but also need to take into account the shifting of borders and the differential access to territory. The process needs to be examined not only as the downfall of ideologies but also at the more prosaic level of the breakdown of totalizing state structures that helped determine ethnic identity through legal categorization, administrative procedures, and the restriction of mobility and access to territory. A historical analysis of concrete situations focusing on whether, and how, ethnic identification is produced by precisely these universalistic ideologies and the practices associated with them, appears to be in order. This is especially the case with the 'new' peoples who do not produce the dominant narratives and who are only just entering the global imagination through violent means and seemingly mysterious ends. The nationalisms coming into play cannot be simply explored within the space occupied by the populations now interrogating old boundaries. Rather, the

---

3. Positioned as I am in Middle Eastern studies rather than Soviet studies, it is fascinating and disturbing to see the assimilation of these areas into the realm of Islam and Orientalism. The predominant identification of Islam with the Middle East leads to interesting permutations such as calling the Trans-Caucasus and Central Asia 'The ex-Soviet Middle East' (Hooson, 1994: 138). Furthermore, despite two decades of powerful arguments for more sensitive and historically informed interpretations of Islam in the Middle East, essentialism holds sway in the post-Soviet space.

contemporary configurations of past diasporas and population dispersals also have to be taken into account.

A PEOPLE AND THEIR GEOGRAPHY

The Circassians, or the *Adyge* as they name themselves, trace their descent from the indigenous peoples of the North-West Caucasus. Pushed out by the Tsarist Russian expansion into the Caucasus, and encouraged by the Ottoman Empire, large numbers of Circassians, possibly up to 1.5 million, left for the Ottoman domains (see Berkok, 1958; Karpat, 1972, 1990). Mass migration started in 1864 (Karpat, 1985) and the immigrants were settled by the state in order to form agricultural communities in various parts of the Empire, first in the Balkans and later in Anatolia and the Syrian Province (Shami, 1992). Today, the Circassians form communities of different sizes and characteristics in some Balkan countries and in Turkey, Syria, Jordan and Palestine/Israel.[4] In the Russian Federation, they live primarily in the three newly formed republics, previously autonomous regions, of Kabardino-Balkaria, Karachaevo-Cherkessia and Adygeia, as well as in some villages and towns within the republic of Ossetia and others linked to the administrative districts of Krasnodar and Sochi.[5]

Secondary migrations to Germany, Holland (mainly as labour migrants from Turkey) and the United States (New Jersey and Orange County, California) adds to the list of major locations where Circassians live today.[6] Circassians are Muslim except for those in the Ossetian Republic who comprise four Christian villages and one town. In addition to Circassians, other North Caucasian groups such as the Chechen, Daghestanians, Ossetians, Abkhasians and Ubykh also formed part of the nineteenth century migrations and are found in the same countries of the Middle East.

---

4. It is difficult to know the number of Circassians in these countries. Impressionistic sources put the population in Turkey at around 1 million (Andrews, 1992), 50,000 in Syria, 30,000 in Jordan and 2000 in Palestine/Israel. The figure for Turkey is probably underestimated. In the Balkans, a few villages are reported in Albania, Yugoslavia, Hungary and Bulgaria.
5. The Circassian/Adyge population in the Caucasus can be estimated by adding the numbers given for the Cherkess, Kabardians and Adygei populations based on the 1989 census. This totals 476,900 in Olcott (1990) and 499,372 in Teague (1994). However, since these figures do not include all those who might identify themselves as Adyge outside the boundaries of these republics and do not include the villages tied to the Russian regions mentioned above, the total is underestimated.
6. Another Circassian presence, but of a different and complex order, is in Egypt. Here individuals and families tracing their ancestry to a rich mixture of Circassians, Turks, Bosnians, Albanians etc. (from the Circassian and Turkish Mameluke slave dynasties of the thirteenth–sixteenth centuries, as well as later Ottoman influxes), represent the remnants of a 'creolized' ruling élite, now marginalized by half a century of nationalism, socialism and 'open-door' capitalism. Interestingly, here too, events in the post-Soviet space have touched lives and revitalized interest in the search for 'pure' identities.

Convergence between different groups took place in the places of settlement. For example, the Abkhaz and Ubykh are usually glossed as Circassian/ Adyge in the communities outside the Caucasus. Intermarriage between the various groups outside the Caucasus also blurs distinctions between them while reinforcing their common identity *vis-à-vis* the 'majority'.

While a Circassian identity persists in these various localities, its cultural content and socio-political parameters differ according to context.[7] In Turkey, for example, the large number of Circassians means that they are found in every walk of life, in urban as well as rural areas, leading to complex permutations of identity. Turkey is a country which has witnessed, and continues to develop, an extremely powerful nationalism. This nationalism is based on a Turkish ethnicity, representing itself as secular but including a not-so-subtle imbrication of Islam, and is reproduced forcefully through education and the media. For Circassians and others who conceive of themselves as non-Turkish, assimilation into a Turkish identity is a clear option and one which, over the generations, vast number of Circassians, especially in the cities, have taken. Some simply retain a memory of a Circassian origin with a rather hazy conception of what that 'means' or where Circassians are 'from' and whether they have a 'language' or a 'culture'. Others have been active in forming associations which advocate right-wing nationalist politics or, more recently, Islamist programmes. During the turbulent decade of the 1970s the politics of identity in Turkey produced two dominant formulations among Circassians. The *devrimci*, or revolutionaries, argued that the betterment of Circassian rights would be achieved through a socialist revolution in Turkey. The *dönüşcü*, the 'returnists', on the other hand, advocated a return to the Caucasus. They accused the right-wing groups of simply promoting the state's assimilationist policies. Their reply to the *devrimci* group was that by the time Turkey became socialist there would be no Circassians left, that is, the historical memory, the culture, the language would have disappeared. Circassian associations in the cities and the towns of Turkey played an extremely important role in developing this platform, mobilizing rural migrants and especially young people. While the *dönüşcü* saw themselves as leftists, their programme was essentially Circassian nationalist and a number of them migrated back to the Caucasus after 1989.

In Jordan, a completely different scenario of identity politics plays itself out in a context where Circassians are largely a middle-class urban community with favourable representation in government bureaucracy, parliament and the military. The dominant trend was articulated in 1979 by a thirty-five year old Circassian man as follows: 'What the Circassians need to do is to become a tribe, because this is a country of tribes and they have to find a leader who can nag the government for them and put the benefit of the Circassians

---

7. For more ethnographic detail on some parts of this and the following section, see Shami (1995).

foremost'. The perception that tribalism is the predominant political idiom and process in Jordan led in 1980 to the formation of a Circassian–Chechen Tribal Council. In one of the early organizational meetings, a speaker pointed out the basic aim of the Tribal Council: 'We want to unite the two tribes, to be like the others'. Tribalism was not the only vision of the future within the Circassian community, but for a while it became the prevailing, if contested, one. The dominance of one particular conception of Circassian ethnicity and the ability of the holders of this conception to translate it into organization is directly related to hegemonic discourses and political practices at the national level. A variety of colonial and state-building practices and policies led to the increasing 'modernization' of tribal identities as a constitutive component of Jordanian national identity (see Layne, 1994). In addition, tribes were becoming institutionalized. All the major Jordanian 'tribes' now have a Tribal Association, and of course all those that have an association thereby prove that they are a major tribe. The tribe, thus constituted, aims to create political consensus and to act as a redistributive centre for resources. These tribal associations are officially registered with the state and have headquarters in the various cities.

In Jordan, Circassian identity presents itself paradoxically as tribalism, while in Turkey it takes the form of minority politics. Both communities imagine themselves as unambiguously 'Circassian' but the formulations, content and discourses of this identity and the constructions of the past and future that they espouse are divergent. For example, the Circassians in Jordan who advocated the 'tribal solution' emphasized that the reason for the nineteenth century mass migration was religion and the desire of Circassians to live in a Muslim society. This leads them to seek integration into their current societies. Conversely, the *dönüşcü* Circassians in Turkey emphasized that their ancestors had been expelled from their homeland and had been pawns in the political machinations of the Russian and Ottoman Empires. They conclude, therefore, that a return to the homeland is imperative.

Although these identities were constructed in constant reference to a space, a 'homeland' in the North Caucasus, this space was devoid of geographical detail, of territoriality. Cut off from the Caucasus by 130 years of history and boundary construction, Circassians of the Middle East were only dimly aware of the Circassians in the Caucasus and the trickle of emigrants who came after 1917 and after World War II gave accounts of forced Russification. In the Caucasus, the Circassians having failed to qualify as a 'nation' instead became the titular nationality in one republic and two autonomous regions. The three 'nationalities' that were formed, Cherkess, Adygei, and Kabardian, were minorities within their republics and today constitute only between 10 and 48 per cent of the inhabitants of each republic (Teague, 1994).

Contacts between the inhabitants of these three republics were at a minimum throughout the Soviet years and divergences marked the evolution of language and identity. Disjunctures were created and maintained by a politics of philology. For example, the three 'nations' were regarded as speaking different 'languages' and separate Cyrillic-based alphabets were devised for each one. Today, many Kabardians state that they are not Adygei and when speaking Russian or English will refer to their language as Kabardinian as opposed to Adygeian. When actually speaking this language, however, they will refer to it as *Adygebze* (the tongue of the Adyge) and to their traditions as *Adygekhabze* (the customs of the Adyge).

Other markers of identity also exhibit interesting ambiguities. In Soviet times, the various republics and 'nations' all had their folklore dance troupes and every local village and town had youth dance groups that served as a recruiting site for the official troupes. The Caucasians (especially the Kabardians and the Georgians) were notably successful in winning all-Union contests and representing the Soviet Union abroad. Folklore was thus elaborated and celebrated and research was conducted into dance forms, as well as into local customs that could be symbolically performed through dance. Yet Circassians in the Caucasus today argue that this was not a celebration of identity or a perpetuation of tradition because the performers in these groups were not necessarily Circassians. The majority in fact were not, but could be Russians, Armenians or any individual on the basis of skill rather than ethnicity.

Soviet studies paid little attention to the micro-politics of the construction of identity in the Soviet period, in spite of an initial extensive literature on 'the question of the nationalities' (see Szporluk, 1994). These tended to focus on the nationalities that were embodied in the republics of the Union (for example, Azerbeijan, Armenia, Georgia, etc.) and generally ignored the varied peoples within them as well as those within 'Russia' such as the peoples of the North Caucasus (Olcott, 1995; Suny, 1995). The impact on ethnic identity of Soviet practices of deportation, collectivization, the creation of enclaves and the severance of people and territory, was also overlooked (IOM et al., 1996). With the explosion of ethnicity and the 'emergence' of 'new' peoples, attention has been riveted to retroactively understanding processes and limits of sovietization and Russification.

As Singh points out '... no existing theory of nationalism is founded on the Soviet experience and applying current theories, blindfolded, to the Soviet and post-Soviet states may not leave anyone the wiser' (Singh, 1995: 199). Scholars have moved from arguing that the Soviet state successfully sovietized (with its implied Russification) the various 'nationalities', to arguing that sovietization was simply unsuccessful leading to the persistence of ethnic and religious identities, themselves seen as unchanged.[8] This persistence is seen as the result of the 'inherent' strength of ethnic identities especially when reinforced with religious identities which are commonly

---

8. Also see Teague (1994: 48) for an argument that it is regionalism or localism and vested interests rather than nationalism that is currently operating in the Russian federation. While this reduces the 'primordialism' of the prevailing arguments, and introduces the pragmatic aspects of the current conflicts, it evades the question of identity construction.

perceived as 'stronger' than ethnic ones. It is in the feminist literature that more interesting ways of conceptualizing ethnic/religious and national identities are being formulated. The 'woman question' and the domestic sphere have been identified as important sites for resistance to sovietization and for the 'perpetuation' of ethnic and religious identities (see Lubin, 1982; Massell, 1974; Tett, 1994; Tohidi, 1996). In general, however, not only do the 'national' labels and categories of analysis remain those of the Soviet state, but also the continuous construction of identity and the sites of its production are given little attention. In this way, the 'black box of primordialism' (Appadurai, 1996: 139) remains unpacked in the post-Soviet space.

SHOCKS: ENCOUNTERS WITH THE HOMELAND

The Circassian homeland in the Caucasus has now become directly accessible to the communities outside for the first time in 130 years, although in Jordan and Syria a trickle of students had been going to study in the Caucasus since the 1970s and a series of 'official visits' were taking place between officials of the Soviet republics, folklore groups, and leaders of Circassian organizations. Since 1989, however, large numbers of Circassians from all the countries they live in, have been going to the Caucasus, usually during the summers, to visit, to find long-lost relatives and home villages. A World Circassian Association and an International Circassian Academy of Science have been established, which have had a series of conferences and meetings attended by delegates from all the communities abroad. In addition, an estimated 200 families have migrated back, largely from Syria and from Turkey, and a few from the US have settled in the republics of Kabardino-Balkaria and in Adygeia. The Caucasus has become a site for many encounters: of people from the diaspora communities with the homeland, but also of the various diaspora communities with one another. These encounters engender lively debates about future possibilities and scenarios and throw into relief the variety of identities that have emerged in diaspora.[9]

The most salient sentiment that the encounter of Circassians from the diaspora with the homeland is engendering is one of shock. Ethnicity is suddenly experienced not as a fact but as a contradiction. To emphasize the 'suddenness' and disconcerting effect of such encounters is not to imply that a homogeneous, unified conception of Circassian identity existed in any locality prior to the encounter with the homeland. However, new and

---

9. My sustained fieldwork has been in Jordan, Turkey and the Caucasus although I have also often visited Circassians in Syria and the USA and, in the Caucasus, one now meets Circassians from all countries. Still my main sources of information are from the three fieldsites. Also, as is clear in the following discussion, my focus is not so much on the Circassians of the Caucasus as on the experiences of the diasporans in their encounters with the homeland.

unexpected disjunctures have emerged that lead to a new questioning of identity. Previous, older contradictions had been routinized: Why did we leave the Caucasus, were we pushed out by the Russians or pulled in by the Ottomans? Are we primarily Circassians or Muslims, and how does this inform our relationship with Arabs and Turks? Does intermarriage lead to the disappearance of community or to the consolidation of alliances? How can we have political clout through participation while preserving our cultural integrity? These questions had not been resolved but the debates around them had settled into well established grooves. Different questions and different grooves had appeared in the different localities, but the distinctions by locality were seen by many Circassians as expressions of a common (though not collective) endeavour for the perpetuation of a naturalized ethnicity. Encounters with and in the Caucasus are marked by a heightened awareness of contingency and choice as well as mixed emotions.

As Circassians journey to the Caucasus, the experience of locating and contacting their kin is overwhelming.[10] The excitement, warmth and joy of these occasions is experienced as a deeply moving encounter. In the hotels of Nalchik and Maikop, particularly in the summer, bus-loads of Circassians arrive from various countries and meet one another and look for their kin. When word spreads that a group is arriving from Jordan or Turkey or elsewhere, people converge on the hotel lobbies to ask whether there is anyone from this family or the other. As the evening wears on, the space in front of the hotel begins to look like a big party. Someone may drive up in a car and start selling liquor from the boot. Next someone brings out an accordion and all join in a *djeg*.[11] Subsequently, the 'found' relatives from the diaspora are taken to the 'home' village. There follow days of feasting, dancing, and visiting of all possible relatives. There is usually also an attempt to locate the house, or more usually the location or plot of land where the house of the common ancestor who had emigrated once stood.

After this first discovery of commonality, however, more intensive contact and ensuing visits bring the discovery of divergence.

Definitions of ethnicity have suggested that the ethnic community is conceptualized as an extension of the self. In other words, a common ethnicity is experienced or expected to constitute a 'sameness', a familiarity. However, the more salient experience of most of those who journey to the Caucasus, men and women, is generally one of shock, of non-recognition and the encounter of 'the self as other'. The self, in addition to being conceptualized in abstract terms of cultural characteristics or symbols of identity, is also perceived as having particular physical characteristics, of being linked to a

---

10. Relatives are usually identified through common family names or through the village of origin, if the memory of the latter was retained. The genealogy is generally constructed through a presumed sibling relationship in the generation of the emigration.
11. The word *djeg* means dancing but also contains the meaning of 'games' as well as weddings, as the main context for dancing and games of skill.

particular kind of body. Circassians coming to the Caucasus from the outside soon come to feel estranged at all levels of this encounter.

First, and most problematic to their ethnic identity, is the statement that 'they' (Circassians in the Caucasus) do not look Circassian (unlike 'us'). Circassians in the Caucasus see themselves as dark ('the dark Southerners') and are described as such by the Russians, while Circassians in the Middle East are seen by Turks and Arabs as fair and beautiful (a vestige of their historical relationship to Ottoman courts and harems). Therefore, Circassian visitors from the Middle East see themselves as blond and the locals as dark. This perceived physical difference is not accepted as a reasonable diversity within a common biologically-imagined ethnicity but as an opposition, a difference. Aspects that are perceived as cultural rather than biological are also not recognized by those coming from abroad. The language is hard to understand, since Russian, Arabic and Turkish have made their impact respectively and in the Middle Eastern settlements different dialects have converged while in the Soviet republics they diverged. Equally shocking, Circassian dances are unsettlingly different. People known to be very good dancers in Jordan or Syria suddenly seem awkward and clumsy in the Caucasus. While dance is a main and subtle vehicle for courtship, young men and women are unable to communicate their admiration and feelings for one another when trapped in the unfamiliar melodies, tempos and motions. More generally, marriage customs, food, hospitality and reciprocity are misunderstood by both sides, and behaviour and expectations at such occasions are fraught with difficulties and feelings of social awkwardness.

The list goes on, but the most important element underlying these various aspects of the alienation from the self, as experienced by the returnees to the Caucasus, is the lack of trust. Alienation translates into mistrust. This is not a mistrust of particular individuals but of the situation and the society as a whole, which they describe as 'immoral'. This is not helped by the upheaval that these societies are undergoing, the general lawlessness, increasing poverty and deterioration in standards of living and safety, accompanied, apparently, by a concomitant rise in divorce, in alcoholism and domestic violence.[12]

In addition to these disconcerting relations with the Circassians of the Caucasus, those coming from the various countries on the outside also experience difficulties in finding commonalities with one another. Reactions to the current political situation in the Caucasus, and visions of the future, tend to differ according to the country from which the individual comes. Some Circassians from Syria, for example, are positive about the communist past of the Caucasus and decry the present as the disintegration of a powerful

---

12. I cannot say with any certainty that violence and alcoholism have increased or claim the relationship of such phenomena to the collapse of the Soviet Union. Some Circassians in the Caucasus asserted that this was the case.

system. Many coming from Turkey tend to advocate 'Westernization', arguing, for example, that the Cyrillic alphabet used for writing Circassian should be replaced by a Latin one. Circassians from Jordan often stress the need for religious education and some contribute money for the building of mosques in their villages of origin.

For those families who have migrated back, socializing tends to take place amongst those who come from the same country. They may even on occasion refer to each other as 'the Turks', 'the Syrians', 'the Jordanians' and to the Circassians of the Caucasus as 'the Russians'. As one young woman who emigrated from Turkey said, 'We left Turkey not to become Turks, only to become Turks here'.

Clearly, the coming together in the very location where Circassians expect to find commonality and a naturalized ethnicity, instead generates an experience of difference, disjuncture and a sense of rupture. This is hardly the portrait of ethno-nationalism displayed in scholarly or popular representations.

In spite of these highly divergent and problematic relations, however, one can also discern a number of emerging arenas that provide the space for exploring commonalities and unifying discourses. The most obvious arena for integration that has emerged is the World Circassian Association. Disagreements arise within this forum and long discussions reveal that those from outside the Caucasus tend not to appreciate the difficulties experienced by the three tiny Circassian republics in re-negotiating their links with Moscow.[13] Still, however, the meetings take place, one after another. Although little programmatic action is adopted, and less executed, the meetings provide the opportunity for the development of a common discourse, one with clear overtones of nationalism. In the July 1993 meeting of the World Circassian Association at Maikop attended by several hundred people, one delegate from the Adygeia Republic was given a standing ovation as he said:

> Now that we are [finally] meeting, we have hope that we can get closer together ... We have to do everything to help them [those in the diaspora] to come back. We should help them settle here, it is enough the problems they have had [in the diaspora] ... [The Russians] don't consider us important because we are few. We are few not from our own actions, but because they made us few.[14] We want Russia to be a democratic country. We should not be reluctant to respect other peoples [nations] but we expect to be respected in return. The war being waged [in Abkhasia] is an oppressive war. Finally, we send our greetings to our parents who are in diaspora [and look forward] till when we will be one big family and one people [nation].

Given the divergent and fragmentary conceptualizations of present realities and future scenarios, however, could the Circassians, across the localities

---

13. The war in Abkhasia (1993) and the war in Chechnya (1994–6) clearly demonstrate the complexity of the relationships between the non-Russian peoples within the Russian Federation and the CIS.
14. The reference here is to deportations and exile during the Stalinist period.

within which they find themselves, in any way be seen as fragments of a nation? Even a brief description highlights the permutations of Circassian identity engendered by different contexts as well as by the encounters with, and in, the Caucasus. The homeland that the Caucasus presents to its diasporic descendants, is itself a fragmented and contested terrain. Circassians within the Caucasus are scattered, divided by borders, interspersed with other ethnic groups and have experienced successive displacements and exile. Arguments abound about where the centre of gravity lies for Circassians and to which republic or city the diasporans should migrate back. Clearly, current ethnic identification is not simply an intensification, or a 'violencing' of an older persistent identity.

To understand the new constructions of Circassian identity, it is not enough to examine conceptions in one locale or even to compare across a number of locales. Rather, the socio-political relationships and cultural representations linking the multiple locales and the homeland with one another should be seen as constituting a field of transnational intersections. An emphasis on transnationalism shifts the focus from how these identities are imagined to how they are organized.

A powerful example is the war in Chechnya, which started in December 1994. The implications of this conflict for the Russian Federation and its political leadership are generally well examined by international journalists and commentators and some attention is given to the ramifications in the rest of the Caucasus. However, how the conflict is perceived by the Caucasians themselves and how Caucasian diasporas outside the region may react or contribute to such perceptions, is given little attention. During the crisis over the hostages taken by Chechen fighters in Daghestan in January 1996, the parallel dramatic hijacking of a Turkish ferry-boat in the Black Sea was represented in the media (and by Russian officialdom) as the 'spreading' of terrorism 'across borders' and the hijackers were labeled as 'Chechen sympathizers'. The roots and conditions of such a 'sympathy', that several of the hijackers were not Chechen but of other North Caucasian groups and that they were Turkish nationals and residents was hardly noted. Rather than a 'spread across' borders, such simultaneity of political action and expression in different locations should lead to a re-examination of notions of borders and the arenas of political action.

Hardly existing in a vacuum, therefore, constructions of identity and the concomitant politics are taking place in a global context characterized by ambiguously articulated but powerful ideas and by very specific skeins and relationships attaching people to one another and to particular spaces and places. This global context is marked by shifting boundaries which bring into question matters of personhood and belonging to social groups. The geography of identity, the linkage between territory and belonging, becomes important to conceptualize in addition to its modes of articulation, textualization and persuasion.

ROUTES AND JOURNEYS, LIVES AND NARRATIVES

As the encounters in the Caucasus produce emergent discourses, similarly the recurrent journeys back and forth to the Caucasus produce an emergent geography. Tracing the routes that have opened up between the Caucasus and the Middle East, and observing who travels along them, highlights the intersections between identities, territories and boundaries. Shifts in identity are not simply reactions and counter-reactions to 'contexts', whether local, national or global, but are also continuously constructed through meaningful encounters brought about by different forms of mobility. These pathways to identity, the routes and journeys that transform selfhood and ethnicity, have changed dramatically for Circassians since 1989. Conceptualizing the formation and transformation of identity through pathways implies that, in addition to the encounters at the point of arrival, the journey itself constitutes a meaningful experience of, and for, identity.

In the travels undertaken by Circassians to the Caucasus, the mode of transport (bus, ship, plane), whether the travellers come individually or as families, whether they travel as part of organized tours or along their newly-discovered kin networks, all these mark the experience of the journey and its interpretation. The difficulties of travel and access make the routes to the homeland particularly fraught with symbolism. Visas continue to be a complicated process at Russian embassies. International scheduled flights entail a difficult transfer to domestic flights and at least one ominous night in the volatile city of Moscow. The planes that fly directly to the cities of the Caucasus from Istanbul, Damascus and Aleppo are charters with random schedules and unpredictable booking policies. Getting onto the plane and finding a seat is often a matter of the 'survival of the fittest' and may entail physical scuffles. Buses may have to traverse war zones, often break down and entail long border waits. Unreliable hotel reservations en route may mean sleeping out in open fields or beaches. Ships are overcrowded and equally unpredictable and when the travellers arrive at ports they are faced with few amenities and unsavoury hotels as well as further inland journeys by bus or train to get to the principal cities. Seemingly arbitrary and indecipherable 'regulations' at border points makes each crossing an adventure in negotiation, bribery, confiscation of belongings and extraction of fines and taxes.

These difficulties, while not getting less in any formal sense, are being tamed over time into some sort of predictability through frequent travel, through making connections with people who can help at the various junctures and through the slight improvements in the quality of hotels and eateries. At the same time, however, the increasing insecurity in the cities and the continuing wars in the region still make each journey undertaken an adventure and a calculated risk. The conditions that face travellers en route to their homeland accumulate into a collective experience that feeds into a sense of community, a sense that is being continually transformed by these experiences. People trade stories of difficulties and achievements and flaunt their current expertise and abilities. They exchange useful information on helpful intermediaries, what foods to carry and how to obtain necessities. By now, reactions, responses and perceptions have formed that create expectations and frame understandings even for the first time traveller.

At first, it would appear that the frequent travellers to the Caucasus fall easily into distinct categories. It seems possible to dissect the political, economic and cultural dimensions of transnationalism through 'the' motive informing the journey. For example, 'militants' seek to invigorate ethnic solidarity by encouraging a return migration from the diaspora locations back to the homeland. They are active in forming associations that transcend borders, they bring together a variety of people in different locations and are vocal in a variety of forums concerning regional political events. In the meantime, 'traders' are exploring the new markets and commodities made available through the opening up of borders and 'transition economies'. They range from itinerant entrepreneurs and 'suitcase peddlers' to founders of large-scale import–export companies. 'Scholars' are equally active travellers seeking to explore new terrains of knowledge. Those from the Caucasus re-examine notions of culture, tradition and language by investigating the 'mutations' that have occurred in the diaspora, while those from the Middle East journey in search of the roots and authentic origins of contemporary cultural forms.

A closer look at individual life histories, however, reveals the difficulties of isolating and classifying the activities and identities of the sojourners. Even with the formation of collective approaches to the homeland, the people who journey back and forth, their motivations, aims, representations and the kinds of landscapes they construct as they travel these circuits vary significantly.[15] The countries that they come from, the class and gender politics that they embody also frame their encounters. Narratives of these journeys are one way of looking at the intersection of individual particularities and the connections to the collapse of states, regional blocs and empires.[16]

Consider, for example, Emine's journey from a provincial Turkish town to the city of Nalchik in Kabardino-Balkaria. Emine was a high school teacher and in her mid-thirties when she decided, in 1992, to return to the Caucasus. In explaining her decision, she starts from her childhood and youth. She says that as she was growing up she never thought much about being Circassian. They did not speak Circassian at home because their parents wanted them to do well in school and not be 'confused' by different languages. She had Circassian friends but also Turkish friends and she thought of herself as being both. When she went to Ankara to study at the university in the early

---

15. This idea of landscapes constructed and circuits travelled is inspired by the work of Roger Rouse (1991, 1995) on Mexican migrants in California.
16. In the following accounts, 'Emine', 'Engin' and 'Omar' are pseudonyms. I have tried to give a feeling for their own style and emphases in the narratives and the key Turkish, Arabic and Circassian words they used.

1970s, she was influenced by leftist student politics. She also began to go to the Circassian Association regularly because she had no friends in Ankara and because her older brother was an active member. She gradually saw that what was being said in the association about the importance of the return to the Caucasus was logical. She therefore broke off with her *kashen*, her Circassian boyfriend, after a discussion in which he said that he would not return to the Caucasus even if it became possible. She felt that she could not marry someone who was not a *dönüşcü*. Although she had other *kashen*s, she is still single and says, 'Well, you also cannot marry someone simply because he is a *dönüşcü*'. She adds:

> I knew when I became a *dönüşcü* that it may mean my remaining single, and I definitely knew that this would be the case when I immigrated here. But my being here is a model for others; they can see that it is possible to return. There are many families who have migrated and they have small children. I regard them all as my children and the ones that will be born here will be my children as well and that satisfies me.

Emine says that her parents were not very nationalistic but that she and her two brothers were and would never marry a *yabancı*, a foreigner, a non-Circassian. Her mother had been against her coming and settling in the Caucasus but her brothers supported her and were also planning to come. Emine reserves her anger for association activists who appeared to be strongly *dönüşcü* when in Turkey and sought leadership on that basis and now were finding all sorts of reasons for not emigrating. She says that it is clear that what they were really seeking was their own political promotion in Turkey and not the benefit of the Circassians.

Emine describes how she and two others, a woman and a man, had first come to the Caucasus by bus. They had to walk across the Turkish border and take another bus because at that time buses did not come through the border. So they had to carry everything with them. A friend waited at the Turkish border to make sure that they got through, that the Turkish police did not give them any trouble. At the Russian border, the customs official was surprised by how much they had in their luggage and wanted to charge them customs. They told him that they were not trading (as he had assumed) but that they were immigrating. He was so taken aback at the thought that he just let them through with no trouble.

With her savings from Turkey, Emine bought a flat in the city from an elderly ethnic German woman who was returning to Germany.[17] She lives off her savings and her share of the family farm and businesses in Turkey while trying to establish some sort of enterprise with other returnees from Turkey.

---

17. Germans migrated to the Volga region, the Caucasus and other parts of the Russian Empire in the eighteenth century. Their return has been greatly facilitated by Germany and they constitute one of the major groups of migrants out of the Russian Federation, numbering 850,000 since 1992 and 1.4 million since 1961 (IOM et al., 1996).

They have imported equipment and goods from Turkey for their various ventures (an ice-cream making and vending machine, a teashop, a sheet sewing workshop) but so far have not been successful. She attends the meetings and rallies of the Circassian associations but is frustrated by the lack of energy and plans for working towards independence from Russia.

Emine has clear ideas on what should be done to build a Circassian society in the Caucasus. Once, when I said that as an anthropologist I studied contemporary societies, she said that there was no contemporary Circassian society, it has yet to be formed. In order to do this, Circassians from the diaspora should come back to the Caucasus. They should settle in the city of Nalchik, rather than Maikop, because in Nalchik Circassians have more weight as they are a more significant percentage of the population. In Maikop and the Adygeia republic (where they constitute only 22 per cent of the population) they would just melt among the Russians. She said that at this point in time they needed to focus on one place, to increase the Circassian population there and get a republic: once every town had become part of the Circassian republic, then it would not matter where people settled. Since Emine herself is Ubykh, she should actually settle in the city of Sochi,[18] but says that if she did that, it would have no meaning at all. Her real homeland is Sochi, with Nalchik in second place, but Nalchik is better: there are more job opportunities and life in general is better among the immigrants. In Maikop there were lots of fights. Emine said that she thought it was in the Russian government's interest to get people to settle in Maikop where the immigrants would melt into the wider society. Again, once a Circassian republic has been formed, the official language is Circassian and so on, it will not matter who marries whom because the children will be Circassian (by nationality and citizenship). At the present time, however, there is a need for chauvinism and Circassians should only marry each other.

When Emine first came to the Caucasus, she and others were able to obtain residence permits without much difficulty, however obtaining a passport and Russian citizenship was another matter. After an appearance on a local television show where she and two other 'returnees' complained that their homeland was not making them feel welcome, they embarrassed local authorities into providing them with citizenship. As she says, 'When I came here, I gave up my Turkish nationality forever'.[19]

---

18. The Ubykh are traced historically to the western coast of the Caucasus. They were decimated by warfare and then deported en masse in the nineteenth century. Scattered in the countries of resettlement, they merged with other Adyge groups and their language is no longer spoken. The coastal areas were the first to be cleared by Russian settler-colonialism with the inhabitants either deported or pushed into the mountains. Sochi, a famous port and spa city in Tsarist and Soviet times, is administratively within the Russian republic and not in Adygeia.

19. In Turkish 'Türk vatandaşlığımı gözden çıkardım': literally, 'I eliminated my Turkish nationality from my sight'.

Emine says that she has adjusted quite well to living in the Caucasus, but that she does not like living alone. She misses her family and the movement of people in and out of the house. She does have good friends, however, who always look out for her and never leave her on her own. After the first year, Emine was spending at least three or four months of each year in Turkey. Her widowed mother needed her, she said. Although Emine had tried to persuade her mother to come and live with her in Nalchik, her mother said she was too old for the rigours of life in the Caucasus. Emine's help was often needed, and she was called to Turkey to supervise the harvest, or because her sister-in-law was giving birth, or because her younger brother was getting married. 'I want to be in the Caucasus winter and summer', she says, 'but so far it has not been possible'.

Unlike Emine and other returnees, some travellers to the Caucasus, especially those who are engaged in import–export activities, do not deploy the language of absolute return but see themselves as straddling two places and building bridges between them. Engin, for example, is in his early forties and owns five companies in several cities in Turkey. In 1993, he and a relative were attempting to establish a base in the Caucasus. They formed a company with capital raised from five relatives and were exporting leather, wood and PVC and importing commodities. They have hopes of eventually winning contracts to set up telecommunications systems, and build roadworks and tourist facilities.

Engin emphasizes that his goal in these activities is not profit since he was doing very well already in Turkey. He describes the hardships and frustrations of trying to establish a business in the inefficient and 'corrupt' environment of the Caucasus. In spite of these difficulties, Engin sees it as his duty to try to help the economy of his homeland and to introduce its inhabitants to modernity. He is willing to risk the capital of $100,000 that he and his relatives have jointly formed, but not more, towards this end. He is planning to open stores in the Caucasus that are clean, bright and modern, run through modern management techniques and providing guarantees and maintenance services. He wants to establish an honest and prosperous enterprise and train people in proper business techniques '... so that everyone can see this and say: here is what the people who came from Turkey did.'

In explaining his decisions, Engin says, 'My father lived all his life completely as a Circassian.[20] I am half a Circassian but trying to be one [whole]. I owe it to him and the way he lived to try to do this'. To fulfil his obligation to his father, Engin will try to perpetuate the Circassian identity of his own children, but, he says, he does not agree with those who say that one should drop everything and migrate back. He will not bring his family to the Caucasus as it is not fair to his wife and young children. She does not speak

---

20. In Turkish: 'dört dörtlük Çerkez idi': literally, 'He was a four over four Circassian' — that is, in the full meaning of the word, totally, 100 per cent.

Circassian and has her environment in Turkey — what would she do here? The children do not speak Circassian either and they are studying in good schools. He will not move them away from Istanbul but, in the Caucasus, he will establish a base for his children that will enable them to choose, when they come of age, whether or not to return to their homeland. Business is what he is good at and what he can contribute to the homeland. If he succeeds, others will follow and his children will have the alternative, when they are eighteen or so, of remaining Circassian if they wish, or becoming Turks.

Engin thinks those who say that the Russians could be removed from the Caucasus are simply naïve. Over the past century, Russians have been settled in between the Circassian territories in a deliberate attempt to divide the Circassians. Moreover, Kabardino-Balkaria does not have the economic ability to demand independence, unlike Chechnya which has oil as well as weapons manufacturing plants. But there are great opportunities in the Caucasus. Engin describes the difficulties of life in the village in Uzunyayla in central Turkey where he was born: 'The situation of our villages is terrible. Everyone is leaving, or else one person sacrifices himself and remains for the land and the rest go to the city. The villages are emptying ... It is winter for eight months and you have to squeeze the four seasons into the remaining four months ... Although we were from the lucky ones with more land and close to the river yet I do not remember a single winter that we started with some money saved, just food for ourselves and the animals'. He continues, with tears forming in his eyes:

> My father was always up before the dawn breaks ... My mother used to work till after everyone was asleep. There were times when I would wake up in the morning and find her asleep sitting in the kitchen because she was too tired to go to bed. She should go straight to heaven for the way she worked for us so that we would be fed and clothed ... Here it is like a heaven, the earth here is so giving, you just have to plant and wait, there is no need for irrigation or anything. If you mechanized agriculture a little, it could produce incredibly. They just need a little technology ... If (and when) they begin to distribute land, then the peasants of Uzunyayla would come. They would sell what they have and come because what they have is worthless anyway. When you tell people about the land here, they listen to you as though it is a fairy tale — they cannot believe it because they have not seen anything like it. A peasant cannot afford the price of a ticket. Every person who can, like me, should pay the expenses of one peasant to come here. And when they see what is here and they tell the people (and they will believe it from the peasant more than from me) they will all come back.

In his home in Istanbul, with his family around him, Engin eloquently elaborates the same points he had made in Nalchik. His seven-year-old son, however, when asked if he would like to live in the Caucasus, simply purses his lips and responds with a long, wet and negative 'tttuuutt'.[21]

These two lives, Emine and Engin, illustrate how the politics and economics of the 'return' to the homeland are translated and refracted through the lives of individuals into a prism of expressions and representations.

---

21. A sound signifying 'No' which is well understood in all of the Middle East.

Regardless of their own attempts to classify themselves as one 'type' or the other, the narratives of such individuals supply a rich array of reasons and legitimations of their journeys to identity. These journeys start within Turkey and the pathways that they forge to the Caucasus are informed by earlier transformations and ruptures.

Emine starts out from a comfortable accommodation of her Circassian and Turkish identities until her journey from town to city in Turkey 'makes' her a *dönüşcü*. Only, however, if she finds the conditions to maintain and perpetuate Circassian identity will she stay in the Caucasus. Although she had given up her Turkish passport initially, she eventually re-obtained it in order to facilitate travel and her stays in Turkey. Engin, on the other hand, moves from the wholeness bestowed by his peasant parents in the village to the industrial sector of Istanbul which fragments his identity and that of his children. His vision of the homeland is that of economic prosperity and opportunity, of telecommunications systems and roadworks that will connect, though not conjoin, physical, external and internalized divides.

A store which sells candy and processed foods, washing machines and electrical appliances imported from Turkey and which was established in downtown Nalchik in 1995 is a site for the production of these kinds of connections. Established by Circassian businessmen from Turkey, and employing returnees and locals, it is called Elbruz/Bosfor in reference to the prime geographical landmarks of the two countries. Elbruz is the highest mountain in the Caucasian range and historically an insurmountable barrier to the invading imperial armies of the south. The Bosphorus straits in Turkey, while dividing Asia from Europe, have historically been a passage-way and trading route. The store, and the goods within it, geographically, economically and symbolically link the two locations and simultaneously invoke barriers and routes, boundaries and passageways.

NATION OR DIASPORA?

The ambiguities of ethnicity and nation-ness in a transnational world are particularly clear with returnees who state that they are back to stay in the homeland, and argue that it is the duty of all Circassians to help forge a national entity in the Caucasus. These nationalists themselves are forced to be transnational. This is not only because of the diasporic nature of the potential constituency of this Circassian nation, but also due to the nature of the 'transition economies' on which this nation is to be built. The only economic space for returnees to the Caucasus is in trading and entre-preneurial activities. The only comparative advantage for those who have little capital comes from exploiting social capital, which in this context means kin networks. Thus it is only through forming transnational trading net-works based on trust and reciprocity emanating from, and legitimated by, kinship and common ethnicity, that these returnees can insert themselves economically into the homeland. These networks are not easily created, however, in the context of the complex and sometimes adverse relations and reactions that are resulting from the encounters between Circassians. Newly discovered kinships in the Caucasus are often not able to sustain rapid commodification. Similarly, older kin networks may crumble under the weight of their new functions and the intensified and magnified obligations resulting from the expanded and fragile extension over space.

The interplay between nation and diaspora also appears clearly in the issue of residence and travel. Returnees and frequent travellers to the Caucasus attempt to obtain residence permits in the republics of North Caucasus that give rights to own property and to work. There are rather lengthy bureaucratic procedures to obtain these permits, but associations in the Caucasus help those from the diaspora to obtain them on the grounds of their Circassian ethnicity. Citizenship and a Russian passport, on the other hand, are obtained only with great difficulty. While all returnees were vocal in their criticism of the difficulties of obtaining Russian citizenship, they were reluctant to jeopardize their other passports and citizenships, given the uncertainty of the future. In addition, most returnees from Turkey, now 'resident' in the Caucasus, seek to obtain 'migrant worker' Turkish passports. This gives them certain tax breaks and enables them to move goods and hard currency across borders without paying customs dues. This is particularly useful for the export–import activities in which most of them are engaged.

The economics and politics of identity, however, do not capture all of the moments of transnationalism that are to be found in the Caucasus today. The value of a Russian passport, and the ambiguities of transnational identities, emerge in an unexpected way in the narrative of Omar, who came to the Caucasus from Jordan in 1993 at the age of twenty-three.

When asked about his reasons for coming to the Caucasus, Omar was hesitant at first and then began speaking rapidly and continuously. He said that he was here in the Caucasus because he wanted to get a Russian passport to go to Saudi Arabia to study Shari'a in Medina. To explain this startling statement he had to go back a few years to a major turning point in his life.

After he finished high school, Omar worked on the Maan–Aqaba railroad in Jordan.[22] One night he was sitting and drinking with the other workers, as they did every night, when one man started talking about religion and asked: who will get up and pray with me? Omar was the first to get up and pray and after that he stopped drinking and became religious.

He did not join any organizations or Islamic movements. He used to go from home to work to the mosque and that was all. He started to read in the magazines that came to Jordan about Afghanistan and how the Muslims

---

22. This in itself is an unusual and rare occupation in Jordan, given that there is only one track in the whole country with a once-weekly train — the one that Lawrence of Arabia is famous for blowing up.

were being killed there, women and children. There were pictures of people
with their limbs cut off. He took a plane and went to Peshawar, by himself,
where there was another Circassian that he knew from Amman. The very first
night he was there they brought in somebody who had lost a leg. Omar felt
shaken and thought that it would be one thing to be wounded or to die but
how would he feel losing a leg? A few months later the same man was playing
football. They fitted him with a plastic limb and he was left with only a slight
limp.

Omar joined an organization funded by Saudi Arabia. He spent six
months being trained. They would wake up for the dawn prayer, then have
fifteen minutes of exercises (which he always tried to avoid), and then break-
fast. They were trained on tanks, automatic weapons and mines and how to
forge passports. There were specialists from all over the world to teach them
these things.

He stayed for a year and a half but then left because someone he respected
told him that the organization was funded by Saudi Arabia, the CIA and the
Mossad. He went to his Amir[23] and asked him. The Amir said it was true
about Saudi Arabia and the CIA but not the Mossad. They had not sunk so
low, he said.

Another thing Omar did not like was that the organization he belonged to
was a rich one and they would get fancy food and blankets. Hot meals came
to them at the front lines, whereas those who were from Bangladesh and were
doing exactly the same thing would hardly get any food. Why should there be
this kind of differentiation? When the trucks with food came, it should have
been divided amongst everybody and not according to which organization
they belonged to. He gained 25 kilos there.

On the way back to Jordan, Omar passed through Saudi Arabia and
decided that he wanted to study Shari'a. He wanted to study in Medina where
there are shaykhs who teach the real religion and not that of the state and the
state cannot do anything to them even though they kill a few of them every
year. He liked Medina very much but as an Arab he had to wait a year to be
accepted into the school. He came back to Jordan. There was nothing to
do — there was no work. He was sitting one evening with his parents, joking,
and his mother said, why don't you go to Russia? He thought that this was a
good idea since, as a Russian, he would be accepted immediately to study
Shari'a.

Now he had been in the Caucasus for six months and he still didn't have
the passport. He was such a fool: if he had registered in the school back then
he would have been accepted by now. Instead it had been six months and he
still hadn't got the Russian passport. He discovered that there was no way to
get the passport except to get married. He was going to marry a girl in

---

23.   Amir literally means 'prince', 'leader' and is commonly used in Islamic organizations to
      denote section leaders especially of youth groups.

Maikop, everything was arranged and then her grandfather died. This meant, 'according to their customs', that she could not get married for six months. He came to Nalchik and found another woman to marry: she was thirty-seven years old and a lawyer, and had an adopted son Hajmurat.[24] Then her grandfather also died. He told her that he would not wait six months. Now, it had already been three months and she said that soon they would get married.

I asked whether she would be willing to go to Saudi Arabia. Omar answered that in the Caucasus, girls were willing to marry anyone just to get out of the place. He knew a prostitute who was willing to go to Saudi Arabia and wear a veil and everything just to get out. The girl he wanted to marry in Maikop also had a child, a girl whom she gave to her parents to raise. She said that her parents made her get married very young and then she divorced. This was according to what she said, but her word was not very trust-worthy.[25] She was probably a prostitute, otherwise who were all these people who kept coming in and out of her house? How many cousins could one person have? Coming in and out constantly.

Omar said that he had lost everything here. He lost 25 kilos. He had one drink and then it was all over. He managed to hold out for four months, but a person is made of flesh and blood and he surrendered to temptation. But he still prays. If he forsakes that as well he will no longer be a Muslim.

He said he had to go pick up Hajmurat from kindergarten. He said good-bye and left.

Three and a half years later (in January 1997), I had a chance encounter with a friend of Omar's in a shop for musical instruments in Amman. He had come in with three Circassian musicians from the Kabardinka folklore group of Nalchik who were performing in Amman and wanted to buy recorders. He said 'Do you remember that day we met in Nalchik there was that young man with glasses? He was martyred in Chechnya. Well, I guess he was martyred ... we have to say he was martyred. You know he used to drink and pray, drink and prostrate himself'.[26]

What does a short life like Omar's, spent in restless movement between various countries and border zones, prey to contingencies, earnest whims and random strategies, tell us about nationalism and ethno-nationalism? Omar stumbles across Islam on a railway track in Jordan. Travelling to Afghanistan to fight for Islam, women and children, he learns that passports can be forged

---

24. Haji Murat is the name of a Caucasian hero in Tolstoy's 1896 novel with the same title. Haji means one who has undertaken the pilgrimage to Mecca. Here the title and the name were collapsed into one name for the little boy.
25. In colloquial Arabic: 'ala dhimitha wa dhimmitha wasi' jiddan': literally, 'according to her conscience and her conscience is very broad'.
26. In colloquial Arabic: 'yishrab wa yisjid, yishrab wa yisjid': literally, 'drinks and prostrates, drinks and prostrates'.

and limbs can be replaced by technology. The route to the passport that he needs in order to seek true Islam goes through his ethnic identity. As a Circassian, he can transform himself from an Arab to a Russian for the purposes of acquiring Islam. The Caucasus for him is not a homeland, it is just a stopover, a transit way station. En route to Islam via the Caucasus, he is overcome by the place, its women and children. He has one drink and 'loses everything'. Finally, in Chechnya, he loses his life for the cause of Chechnian Islamic nationalism, though he is neither a Chechen nor a nationalist and perhaps no longer really a Muslim.

CONCLUSION: THE PRODUCTION OF DIASPORIC SPACES

It is not only the mobility of people beyond national boundaries that transforms identity but the problematization of the nature of boundaries and borders that creates the possibility for, and may impose, a condition of post-nationality. This condition is marked by the production of 'diasporic public spheres' and 'nonterritorial principles of solidarity' (Appadurai, 1996: 147, 165). Badie (1995) argues that the transcendence of the nation-state means that territoriality can no longer be regarded as the prime regulator of the international order. The resultant 'disorder' is marked by 'the end of territories', by a transition from territory to space, or to 'aterritoriality' (Badie, 1995: 14). In the case of 'ethnoscapes', however, perhaps in a different way than for 'mediascapes', 'technoscapes' and other post-modern landscapes (Appadurai, 1996: 33), there continues to be a place for territory and geography. This is particularly clear in the production of diasporic spaces.

The breakup of the Soviet Union meant, among other things, that 'In December 1991, Soviet citizenship ceased to exist leaving 287 million people in need of a new identity' (IOM et al., 1996: 17). In addition to the effect on the millions inhabiting the ex-Soviet space, the shock-waves engendered by these critical changes have spread into very local situations around the world and have affected small and scattered populations, whose histories are connected in numerous ways to that geographical region. While the experience of many of these groups is sometimes of little consequence for global politics, they themselves experience it as momentous.

Shapiro (1994) suggests that an 'ethics of post-sovereignty' may be generated through privileging the 'moral geographies' of peoples whose histories have hitherto been marginalized. In the post-Soviet space, the current '164 ethno-territorial disputes and claims' (IOM et al., 1996: 4) indicate that 'The end of ideology and imposed centralization has meant the return of geography, just as it signals the return, rather than "the end" of history' (Hooson, 1994: 134). Ethnography further reveals that while transnationalism has certainly transformed identity politics making them more fluid and less bounded, the geographies upon which these identities are inscribed continue to exercise the coerciveness of territoriality.

For Circassians, more than the fall of Soviet communism per se, it is the sudden porousness of borders and accessibility of territories that had been largely closed to them, that has been of transformative importance to concepts of ethnic identity. While the collapse of powerful ideological systems and the apparatus that sustained them is dramatic, yet equally dramatic have been the struggles over borders and boundaries. For many Abkhasians, Chechens, Circassians, Daghestanians and Ossetians in Turkey, Jordan, Syria, Israel, Holland, Germany, the United States and so on, the accessibility of their 'homelands', together with the conflicts within and around them, has had a galvanizing effect. It has transformed them from minorities encapsulated within their respective states into self-conscious transnational diasporas which seek to re-interpret their history, their present spatial distribution, and their connections with their various localities as well as with the homeland. The North Caucasus is now an arena for a variety of transnational encounters that question and contest past and present alignments of community, identity, and loyalty.

When the homeland was inaccessible it formed a point of reference, an explanation for what made Circassians distinctive from others and similar to one another. It was perceived of as a space out of time, a space that stood for the timeless qualities of Circassian ethnicity. Furthermore, it stood for the immemorial past. Its geographical features, its boundaries and divides were vague and ill-defined. The encounter with the homeland has brought this space back into time and has made it into a territory. It has also changed its quality as a referent. From being a highly abstract point of origin that did not directly inform present-day conditions, the accessibility of the homeland means that any future scenario for the emergent diaspora must necessarily be formed, to some degree, in relation to the Caucasus. At this moment, to remain as scattered minorities appears as the end of community, either by 'becoming Arabs', 'becoming Turks' or 'remaining Muslims'.

All this supports Clifford's generalization that 'Diasporic language appears to be replacing, or at least supplementing, minority discourse' (Clifford, 1994: 311). Clifford points out that diasporic discourses are polythetic and that 'diasporic cultural forms can never, in practice, be exclusively nationalist' (ibid: 307). The examples of Circassian ethnic politics in Turkey and ethnicity as tribalism in Jordan show that minority discourses, though constructed in reference to a 'majority', are not exclusively nationalist either and are never unified. The interpenetration of minority and diaspora discourses, the way they inform and implicate each other, shows up in the narratives of individuals as they seek pathways to identity in the contemporary global order..

While stressing the multiple attachments of diaspora populations and their accommodation to host countries, Clifford attempts to widen the concept of 'diaspora' from connections 'articulated primarily through a real or symbolic homeland' (ibid: 306). Taking seriously, however, his suggestions to study 'specific, discrepent histories' (ibid: 302), 'roots *and* routes' (ibid: 308, emphasis in the original), 'travelling rather than dwelling' (ibid: 313) and 'the routing of diaspora discourses in specific maps/histories' (ibid: 319), indicates that the homeland cannot easily be disarticulated from diasporic circuits.

The homeland, for the Circassians, is now being produced through the routes that link it to the locations of the diaspora and the journeys and encounters that take place along these routes. While the transformation of the Caucasus from space to territory has made it accessible imaginatively, difficulties of transportation, visas, border crossings, residence permits and living conditions quickly dispel any romantic notions of an in-gathering. Furthermore, the fragmented and complex identities of the diaspora and the variety of motivations in the journeys to the homeland do not translate into a primordial ethno-nationalism. Still, the impact of the access of the homeland on the sense of collectivity and community is fundamental. The ethnic community is now visualized as comprising intersecting transnational networks and specific nodes, with the Caucasus itself presenting the main arena for interaction.

Such a view of 'globalization from below' (Clifford, 1994: 327) rescinds simplified distinctions between retrograde 'ethnic nationalism' and cosmopolitan 'civic nationalism'. Deviating from a self-acknowledged bias for North America and the Atlantic (Appadurai, 1996; Clifford, 1994) also reveals new arenas, sites and terrains of post-nationality. The life histories and trajectories of individuals travelling the routes to the Caucasus show the contemporary confluence of nationalism, ethnicity, commodification and globalization. This confluence is marked by disjunctures in ethnic identity, shifting classifications constructed by individuals as to their aims and motivations, and the material and discursive production of diasporic spaces.

As long as borders are tight and exclude physical and imaginative transgressions, the ideologies and politics of identity may be equally introverted. In an emergent transnational and post-national era, however, our understandings of nationalism and 'ethno-nationalism' must keep up with the times. Looking beyond and travelling beyond the national boundaries within which they had been (imaginatively) encapsulated, has had a particular impact on Circassians: while it has expanded the geography and space of their identity, it has also reinforced the sense of diversity by locality. The question that is now posed to the newly formed diaspora is not only 'how', but also '*where* can one be truly Circassian?'. Geography is transformed but loses none of its centrality in the definition of identity. The force of history, as constructed and mediated through memory and imagination, acts upon diasporas through specific geographies and territories. In the new geography of Circassian identity, the 'homeland' in the Caucasus emerges as a pivotal place. The globalization of the Caucasus with its social, economic and political complexities, presents the Circassians of the diaspora not only with revelations of their pasts but also with visions of their futures.

REFERENCES

Anderson, B. (1991) *Imagined Communities: Reflections on the Origin and Spread of Nationalism.* London: Verso.

Andrews, P. A. (1992) *Turkiye'de Etnik Gruplar.* (Trans. Mustafa Küpüşoğlu) İstanbul: Ant Yayınları.

Appadurai, A. (1996) *Modernity at Large: Cultural Dimensions of Globalization.* Minneapolis, MN: University of Minnesota Press.

Badie, B. (1995) *La fin des territoires: Essai sur le désordre international et sur l'utilité sociale du respect.* Paris: Fayard.

Berkok, I. (1958) *Tarihte Kafkasya.* İstanbul: İstanbul Matbaasi.

Clifford, J. (1994) 'Diasporas', *Cultural Anthropology* 9(3): 302–38.

Conner, W. (1994) *Ethnonationalism: The Quest for Understanding.* Princeton, NJ: Princeton University Press.

Hall, S. (1991) 'The Local and the Global: Globalization and Ethnicity' and 'Old and New Identities, Old and New Ethnicities', in A. D. King (ed.) *Culture, Globalization and the World System*, pp. 19–68. New York: SUNY Press.

Hooson, D. (1994) 'Ex-Soviet Identities and the Return of Geography', in D. Hooson (ed.) *Geography and National Identity*, pp. 134–40. Oxford: Blackwell.

Ignatieff, M. (1993) *Blood and Belonging: Journeys into the New Nationalism.* New York: Farrar, Straus and Giroux.

IOM, UNHCR and OSCE (1996) *CIS Conference on Refugees and Migrants.* Geneva: UNHCR Public Information Section.

Karpat, K. (1972) 'Ottoman Immigration Policies and Settlement in Palestine', in I. Abu-Lughod and B. Abu-Laban (eds) *Settler Regimes in Africa and the Arab World*, pp. 57–72. Wilmette, IL: Medina University Press International.

Karpat, K. (1985) *Ottoman Population 1830–1914: Demographic and Social Characteristics.* Madison, WI: University of Wisconsin Press.

Karpat, K. (1990) 'The *hijra* from Russia and the Balkans: The Process of Self-definition in the Late Ottoman State', in D. F. Eickelman and J. Piscatori (eds) *Muslim Travellers: Pilgrimage, Migration, and the Religious Imagination*, pp. 131–52. London: Routledge.

Laclau, E. (1994) 'Introduction', in E. Laclau (ed.) *The Making of Political Identities*, pp. 1–8. London and New York: Verso Books.

Layne, L. (1994) *Home and Homeland: the Dialogics of Tribal and National Identities in Jordan.* Princeton, NJ: Princeton University Press.

Lubin, N. (1982) 'Women in Soviet Central Asia: Progress and Contradictions', *Soviet Studies* (April): 182–203.

Massell, G. (1974) *The Surrogate Proletariat: Moslem Women and Revolutionary Strategies in Soviet Central Asia (1919–29).* Princeton, NJ: Princeton University Press.

Olcott, M. B. (ed.) (1990) *The Soviet Multinational State: Readings and Documents.* Armonk, NY: M. E. Sharpe Inc.

Olcott, M. B. (1995) 'Soviet Nationality Studies between Past and Future', in Daniel Orlovsky (ed.) *Beyond Soviet Studies*, pp. 135–48. Washington, DC: The Woodrow Wilson Center Press.

Rouse, R. (1991) 'Mexican Migration and the Social Space of Postmodernism', *Diaspora* 1(1): 8–23.

Rouse, R. (1995) 'Interpreting Transnationalism: Contending Visions of Social Space in a Mexican Migrant Circuit'. Paper presented at the American Anthropological Association Annual Meeting, Washington DC (15–19 November).

Shami, S. (1992) '19th Century Circassian Settlements in Jordan', in *Studies in the History and Archaeology of Jordan IV*, pp. 417–21. Amman: Department of Antiquities.

Shami, S. (1995) 'Disjuncture in Ethnicity: Negotiating Circassian Identity in Jordan, Turkey and the Caucasus', *New Perspectives on Turkey* 12 (Spring): 79–95.

Shapiro, M. J. (1994) 'Moral Geographies and the Ethics of Post-Sovereignty', *Public Culture* 6: 479–502.

Singh, A. I. (1995) 'Managing National Diversity through Political Structures and Ideologies: The Soviet Experience in Comparative Perspective', *Nations and Nationalism* 1(2) (July): 197–200.

Smith, A. D. (1991) *National Identity*. Reno, NV: University of Nevada Press.

Suny, R. G. (1993) *The Revenge of the Past: Nationalism, Revolution and the Collapse of the Soviet Union*. Stanford, CA: Stanford University Press.

Suny, R. G. (1995) 'Rethinking Soviet Studies: Bringing the Non-Russians Back In', in Daniel Orlovsky (ed.) *Beyond Soviet Studies*, pp. 105–34. Washington, DC: The Woodrow Wilson Center Press.

Szporluk, R. (1994) 'Introduction: Statehood and Nation Building in Post-Soviet Space', in R. Szporluk (ed.) *National Identity and Ethnicity in Russia and the New States of Eurasia*, pp. 3–17. Armonk, NY: M.E. Sharpe.

Teague, E. (1994) 'Center-Periphery Relations in the Russian Federation', in R. Szporluk (ed.) *National Identity and Ethnicity in Russia and the New States of Eurasia*, pp. 21–57. Armonk, NY: M.E. Sharpe.

Tett, G. (1994) 'Guardians of the Faith: Women in Soviet Tajikistan', in Camillia El-Solh and Judy Mabro (eds) *Muslim Women's Choices*, pp. 128–51. London: Berg Publishers.

Tohidi, N. (1996) 'Soviet in Public, Azeri in Private: Gender, Islam and Nationality in Soviet and Post-Soviet Azerbaijan', *Women's Studies International Forum* 19(1–2): 111–24.

Williams, B. (1989) 'A CLASS ACT: Anthropology and the Race to Nation Across Ethnic Terrain', *Annual Review of Anthropology* 18: 401–44.

Transnationalism in the Era of Nation-States: China, 1900–1945

Prasenjit Duara

INTRODUCTION

This volume elaborates upon the idea that the globalization process repeatedly encounters the problems of 'flux' and 'fixity'. Indeed, nationalism may well be seen as an effort to fix, or more precisely, *authoritatively* regulate, the flow of global capital and its attendant processes in the interests of the nation or nation-state. In the era before 1900 or so, these flows were enabled by colonialism. During the subsequent era of 'high nationalism', up to around the 1980s (see below), nation-states claimed this authority in the name of sovereignty over a delimited, but maximized territory — the *terra firma* — in a world of ever more rapidly circulating resources and people. Sovereignty, in turn, derived from the historical claim of a people to this territory who were represented by the nation-state.

Yet for most nation-states and particularly the 'new' states seeking to join the emergent global system of nation-states from the beginning of the twentieth century, this territory was far from firmly secured. It was particularly difficult to match territory with a people since many peoples within the claimed territory refused to be represented by their purported nation-state. Conversely, there were also people beyond the sovereign territory upon whom the nation-state sought to make claims. For this and other reasons discussed below, the territorial nation was not adequate to the nation-state's claim of sovereignty. It necessarily had to supplement its sovereignty claims by appealing to alternative narratives of political community based on a racial or cultural primordialism and authenticity. The immediate goal of this article is to examine the relationships between these different conceptions of political community and the implications for the notion of territorial sovereignty in twentieth century East Asia. Its wider aim is to suggest a periodization scheme that grasps the changing status of territorial sovereignty in relation not only to these alternative narratives but to global capitalism itself.

Around the early years of the twentieth century, modern nationalism became a dominant force in China and many other parts of the colonial and semi-colonial world. Precisely because this nationalism was a reaction to

An earlier version of this essay, entitled 'Transnationalism and the Predicament of Sovereignty: China 1900–1945', appeared in *American Historical Review* 102(4): 1030–51 (Oct 1997).

imperialism, it was built around the idea of territorial sovereignty and the territorial model of sovereignty remained the dominant conception during the period of 'high nationalism' which extended until approximately the 1980s. In China this model began to change with the reforms and 'opening' launched by Deng Xiaoping in 1978; more generally, its decline can be traced to the collapse of socialistic and autarkic nationalism that took place through the 1980s in large nation-states like the Soviet Union and India. In the discussion today of the emergence of the 'deterritorialized nation' we may be seeing not only the transformation of this kind of nationalism but a predicament for nationalism as we have known it. As I understand it, the 'deterritorialized nation' is one in which the state tends to value extraterritorial loyalties (of race or culture) over territorial ones.[1] While the deterritorial nation may represent a better response to global competitiveness today, the conception of territorial citizenship entailed by the older concept of sovereignty remains politically very significant, particularly for those outside the core cultural and racial groups of the nation.

In the global system of nation-states during the first eighty years of the twentieth century, sovereignty resided only in territorially limited states and this conception was necessary to the system as a whole. Sovereignty was the principle which a territorial state invoked to defend itself against external attack (Laski, 1968: 26–8; see also Hinsley, 1986: 176); but sovereignty also had an internal or domestic dimension. The sovereignty of the territorial nation-state in modern Europe was thought to be built upon the 'common ground of identical citizenship . . . The state embraces all men by its territorial nature. It is universal because it is the one compulsory form of association' (Laski, 1968: 26–7). In other words, the territorial model of state sovereignty also carried within it a model of citizenship. None the less, prominent critics of the idea of sovereignty, like Laski, believed that the idea permitted the state to expand its prerogative *within* domestic society. Curiously enough, while for Laski the class stratification of national society belied the universalist pretension of state sovereignty, this critique did not affect the legitimacy of the sovereign territorial state in the external sphere of international relations (ibid: 27–8).

Defenders of the notion, such as Hinsley, see an intimate connection between sovereignty in its internal and external senses, arguing that just as citizen and community exercise political and ethical restraints upon the sovereign modern state, so too does the inter-state system historically limit the absolute sovereignty of the state externally. Moreover, Hinsley is convinced that the idea of internal sovereignty founded upon political society and identical citizenship is prior to external sovereignty which is dependent

---

1. According to Basch et al. (1994), deterritorialized nations are ones in which national governments count upon the loyalty, wealth and influence of their expatriates for national ends. In certain small nations like Grenada, these expatriates make up a larger number than the population at home. See especially Basch et al. (1994: Ch. 8).

upon it (Hinsley, 1969: 279). From my perspective, by the period of 'high nationalism', the sovereignty of the nation-state in the inter-state system, had, at least doctrinally, become significantly dependent upon the internal idea of 'identical citizenship within the territory', or civic nationalism. Causally, however, the experience of nation-states like China and others during this period suggests that the possibility, if not guarantee, of 'identical citizenship' is perhaps also necessitated by the nation-state's prior claim of territorial sovereignty, particularly over territories inhabited by racially or culturally dissimilar peoples. Thus, territorial nationalism embedded in sovereignty was not simply an evolutionary outcome of national history, but represented, crudely speaking, a promise, however compromised or disingenuous, of citizenship and its rights to those transcultural peoples in the vast peripheries. This may be the best way to understand the policy of the People's Republic of China (PRC) of extending privileges to ethnic minorities.

Yet, if this form of territorial nationalism became necessary in principle, recent scholarship on nationalism tells us that there is no nation-state or nationalism in the world that relies solely on this 'civic nationalism'. All nationalisms employ either more exclusive or wider narratives of historical community, based on common race, language or culture, to create an affective identification of the people with the nation. The problem with territorial nationalism is that while it is the only acceptable expression of sovereignty in the modern world, it is an inadequate basis of identification within the nation-state. Thus it is that the modern nation-state and nationalists have to appropriate a variety of historical, non-territorial and often incommensurate conceptions of political community to try to 'make' the territorial nation racially and/or culturally cohesive.[2] Transterritorial, and indeed, transnational phenomena become both obstacles and opportunities in this project.

At the same time, the language of 'appropriation' captures only one side of this political process. The imagery of 'common citizenship within the territory' is inadequate also because nationalism most often seeks its ultimate value and justification beyond its territorial figuration. Despite its blustering self-confidence, nationalism has never been fully comfortable as a self-contained, self-justifying, and self-glorifying ideology. Even Nazi Germany drew its rationale from a civilizational narrative of a transcendent, aesthetic, racialist ideal (see Balibar, 1991). Among those narratives that exceeded the geobody were, of course, those that celebrated imperialism in the name of a higher civilization or as the destiny of a superior race, but also those that celebrated a transnational ideal. Rising almost simultaneously with

---

2. This dynamic between historical conceptions of race, religion, culture, and so on, often tied up with practices of everyday life, and the new territorial conception, is a more complex way of grasping the relationship of nationalism and history than recently popularized notions of 'invented' or 'imagined' histories. Although the powerful new territorial form will try to channel these historical engines towards its own goals, as this article will try to show, these histories can also exceed it.

nationalism as a global ideology in the late nineteenth century were various transnational ideologies such as pan-Europeanism, pan-Asianism, and later pan-Arabism, pan-Africanism, and so on.

The remainder of this article examines three instances of transterritoriality: the first, a transnational vision of community among a variety of social groups and the state in Manzhouguo; the second, a pan-Asian ideology of the KMT state which was also directed towards the many transcultural peoples in China's vast, inner peripheries; and finally the nationalist appeals to the overseas Chinese, a transterritorial group with multiple loyalties. In each of these cases, I examine the relationship between the territorial nation-state and the wider transnational or transterritorial conceptions of community which the former needed to mobilize, but in a way in which it could contain the effects on its claim to territorial sovereignty. In the conclusion, I discuss the impact of the contemporary, deterritorialized nation upon the model of citizenship in the territorially sovereign nation.

REDEMPTIVE TRANSNATIONALISM, NATIONALISM AND IMPERIALISM

In China, transnational ideologies began to make their appearance at the same time that modern nationalism began to take hold, at the turn of the twentieth century. Indeed, nationalism was often justified as a stage on the way to a universalist ideal. There were at least two types of transnationalism: modern radical, utopic ideologies of anarchism and communism (which tended to move away from a transnationalism to an internationalism celebrating the comity of homologous, but separate nation-states); and another trend which I shall identify as a 'redemptive transnationalism'. This article deals only with the second, even though there are many interesting issues that relate it to leftist utopic thought. Although they identified themselves as basically modern, the advocates of this latter type of transnational ideology sought to locate themselves as inheritors of the tradition of Confucian and/or Buddhist universalism. There were several variants of redemptive trans-nationalism, but most were identifiable with groups of modern urban, élite-led, though often popularly-based, associations.

These associations include in their numbers the Morality Society, the *Dao Yuan* (Society of the Way) and its partner, the *Hongwanzihui* or Red Swastika Society, the *Tongshanshe* or the Fellowship of Goodness, the *Zailijiao* (The Teaching of the Abiding Principle), the *Shijie Zongjiao Datonghui* (Society for the Great Unity of World Religions, first organized in Sichuan in 1915 as the *Wushanshe*), and the *Yiguandao* (Way of Pervading Unity), among many others. Some of these claimed a following of many millions: the Fellowship of Goodness claimed to have 30 million followers in 1929 (Suemitsu, 1932: 252) and the Red Swastika Society 7 to 10 million in 1937 (Takizawa, 1937: 67). While these claims are likely to be exaggerated, Japanese sources of the time believed that these associations commanded very significant followings in several parts of the country.

The great majority of these societies were premised upon an East versus West polarity, where the West represented science and material culture and Eastern or East Asian civilizations represented the hope for spiritual and moral regeneration of the world. The associations, most of which were established or flourished at the time of World War I, sought to bring peace and morality to a world devastated by war and greed, by supplementing the material civilization of the West with the spiritual civilization of the East. Their spiritual solution came in the form of a religious universalism in which all major religions of the world — Confucianism, Daoism, Buddhism, Islam and Christianity — embodied the same universal spirituality. Their redemptive message drew on a rich vein of late imperial gentry syncretism (*sanjiaoheyi*) which first gained popularity in the late Ming period in the late sixteenth and seventeenth centuries. This movement, which merged Confucian precepts with Daoist and Buddhist teachings, was inspired by Wang Yangming's commitment to the self-transformation of ordinary people and urged moral engagement and the extinguishing of worldly desires (Chow Kai-wing, 1994: 21–5).

Of course, in the twentieth century these syncretic societies came to resemble other modern religious and morality societies all over the world. They were organized with charters and by-laws, armed with a strong this-worldly orientation and a modern rhetoric of global redemption. Perhaps their participation in a modern discourse is revealed most clearly by their allegiance to that most fundamentally modern discourse: evolutionism or the linear history of progress. Many of their arguments and propositions were framed by this discourse of evolutionary history, although the scope of this history was not confined to the nation. They argued that human evolution (*jinhua*) would stall and become even more destructive if the present trend towards hedonistic materialism (exemplified by the West) was not countered by moral and spiritual regeneration (MMS, 1934: Part 4.1; see also Takizawa, 1937: 67). Thus their spiritualism was dedicated to restoring humanity's evolution to perfection.

The modern spiritualism of these societies encoded a universalizing impulse that sought to transcend national boundaries in search of the ultimate moral and spiritual community. Thus, while the red swastika of the society with that name could and should be understood in Buddhist terms, it was also modelled upon (an Eastern equivalent of) the Red Cross Society (Suemitsu, 1932: 354). Many of these societies were committed to benevolent works and philanthropy (*cishan shiye*) including traditional charities such as soup kitchens and poorhouses, and also modern hospitals, schools, and contributions to relief works. In their efforts, there was an insistent urge to break through national barriers. Thus, for instance, the *Hongwanzihui*, which had branches in Paris, London and Tokyo and had professors of Esperanto among its members, contributed substantially not only to relief works in China but also to those following the Tokyo earthquake and natural disasters in the Soviet Union (ibid: 292–305).

Consider the role of one such redemptive society, the Morality Society (*Daodehui*): this Society had a strongly syncretic religious and moral character and a salvationist rhetoric that was universal in scope. It argued that morality alone gave meaning to the universe, and it was the morality of the East that would save the universe from the materialism and destructiveness of the West (MMS, 1936: Part 3.1). The society was founded in Shandong in 1918 and the philosopher Kang Youwei served as its President in the 1920s, until he died in 1927 (MMS, 1934: Part 1.1). Kang Youwei was perhaps the most prominent name associated with the philosophy of 'redemptive transnationalism'. Kang's philosophy became widely known because of his leadership of the ill-fated 100 Days Reform movement of 1898 which was quashed by the imperial court; Kang and his associates were forced to live in exile until the overthrow of the Manchu dynasty in the republican revolution of 1911.

Kang's philosophy developed out of the New Text school of Confucian thought which believed that political action must adapt to the needs of a given time. He was thus able to argue for modern institutions, and ultimately even for a modern nation-state, while remaining within a universalist Confucian perspective. For Kang, the ultimate significance of the nation-building project arose from its self-transcendence in the universalist utopia, *Datong*, where there would be no barriers of class, gender, culture and nations (K'ang Yu-wei, 1958). It was a utopia which was not only inspired by Confucian ideals of universal love, but which also represented a 'transcendent universalization of Confucian values' (Grieder, 1981: 265). Like Liang Shuming, Kang saw himself as the Confucian sage, the transmitter of the Way, the agency whereby the ancient and universal truths of the world will be revealed. The *Datong* philosophy of Kang Youwei harmonized well with the transnational and salvationist impulses of the society.

How did the Chinese nation-state respond to these societies? The Kuomintang (KMT) government (1927–49) treated all these redemptive societies, as it did the Morality Society, with extreme hostility and banned them (Ōtani, 1937: 69, 123; see also Suemitsu, 1932: 251, 255). In some ways it was an ironic move, because the KMT also espoused a similarly dualistic, redemptive modernity, as we shall see below, but significantly the source of the spiritual mission which would enable it to redeem the world lay specifically in China. The KMT declared its opposition to these societies because it claimed that they were riven by superstitions and dominated by local bullies and warlords. Behind this rhetoric, however, lay a strategic representation of modern religion and national tradition. In this strategy, the KMT produced a realm of legitimate spiritualism into which it incorporated modern, licensed religions and designated them as part of China's *national* tradition. Obversely, many popular religious traditions were condemned as superstition and banned — in part at least to uproot the historical, political power of religious heterodoxy (Duara, 1995a: Ch. 3). In the view of the KMT, the transnational spiritualism of these redemptive societies not only transgressed the national boundaries of spiritualism that it had devised; it also suspected these societies of promoting a politics of counter-nationalism. Certainly the cultural bonds of these societies with similar Japanese societies made them susceptible to such attacks.

Despite the feverish development of nationalism in Japan, the Meiji period (1868–1912) was not wanting in redemptive pan-Asian movements which both fed and resisted the nascent imperialism of that nation (Hashikawa, 1980: 331–41). Among imperial powers, Japan was in some ways unusual because it did not distinguish itself racially and culturally from most of its colonies. Japanese pan-Asianism thus dramatized the uncontainability of the nation whose narrative of history shuttled between an impulse to regard its empire in East Asia as its cultural womb and thus to assimilate its subjects as citizens of the Japanese imperial nation itself, and the equally powerful drive to distinguish itself from its backward Asian colonies who were not capable of attaining modern civilization (Tanaka, 1993). Japanese narratives of the nation, which appeared to have been so rigorously internalized by its citizens through various disciplinary regimes, were in fact caught between the search for roots beyond the national territory — in northeast Asia, East Asia, Asia — and an anxious desire to belong to the civilized, Western world. In both cases, the nation sought its fullest meaning beyond itself.

Redemptive societies in Japan similar to those in China, such as the *Shibunkai*, offering Confucianism and Shinto as the spiritual alternative to excessive materialism and individualism, began to grow in strength from the 1920s, particularly as economic conditions worsened and social unrest grew. Asiatic moral systems emphasizing ethical responsibilities were celebrated as alternatives to capitalism and Marxism, both Western doctrines (Smith, 1959: 123–6). By the 1930s, the redemptive rhetoric of élite Japanese Confucian societies and the right wing nationalists and militarists not only began to come together but were also assimilated in an active political and educational programme by the Japanese government (ibid: 154–6). The most systematic and sustained effort to formulate a redemptive pan-Asianism, however, was undertaken by the young officers and intellectuals in the Kwantung army in Manzhouguo.

Manzhouguo was the Japanese puppet state in Manchuria which existed between 1932 and 1945. The Morality Society flourished in Manzhouguo because of state patronage of its activities and those of similar organizations. Thus it was that the Manzhouguo state, the real power behind which was the Japanese military, had at its disposal an ideology and language of trans-nationalism with which to forge an alliance with the redeemers of modernity in northeast China. The most important doctrine of statist pan-Asianism was the 'kingly way' or *wangdao*, a Confucian historical notion of rulership based on moral example that was contrasted to the hegemonic way or *badao*. Some six years before the establishment of Manzhouguo, none other than Sun Yat-sen had urged the Japanese to pursue the kingly way in contrast to the Western imperialist nations who persisted in the immoral hegemonic path. Sun's advocacy had now been appropriated by the Manzhouguo state. The message of the kingly way, or moral and spiritual salvation of the world by the East, was one that well suited the world view of the leaders of the Morality Society who were the successors of the old gentry élite. The Morality Society was perhaps the most élite Chinese organization among all such societies in Manzhouguo. Its membership and office-holders boasted top officials, merchants, and landowners at all levels of Manzhouguo society from the major cities to the sub-county townships. Through its propaganda activities in schools, in lectures, in spreading *baihua* commentaries of classical morality, in establishing popular enlightenment societies to 'reform popular customs and rectify the people's minds and hearts', the Society propounded a strong rhetoric of reaching out to all — rich and poor, men and women (MMS, 1934: Part 2: 36–42; Part 4: 117, 118; Part 8: 22–3). By 1934, the 312 branches of the Manzhouguo society operated 235 'righteous' or 'virtuous' schools, 226 lecture halls, and 124 clinics (ibid: Part 1: 21).

While the Manzhouguo regime advocated modernization and, indeed, carried out one of the most comprehensive modernization programmes in Asia outside of Japan, its pan-Asianism was designed significantly to restrict the penetration of 'Western' moral, cultural and political ideas into society. One of the most important means through which both the Manzhouguo state and the Morality Society sought to restrict Western cultural penetration was by the disciplining of family and gender roles within it. It promoted the representation of the new family: pure, selfless, and committed to the moral regeneration of the world by adherence to the kingly way. In this project, women became the principal vehicles of the new morality. As repositories of all that was good and essential in East Asian traditions, women's bodies and minds became the sites for a discourse of self-sacrifice, righteousness and moral regeneration. The figure of woman, though mediated by much complexity, came to stand for Eastern purity and cultural inviolability (Duara, 1995b).

A look into some of the personal narratives of the Chinese women lecturers of this society reveals some of the motives, practical and spiritual, that led them to the Morality Society. A recurrent theme is the importance of the Buddhist faith in their lives and the way in which the Morality Society, which demanded a commitment to public service to the point of self-sacrifice, had opened up for women this path of service to the world. For the first time, says one woman, women, like men, could devote themselves to the social good. Once a woman had satisfactorily served the in-laws, it was incumbent in the next phase to serve the world, in accordance with Buddhist teachings (MMS, 1936: Part 4: 134–5). A Mrs Chen emphasizes not only the value of self-sacrifice that women had cultivated in the home, but also how these values could purify the world once women engage in public service (ibid: 181). This same woman later reveals the different ways in which her parents were good people and the way in which she could be a morally pure person. Her parents were good people of a village or a county; she is a good citizen of the nation and the world (ibid: 227–8). It is true that such declarations were often mixed with instrumental goals and also served the regime's purposes: none the less, the commitment to the older Buddhist ideal of striving for universal salvation — which had a curiously liberating effect because it only now became possible for women to pursue this idea outside the home — was an unmistakable element in the self-perception of these women.

Pan-Asianism in East Asia embedded a vision of community that sought to transcend the territorial nation-state and redeem and regenerate the world through Eastern spiritual morality. This vision was constructed in the image of Western civilization (to which Western nations were also indebted) and served as an important source of authority for the political programmes of many groups — nationalist, transnationalist, and others. As it turned out, redemptive transnationalism in this area, and era, was pressed into service by Japanese militarists and imperialists. It is perhaps the general condition that transnational entities and ideologies, which almost by definition lack defensive political organizations will, when possible, be appropriated by states and militaries for their own purposes.

STATIST TRANSNATIONALISM AND THE GEOBODY

Transnational imaginings were not the exclusive domain of the redemptive societies. Despite its committed nationalism, at some levels, KMT ideology also drew upon transnational sources of authority to endow the nation with higher meaning. Thus ideologists like Chen Lifu argued that the Chinese spiritual tradition had evolved parallel to the Western material tradition. Once the two became fused in the Chinese republic, history could be propelled into civilizational perfection, to be embodied in the universal *Datong* or the Great Unity (Chen, 1976: 133). Perhaps the most significant pronouncement on the transnational ideals and roots of the Chinese nation was made by Sun Yat-sen himself in a 1924 speech to Japanese merchants in Kobe, just months before his death. It is of particular interest not only because of its foundational character, but because it mirrors the very intertwining of race and civilization that Western imperialism had itself employed to suppress the emergence of modern nations in the colonized world.

In the speech, called *Da Yaxiyazhuyi* or 'Great Asianism', Sun invokes the monumental significance of Japan's victories over Western imperialism, first in overcoming the unequal treaties some thirty years before and, most of all, in the Russo-Japanese war in 1905. He narrates a personal testimony to the impact of this victory: he was in a ship crossing the Suez canal soon after the victory when some locals enthusiastically mistook him for a Japanese. Even after discovering their mistake, however, they continued to celebrate their solidarity with him against the imperialist powers. In the speech, Sun develops the theme of a racial or colour war against the white race for whom, (he cites in English) 'blood is thicker than water', which is why the British were saddened by Russia's defeat despite their political alliance with the Japanese (Sun, 1930). The theme of common coloured-ness (*yousede minzu*) among the oppressed Asians is braided with, and finally yields to, another unity: common culture and cultural resistance. When the 900 million Asians realize that the culture of the West has been arbitrarily imposed upon them and that they too have a powerful and independent culture and philosophy, they will put up an unyielding resistance (ibid: 4).

From this point in the text, Sun discusses the notion of the Asian kingly way (exemplified by the Chinese imperium) versus the hegemonic way of the West. To illustrate the effectiveness of the morally based *wangdao*, he cites the example of Nepal which continued to pay tribute to imperial China despite the precipitous decline of China's political power in the nineteenth century, while the politically powerful British, on the other hand, were compelled to subsidize the Nepalese monarchy to retain the flow of Gurkhas into the British army. Rather than analyse the situation in terms of the maintenance of the balance of power, Sun chooses to interpret it as a moral lesson in Asian nurturing of ethical values (ibid: 5). Towards the end of the speech, Sun returns his attention to Japan where he predicts an apocalyptic culture war between the forces representing the aggressive militarism of the West and the moral pacifism of the East and urges his listeners to strengthen the forces of peace in their nation (ibid: 7).

We may pause to reflect on the fateful irony that it was precisely the notions of *wangdao* and Eastern culture that the enemies of Chinese nationalism in Japan and Manchuria also sought to deploy. Lest we think it was only appropriated by imperialists, however, there is evidence that as alternatives to Westernized modernity, these notions had considerable popularity in China. Thus, apart from redemptive societies, secret societies and peasant rebels continued to use the rhetoric of universalism and pan-Asianism. In particular, they used it to oppose the modern nationalism of the KMT and others, who they believed were bent upon uprooting their cultural and material world (Mitani, 1979).

Before going on to examine the ways in which the nation-state sought to use Sun's pan-Asianism, I want to examine the manner in which Sun constructs pan-Asianism discursively. In his formulation, the territorially delimited notion of Asia is symmetrical with Europe (or East with West), the racial or physical attribute of colour contrasts with whiteness, and the superior Asian civilization built on morality and spirituality forms the perfect counterpart to European material civilization. In this mirror image, the nation derives its strength by returning to its wider territorial, racial and cultural roots. What is the source of this discursive construction and how does it function? Race, civilization and territory had provided the bases both of imperialism and nationalism in the non-Western world in the early twentieth century. The particular matrix of these ingredients in this period took the form of social Darwinism.

Social Darwinism justified colonial intrusions by arguing that the imperial races with territorially sovereign states possessed a superior, enlightened civilization or history. This configuration justified conquest of inferior races with no history or national territory, and colonial apparatuses of knowledge worked to reproduce this sociology. Non-Western nationalism, at least in East Asia, was produced within the general terms of this social Darwinist configuration. Nationalist élites in these societies responded by formulating the present or desired territorial nation (what Thongchai Winnichakul has called the 'geobody'; Thongchai, 1994) as the subject or agent of history to which belonged the entire past that had occurred on this delimited but maximized surface. In the ideal of self-contained nationalism, which Sun's party had once advocated, the territorial nation was to be perfectly co-extensive with a homogeneous community (race) and a common culture, so that this sleek body moving in historical time could be perfectly poised to lunge successfully into the future (Duara, 1995a: Ch. 1). New nations were thus produced in the matrix of the old discourse. Sun's formulation of pan-Asianism develops in great part within the same matrix; but where in nationalism, race and culture are locked into the nation-state, here they remain unbounded by the territorial state. At one level, we could say that pan-Asianism responded more directly to the discursive conditions that produced nationalism: transnational imperialism. It sought to address problems and anxieties that nationalism could not resolve within its own bounds.

In late 1930, the new journal *Xinyaxiya* was founded by the KMT thinker Dai Jitao to fulfil Sun's ideals of pan-Asianism. The mission of the journal proclaimed that it sought to address the problem of nation-building in relation to the border question and in relation to the liberation of the nations of the East: 'In order to reconstruct China it is necessary to develop China's border areas; in order to liberate the nationalities (*minzu*) of Zhonghua [China composed of the Han and other minorities], it is necessary to liberate the nationalities of the East alike' (from the preface of the first issue of *Xinyaxiya*, 1930). One of the central concerns of the journal was to stabilize and secure the vast border regions of the Republic which constituted almost two-thirds of the territorial surface of China and included Manchuria, Mongolia, Xinjiang, Qinghai, Tibet, and the Southwest. Populated as they were until recently by non-Han peoples, political resistance to the Republic of 1912 had been experienced in almost all of these areas.

The border question dramatized a classic problem of modern nationalism. In positing the nation as an evolving unity, national histories project the 'geobody' into the past. The Chinese nation-state was no exception and claimed sovereignty over peoples in these lands despite the fact that the modern notion of sovereignty was irrelevant to the relationship between the Chinese imperial centre and these local polities. The peoples in these regions had multiple and overlapping relations with several polities, including the imperial Chinese state. Moreover, their perception of the imperial Chinese state differed greatly from modern understandings of the sovereign territorial state. As the Mongols seeking independence from the impending Republic declared in 1911, their relationship with the Qing empire was one with their fellow Central Asian Manchus, not with the Han Chinese of Kitad. They believed that they were at the same level as the Han Chinese within the empire and now that the empire had dissolved, each should go its own way (Nakami, 1984: 146–7).

It was precisely in response to this kind of problem, which worsened with the virulent anti-Manchu racialist nationalism of the period until 1912, that the new Republic of 1912 was declared to be the Republic of the Five Races or Nationalities, thus establishing the juridical notion of equal membership in the territorial nation. Such declarations in the Republic seemed hollow, however, as they were accompanied by increasing Han settlement of the border areas. If anything, tensions between the local peoples and Han settlers, soldiers, administrators and merchants in these regions appeared to have been exacerbated during the Republic (Ma, 1930).

Thus, territorial nationalism, despite its promise, could not by itself resolve the problem of political resistance by the 'minorities' as these trans-cultural peoples came to be called. Dai's pan-Asianism (more anti-imperialist than redemptive), on the other hand, could provide an alternative basis for solidarity with the non-Han. By emphasizing a strongly culturalist and weakly racialist (coloured peoples versus whites) basis for solidarity, ironic-ally, pan-Asianism could be mobilized to secure national solidarity. This is, I believe, the only way to understand the journal's mission of deliberately juxtaposing the liberation of the minorities with that of Eastern nationalities. However, the essay mentioned below reveals that it is not enough to see nationalism as simply appropriating transnational ideas. Just as critically, nationalism reveals its own insufficiency when it depends upon transnation-alism not only to resolve certain problems, but to establish its *raison d'être*.

An essay in the journal entitled 'The evolution of Asian culture and its new opportunity', while not very reliable for its scholarship, provides an instance of this mutual dependency. The author, Zhang Zhenzhi, traces the origins of world culture to mountainous regions and plateaus, and specifically to the Pamir Plateau in Central Asia. He declares that three of the four oldest cultures of the world are Asian (China, India and Mesopotamia), while the fourth, Egypt, has had close ties to Asia. Zhang next cites the older philosophies of Asian, and specifically Chinese, civilizations and their great inventions as signs of early Asian superiority which had made possible the modern age in world history. Lamentably, in the last thousand years or so, Asian civilizations have declined and been overtaken by the Europeans. He locates this decline within a sociology of natural and cultural races. The natural races are barbaric peoples whose blood is relatively unmixed, whose physical stature is robust, and whose spirit is courageous and fierce. The cultural races belong to old cultures with mixed blood, are literary rather than martial, and are without the former's spirit. They cannot avoid decline. All Europeans are of the first type, but, notably, they also have civilization. The weakness of Asian cultures is revealed in the thought of their philo-sophers, Confucius, Mencius and the Buddha, which is deep, but unpractical and other-worldly. Thus society became monkish and dilettantish. In China the Han people were conquered by the natural, barbaric Mongols and Manchus raised in the wilderness. The Han were pushed south to the Yangzi river and from there still further south to the Pearl river. Thus, the land of the origins of Chinese culture in the Yellow river basin was transformed into a desolate wilderness (Zhang, 1930: 81–6).

Reviving Asian culture, according to Zhang, depends on the ability to absorb the new world culture on the foundations of the old Asian culture (ibid: 87). Indeed, this absorption cannot be seen as a surrender to the West since the West itself is harvesting the yield which has grown multi-fold from the seeds and sprouts of Asian culture, the originator and early leader of world civilization. This circular motif of the return of greatness to its origins is elaborated much more fully in a remarkable sub-narrative in which the fate of the Chinese nation becomes inextricably linked to revival of Asian greatness. Only the Three People's Principles of Sun Yat-sen can lead to Asia's revival. That is because Sun was from Guangdong (the Pearl River delta) which is historically the meeting point of Asia and the West: both the eastern and western routes to China from the West enter through Guangdong. At the same time, because the Han people were pushed south by barbarians, Guangdong became the southern-most foothold of these people. This synthesis of East and West could be glimpsed in the nineteenth-century Taiping rebels from the south who espoused Christianity, but they did not understand the true meaning of modern revolution. Only Sun understood both ancient China's civilization and modern revolution. Thus he urged us to study Western science, not its politics or philosophy. Once we do so and revive ancient Asiatic culture, we can catch up with the West. Only when this new harmonization of the old and the new circles back from the Pearl river to the Yangzi to the northwest and from there to the Pamir plateau, will world civilization find its final settling place and be perfected (ibid: 89).

There is no question that this rather fanciful historical narrative secures the role of the Chinese nation as the saviour of Asian, and indeed, world civilization. It recalls the way in which Sun himself equated Asiatic values principally with *wangdao*, a Confucian category, which leaves us with no doubt as to the centre of Asiatic culture, and is an expression of how national histories co-opt transnational ideals. Yet the need felt to build this role within the framework of Asian culture should not be dismissed. The tale of the hero who returns a culture to its original greatness endows greatness to the hero, but only on condition that the culture itself is great. Both the hero and the culture he revives empower each other. Note here how China figures as an intermediary, both as historical agent — since the hero is Chinese, agency is transmitted through synecdoche — and as object of agency — the fallen culture which the hero will have to first uplift before going on to the ultimate task of reviving Asia. Thus the tale cannot simply be viewed as a nationalist appropriation because the authorizing function of the wider culture has itself to be explained.

CHINESE TRANSNATIONALS AND NATIONALIST IDEOLOGY

In the discussion above we have seen how imperialists and the nation-state rejected, required and commandeered the ideology of transnationalism. Here I will explore how Chinese transnational communities — a lived reality of transnationalism — negotiated the claims of loyalty made by nationalist ideology upon them. I will consider the phenomenon of overseas or migrant Chinese communities in southeast Asia and America in the early twentieth century when modern Chinese nationalists first recognized their significance to the nation-building project. In the period from 1900 to 1911, three groups of Chinese nationalists (the imperial Manchu state itself, the constitutional reformers like Kang Youwei and Liang Qichao, and the revolutionaries like Sun Yat-sen) made extensive efforts to raise contributions and investments among the increasingly wealthy Chinese overseas for projects within or related to China.

In the emergent ideology of the nation-state system, the territorial conception of the sovereign nation-state could not include the Chinese overseas in the political community (the notion of extraterritoriality and dual citizenship were exceptional provisions that confirmed the rule). On the other hand, it was precisely the discourses of race and culture — pressed (and fitted) into the service of the territorial nation, but always exceeding it — which provided the grounds for nationalists to appeal to these overseas communities. The nationalists made their appeals to the Chinese overseas on the grounds of older, pre-national or non-territorial discourses of community such as Confucian culturalism or Han racism. These older discourses were now recast as historical narratives that stressed rootedness and belonging to the territorial nation-state.

The problem for the nationalists, however, was two-fold: first, they themselves were deeply divided as to what China or Chinese-ness meant; secondly, while they assumed that they were appealing to a Chinese-ness, they were, in effect, building a conception of Chinese-ness among people who, to the extent that they had it at all, had a very different sense of it. These primordialist narratives of belonging and rootedness, with deep rifts within themselves, fought an uphill battle against dispersion and division, deracination and deculturation, localization and globalization among the Chinese overseas. Yet in some ways, they also succeeded in cultivating a vague, contextual, and ambivalent yearning for a Chinese-ness that reminds us of the 'national' in 'transnational'.

Emigrants from China often organized themselves as several simultaneously different communities: as linguistic groups such as Cantonese *bendi*, Hakka, Chaozhou and Hokkien, which were mostly mutually incomprehensible; as surname groups; as territorial or native-place communities; as secretive versus public sodalities; and as class differentiated groups, among others (see Duara, 1997; Freedman, 1979; Ma, 1990: 7–29; Yen, 1976: 4–15, 286–9). An individual might have belonged to several of these communities, thus crossing some permeable boundaries, while encountering other harder boundaries. At the same time, emigrant communities were also differentiated by how they perceived their boundaries with the surrounding communities and cultures — depending often on the nature of the indigenous or colonial polity and racial division of labour (Alatas, 1977: 75–6, 85–9). Thus Chinese in Thailand tended to assimilate with local Thais (or exhibit a biculturalism), Peranakans in Indonesia to remain aloof from the local culture, and Chinese in the Philippines to emerge as a *mestizo* group half-way between the above two (Lee, 1978: 4–5; Purcell, 1965: 30–6). Chinese Christians in North America (Ma, 1990: 21–2, 36) or Malaccan Babas and other straits-born Chinese who intermarried with local Malays and later became Anglicized, had different and changing attitudes from those more recently arrived (*xinke*) from China (Freedman, 1979: 63–4). If we imagine a baseline scenario of these communities before the arrival of mainland nationalist forces, it would be this image of multi-strandedness and shifting boundaries. The activists sought to transform these mobile, transnational lives into a Chinese-ness that eliminated or reduced internal boundaries on the one hand, and hardened the boundaries between Chinese and non-Chinese on the other. From this period, these emigrants who had had no single name for themselves came to be known as *huaqiao* or sojourning Chinese.

When nationalist organizers, especially revolutionary republicans, arrived in the early 1900s in southeast Asia and the Americas, they were appalled by this absence of a Chinese-ness among the 'Chinese'. Revolutionary leader Hu Hanmin, who was sent to organize Chinese overseas for the revolutionary cause in 1908 (Hu, 1931), was struck by two phenomena: the extent to which many overseas Chinese had lost their Chinese identity, and the extent to which those who remained Chinese were under the spell of imperial Confucian culture. The amazement or grief about the loss of Chinese-ness among overseas Chinese is a recurrent theme among revolutionaries and indexes the rapidity with which the idea of national loyalty had become naturalized or de-historicized among them. Hu reports that many overseas Chinese from Fujian would find it strange if he asked them their Chinese names (Hu, 1931: 6). Another revolutionary, Lu Hun, complained that when asked, those Chinese residing in Java would reply that they were Javanese; those in Singapore, Singaporeans, and so on (Lu, 1910: 3981). Moreover, Hu found them greedy for the honours and titles of the imperial state. Such was the extent of their identification with the imperial Confucian orientation, that the only way to identify them as Chinese was by the queues that they sported — a sign, in fact, of submission to the Manchus in China! While Hu on the one hand decries their lack of a modern republican sensibility, he is thankful that the queue at least continues to identify them as Chinese. Yet his predicament is clear in his subsequent comment that he would have them cut off their queues after they had been made sufficiently Chinese (*zhongguohuale*) (Hu, 1931: 7).

In 1910, the revolutionary Xihuang Zhengyin's influential history of the overseas Chinese in Nanyang was published in the republican journal

Minbao. The author and Lu Hun, who wrote a preface framing the text tightly within the following narrative, lament the loss of Chinese identity among the overseas Chinese and seek the origins and history of overseas Chinese settlement in order to rally Chinese people both within and outside China to resist the Manchus. Xihuang develops two intertwined narratives which address two dimensions of a social Darwinian nationalism. The first is the narrative of the *huaqiao* as the last loyalists of the Han race who resisted the two principal barbarian invaders, the Mongols and the Manchus. The text dwells at length on the resistance by the southerners led by Koxinga against the Manchus. These Ming loyalists finally fled to Southeast Asia where they were persecuted by the Dutch colonialists in active collusion with the Manchus (Xihuang, 1910: 4002–10).

If the first narrative deplores the victimization of loyalist heros by foreigners, both barbarian conquerors of China and western colonialists, the second narrative seeks to remind *huaqiao* of their glorious role as pioneering colonizers. Xihuang writes that geographically, Nanyang has been China's southern screen of defence; historically, it has been China's territory (*lingtu*) for thousands of years; and finally, it has been a place of colonial settlement for no less than seven million (sic) Han people. Despite their great numbers, however, the *huaqiao* have succumbed to the tyranny of a small number of Europeans and Americans (ibid: 3986–7). Central to this narrative are the reigns of the first two Ming emperors who conducted the great maritime expeditions across the Indian Ocean, revived Han power in Southeast Asia and re-established colonial settlements there. The Ming represented the culmination of an early and interrupted history of Chinese colonization of Nanyang; it was a time when settlers in Nanyang after 90 years of Mongol rule were once again able to see the light of day (ibid: 3994–6). By their great enterprise of colonizing distant lands (*yuanluo*), these two emperors are 'the great men of national imperialism in world history' comparable not only to the founders of the Han and Tang dynasty, but to Columbus, Magellan and others (ibid: 4110). Indeed, according to Lu Hun, Nanyang has been China's new America for centuries (Lu, 1910: 3981). As for the settlers, Xihuang recounts the stories of the great pioneers who ruled Southeast Asian states, and concludes that despite all odds, these settlers have continued the legacy of the Ming. They have conquered the savages, reclaimed land, and dominated commerce; the greatness of their civilizing purpose — evidenced by their support for education — is unmatched. In conclusion, he quotes Theodore Roosevelt to the effect that the Chinese, with their adventurous and enterprising character, are most capable of developing the barbarians (*kaipi caolai zhi renmin*) (Xihuang, 1910: 4112).

The two narratives are joined together causally: the reason that *huaqiao* were not able to defend these southern lands from the Western colonizers is not because they are deficient in any way. It is because they have been denied any support or encouragement from the Qing government, and worse, they have been vilified, sabotaged and persecuted by it. Colonial expansion by the

Western powers was only made possible by the support of each of their states, Portuguese, Dutch or English. The present condition of the *huaqiao* is the consequence of despotic rule by an alien race (ibid: 4111). Thus to restore the Han to their pristine greatness in the progress of world history towards which the *huaqiao* have made such great contributions, it was now incumbent upon all Chinese to overthrow the Manchus. The image of Chinese-ness that the revolutionaries offered the Chinese transnationals was one associated not with high cultural traditions, but with newly discovered Enlightenment values of adventurousness, enterprise, and expansionism. The narrative of national greatness focused upon Han racial superiority over primitive peoples unlimited by territorial boundaries.

For all of their discursive ingenuity, the revolutionaries were unable to generate support from more than a very small segment of the populace until 1911. One of the more sympathetic accounts of the republican efforts indicates that even at the time of the 1911 revolution, no more than 0.3 to 0.5 per cent of the Chinese transnational population in Singapore and Malaya supported the revolutionary parties (Yen, 1976: 263).[3] During this period the Qing imperial state as well as the constitutional reformers were more successful in gaining the attention of the Chinese overseas. Both employed the older Confucian cultural narrative of community through which they tried to channel the emigrants' loyalties to the new territorial nation.

Although the Qing state was initially hostile to those who left the imperial realm, and at best, indifferent to the fate of the Chinese overseas, by the late nineteenth century when it began to try to participate in the nation-state system, it quickly recognized the advantages that Chinese overseas could bring. They could be useful to the nation-building effort because of their technical knowledge, as spies, and ultimately for their wealth which could be tapped for both investment and revenue purposes. The imperial state couched its nationalism in the model of Confucian gentry culturalism. For many of the Nanyang Chinese who came from modest merchant or would-be merchant backgrounds, this model had more appeal than the one the revolutionaries offered. In late imperial China, merchants had emerged as among the most persistent emulators and patrons of literati culture and ritual especially in peripheral, 'barbarian' regions such as Yunnan and Guangxi (Naquin and Rawski, 1987). Despite undoubted differences, the cultural pattern established by the emigrating or sojourning merchants continued to have some force in Southeast Asia. While the political power of colonial regimes and the social ties with the local communities did exercise a pull on these merchants, the blockages or limits — in particular, the racial bound-aries laid by colonial rulers — on these same pull factors, the continuing

---

3. Support for republicanism had to await the establishment of a republican administration in 1911 and especially 1927 when the KMT regime promoted the spread of (Mandarin) Chinese schools across Southeast Asia.

links with Chinese communities and families, and, from the late nineteenth century, the unexpected attention from the imperial establishment in China made this civilizational model of Chinese-ness very attractive to the merchant community.

From the 1890s until the Republican revolution in 1911, the Qing regime sold countless brevet ranks and titles to eager buyers. After 1907, those who invested over 2000 yuan in a modern enterprise in China received the first rank (Zhuang, 1989: 257–8). Titles were also purchased for three generations of ancestors and ranked Chinese transnationals could don 'dynastic costumes' when receiving Qing delegates and celebrating imperial holidays (ibid: 255–7). The popularity of these imperial symbols must be understood in the context of a larger effort, indeed, campaign, by the imperial Confucian establishment to instil Confucian virtues among the overseas Chinese in Asia. Literary and charitable gentry-style societies, Confucian temple-building, the teaching of the imperial maxims in community centres, among other activities, were financed by local merchants, directed by imported scholar-officials, and often sponsored by local consulates. The idea was to wean overseas Chinese away not only from both Malay-ization and Westernization or Islam and Christianity by introducing an upper-class or gentry model of Chinese-ness, but also, by the late 1900s, to compete effectively with the narratives of both the reformers and the revolutionaries (Huang, 1993: 273–81).

The last group of nationalists to appeal to the Chinese overseas were the constitutional reformers who were also more successful than the revolution-aries even though they did not possess the political advantage that the Qing regime possessed as rulers. The same reformer and philosopher Kang Youwei, who was later to head the Morality Society, was able to formulate a vision and programme of modernity within the framework of Confucian civilization and constitutional monarchy (*xujun gonghe*). During his years of exile from China in the 1900s after the failure of the 1898 reforms, this vision was embodied in the *Baohuanghui* (The Society to Protect the Emperor) which had many chapters all over Nanyang and America. The focus on the emperor — especially a constitutional emperor who also stood for change — as symbolic of Chinese civilization gave Kang a political advant-age at the time among Chinese transnationals. He could appeal to the monarchism or prestige of imperial state and the symbols of that ideology in a way that was not available to the revolutionaries, and yet promote reform. On the other hand, the reformers — who were not in power — were not constrained in the way that the imperial state, which sought to graft a modern nationalism onto an older discourse of civilization, was constrained in how far it could reform itself without losing power. In their synthesis of the necessity of the old and the new, the reformers were able to attract those merchants, would-be merchants and others drawn to the imperial Confucian model, while appealing to the changing consciousness of the people who were, despite or perhaps because of Chinese nationalist education, becoming more aware of the necessity of change.

The reformists, especially the *Baohuanghui* in America, also incorporated an economic vision of China and Chinese people which responded to the interests of the Chinese transnationals. The economic wing of the *Baohuanghui*, the Commercial Corporation, sponsored investment ventures in China, America, Canada, Mexico, as well as in Southeast Asia (Lo, 1967: 195). Thus at least until the end of the decade, the reformers offered a vision of gradualist modernity in which Chinese moral and cultural values were commensurate with an élitist constitutional polity and expanding capitalism. One might say that this vision of modernity could be associated with the gentry-merchant élites in China who were the force behind the movement for provincial constitutional assemblies in the 1900s and the proliferation of philanthropic, 'redemptive' societies in Republican China. It is hardly a coincidence that Kang Youwei was the key figure in both of these milieux. While in China during the first half of the twentieth century, this vision of modernity was frustrated by warfare and obscured by revolutionary narratives of modernity — first of the republicans and then of the May 4th movement — in some ways, the vision or model, if not the activists themselves, had greater staying power among the Chinese transnationals where merchants and would-be gentry-merchant élites were more influential in the communities. Indeed, this vision may be the most proximate ancestor of the phenomenon called 'Confucian capitalism' in the Pacific Rim today. Both because of economic and ideological imperatives, this vision was suffused with transnational urges.

Finally, let us briefly consider a text by Ou Qujia, called 'New Guangdong', which elaborated for the Chinese overseas a narrative designed to appeal less to their purported national identity and more to their regional or provincial identity (Ou, 1971/1902). Ou developed an argument for the independence of Guangdong, a region from which the overwhelming majority of overseas Chinese hailed, from an ingenious application of social Darwinism. He advocated the independence of China's provinces so that the supposedly greater ties of intimacy within the province could promote a closer unity internally and a competitive drive with other provinces. Through such competition, the successful provinces could absorb the weak and China could ultimately become strong.

I believe the significance of this text emerges from its tacit acknowledgement of the indeterminacy of political loyalty. Ou is not overly anxious about the chances of eventual unity. To critics who point out that his plan will do the work for the imperialists by getting the Chinese to slice the Chinese melon themselves, he responds that when a people voluntarily secede, it is easier for them to re-establish a federated unity on the model of a German federation and better protect the great unity (*dayitong*) (ibid: 46–8). The issue of Chinese national unity provides a kind of ultimate framework, a distant, deferred horizon — a deferral with which many Chinese transnationals presumably did not feel much discomfort. The narrative of racial community sanctioned a flexible framework of territorial belonging to locality and region that was indifferent to the territorial loyalties demanded by the nation-state. In such ways, the text revealed the insufficiency of the nationalist model for communities of transnationals with multiple identities pulled by global forces as much as by their need for a sense of home that was itself quite elastic.

CONCLUSION

When nationalists deployed their narratives to nationalize transnationals, they revealed the constructedness of nationalist ideology which had to be taken apart in order to separate out the narratives of race, culture, and native place from their 'natural' belonging in the territorial nation-state. This deconstruction is revealed not only by the competing narratives of different nationalists emphasizing one sort of primordiality against another, but also in that race and culture produced nations that were very differently contoured from the territorially sovereign nation. Certainly, older Chinese narratives of race and culture did possess a cultural geography with a centre and peripheries, such as the notion of *zhongyuan* (central plain) or the concentric spheres of inner and outer realms; but neither was territorially delimited nor unchanging.

In relation to Chinese transnationals, nationalists first engaged these transterritorial discourses to establish a bond. Next, they sought to turn the loyalties of these forgetful 'sojourners' back to the geobody by appropriating or inflecting these older discourses of race and culture to create sentiments of rootedness in the new territorial entity. Doubtless, these narratives of primordiality needed to press into service not only fragments of memory, such as anti-Manchuism or native-place ties, but also contemporary aspirations, such as association with imperial prestige or secure returns on investment. Be that as it may, nationalist ideology develops a strategy that will both deploy and overcome its own transnationality.

The case studies presented here reveal that national and imperialist states occasionally succeeded in this two-part strategy of 'domesticating' transnationality whether by enlisting pan-Asianism to incorporate peripheral peoples into the geobody and colonized peoples into the empire, or by employing Han racialism and Confucian culturalism among Chinese transnationals. In each of these cases, however, the self-confident closure of the territorial nation was repeatedly deferred. Perhaps because nations are genetically and discursively so bound up with transnational race and culture, they frequently seek their sources of authority in these discourses even as the source of their sovereignty continues to lie in the inter-state system's principle of territorial citizenship.

Thus while territorial nationalism needs the discourses of race and culture for its own adequacy, it is not fully capable of containing them within itself. These discourses can also produce belonging to the historical communities they once defined or they can irrigate the imagining of new, deterritorialized communities. As we approach the end of the period of high nationalism in Asia, when the rationale for territorial nationalism has begun to weaken under the onslaught of a reinvigorated transnational capitalism, we are beginning to hear about the emergence of 'deterritorialized nations'. Certainly the emergent narrative of Greater China, made up of Han Chinese all over the world, has strong material underpinnings given the enormous capital investments that Chinese transnationals have made in China. This narrative assimilates many rhetorical figures encountered in the early part of the century regarding Han racial community, Confucian capitalism, redemptive modernity, moralistic states, cultural inviolability and intra-Asian historical networks, among others. Indeed, it is as if these culturally authoritative stories were liberated from the supplementary role they were forced to play within the scaffolding of territorial nationalism.

Today, it is not only among the Chinese that we can see the power of other historical forces that had been obscured by the dominant political form (of territorial nationalism). Everywhere, administrators, merchants and intellectuals are trying to patch together creative, workable identities from older regional or non-territorial ideologies and networks in response to this latest turn of capitalist globalization. To an outsider, it seems clear that European union would not have a chance without a strongly developed historical consciousness of European-ness *vis-à-vis* the rest of the world. Indeed, it was from the earlier European construction of Asia as its 'other' that Japan derived its very conception of 'Asia' in the nineteenth century (although it had a clear awareness of the 'Eastern sea' or *tōyō*) (Yamamuro, 1993: 3–5). By the late nineteenth and early twentieth centuries, Japan had already developed a primordialist discourse of Asiatic civilization which it needed both for purposes of domination and self-completion. Although the geography and politics of contemporary Japanese pan-Asianism, fuelled by a non-militarist capitalism, is significantly different from its pre-war counterpart, the figure of Asia as a deeply meaningful mirror appears to have been indelibly inscribed in modern Japanese consciousness. Others, like the Indian government, emulating the Chinese model, are trying to mobilize the long history of trade and cultural networks around the Indian Ocean and beyond to reach out to the Non-Resident Indians or NRIs. Perhaps just as significant is the formulation of the deterritorialized Hindu nation by transnational and diasporic groups who have been quietly spreading their influence beyond the Indian Ocean core since early in the century.

Thus, the deterritorialized nation is not necessarily dissimilar in structure to the territorial nation. It may, after all, also be a bounded, exclusive community sustained by an active distinction between self and other; only its territorial boundaries need be replaced by the hard cultural boundaries of say Han-ness or Hindu-ness. On the other hand, the forces of globalization are such that it may be difficult to sustain boundaries of such (or any) kind. Whatever the effects of the deterritorialized nation, it is likely to place the territorially sovereign nation in a painful predicament. The devaluation of the geobody entailed by the new racial or cultural nation will mean that its ideal of 'common citizenship' becomes less and less meaningful to the different peoples of its inner frontiers.

REFERENCES

Alatas, Syed Hussein (1977) *The Myth of the Lazy Native*. London: Frank Cass.

Balibar, Etienne (1991) 'Racism and Nationalism', in Etienne Balibar and Immanuel Wallerstein (eds) *Race, Nation, Class: Ambiguous Identities*, pp. 37–67. London: Verso.

Basch, L., N. G. Schiller and C. S. Blanc (1994) *Nations Unbound: Transnational Projects, Postcolonial Predicaments and Deterritorialized Nation-states*. Luxemburg: Gordon and Breach.

Chen Lifu (1976) *Xin shenghuo yu minsheng shiguan* (New Life and the Minsheng conception of history) in *Geming Wenxian* vol. 68: *Xin shenghuo yundong shiliao*, pp. 126–46. Taipei: Zhongguo guomindang zhongyang weiyuanhui dangshi weiyuanhui.

Chow Kai-wing (1994) *The Rise of Confucian Ritualism in Late Imperial China: Ethics, Classics, and Lineage Discourse*. Stanford, CA: Stanford University Press.

Duara, Prasenjit (1995a) *Rescuing History from the Nation: Questioning Narratives of Modern China*. Chicago, IL: University of Chicago Press.

Duara, Prasenjit (1995b) 'Of Authenticity and Woman: Personal Narratives of Middle-class Women in China', unpublished ms.

Duara, Prasenjit (1997) 'Nationalists among Transnationals: Overseas Chinese and the Idea of China, 1900–1911', in Aihwa Ong and D. Nonnini (eds) *Ungrounded Empires: The Cultural Politics of Chinese Transnationalism*, pp. 39–60. New York: Routledge.

Freedman, Maurice (1979) 'Immigrants and Associations: Chinese in Nineteenth Century Singapore', in Maurice Freedman *The Study of Chinese Society* Selected and introduced by G. William Skinner, pp. 61–83. Stanford, CA: Stanford University Press.

Grieder, Jerome B. (1981) *Intellectuals and the State in Modern China*. New York: Free Press; London: Collier Macmillan.

Hashikawa, Bunso (1980) 'Japanese Perspectives on Asia: From Dissociation to Coprosperity', in Akira Iriye (ed.) *The Chinese and the Japanese: Essays in Political and Cultural Interactions*, pp. 328–55. Princeton, NJ: Princeton University Press.

Hinsley, F. H. (1969) 'The Concept of Sovereignty and the Relations between States', in W. J. Stankiewicz (ed.) *In Defense of Sovereignty*, pp. 275–90. New York: Oxford University Press.

Hinsley, F. H. (1986) *Sovereignty*. Cambridge: Cambridge University Press (first published 1966).

Hu Hanmin (1931) 'Nanyang yu Zhongguo geming' (Nanyang and the Chinese revolution) in *Xinyaxiya* 1(5): 6–11. Taipei: Zhengzhong shuju.

Huang Jianchun (1993) *WanQing XinMa huaqiao dui guojia rentongzhi yanjiu* (Studies of overseas Chinese attitudes in Singapore and Malaya towards national identity in the late Qing). Taipei: Zhonghua minguo haiwai huaren yanjiu xuehui.

K'ang Yu-wei (1958) *Ta T'ung Shu: The One World Philosophy of K'ang Yu-wei* trans. from the Chinese with Introduction and Notes by Laurence G. Thompson. London: George Allen and Unwin Ltd.

Laski, Harold J. (1968/1921) *The Foundations of Sovereignty and Other Essays*. Freeport, NY: Books for Libraries Press.

Lee, Poh-ping (1978) *Chinese Society in Nineteenth Century Singapore*. Kuala Lumpur, New York: Oxford University Press.

Lo, Jung-pang (ed.) (1967) *K'ang Yu-wei: A Biography and a Symposium*, with translation. Tucson, AZ: University of Arizona Press.

Lu Hun (1910) 'Xu' (Preface to Xihuang), *Minbao* 25: 3981.

Ma, Eve Armentrout (1990) *Revolutionaries, Monarchists, and Chinatowns: Chinese Politics in the Americas and the 1911 Revolution.* Honolulu, HI: University of Hawaii Press.

Ma Hongtian (1930) 'Kaifa xibei shi jiejue Zhongguo shehui minsheng wentide genben fangfa' (Opening up the northwest is a basic means of solving the problem of livelihood in Chinese society), *Xinyaxiya* 1(1): 37–9.

Mitani Takeshi (1979) 'Kōhoku minshu bōdō (senkyūhaku nijūkyū nen) ni tsuite' (Concerning the popular riot of 1929 in Jiangbei), *Hitotsubashi Ronsō* 83(3): 137–57.

MMS (Manzhouguo Morality Society) (1934) *Manzhouguo Daodehui nianjian* (Yearbook of the Manzhouguo Morality Society). Wanguo Daodehui Manzhouguo zonghui bianjike ed. Xinjing: Manzhouguo Daodehui huijike.

MMS (Manzhouguo Morality Society) (1936) *Disanjie Manzhouguo Daodehui daode jiangxi yulu* (Oral Records of Morality Seminars of the Third Manzhouguo Morality Society). Manzhouguo Daodehui bianjike (Manzhouguo Morality Society editorial department) ed. Xinjing: Manzhouguo Daodehui huijike.

Nakami, Tatsuo (1984) 'A Protest against the Concept of the "Middle Kingdom": The Mongols and the 1911 Revolution', in Eto Shinkichi et al. (eds) *The 1911 Revolution in China*, pp. 129–49. Tokyo: University of Tokyo Press.

Naquin, Susan and Evelyn S. Rawski (1987) *Chinese Society in the Eighteenth Century.* New Haven, CT: Yale University Press.

Ōtani Komme (1937) *Shūkyō chōsa shiryo* (Materials from the survey of religions) vol. 2: *Kirin, Kento, Binko, kakusho shūkyō chōsa hōkoku* (Report on religious surveys of the various provinces of Jilin, Jiandao and Binjiang). Xinjing: Minshengbu shehuisi.

Ou Qujia (1971/1902) 'Xin Guangdong' (New Guangdong), in Zhang Yufa (ed.) *Wan Qing geming wenxue*, pp. 1–49. Taipei: Xinzhi zazhishe.

Purcell, Victor (1965) *The Chinese in Southeast Asia.* Kuala Lumpur, New York: Oxford University Press.

Smith Jr., Warren H. (1959) *Confucianism in Modern Japan: A Study of Conservatism in Japan's Intellectual History.* Tokyo: The Hokuseido Press.

Suemitsu Takayoshi (1932) *Shina no himitsu kessha to jizen kessha* (China's secret societies and charitable societies). Dalian: Manshu hyoronsha.

Sun Yat-sen (1930) 'Da Yaxiyazhuyi' (Great Asianism), in *Xinyaxiya* 1(1): 2–7.

Takizawa Toshihirō (1937) *Shūkyō chōsa shiryo* (Materials from the survey of religions) vol. 3: *Minkan shinyō chōsa hōkokusho* (Report on the survey of popular beliefs). Xinjing: Minshengbu shehuisi.

Tanaka, Stefan (1993) *Japan's Orient: Rendering Pasts into History.* Berkeley, CA: University of California Press.

Thongchai Winnichakul (1994) *Siam Mapped: A History of the Geo-Body of a Nation.* Honolulu, HI: University of Hawaii Press.

Yamamuro Shinichi (1993) 'Ajia ninshiki no kijiku' (The axes of perceiving Asia), in Furuya Tetsuo (ed.) *Kindai Nihon no Ajia ninshiki* (Modern Japan's Perceptions of Asia), pp. 3–45. Kyoto: Jimbun Kagaku Kenkyujo.

Yen Ching-hwang (1976) *The Overseas Chinese and the 1911 Revolution. With Special Reference to Singapore and Malaya.* Kuala Lumpur, New York: Oxford University Press.

Xihuang Zhengyin (1910) 'Nanyang huaqiao shilue' (A brief history of overseas Chinese in Southeast Asia), *Minbao* 25: 3983–4011; *Minbao* 26: 4087–126.

Zhang Zhenzhi (1930) 'Yaxiya wenhuade bianhua yu qi xinshengji' (The evolution of Asian culture and its new chance), *Xinyaxiya* 1(1): 81–6.

Zhuang Guotu (1989) *Zhongguo fengjian zhengfu de huaqiao zhengce* (The Policies of China's feudal governments towards overseas Chinese). Xiamen: Xiamen Daxue Chubanshe.

The French Colonial Policy of Assimilation and the Civility of the *Originaires* of the Four Communes (Senegal): A Nineteenth Century Globalization Project

Mamadou Diouf

> "We have left Senegal, the ballot boxes colony,
> Blaise's Kingdom, the ten thousand citizens
> of the four 'fully empowered' communes — empowered
> to practice *prestidigitation*, boxing and kickboxing!
> Here are the Blacks, the real ones, the pure ones,
> not the children of universal suffrage, but those of
> Old Cham. How polite they are!
> They rush out of the bush to say Hello to you!"
> (Albert Londres, *Terre d'ébène*, 1929)

This study[1] is part of a broader project of rewriting the history of the French policy of assimilation and its outcomes[2] in Senegal's Four Communes (Saint-Louis, Gorée, Rufisque and Dakar). The article traces, in places under colonial domination and among populations with heterogeneous memories, the emergence of an indigenous civility that is no less distinct from autochthonous Senegambian traditions than it is from the prescriptive lessons of the 'colonial civilizing mission': a civility that bears witness not to an assimilation that has been identified, following Léopold Sédar Senghor,[3] with alienation and a loss of cultural memory,[4] but rather to a profound cultural reconstruction that expresses a hybrid culture peculiar to groups of *habitants* or *originaires*.[5] The first president of the Senegalese Republic drew

---

1. This article is a heavily revised version of a piece that will appear in V. Y. Mudimbe (ed.) *Encyclopedia of African Religions and Philosophy*, under the title 'Islam, christianisme et assimilation: Histoires des religions dans les Quatre Communes du Senegal'. I thank René Collignon, who agreed to read and comment on this paper. Translated from French by Luca D'Isanta.
2. On this, see the classic studies of Michael Crowder (1962) and G. Wesley Johnson (1991/1971). The prevailing interpretation stresses that the natives lost their African identity.
3. Léopold Sédar Senghor, Senegalese poet and thinker, was the first president of independent Senegal (1960–80). On his life and work, see Janet Vaillant (1990).
4. The *negritude* movement, of which Senghor was a promoter, had as its goal precisely the restoration of the values of the Black world that had largely been undermined by the policy of assimilation.
5. *Habitants* or *originaires* are African people and mulattos residing in the Four Communes who accumulated enough wealth and capital to go into business and other activities and were granted French citizenship status. They did not consider themselves and were not considered natives (*indigènes*). They were different from French colonial administrators and commercial agents (metropolitans) posted and operating in the colony.

heavily on a reading of the history of the Four Communes that emphasizes the loss of Black cultural values and the appropriation of French culture by the *originaires*, with his gripping expression 'assimilate, don't be assimilated' (*assimiler et non être assimilé*) (Senghor, 1964).

The Four Communes of Senegal are the result of the French presence on the western coast of Africa, beginning with their settlement in Saint-Louis in 1659. Although the French presence in that region of Senegambia was interrupted by English occupations of the French colony during the French Revolution and Napoleonic Wars, the French took definitive possession of their colony of Senegal in 1817. The development of this area, urbanized very early in the cases of Saint-Louis and Gorée, was driven by territorial conquest, European rivalries, and the workings of an often indecisive administrative organization. It was marked by two significant turning points. One was the drafting of the Register of Grievances by the prominent men of Saint-Louis, and its dispatch to the States General of Versailles during the French Revolution. The Register's principal demands were: the abolition of the Compagnie du Sénégal's trade privileges, the abrogation of the colonial pact restrictions that worked against the *habitants* to the benefit of metropolitan merchants, and freedom of trade. During the French Revolution and Napoleonic Wars, following the colony's isolation as a result of English occupation, the first local assemblies emerged.[6] They served as foundations for municipal institutions in Saint-Louis and later in Gorée. From then on, the Four Communes were granted the same rights as their counterparts in the metropolis (Johnson, 1991; Marcson, 1976). The rationale for this situation, which distinguishes the *originaires* from the Africans of the interior, was: 'the contributions made by the African Muslims for generations in Saint-Louis and Gorée . . . In fact, they pay the blood tax, which none of the other colonies pay, by fighting in our colonial armies' (quoted in Johnson, 1991: 44). The crux of the political struggle was repeated attempts on the part of the colonists to strike the Muslim *habitants* from the electoral lists (Boilat, 1984/1853; Marcson, 1976: Ch. 1). The latter claimed French citizenship without submitting to French cultural and civil codes, claiming a special status conferred by Islam.

The other turning point was the impact of the Revolution of 1848 on the French colonial empire, with the Second Republic's decision to offer its colonies, including Senegal, the power to send a representative to the French National Assembly. This power resulted in a general election in Saint-Louis and Gorée: all *habitants* who could prove five years' residence could participate. The decision of 1848 lent more legal and regulatory formality to practices of political representation, at the same time that slavery was abolished. As Johnson argues: 'Although French Senegal had evolved its own municipal institutions and had been given a General Council and an

---

6. On this point, see Marc Marcson (1976).

advisory representative to the Ministry of Marine in 1840, the election of 1848 was the first time the general populace actively engaged in a political contest' (Johnson, 1991: 26).

The colonial administration showed a certain reticence with respect to this policy, as witnessed by the reaction of the colony's governor, Captain Baudin:

> I don't share the view of those in France who think universal suffrage an admirable thing; here [in Senegal] I would go further and call it absurd and nonsensical. If it were possible to explain how the election for the colony's representative took place here, it would frighten even the most dedicated partisans of universal suffrage. The poor blacks were beset by the agents of all the candidates. Ballots printed in advance were handed out to some, torn up by others, redistributed, and recirculated perhaps fifty times in the days preceding the election. On election day, the battle was even more murderous; it got to the point where I would defy any black to know positively which candidate he voted for; and if such a business should take place often, all the paper manufacturers in Europe would not be able to meet Senegal's needs (Baudin, quoted in Johnson, 1991: 26).

Nevertheless, the movement continued, and on 1 August 1872, a decree was signed granting Gorée and Saint-Louis the same municipal prerogatives and rights as French communes. Thus they became fully empowered communes (*communes de plein exercice*). Combined with this participation by the Saint-Louisians and the Goréans in a European-style political activity, which constitutes the central characteristic of assimilation, a twofold movement began with General Faidherbe's nomination as Governor in 1854: the acceleration of the conquest of Senegambia and the consolidation of possessions on both the economic and the political fronts. The exploitation of the peanut crop intensified the commercial activities and the urbanization of the coastal regions. Rufisque was the first locality to benefit from these new economic conditions, attracting shopkeepers who used to set up commercial operations from Gorée. According to Johnson (ibid: 32):

> Rufisque soon became the commercial centre of southern Senegal. Although not endowed with a good harbor, it was close to the inland areas that were now producing peanuts for market. Unlike Dakar, it was an established city; and it had space for warehouses, offices, and depots that could not be built on the small island of Gorée.

Because of the economic importance the city had acquired, Rufisque joined Saint-Louis and Gorée during this period, becoming a fully empowered commune in 1880. For the same reasons, Dakar would be included within the circle of fully empowered communes in 1887.

Thus in the course of the nineteenth century 'the three primary institutions of local government were established: the municipal councils and mayors, the deputyship, and the General Council of Senegal' (Johnson, ibid: 38). In contrast with the establishment of the legal framework of the Four Communes, which granted the *habitants* the status of French citizens, the lands of the protectorate (*pays de protectorat*) fell under the authority and arbitrary power of the French colonial administration, which most often relied on traditional chiefs — ethnic leaders or marabouts — to establish its domination. The natives of these regions had the status of French subjects, and were subject to the Native Code (*le Code de l'indigénat*).[7]

The dates marking the definitive establishment of the Four Communes are the following: in 1840 a General Council of the colony was established; in 1848, Senegal was granted a seat in the Chamber of Deputies in Paris; on 10 August 1872, the decree was signed that registered the creation of the communes of Senegal. Finally, Rufisque (1880) and Dakar (1887) also benefited from these privileges, achieving the status of fully empowered communes.

In the areas of demography and social structuring, there were two sharply different situations. In Saint-Louis and Gorée, the population was composed of metropolitans, *habitants*, and, depending on the period, freed slaves or captives. Among the *habitants* were mulattos, *gourmets* (Catholic Blacks), *signares* (women living with or having affairs with European merchants), and Muslims. The freed slaves were considered animists, but after staying in the colony for an extended time, they would convert to one of the revealed religions. In contrast, the populations of Dakar and Rufisque were much more homogeneous ethnically: they were *Lebu* and *Wolof*. The composition of the population is indicative of the religious membership of the social groups. While few Muslims were listed in Gorée, in Saint-Louis, Dakar and Rufisque, by contrast, the African population proclaimed allegiance to an Islam very heavily modified by local beliefs.

The civil and civic status of the *originaires* caused a prolonged conflict between the colonial magistrates and the colonial administration. The crux of the conflict was whether or not the *originaires* should be eligible for French citizenship which would both accord them political rights and shield them from the rigours, if not the universality, of the French Civil Code. Their refusal to submit to the Civil Code was connected with their stubborn defence of their special status. This illustrates the various issues pertaining to citizenship which characterized the players in the Senegalese colonial scene: a nit-picking, universalist magistrature; a colonial administrative power; and the *originaires*; all joining together only in affirming the gap within the empire between the colonies and the metropolis.

These configurations, revealed in the overlap of contradictory elements and the spectacular events that they fostered in areas that were so non-African, have had the effect of isolating this urban area and its *habitants* from sociological, anthropological, and even historical studies. Their

---

7. The terms *originaire* and *habitant* are equivalent. They describe the status of the residents in the cities of Saint-Louis, Gorée, Rufisque and Dakar when they obtained the status of fully empowered communes and their *habitants* acquired citizenship. They also establish and make clear a difference between the *originaires* and the metropolitans with whom they live, and the Senegambians (the natives), their neighbours, subject to autochthonous powers before their conquest, then integrated into the colonial arena as *subjects*.

globalization, both economic and religious, has certainly contributed to their marginalization. The social sciences have paid little attention to their evolution and they have been allowed little space in studies on Senegal. Considered detribalized and overly assimilated, the *originaires* had little appeal for an eye in search of the exotic.

However, the Africa that is revealed in the social, cultural, political, and economic practices of the *originaires*, as well as their very diversity, is neither the Africa of the villages nor that of the local religions. On the contrary, those practices are expressed in an urban space, incorporated in a French imperial economy that determines its ebb and flow, with its conflict of interests. On the other hand, the intellectual appropriation of Islam and Christianity, the two religions in the native area, produces an original structuring of the representations and symbols of identity of the *habitants* of Saint-Louis, Gorée, Rufisque and Dakar. Thus the identities that they produce is part of the story of colonization and the religious, political and economic pattern of the French colonial empire, while at the same time borrowing elements from an autochthony revised by colonial contact. It is in this perspective that one must understand the central idea in the *originaires*' struggle: special status. At the same time that they were proclaiming allegiance to a French citizenship on which were based their rights, duties and individual pursuit of wealth and the defence of their commercial interests, they buttressed themselves with a culture all their own — they were not French culturally, but they were French politically and economically.

The aim of this article is to contribute toward an investigation connected with new intellectual territories, and the opening of at least two fields: postcolonial studies[8] and cultural studies (see Dirks et al., 1994). These new fields are particularly concerned with the relations between the West and the Third World and in the ways in which the former has constructed the latter; modes of appropriation, derivation (Chatterjee, 1986, 1993), and hybridization (Young, 1995); and/or the rejection of the processes by which colonial empires were created and deconstructed.

The contribution of this study in these new areas is centred on the following concern. The prevailing readings of the French imperial experience, especially in Senegal, emphasize the policy of assimilation. In contrast to the English policy of indirect rule, the policy of assimilation followed Enlightenment Philosophy, which promoted both a unilinear evolutionism and the unity of reason, and so considerably reduced the possibility of preserving an African identity. Assimilation, it is argued, could only mean the loss of a historical initiative and of a cultural creativity, because of total subordination to the metropolitan culture. In contrast, this study defends the thesis that assimilation as a policy did not reduce the areas of innovation and creativity

---

8. For a general overview, see among others Baker et al. (1994); Bhabha (1990); Chatterjee (1986); Monga (1996); Said (1979); Spivak (1993); Young (1991).

available to the colonized. On the contrary, in the colonial experience that most fervently emphasized the cultural side of the civilizing mission and the colonial enterprise, people possessed and indeed exploited possibilities for hybridizing and selecting modes of acculturation. Here 'acculturation' means the recreation of a culture and a society in the context of the colonial experience, an original production built on the continual reorganization of precolonial and colonial experiences. It is expressed by a continued tinkering with unstable constructions of identity, which were assembled from different social codes, modes of belief, forms, representations, and staging of politics, and the celebrations, commemorations and feasts that directed social relations in colonial Senegal.

The article is organized around three themes: urbanism, religion, and citizenship. Urbanism is composed of expressions of life in cities. Cities appear to be unique locations in the African environment, departures from the traditional and the tribal, for cities exist in a universal geographic context. As 'colonization areas' — Coquery-Vidrovitch's *lieux de colonisation* (1993: 11–22) — they participate in the economic, political and social project of a colonial empire; in this case, the French colonial empire. In the Senegalese context, this urbanity appeared at the precise moment that Johnson called 'the birth of contemporary Senegal'. The new model that emerged after the trading-post stage was characterized by the development of the peanut-based economy and the institution and consolidation of a colonial area and urban system controlled by the Four Communes. These events opened up spaces in which a threefold modernity blossomed: Islamic, Christian, and political. The dialectic of land and territory[9] explains to a certain extent socio-spatial dynamics and architectural forms, and provides a context for the political struggles. Land is a geographic and spiritual reality, which unfolds a totalizing world made of coherence and balance, whether real or fictitious (Diouf, 1992: 274, note 3). It is at the same time a community and an imagined world that appropriates a space in a discriminatory and exclusive way. It is first and foremost an ethnic space, in opposition to a *territory* which is more open and heterogeneous, in which the signs, in this case analysed as Islam and colonization, each proclaim allegiance to a universality that is an act of dispossession (Berque, 1964), through openness and conversion (either by colonial violence or its 'scientific' rationality), driven by their desire to classify and construct the other. From the confrontation of homeland and territory are derived phenomena that are either processes of transforming and/or destroying of homeland — deterritorialization — or processes of adapting, redefining, or inventing new modalities — reterritorialization — in order to adapt to the territory. To account for this twofold process, while stressing the capacity of African societies for

---

9. For a clarification of the notion of communal land/homeland versus territory, see Diagne (1992) and Diouf (1990).

initiative and innovation, MBembe (1988: 29) uses the concepts of 'unruliness' and 'intractableness' (*indiscipline* and *indocilité*).

The second theme is the total domination in the *originaires*' urban space of the revealed religions, Islam and Catholic Christianity, although these had taken on a local colouring. The two religions, through their mission of conversion and their claims of universality for their rites, texts, liturgy and ethics, had the presumption to erase local laws and social structures or to revise and subvert them. The characteristics of exegetical and intellectual Islamic religiosity, which exhibits a scholastic arrogance, are radically different from those of the rural Senegalese offshoots of Islam, which are charismatic, organized in brotherhoods, and rooted in the beliefs and practices of the local cultures and religions. Certainly, expressions of religion (beliefs, imagined worlds, knowledge and practices) participate in a discontinuous space where local practices are entangled with the Islamic and Christian professions of faith. Those practices include the disparate and multifarious memories of the *originaires*, specific ways of appropriating space, architectural productions, the organization of culinary art, ways of perfuming and arraying oneself (clothes and jewellery), as well as usages deployed in Senegalese novels.[10]

The third theme relates to the consequences of the colonial policy pursued by France in Senegal. It has already been pointed out that the Four Communes are the products of two apparently contradictory enterprises: on the one hand, a colonial project founded on the logic of French assimilation, of which Catholicism has in certain eras been the religious side; and, on the other hand, a long historical accumulation of many commercial transactions between the two banks of the Sahara which hatched different variants of Islam. In this perspective, citizenship is the expression of political status: the *originaires*' right to elect a municipal council and a General Council, and to send a representative to the National Assembly, while continuously refusing to submit to the French Civil Code. In some ways it is a problematic citizenship stated in terms of political rights and special status.

CHURCHES AND MOSQUES: A MONUMENTAL ESTABLISHMENT OF ORDER

Establishing religious order by erecting monuments stems from a desire for visibility, for the public display of worship. In colonial urban logic, it tries to combine architecture with a city product that together can identify the communities and also inscribe in the soil a text that can be read at first glance. The search for an identity construction that delineates the spaces of life, leisure, work, and religious practices had an impact on the morphology of the

---

10. I am thinking especially of the novels of Ousmane Socé Diop and Abdoulaye Sadji.

Four Communes. In particular, a spatial translation of religious practices has innumerable effects on religious worship. It especially explains the transactions between the religious symbolic orders, commemorations and languages of Muslims and Catholics, and the connections between the appropriations of those two religions and the ancestral cults, which refer to patterns that are hard to inscribe in the urban topography.

Both Muslim and Catholic forms of worship asserted themselves over genies and ancestral spirits, which from then on retreated into private space, obscure regions of the memory, of the seaside (Gorée, Dakar, Rufisque), and of the river (Saint-Louis). The reorganizations and interference between public and private space in religious transactions are translated into processions and libations linked to the genies of urban lands: Maam Kumba Bang (Saint-Louis), Maam Kumba Castel (Gorée), Maam Kumba Lambaay (Rufisque) and Lëk Daawur (Dakar). It is presumptuous of buildings to try to contain them, and this leads to a growing tension with urban monumentalism (Sinou, 1993).

The transactions and accommodations between the Muslim and Catholic religious practices did not preclude competition in the occupation of public space — deciding who should dictate the urban syntax and grammar — any less than in determining the definitions and practices of citizenship, that is, the ability to exercise political (and especially electoral) rights and duties. The tension between citizenship and inscription in the city is apparent in the search for a discriminatory organization of space in relation to religious practices and the provoking desire to convert, the acceptance of the civil law and, by way of consequence, the systematic adoption of monogamy and the European way of life.

Having sought a public display since 1819, the Catholic priests acquired some land and mobilized wealthy mulattos to erect a church, which was finished in 1828. Located in the reputedly Christian South Quarter of Saint-Louis, the religious building lacked architectural originality (Sinou, 1993: Ch. 7) because the missions wanted to reproduce a universal symbolism, especially since they were in a 'barbaric land' of 'moral turpitudes'. In the same period, a church was built in Gorée in an identical style. In 1930, after the discovery of 'Sudanese' architecture with its decorative lines, a Sudanese colonial architecture was invented, symbolized in the religious sphere by the cathedral of Dakar, which is Sudanese in the buttresses of the façades, Byzantine in its cupola (Sinou, 1993: 339).

The Islamic logic of public display was somewhat different. In Dakar and Rufisque, whose populations were predominantly Muslim, the mosque functioned as the centre of gravity in the composition of social space. In Gorée, where Muslims were in the minority, the small, very discreet mosque backs onto the sea, almost invisible and out of place. By contrast, in Saint-Louis, the Muslim community demanded a plot facing the Catholic church's monumental inscription in the public space. It got one in the North Quarter of the reputedly Muslim island, but since it was unable to raise the funds to build a mosque, the colony stepped in for the 'Mahometan' (that is, Mohammedan, Muslim) community:

> The edifice constructed between 1844 and 1847 is somewhat evocative of the church of Saint-Louis ... The steeples turned into minarets, and the signs of Islam, taken from the architecture of the Arab world, are limited to the arcades and the embryonic cupolas placed at the top of each tower. (Sinou, 1993: 135–6)

The stylistic influences on religious monuments are expressions of culture in the process of formation and purification. If Sudanese architecture was invented in Catholic edifices, Muslim buildings purged Christian forms and adopted North-African Arabic forms after independence. The Great Mosque of Dakar is the best illustration of this nationalist style. Echoing the Catholic indigenization was the pressure towards an Arabism (*arabité*) invented by the Muslim intellectuals of the Four Communes. In its plenitude and arrogance, their religious architecture expresses an original culture in its design, which tells of an exegetical and élitist liturgy.

The topography of religious monuments illustrates both the output of the Four Communes and the modalities of inscription in those spaces by communities whose identities are revealed in their adopted religions. Nevertheless, if the Catholic community posed fewer problems precisely because it adopted the religion of colonization, it did not distance itself from the *originaires'* culture with which it combined in its own way. That brought it closer to the Muslim community than to the priests and metropolitan missionaries. In this sense conversion was not a way of insinuating oneself into a colonial society, which was composed of many fragments. Precisely because emphasis was placed on a common culture despite religious differences, and because of the long distance involved in its link with the metropolitans and their culture, the Catholic community was able to join in the secular and anticlerical policies of the administration. That helped delineate an *originaires'* space where religious display was essential without being competitive or proselytizing.

STYLES AND HYBRIDS: FRAGMENTS OF RELIGIOUS CULTURES

The indigenization of religious architecture resulted from the quest for a local rooting for Christ's message, a rooting rejected by Father David Boilat (1984/1853: 14). For Islam, however, the constraints of the colonial policy of assimilation and an opposition to the Islam of brotherhoods of the Senegalese countryside produced an intellectual Islamic tradition, the former relying on the guidance and leadership of a 'marabout', the latter based on the reading and interpretation capabilities of literate Muslims (Diagne, 1992: 290).

Father Boilat mentions the existence, from the very beginning, of Catholic communities in Saint-Louis and in Gorée, composed of mulattos ('Christians from the outset because of their fathers' religion'), *signares*, and 'the most intelligent of the Blacks, the closest to the Europeans' (Boilat, 1984: 5), a group generally referred to as *gourmets*. These are:

> Catholics of either sex who take pride in living apart from the Muslims, of dressing in European fashion, and of being civilized ... According to Lamiral, the name *gourmet* denoted Blacks filling the ships trading on the Senegal River, working as pilots and helmsmen, that is, positions of trust that required professional expertise and heavy responsibilities. (Jore, 1965: 25, note 1)

The captives of Gorée are to be included in this community, at least the captives of Christians, for they were always baptized by their masters. In Saint-Louis, on the other hand, the captives 'were all Mahometans ... The habitants of Saint-Louis always believed that it was not permitted to hold Christians as slaves' (Boilat, 1984: 213).

Father Boilat's testimony is interesting in that it helps us understand the reasons for adopting the Catholic religion. Three factors are adduced: origin (mulattos and *signares*), proximity to Europeans (*signares* and *gourmets*) and subordination (captives). Father Boilat's emphasis was on language. Considering the absolute necessity of offering assistance 'especially [to] girls who need the help of piety and Christian virtues', he lamented the unsuitability of the local language, *Wolof*, for stating Christian dogma:

> This language lacks all theological words; how can one accurately teach them dogma, Christian duties without the French language ... One puts in their hands the most moving prayers, the heroic acts of the saints of their same age and condition, the most moving spiritual readings; they read them with the most frigid indifference ... Many youngsters have been led astray because they lack a clear understanding of French ... Owing to the lack of understanding of the French language, religion is, as it were, still in its birth, so one might be allowed to doubt that it will ever grow. (Boilat, 1984: 14)

It might seem paradoxical that Father Boilat, one of the first three native priests, ordained in 1840 (the other two were Arsène Fridoil and Jean-Pierre Moussa), objected to using the local language to deliver the Christian message. Father Fridoil, the priest in Gorée, was to proceed in a completely different manner. He made numerous conversions among the slaves freed by the decree of 1848, basing his evangelizing on a catechism in *Wolof* that was translated and printed by a certain Father Lambert (Boilat, 1984: 14). Discussing Father Fridoil's results, Boilat again repeats the need to bring the Gospel especially to women and girls:

> Monsieur Fridoil went to the trouble of putting all the Catholic dogma in the form of canticles, and having them sung with the same tunes as Black songs. It is a moving spectacle, hearing the mixed choir attentively singing, accompanied on the organ by Father Luiset, whose talent is well known in Senegal; I myself was touched and moved to tears. How many conversions followed!! Every Sunday and feast day, thirty or forty adults of all ages and both sexes were baptized. A lot of libertines from overseas disliked that catechism, because religion brought more morality to Negresses. For that reason they resorted to gossip, satire and calumny. (Boilat, 1984: 18–19)

The opposition between the approaches taken by Fathers Boilat and Fridoil was only superficial, however, and resulted from the diversity of situations and spiritual transactions in the Catholic community of the Four Communes. The quest to root Christ's message clashed with cultural and colonial habits that were the target of Boilat's ire, and which stemmed from the intermittent presence of priests in the French possessions of West Africa.

Priests did not gain a permanent presence until 1815, when the colony of Senegal was restored to France for good. That presence was consolidated with the beginning of primary education, provided by the Sisters of Saint Joseph de Cluny (1826) and the Brothers of Ploërmel (1841), the establishment of a mission and a school in Dakar by the Brothers of the Holy Spirit, and the abortive attempt on the part of Fathers Boilat, Moussa, and Fridoil to create a secondary school to educate seminarians (1840–9).

Despite its undeniable successes, the main concern of the Church was to impose orthodox religious practices in order to thwart:

> Mahomet [Mohammed] . . . [and] his absurd, regressive religion that destroyed everything. I would only say that a religion that was established by force and promises its followers carnal pleasures as rewards would have to spread quickly: the state of ignominy, stupidity, servitude, and corruption in which all peoples are plunged who have submitted to the law of Mahomet is an obvious demonstration of that. (Boilat, 1984: 232)

The Church wanted to rub out once and for all indigenous and Muslim influences in the colony's Catholic community: Boilat (1984: 207–8) clearly expressed this drive when he called for the Koranic schools to be banned and for children to be obligatorily sent to French schools, where teaching of Arabic would be introduced. According to him: 'So they were Christians by baptism . . . superstitious like the Mahometans and fetishists. Their behaviour was pretty much the same . . . They were Christians without instruction, in a country that was pre-eminently Mahometan' (Boilat, 1984: 214–5).

The constraints Father Boilat ran up against in his quest to purify Catholic religious practices were of a social nature. They were manifested in marriage, baptism, communion and a resorting to mystico-religious protective practices, and they found expression in the indigenous idioms and repertory. Marriages were predominantly traditional local weddings (*mariage à la mode du pays*), in which no mention is made of Christian elements (Boilat, 1984: 221–7; Durand, 1803: 28; Lamiral, 1789). This type of union did not decline until the second half of the nineteenth century. According to Boilat (1984: 226–7), there were fewer than a hundred legitimate marriages in Saint-Louis between 1783 and 1840. The most spectacular manifestation of the indigenous character of marriage was the way in which weddings were celebrated, in particular verifying the bride's virginity, publicly displaying the proof, and retaining polygamy (Marcson, 1976: 43).

Like marriage, the baptism of newborns was closer to *Wolof* practices than to Christian ones. Infants were given their name eight days after birth. In most cases, especially in Saint-Louis, infants were circumcised at birth. Here again, local *Wolof* forms of celebration were the rule, with *griots* (traditional bards), laudatory chants, and gifts. Truly Christian religious practices were very rarely celebrated: excerpts from the registers of Father Fournier, the prefect apostolic of Senegal, give just a few descriptions (Boilat, 1984: 215–16). The first communion ever celebrated in Senegal took place in Saint-Louis in 1823 (ibid: 218).

Not only were the Catholics of the Four Communes circumcised at birth, but *gourmets* as well as mulattos celebrated Muslim religious holidays and carried amulets, *gris-gris* (charms) and talismans made by marabouts, containing verses from the Koran. The available sources mention that the greatest sources of revenue for marabouts were the *signares* and mulatto women, who paid them for making *gris-gris*, telling fortunes, predicting the future, protecting them against the evil eye, providing love potions, and so on (Boilat, 1846; Durand, 1803: 28; Lamiral, 1789: 43). On this matter, Father Boilat passes on Father Fournier's testimony:

> In the evening, before vespers, they returned to the baptismal fonts to renew their baptismal vows there. Father Fournier had succeeded in enlightening those children about the superstitions of Mahometanism, but their parents were not so enlightened. He took away from them and made them take off the *gris-gris*, or talismans, that they were laden with ... but their parents soon gave them back to them, because those *gris-gris* preserved them from witches, devils and illnesses of all kinds ... In the beginning of January 1824, the whole church was filled with people, all of them wearing their *gris-gris* like real Mahometans. The prefect stepped up into the pulpit and explained that those talismans were useless and that they were being deceived by the marabouts, who were abusing the habitants' trust. The speech had its effect. All the venerable ladies of Saint-Louis took off their *gris-gris*, placed them on a big loincloth, presented them to the prefect apostolic, and swore to renounce them forever. (Boilat, 1984: 219–20)

This episode, which was presented as a success, was repeated again and again through time. Nowadays, Muslim and fetishist divination and amulets have again insinuated themselves into the Catholic practice of the natives. They testify to a religious invention, which, according to Marcson (1976: 41) is the distinctive mark of the syncretic nature (with French, Muslim and *Wolof* elements) of the native culture, which is disparagingly referred to as 'being assimilated'. The most spectacular manifestation of the Catholic side of the natives' culture was the religious procession in Saint-Louis, celebrating the Assumption of the Virgin Mary:

> ... organized by the Christian habitants, but which included Europeans and Muslims. Floats were made and the finest costumes and clothing were worn in the procession. In the eighteenth century, these religious processions, celebrated on the day of the Assumption of the Virgin Mary, became a grand tradition of St Louis for both Christians and Muslims. The picture of the habitants that emerges from the evidence is that of a cohesive group tied

together by kinship, common social rank, internal self-government, distinctive culture, and a common role in the economy. (Marcson, 1976: 45)

The testimony of Father Fournier, quoted in the *Esquisses Sénégalaises*, offers the following gripping description of the procession which he organized on 15 August 1823:

> The drum major at the head, with his drums, then the banner carried by three young ladies; after the banner stepped all the girls in two ranks. After the girls, in the middle of the road, came a beautiful ornate cross, all of gold, carried by three young ladies; then followed the women, who had behind them the great cross, carried by three choir children; then right after them the men, in two ranks, the cantors, the priest surrounded by four marching soldiers; and behind him, royal officials of all ranks and branches. A picket of fifty men walked on both sides of the procession. Processions had not been customary in Senegal before then, but ... they are conducted with the greatest order and decency. Marabouts and Mahometans, filled with admiration, followed the procession, saying a thousand *bis milay* [*bismillahi*, in the name of Allah]. They thought that we were portraying paradise on earth. (Boilat, 1984: 217–18)

The indigenization of Christianity in the Four Communes was one of the modalities of struggle against 'Mahometanism' and conversion: acquiring the idioms, repertoires and images found in the collective imagination of the *originaires*. It is in this rooting that 'religious options' (Chrétien, 1993: 239) are made available, which even today make rural Christianity diverge from that of the *originaires*. In this case religious options operate within the imagined world of the revealed religions: a cultural world which, on the Muslim side, is illustrated by the centrality of mastering the text (Koranic reading and exegesis). In this context, the mandatory conversion of freed slaves to one religion or the other was a mode of acquiring citizenship, even though citizenship had no bearing on their social status. Social emancipation was impossible in the *Wolof* conception of slavery, even if there was liberation from providing work for the profit of another, the master. Residency provided a territorialization that furnished access to cultural expressions.

Like Christianity, the Islam of the Four Communes was mixed with elements that came from the cultures of the *Wolof*, *Halpulareen*, Moors and *Lebu*. More than a religion, it is the primary cultural expression of the *originaires*. The Moorish connection to the Islam of Saint-Louis and the role that it played in the formation and spread of *tijaan* religious thought, whose leading figure was El Hadj Malick Sy, added an intellectual impetus to Muslim religious practices.

The brotherhood of *tijaan* was very open to the *umma* (Islamic world community) and Arabic culture; it firmly implanted itself among the *originaires*. It won over a number of *taalibe* (followers) to its cause (Marty, 1917: vol. 1: 208). The pedagogical mission that it undertook as a command line for spreading Islam created the energy to establish Koranic schools. This 'Puritan' insistence on Islamo-Arabic education, reading, and writing was present very early on in Saint-Louis. Father Boilat listed a dozen

Koranic schools, as opposed to just two missionary primary schools, in the 1840s. The same vitality was found throughout the Four Communes at the end of the nineteenth and the beginning of the twentieth century as a result of the programme of moving into the main cities marabouts trained by Malick Sy. The compilation that was made by Marty and partly continued by Johnson attests to the scope of the movement (Johnson, 1991: 164, note 20). It expresses the universalist goal that is at the heart of the unique Islamic modality of appropriation of the *originaires*. This universality is also an entry into colonial society (modernity?) without renouncing one's special status.

In dealing with the *paix française*, this Islam thus opens up to a developing *originaires* élite a way to participate in a universal that cannot be reduced to ethnology and colonial (de)tribalization. It is radically opposed to the presentation suggested in Cheikh Hamidou Kane's novel, *L'aventure ambiguë* (1961).

After Father Boilat's efforts to diminish Islam had failed, the colonial administration took the dynamic of this intellectual Islam into account and tried to develop a French Muslim policy based on it. This policy found a convinced leader in General Faidherbe, who was elevated to the governorship of Senegal in 1857, after a stay in Algeria where he familiarized himself with Arabo-Islamic culture. He took Bou El Moghdad Seck, who had been a cadi and *tafsir* since 1850, and made him the focus of his policy, especially against the jihadist propaganda of El Hajj Umar Tall. With the Colony's support, Bou El Moghdad made his pilgrimage to Mecca (1861). This was the period when state sponsorship of pilgrimages to the Holy Sites of Islam began, a policy which has continued to the present.

This tradition, despite changes that testify to the nature of transactions with traditional religions of the land and with sea and river genies (more significant in the *Lebu* environment of Dakar and Rufisque than in Saint-Louis), attests to the opening to Islamic universality, an opening which found ways of compromising with the colonial order, indeed of taking advantage of it, becoming a side of it. Against the graphic rationality of French civilization learned in school, it opposes, adjoins, or superimposes another graphic rationality, whose concept of the divine implicitly invents an *originaires* identity. Johnson (1991: 164) gives an illustration of this:

> In Senegal, twentieth-century Islam was at the same time conservative and progressive. In rural areas it ended up reinforcing traditional values, whereas in the cities it facilitated the adaptation and unification of Africans who were cut off from traditional society and their family environment.

Social regulation was accomplished by religion, whose graphic expression became an essential element in the culture of the *originaires*. Father Boilat, in his frantic search for a Christian identity cleaned of all the chaff and expressed in impeccable French, was aware of the need to put an end to the embedding of Christian religiosity in the *originaires*' identity, which was stripping away all its orthodoxy.

ASSIMILATION AND PERSONAL STATUS: CIVIL LAW OR ISLAMIC JUSTICE

> "Let's disembark. [From a ship arriving from France.]
> 'Yo! Porter!'
> 'Porter?' answers my companion, 'You have delusions of aristocracy.
> Negroes don't carry luggage in Senegal, they vote.'
> Going down the accommodation ladder, he muttered:
> 'They vote! They vote! And soon they'll be dancing the gavotte ...'
> I'm at the gangplank. I stop. We can't pass. A White and a Black are kickboxing on it.
> 'You hit?' said the Black. 'Ah! You hit? This not France, this Senegal, you understand?
> Senegal my country, my home, you understand?'
> The Negro had been caught checking out the inside of a cabin.
> The lad had seen him out rather more with his feet than with his hands.
> 'This is France', answered the lad, 'and if you get on again ...' He pointed to his shoe.
> 'You, if you get off, me take you to police, you understand? This Senegal, eh? Not France.'
> And he spat, as if to drown in one expectoration the lad, the ship,
> all the Whites, the whole shebang, in the enormity of his contempt."
> (Albert Londres, *Terre d'ébène*, 1929)

It is hard to resist citing these comical scenes written in the cheeky, florid, precise yet militant prose of Albert Londres. They render so well the old-fashioned, precious, yet paradoxically popular aroma of the *originaires*: a free and subversive relationship with the French language; a strong claim and a supreme affirmation of equality with the metropolitans; rights to defend and promote; political rights that express an identity connected with a special status that safeguards a unique civility.

The deep significance of Muslim religion and practices in the everyday life of the *originaires* was manifested in the stubborn quest for a special status from the moment the decision was made in 1840 to apply the metropolitan Civil Code and Penal Code in the colony. While there was now an explicit questioning of the legality of traditional marriages and rules of inheritance, in the domain of the family, however, one observes an informal preservation of Islamic laws.

Before 1840, matters of the administration of justice came down to the following directives: the Letters Patent of 1728, presented to the Director General of the East India Company, giving him the power to judge all crimes and offences, along with the assistant director and three clerks to be appointed by himself (Jore, 1965: 294); and the Instructions of the Duke of Lauzun of 20 November 1778, which mentioned the absence of a court of justice in the colony, requested the application of some simple rules 'almost entirely having to do with policing', and stipulated that only crimes fell under the competence of the metropolitan courts. At the same time, the mayor of

Saint-Louis retained powers of preserving law and order, such as justices of the peace (Jore, 1965: 296).

Customary usage had resulted in a rather lax situation, with an administration of justice that was more the product of evolution and local transactions than a deliberate decision to transfer the metropolitan judicial system. It was rather that people were inspired by 'French laws'. Baron Roger (cited by Jore, 1965: 297, note 1) gave this testimony in 1823: 'It is impossible for judicial organization to be too simple in Senegal; in this nascent society, justice should be administered as it is in a family, not with our European lawmaking . . . To send the entire judiciary from France would be the greatest calamity'.

In the shilly-shallying of the French colonial administration the destiny of the policy of assimilation was played out, the stakes raised by questions of the administration of justice. Three problems were at issue: religion, polygamy and the care of orphans. The administration's procrastination stemmed from the natives' very firm opposition to repeated attempts to impose the French Civil Code from 1827 on. To simplify a complex situation: on one side, the *originaires'* struggle for the recognition of their political rights (citizenship, the rights to elect and be elected, the right to go to court) was part of a permanent challenge of metropolitan civility, whose grammar and repertory is the Civil Code, and whose place of validation is the French civil court. On the other side, the French administration was caught between the demands of the magistrates and the search for the indispensable support of the colony's Muslim community, in the context of the holy wars (jihad) that filled northern Senegambia with fire and blood (Klein, 1968; Robinson, 1985, 1988).

From the end of the 1830s up to 1847, the colonial administration tried to formalize the collection of rules in a situation where the juridical norms of the magistrates conflicted with the political rationales that governed the norms of the colonial administrators. Depending on which group the balance of power would favour, and in line with their immediate concerns, they would develop different responses illustrating a trial-and-error approach to the administration of justice in the colony of Senegal. Those can be traced by reading the numerous ministerial directives, gubernatorial decrees and ordinances. Thus the Decree of 1840 provided that the Civil Code be applied as if Senegal were an integral part of the metropolis. Consequently, every freeborn individual living in Senegal or its dependencies enjoyed the rights of French citizens to the extent that they were guaranteed by the Civil Code (Leroy, 1994: 298). The Decree of 1830 had not produced the desired results (Boilat, 1984: 226): it did not prevent the Muslims of Saint-Louis from regularly sending petitions demanding that a Muslim court be established in the colony. Analysing one of those petitions, from 1843, Schnapper (1961: 94) observes:

> the Civil Code had been promulgated in the colony, but no exception, no distinction had been made for the Muslims. Did that mean that they were subject to French laws in all

details? That it was necessary to apply those laws with respect to marriage, divorce, inheritance? Certainly not, no-one had dreamed such a thing: they were subject to the laws of the Koran which was both their civil and religious law, and the government had never intended to force on them laws contrary to their laws, much less force them to convert to Christianity ... They asked to be granted the rights accorded to the Muslims of Algeria: namely, that it be recognized and decreed that in no case would the Muslims of Saint-Louis be subject to civil laws that were contrary to their religious laws; and that to accomplish that there should be constituted a court made up of their religious leaders, to whom would be referred disputes that are both religious and civil in nature.

During the first half of the nineteenth century, the Algerian model was at the centre of the debate on the administration of justice in the colony of Senegal. As Schnapper indicates, the parallel established between the evolution of Muslim justice in Algeria and the situation in the Senegalese colony made the colony's Muslims determined 'to demand of the French government the same juridical guarantees that the Algerians then possessed' (ibid: 91). This interest in comparing themselves with Algeria is tied to historical events and circumstances: what was at stake was preserving or challenging certain forms of colonial government and cultural and political transactions. Depending on which cause was embraced by the debaters of colonial justice, the Algerian reference allowed them either to defend the need for establishing the French Civil Code without any concessions, or to insist that it be adapted to the environment and history of the subjugated populations. As archives show, for proponents of the former thesis, Senegal was not Algeria. In fact, they opined:

Islam was the only religion that existed in Algeria when we effected its conquest. It was natural as well as wise to respect it and even to facilitate the practice of its laws, despite all the obstacles it would put in the way of our colonization and all the uprisings that it would periodically produce. But it is not the same here, and I am a long way from thinking that we are subject to the same obligations as we had down there. (ANS, 1889: M8, 103)

Proponents of the latter thesis, meanwhile, insisted on the difficulty of distinguishing:

renouncers and non-renouncers among our Muslim natives ... He doesn't see what serious advantage it could bring people, to have the option of abandoning their status in the eyes of all their coreligionists in order to assimilate to us. If the category in question exists in Algeria, there was a distinction that justified it: renouncers were there considered as real French citizens and they alone enjoyed all the prerogatives associated with that designation. (ANS, 1889: M8, 103)

As for the colonial administrators, who were most worried about keeping the peace in the colony, they thought that:

[the] main objective is to draw a very clear line of demarcation between French Justice and Muslim Justice. Recognizing the difference that exists between Muslim laws, behaviour, and customs and our own, he could not agree that one should create a promiscuity that would leave it to our magistrates to judge matters totally alien to our law. He couldn't say

straightforwardly what he would have desired in the bottom of his heart, but he believes the commission took his meaning. According to him, Muslim Justice should operate completely independently, and remain politically under the supreme authority of the head of the colony. (ANS, 1889: M8, 103)

The terms of the debate on the administration of justice sum up very neatly the procrastination on the part of the colonial administration and clearly express the interests at stake throughout the nineteenth century. In this framework, the Algerian reference suggests two solutions, the first being some combination of French and Muslim magistrates, and the second being the possibility of renouncing one's special status as a Muslim. At the heart of these controversies is the question of how to read the individual histories of France in Algeria and Senegal. In one reading, the principal model for the colonial administrators, be they judges, soldiers, or civil officials, is the civilizing mission and commercial benefits. For many of them, however:

> the political conditions there aren't the same as here. In Algeria, Muslim mores have deep and ancient roots, which they do not have in Senegal. Furthermore, the importance of the role that Islam plays there was one of the conditions of conquest and surrender, so one cannot diminish or question it as one can in this colony. One must also take into consideration that our indigenous people are a long way from having the education and abilities of the indigenous Algerians. So shouldn't one avoid letting them play a totally illegitimate role in our organization, which could become highly burdensome at any given moment? By the time danger was recognized, it might be very difficult to put an end to it. (ANS, 1889: M8, 103)

The first reference to Muslim law is found in the Ordinance of 1847, which established an Advisory Council alongside the court of Saint-Louis. It was the first sign of an attempt to create a judicial framework without reference to that of the metropolis. In subsequent discussions about politics and the courts, the question of whether the Advisory Committee's competence was limited to the newly annexed populations was a recurrent theme. It is thus not clear whether the natives were affected by this new judicial structure, which was only consultative (ANS, 1889: M8, 103).

The establishment of the Advisory Council was the product of a long string of petitions from prominent Muslims, of deliberations by committees charged to study and make recommendations on the reorganization of the judiciary in the colony of Senegal, and of very bitter conflicts between the magistrates and the colonial administrators (ANS, 1832: 3E9; 1846: 3E18). It did not put an end to Muslim demands to set up a Muslim court. The difficulty of reconciling the two positions on the administration of justice for Muslims resulted in a reformulation of the competence of the Advisory Committee, which was now 'called on to give its advice on questions of Muslim law, problems that are submitted to it by the courts' (ANS: decree of 9 August 1854, article 35). The Muslim Petition of 1856 (ANS M8 C folio 6: letter of 11 June 1856) contained an almost exhaustive enumeration of the differences between the Civil Code and Muslim law, emphasizing the following points:

[the Civil Code] forbids investigating paternity, the Muslim law authorizes it; the Koran permits and in a way even orders multiple lawful wives, and the penal code denigrates bigamy; the Koran rejects letting natural children be heirs, whereas the Civil Code gives them the same rights as legitimate children; French law does not recognize divorce and repudiation; finally, there are rules contradicted by other laws in the matter of inheritance, gifts, and wills.

Louis L. Faidherbe,[11] named governor of Senegal in 1854, launched the enterprise of creating a modern colony. Drawing on his Algerian experience, he temporarily put an end to the controversies, petitions, and administrative committees by creating a Muslim court in 1857. He thereby assured a written regulation of a body of law inscribed in the Koran and the Sunna. Muslim autonomy in matters of family law was officially acknowledged.

Governor Faidherbe's decision was part of a specific framework, that of pacifying the colony so as to undertake, with the *originaires'* help, the conquest of the independent territories of the colony, especially those that adjoined Saint-Louis and Gorée. The particular context in the surrounding regions was that of holy wars and mobilization under the banner of Islam, particularly under the leadership of El Hadj Umar Tall (Robinson, 1985). As Ndiaye Seck (1984: 11) observed:

The new strategy of El Hadj Oumar Tell in 1855 pushed Faidherbe's Muslim policy in a new direction. The Tukulor marabout was inciting the Saint-Louisians to boycott French trade on the river. In order to avoid a possible response to this appeal and assure the military and commercial co-operation of the Saint-Louisians, on 13 September 1856 Faidherbe supported a Muslim petition that stressed the need for creating a Muslim court in Saint-Louis. The success of his social policy depended in large part on the success of this institution. It constituted his principal means of bringing the two societies together, and in addition was one of the mechanisms in his judicial administration for making Islam lose its social influence.

With the establishment of the Muslim section of colonial justice, Faidherbe reached out to plan Islamic education, Koranic and Arabic. He introduced into the colony the model of the Algerian *médersa* (a religious school), combining Islam with colonial modernity, the French language with Arabic. These were modalities whose public display, exegetical and literate, was expressed in *Wolof* with affected overtones of Arabic and French. This development and its appropriation by the *originaires* radically distinguishes

---

11. Faidherbe, who is considered the creator of modern Senegal, was governor of Senegal from 1854 to 1861 and from 1863 to 1865. He spent part of his career in Algeria, where he learned Arabic. He was the principal architect of the conquest of Senegambia. His knowledge of Senegalese languages, his interest in history and customs, and his publications in geography, history, and languages, all make him, according to Bathily (1976), the founder of French Africanism.

the Islam of the Four Communes from the rural logic of the Islam of the Senegalese brotherhoods. The colony's participation in the institutionalization and monumental inscription of the Muslim community, especially in Saint-Louis, explains the soliciting of religion in constructing the *originaires'* civic and civil identity. The ministerial decree of 20 May 1857 explicitly limited the competence of the Muslim jurisdiction to the purely civil, to matters relating to personal status. Its significance was recalled by a colonial magistrate when the judicial debate was relaunched in 1889:

> It is strange to see not only French subjects but also French citizens having different civil rights, mostly incompatible with the state of being a citizen, unless one tries to go back to what was done in 1857 and remove from the indigenous people who are Muslims by birth or conversion the personal status that was accorded them. Isn't it possible to tighten the ties that bind them to us? Do we have to let them create another state within the State, whose influence we would have all the more reason to fear, that would have no other guide but fanaticism, whose members would be called upon as voters to take part in our public affairs? (ANS, 1889: M8, 103)

The product of a political transaction, the main objective of the decree was to win over the Muslim populations of the colony of Senegal to the French cause, at a time when the colony was concerned about aggressive developments in the Muslim propaganda of bellicose marabouts. When the colonial administration became more firmly established in the greater part of Senegambia, the motivation for compromise disappeared:

> Senegal is a colony created by France; the city of Saint-Louis was constituted by the French, and it is only little by little, gradually and virtually clandestinely that Islam infiltrated the Black population of the city, introduced by the Moors of the river's right bank; so it couldn't have city rights and demand prerogatives analogous to those of Algeria. Here more than anywhere else, the Muslim, because of his profound ignorance developed by his fanaticism, is absolutely recalcitrant with respect to our ideas, our customs, our language, our behaviour, our civilization. He's like a people apart, next to ours, living and growing on our flanks for nearly a century, without managing to be stimulated by our progress and contact with us. To the contrary, he is gaining territory every day toward the south, and it is very much to be feared that if the powers of the Cadi are extended, that expansion will be encouraged, and may end up getting us in the most awkward quandaries in the not-too-distant future. (ANS, 1889: M8, 103)

Similarly, when the cadis' judgements were challenged by recourse to French jurisdictions, especially in matters of divorce, succession of property, and inheritance by women and natural children, petitions would pile up on the desks of the governor and the minister. In the face of these petitions from a Muslim community bracing itself for an intransigent defence of its special status, the magistrates kept trying to reconcile the jurisdiction of the colonial courts with metropolitan traditions in order to restrain or abolish the competence of the Muslim judge, the cadi.

The battle surrounding the organization of Muslim justice rebounded in 1889, when the Muslims sent a petition concerning the treatment of vacant successions and Muslim judicial sales liquidated by the court. In response to this petition, a 'Commission charged to study the reorganization of Muslim justice in Senegal' was instituted. The Commission's report shows that the stakes had not changed, that neither camp had shifted its position. On the contrary, for the first time the colonial administration had to expand the discussion to the second arrondissement (Gorée, Rufisque and Dakar), where demands for instituting a Muslim court became emphatic. This was the rationale that was invoked:

> While the Muslim code governs the indigenous population of the first arrondissement, the Civil Code governs that of the second. It is not acceptable, gentlemen, that in one colony like Senegal there should be two weights and two measures. Our populations of the second arrondissement, composed in large part of children of the Saint-Louisians, are just as religious as the people of the first arrondissement and should enjoy the same prerogatives. I appeal, gentlemen, to your sense of fairness and beg you to express the wish that the Decree of 1857 should be extended to the second arrondissement and that it should get a new Muslim court of the first instance, whose seat would be in Dakar. (ANS, 1889: M8, 103)

The reaction of the colonial magistrature was a reprise of the position that had been adopted with Faidherbe's first mandate. It was based on applying the Civil Code and strictly controlling the growth of Islam, in favour of assimilation. The chief observations made by its representative on the commission are a clear illustration of this position, especially when it came to expanding Muslim jurisdiction to the second arrondissement:

> [He] feels that the populations of the second arrondissement are in general less Muslim than those of the first, and if there is no way to refrain from giving them a judge, then at least we should avoid, in the interest of the French cause, bestowing on them a *tamsir* or Muslim religious leader whose official appointment would contribute to the consolidation and spread among them of the influence of the Islam that unfortunately is already too much implanted in the capital (ANS, 1889: M8, 103)

For its part, the colonial administration, subject to the constraints of the colonial conquest, strove to avoid controversies, in order to ensure the support of the Muslim community (Sarr and Roberts, 1991: 131). Depending on whether the magistrature prevailed over the colonial administration or vice versa, the prerogatives of the cadi were restricted or expanded (Schnapper, 1961). The magistrates thought that any refusal to apply the Civil Code was contrary to Natural Law and the policy of assimilation (Carrère and Holle, 1855). Their aggressiveness was matched by the Muslim community's considerable means of bringing pressure to bear on the colonial administration through representatives, deputies and municipal councilmen, and their position as intermediaries in the trade with Senegambia. The administration, caught between these opposing demands, wavered between connivance with the *originaires* (establishing or re-establishing Muslim courts) and unifying the judicial systems. In 1903, for example, a decree was promulgated that unified the systems of justice and their administration, subjecting *originaires*, metropolitans, and assimilated peoples alike to the authority of the same law, while guaranteeing to the indigenous people that their customs would be preserved in private matters, provided that these did not contravene principles of humanity and civilization (Quellien, 1910: 227). The Decree of 1903 is interesting because it abolished the special status of *originaires* and recognized the Muslim authorities in the same category as 'fetishist' judicial customs, bringing them in a single stroke to the same level, designating them as dominated populations liable to subjection to 'the civilizing mission'. By expanding, or at least including Muslim justice in a geography of custom, the Senegalese colonial magistrature tried to win two wagers: to drive the *originaires* out of colonial society, and to redefine the notions of domination and submission, which had been strongly challenged by the emergence of a plural colonial society and an unstable equilibrium. When the expansion/inclusion did not withstand the petitions from the Muslim community, the administration tried to forbid publishing judgements in Arabic. In reaction, the religious erudition of the *originaires* achieved a cultural hybrid which was expressed in the mastery of Arabic and of theological and judicial sciences, and, paradoxically, the mastery of French. This gave birth to a colonial Islam distinct from the Islam of the brotherhoods and/or Black Islam (Monteil, 1964), strongly dominated by the Sufi outlook: the centrality of the figure of the marabout, holy places and objects, and the abnegation of the Self.

The colonial colouring of the Islam of the *originaires* opened up a new field to the colonial culture, structured in two domains: a public domain subject to French law, and a private domain under the influence of a religiosity that identified the citizen of the Four Communes. Equally, it opened up the universality of the republican tradition of the metropolis, and the uniqueness of its product as colonial subject, inventing for itself a distinction in religion and the judicial system. The demand for instituting a Muslim court should be read not as the struggle for a judicial system that fits in with a religious tradition, but as the delineation of a space for producing an indigenous identity protected from the violence of colonial domination and cultural arrogance. One can trace the objects at issue, around which the opposition between the Muslim community and the metropolitan actors (judges and colonial functionaries) took shape: polygamy, which preoccupied the imagined world of the colonists with the fantasy of a torrid indigenous sexuality, unbridled and fertile; community care of orphans, which brought up problems of inheritance and succession, and conversion, when nobody claimed them; leviratic marriage; and cohabitation. The amount of stress placed on polygamy and the levirate was unusual, but it was part of that colonialist conception of the subjugated as lacking intellectual capacity and as being primitives with an animal sexuality. The extraordinary vitality of the native culture, in its multiple manifestations and complex recompositions, contained those colonial detours, establishing itself as a constituent of the colonial culture.

In 1912, the colonial administration reaffirmed its recognition of political rights and the Muslim community's submission to Koranic law to the exclusion of the French Civil Code. The outbreak of the First World War and the need for African troops in the war effort afforded Deputy Blaise Diagne the opportunity to secure legal recognition of the *originaires'* citizenship through a series of laws known as the 'Blaise Diagne Laws'.[12] To put the finishing touches to the edifice of this new legality, the Decree of 20 November 1932 recognized the exclusive competence of Muslim courts in the civil affairs of Muslim natives and their descendants, such as marriage, inheritance, gifts, wills, and so on (Sarr and Roberts, 1991: 141).

The pluralism and diversity that are so much celebrated in the cultural manifestations of the *originaires*, in religion and in the constant conflicts that set the metropolitan components against the indigenous people of the protectorate, did not withstand the unitary and authoritarian ideology of African nationalism and its Senegalese side, *negritude*.

CONCLUSION

The identity of the *originaires* of the Four Communes is thus revealed in multiple practices, as much in their diversity as in their manifestations in the economic, political and social registers. Their religious expression, especially in cultural idioms and their public display, whether pertaining to the divine or to social and political transactions, is carried out in a space produced by colonial logics, in which social groups and plural practices are expressed. The specific morphology of the colonial space in the Four Communes is the product of these plural logics and of transactions that produced the fully empowered communes of the colony, at the same time that the latter produced fragments of cultures and societies that negotiated their statuses, civil as well as civic. It is in the invention of a culture which is taking on the responsibility of producing a new community that a two-sided religiosity is deployed, Catholic and Muslim, within one and the same *originaires* identity, whose civility is the product of a compromise and of revisions of cultural outlooks, the blending of which is a creole. Therein the culture of the Four Communes presents a religiosity expressed in the design of Atlantic civilization, whose outlines are sketched by the Atlantic slave trade and filled in by European colonization. This design supports an architecture and a civility that is tested in the production of a citizenship opposed to a metropolitan

12. The most important of the Diagne Laws of 1915 and 1916 was the law of 19 October 1915 that gave the *originaires* the right to enlist and serve in the regular army of France (Johnson, 1991: 232). In September 1916, Diagne introduced into the Chamber the following resolution: 'The indigenous people of the fully empowered communes of Senegal and their descendants are and shall remain French citizens, subject to the military obligations imposed by the Law of 19 October 1915' (Johnson, 1991: 234).

civility whose syntax is the French Civil Code. The principal characteristic of the production of a city and an urban civility is at the heart of a globalization project, the colonial civilizing mission, imposing on it the special rhythm of societies that adapt to an economic and political situation in order to secure for themselves a status whose hybrid nature follows from a frenzied resistance to colonial assimilation in its metropolitan version. The *originaires* imposed on the colonial administration and the magistrates the indigenous version of colonial history, that of colonial contact and unstable but continuing transactions between two sides, the one autochthonous and the other foreign. From this dialogue and this opposition were produced the fully empowered communes and the citizenship of the *originaires*.

Colonial violence has always been considered capable of imposing the figures of its domination and hybrid nature by deploying its knowledge of classification and its arrogance, which is rooted in the superiority of its civilizing mission. The *originaires* paths, in their gaudy esthetics, the monumentality of their mosques and churches, and their stubborn rejection of the Civil Code and conversion, reveal histories of identities and transactions where a native pluralism and distinction has established itself at the centre stage of the colonial project: an obvious desire to participate in the world on their own terms.

The paradox of the Senegalese situation is that the postcolonial logics deployed an even more weighty authority to produce a distinction with the colonial project, whether falsely or not, and achieve assimilation within the nation. On the shores and drifts of postcolonialism, it is necessary to pursue those arabesques where, through rips in authoritarianism, protests are expressed with clothing, festive demonstrations, culinary art and the display of social, religious, and economic identities, and a unique history whose landmarks are: the drafting of the Register of Grievances by the population of Saint-Louis, directed to the States General of 1789; the successes in colonial commerce of the traders who followed the troops of Governor Faidherbe and his successors; the election of municipal councilmen and a deputy to the French National Assembly in 1848; resistance and collaboration during the Vichy regime; and an intellectual and enlightened Islam . . . so many signs of a memory required to (again) become African by the philosophy of *negritude* and the *Wolof* ideology of *diggël*.[13]

REFERENCES

Baker, F. et al. (eds) (1994) *Colonial Discoures/Postcolonial Theory*. Manchester: Manchester University Press.

13. A maraboutic prescriptive directive, whether in the religious or political domain.

Bathily, Abdoulaye (1976) 'Aux Origines de l'Africanisme: Le Rôle de l'oeuvre ethno-historique de Faidherbe dans la conquête française du Sénégal'. Cahiers de Jussieu, no. 2, *Le Mal de Voir*: 77–105.

Berque, Jacques (1964) *La dépossession du monde*. Paris: le Seuil.

Bhabha, Homi (1990) *Nation and Narration*. London: Routledge.

Boilat, Abbé David (1846) 'Voyage à Joal 1846'. Paris: Carton B, Société de Géographie de Paris.

Boilat, Abbé David (1984/1853) *Esquisses Sénégalaises*. Paris: Karthala. (1st edn, Paris: Bertrand, 1853).

Carrère, F. and P. Holle (1855) *De la Sénégambie*. Paris: Firmin Didot.

Chatterjee, Partha (1986) *Nationalist Thought and the Colonial World. A Derivative Discourse*. London: Zed Press.

Chatterjee, Partha (1993) *The Nation and Its Fragments*. Princeton, NJ: Princeton University Press.

Chrétien, J-P. (1993) *L'Invention religieuse en Afrique. Histoire et Religion en Afrique noire*. Paris: Karthala.

Coquery-Vidrovitch, Catherine (1993) 'La ville africaine: "lieu de colonisation"', *Afrique Contemporaine* 168: 11–22.

Crowder, Michael (1962) *Senegal: A Study in French Assimilation Policy*. London: Methuen (rev edn).

Diagne, S. Bachir (1992) 'L'avenir de la tradition', in M. C. Diop (ed.) *Sénégal. Trajectoires d'un État*, pp. 279–98. Dakar, Codesria.

Diouf, Mamadou (1990) *Le Kajoor au XIXème siècle. Pouvoir Ceddo et Conquête Coloniale*. Paris: Karthala.

Diouf, Mamadou (1992) 'Le Clientélisme, la Technocratie et après?', in M. C. Diop (ed.) *Sénégal: Trajectoires d'un État*, pp. 233–78. Dakar: Codesria.

Dirks, N. et al. (eds) (1994) *Culture? Power, History. A Reader in Contemporary Social Theory*. Princeton, NJ: Princeton University Press.

Durand, J-B. (1803) *Voyages au Sénégal, 1785 et 1786*, 2 vol. Paris: H. Agasse.

Johnson, Wesley (1991/1971) *The Emergence of Black Politics in Senegal. The Struggle for Power in the Four Communes 1900–1920*. Stanford, CA: Stanford University Press, 1971. (French translation: *Naissance du Sénégal Contemporain*. Paris: Karthala, 1991.)

Jore, Léonce (1965) *Les Etablissements français sur la Côte Occidentale de l'Afrique de 1758 à 1809*. Paris: Société Française d'Histoire d'Outre-mer.

Kane, C. H. (1961) *L'aventure ambigué*. Paris: UGE.

Klein, M. (1968) *Islam and Imperialism in Senegal: Sine-Saloum, 1847–1914*. Stanford, CA: Stanford University Press.

Lamiral, D. (1789) *L'Afrique et le peuple afriquain considérés sous tous les rapports avec notre commerce et nos colonies*. Paris: Dessenne.

Leroy, Etienne (1994) 'Le Code civil au Sénégal', in M. Doucet and J. Vanderlinden *La Réception des systèmes juridiques: Implantation et Destin*. Brussels: Bruylant.

Londres, Albert (1944) *Terre d'ébène*. Paris: Le Serpent à Plumes Éditions (1st ed., Albin Michel, 1929).

Marcson, Marc (1976) 'European-African Interaction in the Precolonial Period: Saint Louis, Senegal, 1758–1854'. PhD Thesis, Princeton University.

Marty, Paul (1917) *Études sur l'Islam au Sénégal*. 2 vols: *I Les personnes; II Les doctrines et les institutions*. Paris: E. Leroux.

MBembe, J. Achille (1988) *Afriques Indociles*. Paris: Karthala.

Monga, Padmini (ed.) (1996) *Contemporary Postcolonial Theory. A Reader*. New York: Arnold.

Monteil, Vincent (1964) *L'Islam noir*. Paris: Éditions du Seuil.

Quellien, A. (1910) *La politique musulmane dans l'Afrique Occidentale Française*. Paris: Emile Larose.

Robinson, David (1985) *The Holy War of Umar Tal: The Western Sudan in the Mid-nineteenth Century*. Oxford: Clarendon Press.

Robinson, David (1988) 'French Islamic Policy and Practice in Late Nineteenth Century Senegal', *Journal of African History* 29(3): 415–36.

Said, Edward (1979) *Orientalism*. New York: Vintage.

Sarr, D. and R. Roberts (1991) 'The Jurisdiction of Muslim Tribunals in Colonial Senegal, 1857–1932', in K. Mann and R. Roberts (eds) *Law in Colonial Africa*. London: Heinemann and James Currey.

Schnapper, Bernard (1961) 'Les Tribunaux musulmans et la politique coloniale au Sénégal (1830–1914)', *Revue Historique du Droit Français et Etranger* 39: 90–128.

Seck, Ndiaye (1984) 'Les Tribunaux musulmans du Sénégal (1857–1914)', Dakar, Université C.A. Diop, Faculté des Lettres et Sciences Humaines, Département d'Arabe, Mémoire de maîtrise.

Senghor, Léopold Sédar (1964) *Liberté I. Négritude et Humanisme*. Paris: Le Seuil.

Sinou, Alain (1993) *Comptoirs et villes coloniales du Sénégal. Saint Louis, Gorée, Dakar*. Paris: Karthala.

Spivak, Gayatri Chakravorty (1993) *Outside in the Teaching Machine*. New York: Routledge.

Vaillant, Janet (1990) *Black, French and African. A Life of Leopold Sédar Senghor*. Cambridge, MA: Harvard University Press.

Young, Robert (1991) *White Mythologies: Writing History and the West*. London: Routledge.

Young, Robert (1995) *Hybridity in Theory, Culture and Race*. London: Routledge.

National Archives of Senegal (ANS)

Documents recueillis, publiés et présentés par Bâ Omar, *La pénétration française au Cayor*. Tome 1 (1854–1861). Abbeville: Imprimerie F. Paillart (1976).

Série M7 Code de Procédure civile au Sénégal, 6 Juilet 1859.

Série M8 Justice musulmane au Sénégal, 1846–1896.

Série 241 Tribunaux Musulmans du Sénégal, 1898–1919.

Série 3E9 à 26 Délibérations du Conseil Privé du Sénégal, 1832 à 1846.

Enforcing the Human Rights of Citizens and Non-Citizens in the Era of Maastricht: Some Reflections on the Importance of States

Jacqueline Bhabha

INTRODUCTION

In 1995, in the third enlargement since its inception, state membership of the European Union (EU) grew to fifteen,[1] two and a half times its original size. Its population grew to 370.4 million, making it 40 per cent more populous than the United States (Bermann and Goebel, 1995: 4), and its sphere of operations expanded from the original economic concerns of the Common Market to include foreign and security policy, and issues related to questions of justice and home affairs. The growth in size, scope and impact of this supranational organization is a striking development of the latter part of this century and part of a global vision of institutionalized interstate co-operation.

As is well known the EU, like the United Nations edifice, has its genesis in the post-war period: in the face of unprecedented destruction of life and property, radical economic disarray and the emergence of a bipolar world order tied into an escalating arms race, the laying of 'foundations of an even closer union among the peoples of Europe' was to be a means of 'pooling resources to preserve and strengthen peace and liberty'[2] and to increase economic, social and political well-being. For the six founding members of the first European Communities,[3] the goals were primarily economic — to aid economic recovery and stimulate growth. However, these were closely linked to political goals both intra-European and international, including

---

I would like to thank Peter Geschiere for his editorial suggestions and Kara Points for her assistance with the manuscript.

1. On 24 June 1994, the Treaties and Final Acts were signed to enable Austria, Finland, Norway and Sweden to join the existing twelve members of the EU. However the Norwegian referendum opposed joining; on 1 January 1995, EU membership thus rose to fifteen (Goebel, 1995: 1093).
2. Treaty Establishing the European Economic Community (hereafter *EC*) March 1957, Preamble.
3. The three Benelux countries (Belgium, Netherlands and Luxemburg), France, Germany and Italy signed the Treaty establishing the European Coal and Steel Community in 1951; treaties establishing the European Economic Community and Euratom were signed by the same six countries in 1957.

(for France) containing potential revivals of German military power, and reducing European dependency on the USA. The philosophy underlying the early development of the Union was that economic recovery and collaborative growth would of themselves fuel political cohesion and social progress by ensuring an improved standard of living and reducing the risk of social discontent or military conflict. Prosperity rather than justice or equality was the prime concern. Combining the forces, energies and resources of individual states would facilitate realization of their common aspirations, something that states on their own had singularly failed to achieve.

Although indirectly invoked,[4] protecting fundamental human rights was not explicitly articulated as a central goal at the outset. However, as the member states of the EU grew from the original six, as the reach of European policy was propelled by the Single European Act of 1 July 1987 to more extensive areas of competence, so recognition that the new European entity had to build on the human rights edifice central to the constitutions of its member states developed. The culmination of this recognition is to be found in the preamble to the Maastricht Treaty on European Union.

This ambitious set of goals for the EU, and the expanding infrastructure and sphere of operations to realize them, can be characterized as part of the post-war phenomenon of globalization. A considerable and rapidly expanding body of scholarship employs this paradigm to analyse significant transformations in the present world order, such as the dramatic increase in transnational corporate penetration, the exponential expansion of information technology, the escalating scale of global flows of goods, capital and persons across state borders (Albrow and King, 1990; Robertson, 1990: 15). At a more theoretical level, it has been argued that the pervasiveness of the term globalization in contemporary social science signifies a spatialization of social theory (Featherstone and Lash, 1995). In fact both the temporal and spatial co-ordinates of the phenomenon are matters of dispute as indeed are its defining characteristics, so much so that it is now common to talk of 'globalizations' in the plural (Nederveen Pieterse, 1995).

A few distinctive positions can be identified from amongst the multiple characterizations and appropriations of the term. For some, globalization is an aspect of post-war transnational finance or corporate monopoly capitalism (Sklair, 1991). From this perspective the phenomenon is a predominantly one-way process of western economic, social and cultural hegemony, epitomized by the power of global finance and McDonaldization, and

---

4. 'Determined to lay the foundations of an even closer union among the peoples of Europe, resolved to ensure the economic and social progress of their countries by common action to eliminate the barriers which divide Europe ... intending to confirm the solidarity which binds Europe and the overseas countries and desiring to ensure the development of their prosperity, in accordance with the principles of the Charter of the United Nations ... have decided to create a European Economic Community'. Preamble, *EC*, 25 March 1957.

captured by the short-hand 'Americanization'.[5] On this view the autonomy and strength of the national state is severely compromised by globalizing forces and asymmetries of power are exacerbated by them. Others have used 'globalization' to signify a more collaborative contemporary process of elaborating shared meanings, and arriving at common 'globally negotiated definitions', over and beyond the understandings embedded in any one national or cultural framework.[6] From this perspective globalization does not necessarily weaken the national state; rather it alters its terms of reference and the temporal and spatial context within which it is embedded. New understandings, more than the sum of the parts so to speak, are an important consequence of this process. With yet a different emphasis, the term has been applied to describe an interactive set of flows and exchanges within and between a range of local, national and regional contexts, characteristic of the last quarter century or so. On this construction globalization, while 'shrink[ing] the distances between elites', nevertheless is not to be confused with Americanization or a more generic homogenization; on the contrary it is here characterized as uneven, 'turbulent', even paradoxically 'a localizing process' (Appadurai, 1996: 9, 17, 150), undermining the importance of states but with historically and geographically specific consequences.

The latter is clearly a critical point. To have meaningful explanatory value, 'globalization' must be tied to a particular context; it can then provide the means for interpreting change in relation to apparently unrelated developments. In this article globalization will be understood to include aspects of all three positions just identified. It is taken to consist of a set of processes characterized by transformed relations between the local, the national, the regional and the global. These processes, while resulting in new, common social understandings, have the ability both to produce distinctive local inflections of the wider process and also to contribute to a more asymmetrical relationship between relatively powerful and powerless agents. The three perspectives on globalization outlined above have different implications for the relative importance of states. The first and the third suggest a weakening of state power, as globalization undermines states' autonomy and impact. The second perspective, by contrast, points in the opposite direction; it envisages a transformation in states' power but no necessary correlation of such change with a reduction in their importance; on the contrary, from this perspective, the result of globalization may be an enhancement of state power and efficacy, a strengthening of state institutions in relation to other sections of the society.

This article approaches the question of the relationship between globalization and state power from a legal standpoint. It focuses on an aspect of

---

5. A regional variant of this perspective is exemplified by the use of the term 'Japanization' to describe the impact of Japanese economic and cultural production on East Asia (see Igarashi, 1996).
6. Das (1996); mimeo on file with the author.

globalization — the European Union — and inquires into its effect on the relationship between individual and state with respect to the enforcement of fundamental human rights. Rather than the ethnographic analysis or historical documentation used elsewhere in this collection, the material relied on here to develop the argument is primarily juridical: the development of case law and judicial reasoning provide the empirical basis for the claims made. This perspective explains the emphasis on the importance of state power in securing access to rights (explored further in the next section), in contrast to other approaches, based more on cultural and technological phenomena, which tend to highlight the declining importance of states.

'SUPRANATIONAL' ORGANIZATIONS AND THE STATE

To what extent does the growth of supranational organizations, and the EU in particular, correspond with a weakening of national bodies, indeed the state itself? It is clear that the multiplication and enlargement of supranational organizations, whether corporate, intergovernmental or non-governmental, is a central characteristic of globalization with profound consequences for the new world order across the domains of culture and society, law, politics and economics. Their influence can be traced from food prices to TV ads, from passport colours to holiday entitlements. Acronyms such as GATT, NAFTA, EC, UNHCR, AT&T, ICJ and ILO need no elucidation in households or newspapers across the globe; they are powerful and prominent players impinging on the daily life of individuals and states, and on the relationship between the two.

On one view, the impact of globalization has so profoundly affected this relationship that the role of the individual state has been decisively,[7] even irrevocably,[8] weakened. According to a recent formulation of this perspective, 'the global is [beginning] to replace the nation-state as the decisive framework for social life' (Featherstone and Lash, 1995: 1–2). Certainly, there are many features of the present era — from fundamentalist to environmental movements, from monopolistic corporations to free trade zones — usefully characterized as post-national, transnational, subnational (Appadurai, 1993: 417; Rouse, 1995: 353). Moreover, especially within the context of developing states, economic liberalization policies and the imposition of structural adjustment measures by international bodies such as the World Bank and the IMF, are typically characterized as aspects or products of 'globalization'. The term in this context is used (in line with the first characterization above)

---

7. 'The state system is being superseded by a series of interlocking social, cultural, economic, political, technological, and ecological tendencies ...' (Falk, 1985: 653).
8. '... we are in the process of moving to a global order in which the nation-state has become obsolete and other formations for allegiance and identity have taken its place' (Appadurai, 1993: 421).

more or less synonymously with monopoly capitalism, to indicate a process of economic integration fuelled by the imposition of free market economics on an ever-expanding area of the globe.

Acknowledging this, however, does not entail the view that the nation state is in decline. The role of the state may not be reduced but simply altered by the emerging global order, as it interacts with a new body of actors and agents (de Sousa Santos, 1995). Intergovernmental policy formation and subsequent legislative enactment among member states of the European Union is a pertinent example. Although member states have conceded inroads into national sovereignty in some areas,[9] these have been circum-scribed by the careful delimitation of community competence,[10] the preser-vation of veto powers over legislation for member states in respect of vital areas of interest, and by states' intransigence in implementing community policies in conflict with national political goals.[11]

In fact it is arguable that the dramatic expansion of information techno-logy and intergovernmental co-operation, certainly one commonly accepted aspect of 'globalization' however conceived, has increased the power and impact of states, severally and jointly, in relation to both individuals and corporations. Within the European Union, sophisticated intergovernmental co-operation and information-storage techniques give immigration officers in Bari, customs agents in Dublin or detectives in Hamburg instant access to detailed personal information about millions of European and non-European citizens (Bunyan, 1993a: 27–33). Globally, technology companies in Europe and North America are selling repressive surveillance technologies to the secret police and military authorities in non-democratic states such as China, Indonesia, Nigeria, Angola, Rwanda and Guatemala, thus enabling them to engage in mass surveillance of populations and strengthening their positions (Privacy International, 1995). In relation to corporations, the growing legislative impact on product regulation and interventionist standard-setting by states increasingly compels multinationals to encourage transnational accords between ever-larger and thus more influential

---

9. Following the period of so-called 'euro-pessimism' in the late 1970s and early 1980s, member states agreed to procedural changes brought about through the Single European Act which increased the scope of majority voting to enact legislation, thus reducing individual states' ability to veto opposed legislation.

10. The fierce debate over the principle of 'subsidiarity' highlighted the delicacy of this negotiation (see Emilou, 1995: 65). According to some, the allocation of competence between the community and member states is no longer a question of a mutually exclusive separation of spheres but rather a collaborative 'shared competence' reflecting the need for shared responsibility in an increasingly interconnected and complex European society (see Dehousse, 1994: 103; Weatherill, 1995: 13).

11. The protracted delays in abolishing internal border controls between member states is a clear case in point. Another example is states' attitudes towards criminal nationals of other member states (see, for example, Vincenzi, 1994: 163).

groupings of states, in a search for harmonization. Arguing for the creation of TAFTA — a Trans-Atlantic Free Trade Zone incorporating NAFTA and the EU — for example, corporate heads urged political leaders to 'end [the] duplicate testing requirements and cut [...] through a hodgepodge of regulations which were far more important to their competitive needs than reducing tariffs' (*New York Times* 3 December 1995: A12). European Union developments, captured in the phrase 'Fortress Europe' confirm this symbiotic relationship between the growth of supranational organizations and the increase in aspects of individual state power.

GLOBALIZATION AND THE ENFORCEMENT OF RIGHTS

It is clear that in the second half of this century, a major reorganization of international life has been taking place through the efforts of politically and economically powerful actors to cope with post-war reconstruction and growing interdependence. One aspect of this process has been the transformation in the status of the individual in international law (for centuries only concerned with inter-state relations)[12] and the creation of a substantial and rapidly growing body of international law concerned with the protection and enforcement of human rights (Meron, 1984; Newman and Weissbrodt, 1990). The complex consequences of this reorganization for social regulation and change depend on the mechanism for intervening and the area of intervention, both substantive and geographical, as much as on the status of the enforcer. The impact of enforcement mechanisms, whether co-operative or coercive, aspirational or compulsory, depends critically on a range of political, legal and socio-economic factors. The acts of states feature centrally in determining these outcomes, so that identical international mechanisms translate into national contexts quite differently.

Thus international standards are only as effective as the means for enforcing them in a given situation: disparities of power, wealth, access to information and expertise can neutralize potentially far-reaching reforms. The Bhopal tragedy is a clear case in point. In 1985, the UN General Assembly adopted Guidelines on Consumer Protection encouraging governments to adopt 'appropriate measures, including legal systems, safety regulations, national or international standards, voluntary standards and the maintenance of safety records to ensure that products are safe for either intended or normally foreseeable use'.[13] The UN General Assembly

---

12. The legacy of this history is evident in the fact that individuals still have no inherent *locus standi* before international tribunals; states can, however, grant such standing, by accepting articles of treaties which grant individuals the right to initiate litigation on their own behalf.

13. Resolution on Consumer Protection, with Annex, adopted by the UNGA, 9 April 1985; UNGA Res. 39/248,39, UN GAOR Supp. (No. 51), Art. 9.

adopted at least three other related resolutions,[14] thus providing the outline of a new international order for hazardous chemicals. Despite these developments, the US based Union Carbide Corporation responsible for the now infamous chemical pesticide plant had dropped safety standards at the Bhopal site considerably below those maintained at a similar site within the United States, without opposition from the Indian government. Moreover the out-of-court settlement reached by agreement with the Indian government following the disaster[15] resulted in awards of only US$3000 to the families of disaster victims — as a journalist put it: 'In the United States this equals the price of ... two high-class pedigree dogs' (Karliner, 1994: 727). As an·enforcer of the Bhopal victims' human rights the Indian state failed both at the stage of prevention and redress. American families in similar circumstances, had there been a disaster, with identical international codes, would have been compensated at a radically different order of magnitude.

The point applies to the rights of individuals as much as it does to corporate acts. Most human rights conventions within the UN system do not create legally enforceable binding obligations which individuals can impose on states' parties (Byrnes, 1995: 193–4); indeed the number of ratifications by states' parties of a particular treaty is often inversely related to its enforceability and the consequent impact on intended beneficiaries of the treaty. The effect of the Convention on the Elimination of All Forms of Discrimination Against Women on women's rights,[16] and the Convention on the Rights of the Child on children's rights[17] bear this out: though large numbers of states have ratified these Conventions, their enforcement potential to date has been

---

14. Resolution on the Exchange of Information on Banned Hazardous Chemicals and Unsafe Pharmaceutical Products, 17 December 1979, GA Res. 173,34, UN GAOR Supp. (No. 46) at 189, UN Doc. A/34/46 (1979); Resolution on the Exchange of Information on Banned Hazardous Chemicals and Unsafe Pharmaceutical Products, 16 December 1981, GA Res. 166,36, UN GAOR Supp. (No. 1) at 193, UN Doc. A/36/51 (1981); Resolution on the Protection Against Products Harmful to Health and the Environment, 17 December 1982, GA Res. 137,37, UN GAOR Supp. (No. 51) at 112, UN Doc. A/37/51 (1982/3).

15. According to government figures over 6600 people died and over 70,000 were injured; citizens' claims suggest much larger numbers — 16,000 and 600,000 respectively (Karliner, 1994: 726).

16. This convention came into force more rapidly than any previous human rights convention due to the rate and extent of ratification. Its impact on the enforcement of women's rights, however, is limited, partly because of the substantial number of reservations entered by signatory states against central articles and against the jurisdiction of the International Court of Justice. The absence of an individual complaints procedure has further severely limited its impact on the enforcement of women's rights (Byrnes, 1995: 189; Cook, 1990: 643–4).

17. This convention was unanimously adopted by the 159 members of the General Assembly of the UN. Ratified by all members of the UN except the USA and Somalia, it came into force even more quickly than CEDAW. Although it contains innovative mechanisms for strengthening the monitoring of state practice through country reports, it contains no individual complaints procedure (Detrick, 1992: 632–40; Van Beuren, 1995: 396).

disappointing and limited. The point can be made with equal or more force with respect to the practice of torture: it is clearly prohibited by international law,[18] yet 'there are probably more States practising torture than States not practising it' (Weiler, 1988: 123.)

INTERNATIONAL NORMS AND LOCALIZING PROCESSES

Although national law cannot be invoked to override international treaty obligations,[19] nevertheless political and legal differences between states have a decisive effect on the impact of treaties on individuals. Indeed, it is clear that there is significant interstate variation: the implementation of international refugee law in Europe exemplifies this 'localizing effect', identified earlier as an aspect of globalization.

The 1951 UN Convention on the Status of Refugees and the 1967 New York Protocol govern international law with respect to refugee protection. In deference to states' defence of their sovereignty and historical prerogative to control access of non-citizens to their territory, the Convention does not impose a binding obligation on signatory states to grant asylum to any individual asylum applicant.[20] It does, however, contain a prohibition on *refoulement*, that is an obligation on states' parties not to send a refugee back to a persecuting country.[21] This clause has become the centrepiece of refugee protection. No international or supranational body is vested with the power to enforce the right to non-*refoulement*; it is a matter of sovereign state control, a reflection of political forces particular to each state. Within this overall frame, in the absence of regulation by any supervisory international

---

18. See Universal Declaration of Human Rights (1948) Article 5; International Covenant on Civil and Political Rights (1976) Article 7, one of only seven non-derogable articles in the Convention; and Convention Against Torture and other Cruel Inhuman or Degrading Treatment (1984).

19. Art. 27 of the Vienna Convention on the Law of Treaties provides that 'A party may not invoke the provisions of its internal law as justification for its failure to perform a treaty', 1155 UNTS 331.

20. The only international instrument to articulate a right to asylum, albeit qualified, is the Universal Declaration of Human Rights, article 14 of which states: 'Everyone has the right to seek and to enjoy in other countries asylum from persecution'. Even this article only describes a right to seek asylum and a right to enjoy it if granted, but no right to demand, obtain or be granted asylum (see Bhabha, 1996: 3). The Universal Declaration, though of great declaratory moment, is not binding on states; most of its provisions have been subsequently articulated in binding instruments, but Article 14 has not.

21. UN Convention on the Status of Refugees, Art. 33. This injunction against forcible return does not necessitate the grant of indefinite refugee status — sending a refugee to another safe country, granting temporary status, even preventing access to the host territory so that no question of asylum can arise, as in the US Haitian cases (*Sale v. Haitian Centers Council*, Inc., 113 S.Ct. 2549, 1993) have all been held by the courts to be acceptable ways of complying with the non-*refoulement* requirement.

tribunal, individual EU states have formulated their own policies, with substantial interstate variation despite their relative homogeneity as a grouping of states.

Recognition rates for asylum applicants exemplify this: in 1991 Germany, Belgium, Italy, the Netherlands and the UK all recognized about 5 per cent of applicants as refugees; France by contrast recognized 20 per cent. Within this overall picture there are significant differences in recognition rates for different nationalities: in 1991 France recognized 91.9 per cent of Vietnamese applicants as refugees whilst Germany recognized only 0.6 per cent; in the same year 67.6 per cent of Sri Lankan asylum applicants in France were granted refugee status compared with only 2 per cent in the Netherlands (Standing Committee of Experts in International Immigration, Refugee and Criminal Law, 1994: 2). There is also substantive variation in respect of the persecution recognized as grounding a successful asylum claim: France, Italy and Spain have not accepted homosexuality as a ground of persecution, whilst Denmark, Germany, and the Netherlands have. Similar differences exist with respect to sexual abuse, traditional practices and cultural norms.

A graphic illustration of the salience of *national* differences, and a consequence of the radically different potential outcomes for individuals with identical situations just examined, has been the growth of 'forum shopping' by asylum seekers, seeking to maximize their chances of a successful claim. Since the difference between states can be a life and death matter to individual applicants risking *refoulement* to persecuting states, this is a logical development. States have responded by adopting a variety of national and intergovernmental policies to eliminate choice and restrict access to asylum (Bhabha, 1995: 29). Formerly asylum applicants had the option of taking advantage of mobility within the European arena to improve the prospects of establishing a successful asylum claim in at least one state.

Intergovernmental mechanisms have been used to counteract this whilst protecting individual states' ability to pursue nationally determined policies. Most notable amongst these is the EU's 1990 Dublin Convention determining States responsible for asylum[22] which is specifically designed to restrict asylum-seekers' choice of forum and allow only one 'bite at the cherry' of international protection (Bhabha and Coll, 1992). This Convention directly addresses the impact of national variation on international human rights by establishing a regionally negotiated and agreed definition of what counts as the 'member state responsible' (Articles 4–8, Dublin Convention). However, this process does not homogenize difference between states or reduce the power of individual states; rather it decreases the power of individual asylum seekers while preserving intact national variation in substantive asylum adjudication. The adoption of 'safe third country'

---

22. Convention Determining the State responsible for Examining Applications for Asylum Lodged in one of the Member States of the EC, signed on 15 June 1990.

policies by EU states to refuse consideration to asylum seekers who have transited, however briefly, through other states is another example of a co-operative use by states of national variations to curb individual rights (Byrne and Shacknove, 1996: 185).[23] Recognition of refugees' transnational strategies has been countered by statist protectionism.

TRANSFERRING POWER TO 'EUROPE'

The development of the EU and the growing impact of European community law on an ever-expanding area of social activity and individual daily life within each of the fifteen member states suggests, in sharp contrast with the situations just outlined, a supranational system undermining the power and importance of individual states. European community law has had a profound impact on a vast area of economic, political, social and cultural life in Europe. It now covers not only the basic Treaty concerns of non-discrimination on the basis of nationality (Article 48 *EC*) and equal rights for women (Article 119 *EC*), and the cardinal four freedoms — the free move-ment of goods, services, capital and persons — but an increasing array of issues from environmental protection to vocational training, from consumer protection to questions of health and safety. Member states have been active partners in the growing impact of European law within their jurisdictions: in the ten years from 1968 to 1978 alone, the number of cases referred by domestic courts to the European Court of Justice for 'preliminary rulings' on questions of interpretation[24] rose from 9 to 119 (Burley and Mattli, 1993: 58).

To what extent does this expansion of EU influence denote a decrease in individual state power? Two points are relevant. First, it is member states, acting through the European Union Council, that have the decisive role in the formulation of legislation;[25] there is no distinct, 'purely European', entity which can impose European law on unwilling member states. Community legislation then broadly[26] reflects a common *member state agenda* and is not a

---

23. In an interesting new development, some national EU asylum adjudicatory bodies are holding that other EU states are not 'safe third countries' because they are found to have 'refouled' asylum seekers returned to them, back to the persecuting country of origin — see for example *Special Adjudicator ex parte Mehmet Turus* (CA), 16 April 1996 (CO-42742-95) (Byrne and Shacknove, 1996: 185).
24. This procedure is established by Art. 117 *EC*, which authorizes national courts to refer questions of interpretation of community law to the ECJ.
25. The European Commission and the European Parliament, to a lesser though increasing degree, also participate in the community's legislative process, but the EU Council, a purely intergovernmental body consisting of the representatives of Member States, is the most powerful player.
26. Since the EEC Treaty of 1957 there has been a progressive shift from the requirement of unanimity in legislative decision-making to various forms of majority voting, brought about by the 1987 Single European Act and the 1991 Maastricht Treaty on European

foreign import imposed by an outside power over which states have no control.

Second, once enacted, community law has supremacy over national law (whether or not it becomes directly effective or requires implementing legislation in the member states depends on the nature of the legislation in question) and therefore becomes incorporated into national law: 'in the sphere of application of Community law, any Community norm, be it an article of the Treaty ... or a minuscule administrative regulation enacted by the Commission, "trumps" conflicting national law whether enacted before or after the Community norm' (Weiler, 1991: 2414). So within this first or community pillar of the EU,[27] the arena in which the ECJ has jurisdiction, member states have agreed to accept a reduction of their autonomy and direct control. Of course, member states have to agree to this transfer of competence to the EU bodies in the first place, and in fact transfer rather than loss of control seems the more appropriate description.

Although recalcitrant states can be forced to implement community law by European community institutions (the European Court of Justice and the European Commission),[28] EC law is primarily and predominantly implemented through national structures, executive, legislative and judicial. Individual citizens have to rely on their national courts initially to enforce their community law rights. They cannot file a case directly in the European Court or force the European Commission to take up their case. Thus if a citizen wishes to challenge the manner of implementation or the interpretation of European law by his or her state, the first recourse is to the domestic courts. In the absence of a satisfactory finding by the national court, to bring the issue before the European Court of Justice, the citizen is dependent on the national court for a 'reference'. *If the national court refuses such a reference the citizen has no supranational or additional legal remedy.* He or she may use political channels to lobby the Commission to bring an enforcement action against the Member State for violation of community law but this complex process depends on a multiplicity of political and institutional factors well outside the individual's control.

Has the introduction of the concept of European citizenship altered this process, so that a new European identity is being created through which citizens can enforce their fundamental rights directly as Europeans, without

---

Union. The main impetus for the changes has been recognition of the stultifying and stagnating effect on European integration and dynamism of the unanimity requirement. There has therefore been some loss of individual state sovereignty as a result of increased majority voting but this does not affect areas of vital interest to individual member states where the unanimity requirement is preserved.

27. The Maastricht Treaty on European Union established a temple-like structure for the European Union, consisting of three pillars and, in the description of one scholar, something resembling a loose tarpaulin covering them (Curtin, 1993: 17).

28. The enforcement procedure under Article 169 *EC*.

reliance on or curtailment by their member state? Such a development might indeed signal a dramatic shift in power from member states to the Union, and therefore be taken as evidence of a weakening of the nation state in Europe.

FROM NATIONAL SUBJECTS TO CITIZENS OF THE EUROPEAN UNION

In the forty years since its inception and in line with more general developments in international law, the European Community and now the European Union[29] has placed increasing emphasis on the importance of individual human rights. The first Treaty Establishing the European Economic Community of 1957 contains no Bill of Rights.[30] Although the European Court of Justice, in a landmark early case, declared 'Independently of the legislation of Member States, Community law ... not only imposes obligations on individuals but is also intended *to confer upon them rights which become part of their legal heritage*',[31] the court was referring to commercial rights in the context of the elimination of customs duties. The emphasis at that stage was on economic development and free trade. The 1987 Single European Act, the next European Treaty advancing the development of the Community, determines, in the Preamble, to 'work together to promote democracy on the basis of the fundamental rights recognized in the constitutions and laws of the Member States, in the Convention for the Protection of Human Rights and Fundamental Freedoms and the European Social Charter, notably freedom, equality and social justice'. Even though the European Community is not itself a signatory to the European Human Rights Convention,[32] and not all Member States have agreed to implement the European Social Charter,[33] this statement marks a significant shift in the conception of the Community as more than a common market. Finally the

---

29. The European Economic Community, now referred to as the European Community, was founded by the Treaty of Rome in 1957. The European Union was created by the Maastricht Treaty on European Union in 1991 and came into effect on 1 November 1993.
30. According to a former judge at the European Court of Justice, '[T]he builders of the European Communities thought too little about the legal foundations of their edifice and paid too little attention to the protection of the basic rights of the individual within the new European structure' (Pescatore in Clapham, 1991: 7).
31. Case 26/62, *Van Gend en Loos v. Nederlandse Administratie der Belastingen, ECR* (1963): 1,12.
32. For a discussion about the advantages and disadvantages of accession see Clapham (1991: 97). The ECJ has, in the context of the 1996/1997 Intergovernmental Conference on the future of the EU, produced an opinion opposing accession by the Community to the European Convention on Human Rights, on the basis that such an accession exceeds the Community's powers under the EC Treaty (Opinion 2/94 of the Court, 28 March 1996).
33. The United Kingdom refused to sign the Social Policy Protocol until the Labour Government won the elections in May 1997 and promptly announced a change in policy.

Maastricht Treaty on European Union confirms the signatory states' 'attachment to the principles of liberty, democracy and respect for human rights and fundamental freedoms and of the rule of law' and introduces the notion of citizenship of the European Union for all member state nationals. This evolution from a common market to a Union of citizens marked the culmination of years of concern about the so-called 'democratic deficit' of the Community and signalled a commitment to address the needs and rights of 'ordinary' citizens.

Article 8 of the European Community Treaty (as amended by the Maastricht Treaty) boldly declares: 'Citizenship of the Union is hereby established. Every person holding the nationality of a Member State shall be a citizen of the Union'. By invoking the concept of citizenship, the EU signalled a new, unmediated relationship with individual Europeans, a development that might be taken to exemplify and prefigure the detachment of citizenship from state territorial boundaries. Although Member States decide individually who qualifies as a national of their state for EU purposes,[34] they have no control over the parallel decisions of other Member States and therefore over the composition of the collective body of EU citizens as a whole. The unification of Germany added 10 million citizens to the EU overnight without any amendment to the existing European Treaties (O'Leary, 1992: 353, 367). Certainly, quite apart from any legal consequences, there are stark political implications in a non-national body, such as the EU, whether supranational, intergovernmental or both,[35] holding out the promise of a body of enforceable rights and duties, distinct from those arising out of citizenship of any individual member state.[36]

The notion of citizens of the Member States having *special* rights as members of the Community can be traced back to 1974, to the earliest moves in the creation of European citizenship.[37] Over the following twenty years the importance of creating a People's Europe, of strengthening the democratic

---

34. This has produced an idiosyncratic collectivity: residents of Macao who have never lived in Europe can naturalize as Portuguese citizens and thus become EU citizens because of Portuguese nationality law, whereas British Dependent Territory citizens in Hong Kong and Turks born in Germany whose families may have been resident in Europe for several generations are not EU citizens.

35. Some argue that recent institutional developments render the distinction between supranational and intergovernmental modes of operation increasingly irrelevant (Snyder, 1994: 87–90).

36. An interesting comparative study could be carried out between the concepts of European Union citizenship and Commonwealth citizenship, following the demise of the British Empire. There are differences and similarities: thus, EU citizenship carries with it the right of free movement throughout the Union territory (subject to certain limitations); no such right is afforded Commonwealth citizens. Both groups have preferential voting rights outside the state of nationality: EU citizens have rights to vote in local but not national elections (Article 8b, *EC*), Commonwealth citizens in the UK have rights to vote in both sets of elections.

37. Working Group established by Paris Summit of 1974 (O'Keefe and Twomey, 1995: 87).

legitimacy of the Community and with it a sense of European identity, were closely tied to debates about the desirable ingredients in European citizenship.[38] There is thus a clear and consistent political impetus linked to notions of democracy and rights, propelling the political architects of European citizenship (Closa, 1992: 1137).

Some writers have envisaged the emergence of a new kind of citizenship 'that is neither national nor cosmopolitan but which is multiple in enabling the various identities that we all possess to be expressed, and our rights and duties exercised' (Meehan, 1993: 172, 185). In terms of the expression of identities, it may be that gradually the sense of being a 'European' or a 'European citizen' will have some subjective salience for individuals in Europe, contradicting Raymond Aron's view that 'There are no such animals as "European citizens". There are only French, German, or Italian citizens' (Aron, 1974: 638). Indeed this sense of European-ness has been considered important as a mechanism for creating the popular consensus necessary to enable the process of European integration to move forward, though as one writer comments: 'it was not clear whether the development of a European identity meant increasing individuals' sense of belonging to the Union or, more controversially, whether it was aimed at making them identify with other citizens of the Union; that is, identifying with fellow citizens to the exclusion of non-citizen residents' (O'Leary, 1996: 39).

WHAT DOES EUROPEAN CITIZENSHIP GIVE THE CITIZEN?

Turning from questions of subjective identification to the enforcement of individual rights considered integral to this new European identity, what does being a European entail over and above being German, Italian or Greek? Given the EU's stated attachment to the 'principles of liberty, democracy and respect for human rights and fundamental freedoms', is human rights enforcement, even if not specifically enumerated as one of the incidents of the new citizenship,[39] a significant element? In other words can individuals rely on their European citizenship to enforce rights that their national citizenship does not afford them? Does being European in and of itself entail a minimum floor of fundamental rights irrespective of national legislation? This question has not yet reached the European Court of Justice

---

38. For an outline of the debates about whether human rights should be explicitly included in the citizenship proposals see O'Keefe and Twomey (1995: 89).
39. Seven rights are enumerated in the provisions on Union citizenship (Articles 8–8e, *EC*). They are the right of free movement; the right to residence; the right to vote and stand for election in municipal elections; the same rights in elections to the European Parliament; the right to diplomatic and consular assistance in countries in which a Union citizen's Member State is not represented; the right to petition the European Parliament; and the right to apply to the European Ombudsman.

or been extensively litigated in Europe, but it was at the heart of two recent British cases. In the first, before the Court of Appeal,[40] the facts were as follows.

A British citizen married an Indian citizen who, at the time of their marriage, was the subject of a deportation order (arising out of her irregular immigration status in Britain). The couple had a child (British by birth) and applied to the British government to rescind the deportation order and grant the Indian spouse permission to remain in Britain as the wife of a British citizen. When this was refused the couple took legal action to prevent the deportation. Since British domestic law provided no remedies, they sought to rely on the fact of the husband's European citizenship and the fundamental rights attached to such citizenship. They invoked the right to respect for family life,[41] and argued for a European citizen's right to reside freely with his family in any of the Member States of the Union, including his own: '. . . just as a *citizen of a Member State* can under national law reside anywhere in that State, so since the creation of *citizenship of the European Union* such a citizen can reside anywhere in the Union, with the result that it is no longer relevant of which Member State he is also a citizen'.

This interpretation of Union citizenship, if upheld, would help put some flesh on the bones of the new legal identity to create a meaningful status related to the project of human rights advancement in Europe. However, the Court of Appeal rejected this argument, and held that no such citizenship rights could be derived generally or applied to 'purely internal' situations such as the present case. Since the applicants had not travelled to another member state they could not avail themselves of the putative benefits of European Union citizenship. Union citizenship did not give rise to a minimum floor of fundamental rights capable of trumping the domestic immigration procedures required by national law. The promise of European Union citizenship as a means for enforcing citizens' rights beyond or above the national regulatory framework did not materialize. The Court of Appeal refused the applicants' request that the case be referred to the European Court of Justice (Berman et al., 1992: 245–74) to review their interpretation of union citizenship rights. In the absence of such a reference the individual citizen has no means of moving beyond the national forum.

---

40. *The Queen v. Secretary of State for the Home Department ex parte Kulwinder Kaur Phul and others*, Judgement of Court of Appeal handed down on 17 August 1995. Quotes in the following paragraph are from this judgement.
41. The third indent to the Preamble of the *TEU* sets out the signatories' attachment to 'the principles of liberty, democracy and respect for human rights and fundamental freedoms'; Article F of the *TEU* provides: 'The Union shall respect fundamental rights as guaranteed by the European Convention for the Protection of Human Rights and Fundamental Freedoms . . .'. Article 8 (1) of this Convention provides: 'Everyone has the right to respect for his private and family life, his home and his correspondence'.

A second case did concern a situation governed by community law: Mr Vitale, a 27-year-old Italian, had travelled to the UK in June 1993; in July 1993 he began receiving state welfare benefits, claiming that he was seeking work. In the absence of persuasive evidence of his job-seeking efforts, the UK government stopped his benefits in March 1994 and informed him that, since he was not 'seeking work with a genuine chance of obtaining work', he was not lawfully resident under EC law and should make arrangements to leave (*The Times* 26 January 1996). Before the Court of Appeal, Vitale argued that the Maastricht Treaty, and in particular the provision on European Union citizenship, confers a *free standing directly effective right of residence*. In particular, Article 8a provides: 'Every citizen of the Union shall have the right to move and reside freely within the territory of the Member States, subject to the limitations and conditions laid down in this Treaty and by the measures adopted to give it effect'. Whereas the pre-Maastricht position had been that member states could determine, within reasonable limits reviewable by the ECJ, the length of time a community national could rely on state benefits while seeking work,[42] Vitale argued that European Union citizenship altered the picture and gave citizens an independent, community-based right of residence. The Court, however, rejected this argument. It held that the right of residence was still qualified by the pre-existing limitations in the Treaty and endorsed the view that 'the TEU does not appear to have added anything to the right of free movement and of residence in existing community law' (O'Keefe and Twomey, 1995: 94). Reasonable national restrictions could curtail the right of residence and the eligibility for state benefits.

These cases illustrate the continuing influence of the individual state on the citizen's ability to enforce his or her European rights. Although both are drawn from British jurisdiction, one concerns a British national and his third country spouse, the other an Italian national: there is nothing peculiar to British citizens about these cases; rather they illustrate the decisive influence of a national jurisdiction on access to the regional, supranational judicial forum. Not only does national law circumscribe the area within which European citizenship rights operate but, through the reference procedure to the ECJ, national courts are the door-keepers to the wider arena. A national judiciary anxious to limit access to European courts or potential rights has considerable freedom of manoeuvre.

THIRD COUNTRY NATIONALS IN THE FIRST WORLD

The salience of the national state for the enforcement of individual rights in Europe is even greater when it comes to non-Europeans, so-called third

---

42. *R v. Immigration Appeal Tribunal ex parte Antonissen* (Case C-292/8).

country nationals (TCNs). Two factors are of significance. First, the free movement provisions and all the measures related to implementation of the single market generally[43] apply only to nationals of member states and members of their family. TCNs therefore have no European community law rights as such.[44] Member states have in fact concertedly opposed the intervention of the European Commission in the formulation of migration and integration policies for non-nationals.[45]

This division had resulted in a multi-tiered system of rights, to mobility, to family reunion, to eligibility for social security payments, which is profoundly discriminatory and politically problematic. While European citizens can move freely within the Union to search for work, to set up a business, to study or to retire, non-Europeans in general, however long-standing their legal residence in Europe, currently have no such rights under EC law.[46] The differences between the legally generous, administratively swift and straightforward family reunion provisions for EU nationals exercising their Treaty rights and the increasingly Kafkaesque restrictions facing third country nationals seeking entry for their immediate relatives are a dramatic and

---

43. Third country nationals may acquire rights within the EU as a result of association and co-operation agreements concluded between the EU and their country; such agreements have been concluded with Turkey, the Maghreb countries, and a growing number of East European states (so-called Europe Agreements). They may also acquire rights as employees of an EU firm providing services in another Member State, *Rush Portuguesa*, C-113/89; *Van der Elst*, C-43/93 (1994), ECR I-3803; (Alexander, 1993: 485).

44. Of course insofar as EC law is implemented into national laws of general application, for example in relation to equal treatment of women workers (Art. 119 *EC*), then its application is not restricted to EU citizens.

45. See *The Concertation of Community migration policy: Joined cases* 281/85, 283, 284 and 285/85 and 287/85, *Germany and others v. Commission*, Judgement of 9 July 1987 (1988) 25 *CMLR* 177.

46. Under the Schengen Agreement, an intergovernmental treaty which includes nine of the fifteen members of the EU, third country nationals do have the right of free circulation: Articles 9 and 10 of the Schengen Agreement provide for the introduction of a uniform visa for TCNs valid for short periods up to three months. Though far from the freedom of movement enjoyed by EU citizens, this limited provision to ensure freedom of travel for brief periods constitutes a gain for TCNs. However, a survey report suggests that the Schengen Common Visa policy is deficient in several significant respects (ILPA and JCWI, 1995). Moreover, the European Commission has been pressing for full freedom of movement for resident third country nationals for some time, on the basis that 'the logic of the internal market implies the elimination of the condition of nationality' for the exercise of this right. Commission of the European Communities, 'Communication from the Commission to the Council and the European Parliament on Immigration and Asylum Policies' (1994) COM(94) 23 final, 34. The European Parliament has also repeatedly called for free movement rights to be extended to TCNs; see for example 'European Parliament Committee of Inquiry into Racism and Xenophobia', Series A Doc. A3 0195/90, 23 July 1990, Recommendation 33. Proposals to grant lawfully resident TCNs European free movement for renewable periods of three months are currently under consideration by the European Council.

particularly poignant example.[47] Differences with respect to protection from deportation, voting and other political rights[48] are also stark. This fundamental, nationality based but racially marked division at the heart of the European project, marks the derivative nature of European rights — their dependence on state-formulated concepts of nationality and with them of inclusion and exclusion. Residence, work, taxation in Europe would have provided more ethically appropriate criteria on which to found a new, supranational basis for entitlements; sovereign member states, however, ensured their continued hegemony over the criteria for inclusion in the first tier of the Union constituency.

Equally significant are the implications for enforcement of rights. While EU nationals are primarily dependent on their national institutions as already indicated, in the area of EC law there is the possibility of supervision and enforcement by both the European Commission and the European Court of Justice. Once EU citizens have successfully used national courts to open access to these fora, they can benefit from a powerful check on national intransigence.[49] Insofar as they are not covered by the provisions of EC law, TCNs have no such supranational enforcement possibility; they are entirely dependent on domestic law. Challenges to oppressive immigration or nationality regulations or to particular decisions about eligibility for asylum are limited to the national structures.

The second point about the salience of nation states in the enforcement of TCNs' rights in Europe relates to the peculiarities of the European Union structure and policy making. In an effort to insulate from 'European interference' those areas of policy considered 'sensitive' and central to questions of national sovereignty and state security, the member states of the European Union have erected a three pillar edifice, only one pillar of which — the 'European Community' — is governed and supervised by the supranational community institutions, the European Commission and the European Court of Justice (Curtin, 1993: 30; Groenendijk, 1993: 391; Weiler, 1991: 2403). The second and third pillars, which deal with foreign and defence policy and

---

47. Whilst EU nationals generally obtain entry visas for dependants within a matter of weeks or months, third country nationals seeking to exercise family reunion rights are experiencing increasing difficulties. In France, for example, as a result of the so-called Pasqua Law of 1993, 'hardly any more authorisations for family reunion are granted by the administrative authorities in Paris. Families are now forced either to live separately, or, as in an increasing number of cases, to live together illegally' *Migration NewsSheet* January 1996: 2. See Bhabha and Shutter (1994: Chs 3, 4, 5, 7).

48. The provisions on EU citizenship have accentuated this difference by granting all EU citizens rights to vote in local elections and stand for political office.

49. See, in the field of free movement of persons, *Diatta v. Land Berlin*, Case 267/83 *CMLR* 2 (1986): 164; *Netherlands v. Reed*, Case 59/85 *CMLR* 2 (1987): 48; *R v. Immigration Appeal Tribunal and Surinder Singh ex p. Secretary of State for the Home Department*, Case 370/90 1 *ECR* (1992): 4265.

'Justice and Home Affairs' respectively, are explicitly excluded from the democratic structures and the public scrutiny and accountability that govern the first pillar. The European Commission has no enforcement or legislative role, the European Court of Justice has no power to supervise or challenge,[50] and the procedures by which decisions are made and policies are established are shielded from public scrutiny (Bunyan, 1993b). The third pillar is where decisions about a common immigration and asylum policy, about external borders and policies governing third country nationals within the EU are made. In this sphere states have proceeded intergovernmentally, evolving policies without public or parliamentary discussion and consultation. Crucial decisions about the criteria for family reunion, employment admission or expulsion have been taken in secret by non-elected senior government officials without any of the democratic safeguards which characterize decision and law making in the first pillar of the Union. This lack of transparency and accountability has attracted severe public censure, including from the European Parliament and a broad spectrum of non-governmental organizations (Standing Committee, 1993).

Reverting to the earlier discussion of EU citizenship, and in the context of the institutional structure just outlined, it is clear that fostering a newly energized sense of 'European identity' is associated with a potentially bleak set of spill-overs. This is of particular concern given the dramatic escalation of racist violence, xenophobia and far-right electoral gains within the European Community during the 1980s and early 1990s. The prospect is that of a new and powerful system for excluding non-Europeans, the 'seventh man' or woman, based on possession or absence of European citizenship, a way of giving a common juridical and civic expression to already prominent chauvinistic forces and significant social and economic realities.

> The potential corrosive effect on the values of the community vision of European integration are self-evident. Nationality as referent for interpersonal relations, and the human alienating effect of *Us* and *Them* are brought back again, simply transferred from their previous intra-Community context to the new inter-Community one. We have made little progress if the *Us* becomes European (instead of German or French or British) and the *Them* becomes those outside the Community or those inside who do not enjoy the privileges of citizenship. (Weiler, 1991: 2403, 2482)

There is indeed substantial evidence that the evolving notion of European citizenship is closely connected to an increasingly racialized sense of European identity. Despite the growing salience of political, social, religious and cultural institutions associated with twentieth century immigration into

---

50. Article K.3(2)(c) of the Maastricht Treaty on European Union does provide that future conventions in the fields of justice and home affairs 'may stipulate that the Court of Justice shall have jurisdiction to interpret their provisions and to rule on any disputes regarding their application', but no such arrangements have been made.

Europe,[51] prominent public voices still argue 'Europe ends where Western Christianity ends and Islam and Orthodoxy begin' (Huntington, 1996: 158). The head of the third largest political party in Austria, J. Haider, recently stated that he wanted the number of foreign workers in Austria reduced by one third which would then make it possible to combat unemployment since posts would be made free for Austrians (*Migration NewsSheet* January 1997: 3). Since nationality of, rather than residence in, a member state is the basis for European Union citizenship, the 'us' of EU citizenship excludes the 10–13 million third country nationals (TCNs) (Peres, 1996: 7) who have cast in their lot with the Union and live there permanently. These TCNs have no coherent set of rights within the EU structure. Most fundamentally, as aliens, their right to permanent residence — however long their stay — is conditional. Whereas a citizen cannot be deported from the country of nationality, whatever his or her conduct, an alien enjoys no such protection. Describing this contemporary exclusionary project at the heart of European consolidation, Etienne Balibar (1991: 7) comments:

> Europe is not something that is 'constructed' at a slower or faster pace, with greater or lesser ease; it is a historical problem without any pre-established solution. 'Migrations' and 'racism' form part of the elements of this problem . . . Discrimination is written into the very nature of the European Community.

Two recent cases highlight the vulnerability associated with this marginal positioning. In one, a Moroccan, who had lived and worked legally in France for twenty-five years, was expelled for keeping the bag of an illegal entrant. The man was charged with aiding and abetting a clandestine immigrant after holding his compatriot's bag for a few days. Convicted in September 1995, he was sentenced to six months imprisonment and banished for five years, and his residence permit was withdrawn (*Statewatch*, September–October 1996: 3). At the same time, the French interior minister J.-L. Debré announced his intention to increase the frequency of collective expulsions (*Migration NewsSheet* September 1996: 4). Following policies first publicized by notorious former Minister Pasqua, Debré recently introduced a new sharply anti-immigrant Aliens Bill in the French Parliament.[52]

---

51. A recent *New York Times* article headlined 'Dutch Turn churches into Shops and Mosques' described the escalating number of churches sold off to Muslim communities as Islamic purchasing power increases and organized Christianity declines (*New York Times*, 10 March 1997: A1, col 1).

52. One of the most contested measures in the first draft of the bill was the obligation imposed on a person offering accommodation to a foreigner to declare at the town hall of his or her borough of residence the departure of the foreigner. Not only did this measure give rise to the risk of vindictive denunciations but to the possibility of criminalizing, as aiders and abettors of illegal immigration, innocent people offering hospitality. This measure has since been softened. The controversy provoked by the Aliens Bill resulted in a serious diplomatic quarrel between the French Government and the European Parliament. See *Migration NewsSheet*, December 1996: 5; March 1997: 3; and April 1997: 4.

In another recent case a nine year old Zairian girl was expelled from the Netherlands only two days after being refused entry without any arrangements being made for someone to meet her in Kinshasa on her return. She had travelled with her aunt, a residence permit holder in the Netherlands.[53] The aunt had fraudulently claimed initially that nine-year-old Francine was her daughter; the child was first expelled to Zurich, where she was held in a Swissair nursery for a week; thereafter she was placed on a plane to Kinshasa, and met by a businessman contacted by Swissair. Unable to find any living relatives, the businessman entrusted her to the Zairian immigration authorities. The child eventually re-entered the Netherlands and was granted a permit to stay with her aunt, two years after her initial expulsion. No EU remedy is available in such circumstances.

Other fundamental rights of third country nationals, such as the right to respect for family life, enshrined in Article 8 of the European Convention on Human Rights, are also excluded from EU protection or ECJ supervision, unless these TCNs happen to be family members of an EU citizen, in which case they enjoy the privileged family reunion rights of citizens.[54] Lawfully resident third country nationals may be separated for long periods from their immediate relatives or prevented from re-uniting within the EU at all, under prevailing domestic immigration provisions. Even the European Court of Human Rights, the body charged with final decision making on the compatibility of state practice with the provisions of the European Convention, has deferred to national sovereignty in allowing several harsh immigration decisions to stand. In a recent case, *Ahmut v. The Netherlands*, the Court upheld the Dutch Government's decision to refuse entry to the nine-year-old Moroccan son of a permanent resident father with joint Dutch and Moroccan nationality, the mother having died. Reiterating an earlier argument advanced when upholding Switzerland's refusal of entry to the seven-year-old only son of a Turkish couple with a right of residence in Switzerland,[55] the Court expressed the view that the father could exercise his right to family life with his son by returning to Morocco. Expressing a dissenting opinion, one judge commented thus on this case: 'in any country, a national is entitled to have his son join him, even if the son does not have the same nationality. How does it come about that in the present case this right was refused him? ... I cannot think that it is because the Dutch father was called "Ahmut". However the suspicion of discrimination must inevitably lurk in people's minds'.[56]

---

53. *Case of Francine Nsona v. Netherlands*, ECHR, reported in *Migration NewsSheet*, January 1997: 2.
54. Art. 10(1), Reg. 1612/68.
55. *Gul v. Switzerland*, ECHR, 19 February 1996.
56. Dissenting Opinion of Judge Valticos, *Case of Ahmut v. Netherlands* (73/1995/579/665) 28 November 1996: 18.

Not only is dual nationality a recognized legal status but with increasing flows of migrants, the establishment and growth of diasporic communities, and the proliferation of second generation immigrants with hyphenated identities, the reliance on essentialized, racially determined notions of 'identity' rapidly turns from neutral archaism to discriminatory presumption. Yet European governments and courts are reluctant to accept the increasingly complex and multifaceted relationship of individuals to territories, one of the aspects of globalization referred to above. In this last case, the prevailing thinking was clearly that Ahmut, despite his Dutch nationality, was 'really' Moroccan, and that 'his' country was the right place for his exercise of family life. Another clear example of this racialized understanding of what constitutes a 'European identity' is provided by a recent Belgian case. In August 1996, the Belgian State Police turned back from a Belgian airport three French children of Algerian origin aged seven, eleven and fifteen. Their Algerian parents were waiting at the airport for them but were not given the opportunity to explain that the children had French nationality before the Belgian authorities refused the children the right to transit to France through Belgium. After six hours of being held at the airport the children were deported to Algeria. Justifying their action the Belgian State Police argued that the children were not being expelled but *sent back* (*refouler*) (*Statewatch*, September–October 1996: 3).

Access of non-citizens within the EU to rights protection and enforcement is thus critically dependent on individual member states. This is particularly significant given the considerable interstate variation in policies and procedures for TCNs seeking access to the Union. In the area of family reunion for example, whereas some states admit dependent children up to the age of twenty-one others limit such admissions to sixteen. Similar variations exist with respect to requirements for support and accommodation by sponsors prior to the entry of their relatives, conditions for establishing the validity of marriages or adoptions, requirements for admission as students, visitors, workers or self-employed persons. TCNs must abide by the requirements in force in their country of desired residence. Although member states of the Union have sought to harmonize their laws in regard to third country nationals in these spheres through joint resolutions[57] and intergovernmental agreements — mainly a process of agreeing to the most restrictive or lowest common denominator of policies in force in any given country — there is still considerable divergence.

A partial but important qualification is necessary at this point. All the Member States of the European Union are signatories to the European

---

57. See for example Ad Hoc Group Immigration, Resolution on the Harmonization of national policies on family reunification (1993) SN 2828/1/93 WGI 1497. Rev 1.; Ministerial Meeting on June 20 1994 in Luxemburg: Council of Interior and Justice Ministers, Resolution on limitations on admission of third-country nationals to the member states for employment; Bhabha (1994: 101); O'Keefe (1995: 21).

Convention on Human Rights[58] and accept the right of individual petition.[59] Because of the scope of protection it affords (including the right to life, the right to respect for family and private life, the prohibition on torture, inhuman and degrading treatment, the prohibition on discrimination, the entitlement to a fair trial and to an effective remedy for violation of any of the Convention rights) and the accessibility of the procedure, the Convention has become a very significant source of human rights protection in Europe. Moreover, unlike European Community Law, the European Convention on Human Rights applies to *all persons* within the jurisdiction of the signatory states. In terms of protecting human rights in Europe it therefore has the broadest application, extending as it does to asylum seekers and third country residents within the signatory states. Numerous cases have been brought to the European Commission and Court of Human Rights in Strasburg on behalf of immigrants, migrants and asylum seekers[60] and some have resulted in significant judgements in their favour.[61] In terms of the rights enshrined in the Convention, the Strasburg institutions function as a partial international court of final instance in Europe, for citizens and non-citizens alike. The European Court of Human Rights can rule that state practice violates the terms of the Convention and that certain human rights should be enforced contrary to existing national legislation. In this it is a powerful forum for challenging the authority of a signatory state and for enforcing individuals' rights. Moreover, judgements of the European Court of Human Rights are binding on signatory states and tend to be adhered to.

However, the scope of the Strasburg Court should not be overestimated. Through the doctrine of 'the margin of appreciation' developed by the European Court of Human Rights, states are accorded considerable discretion and leeway, particularly in 'sensitive' areas of decision making such as public security and immigration. This is clear from several recent judgements, both as regards the family reunion rights for TCNs discussed above and concerning asylum seekers.[62] Moreover, the Strasburg institutions are limited

---

58. European Convention for the Protection of Human Rights and Fundamental Freedoms, (ECHR) 4 November 1950, Council of Europe ETS No. 5.
59. Article 25, ECHR.
60. For a useful compilation of cases in this field see Stevens (1992).
61. See *Abdulaziz, Cabales and Balkandali Case* 15/1983/71/1-07-109 Series A, no. 94 (holding that the UK's immigration rules were sex discriminatory); *Berrehab Case* 3/1987/126/177 Series A, no. 138 (holding that the expulsion of the Moroccan father of a Dutch child by the Dutch authorities violated the right to respect for family life); *Moustaquim Case* 31/1989/191/291 Series A, no. 193 (holding that the Belgian government's deportation following criminal convictions of a Moroccan youth who was under two when he started living in Belgium was a violation of his right to respect for family life).
62. See *Cruz Varas and others Case* 46/1990/237/307 Series A, no. 201 (expulsion of Chilean torture victim and asylum seeker from Sweden upheld; *Vilvarajah and others Case* 45/1990/236/302–6 Series A, no. 215 (removal of Sri Lankan Tamils to Sri Lanka by UK government following evidence of torture upheld); *Vijayanathan and Pusparajah Case* 75/1991/327/339–400 Series A, no. 241-B (holding failure to exhaust domestic remedies

to reviewing questions arising out of the rights covered by the European Human Rights Convention. Many of the developments regarding TCNs within the EU are therefore outside their scope of review. Intergovernmental agreements and the legality of existing or future treaties cannot be reviewed. Examples include decisions about access to the territory of the European Union, including visa requirements, carriers' liability legislation deterring carriers from transporting inadequately documented passengers, the formulation of policies about 'safe countries of origin' and 'safe third countries' to restrict asylum eligibility. Both formally and in terms of substantive decision making, therefore, the Strasburg human rights structures implementing the European Convention only partially limit the role of states as the central forum for the enforcement of rights for non-citizens in Europe.

CONCLUSION

Both the discourse of human rights and the evolving structure of the European Union are aspects of the broad process of globalization. The former is a universalizing discourse that establishes transnational norms (with attendant structural and institutional consequences) about what individuals should be entitled to expect, and how states can be regulated, beyond the confines of a particular time/place context. Aspects of this discourse discussed include transnational norms relating to protection of non-citizens both under international refugee law, and under the family reunion provisions of the European Convention of Human Rights. In both cases the point has been made that international mechanisms do not in practice ensure the access to rights of non-citizens and that individual states have ultimate control over enforcement. Thus asylum seekers fleeing persecution have varying prospects of receiving refugee status depending on which state their application is lodged in, despite the invocation of universal norms set out in the UN Convention and Protocol on the Status of Refugees. Similarly migrants seeking to exercise their fundamental rights to family reunion under Article 8 of the European Human Rights Convention, are affected by the wide 'margin of appreciation' allowed by international courts to states in this 'sensitive' area of domestic policy and sovereignty.

The homogenizing effect of a global discourse of human rights must therefore be understood as establishing common definitions and uniform norms, while permitting profound local variation when it comes to the translation of those norms into legislative and administrative practice. Because international treaty making is a consensual process for states, the balance between a new uniformity and an established domestic order is struck at a point which

---

invalidated application under ECHR). But see also *Case of Chahal v. the United Kingdom* (70/1995/576/662) and *Case of Ahmed v. Austria* (71/1995/577/663).

leaves many of the least just or egalitarian state structures intact. Globalization in this context is best understood as an enabling discourse which creates the possibility for future change and negotiation on the basis of common understandings rather than as a mechanism which of itself profoundly alters the balance between state and individual.

The evolving structure of the European Union is also an aspect of the broad process of globalization. Whether by unanimity or qualified majority voting, states empower their EU representatives to pass legislation with ever expanding scope. In many fields, national courts now implement 'directly effective' community law without national parliaments having been involved in the process at all. It is clear that a substantial transfer of power has taken place and that the relationship between member states and the supranational EU has been irrevocably altered. Community law regulating free movement of workers and their families is an example of this process. Generous rules give EU workers (such as a German working in France) family reunion rights that far exceed analogous domestic provisions (for instance, for an Angolan permanently resident in France). States are thus forced to accord to community workers (or to national workers who have exercised their community law rights and thus have the required 'community nexus'[63]) rights they may not have under domestic law. It has been suggested, however, that this transfer of power does not entail a decisive weakening of individual states, both because of their involvement in the ongoing EU processes and because of the substantial areas of policy and practice excluded from community control.

The central example used to concretize this transformed but not reduced role of member states in relation to the EU is the notion of EU citizenship. As discussed, it is not clear that this new citizenship has so far assisted individual EU citizens seeking to advance their fundamental rights, for example with respect to residence rights if indigent, or in regard to family reunion rights. Not only is there no community definition of a European Union citizen, it being a matter for each Member State to determine which of its nationals will have that status; but, despite the appeal to respect for fundamental rights, attempts to translate this broad vision into concrete entitlements for citizens have been unsuccessful. It appears therefore that EU citizens will be no better endowed with rights in their supranational status than they are in their domestic setting. Member states have been careful not to sow the seeds of their progressive demise, and to cultivate the saplings of post-war rights-endowed citizenry judiciously. National understandings about citizens' rights are clearly informed by discussions and decisions at the European level, so that the globalizing process of evolving shared meanings and structures is a three way one between citizen-litigant, individual state and supranational entity. However, the transformations in power and allocation of responsibility thus

---

63. *The Queen v. Immigration Appeal Tribunal ex parte Surinder Singh*, Case C-370/90 (1992), ECR: I-4265.

produced indicate a complex negotiation about the site for decision making and the parameters of the supranational venture, rather than a reordering of key players in the field of rights enforcement.

September 1997

REFERENCES

Albrow, M. and E. King (eds) (1990) *Globalization, Knowledge and Society*. London: Sage.

Alexander, W. (1993) 'Free Movement of Non-EC Nationals, A Review of the Case-law of the Court of Justice', in H. G. Schermers (ed.) *Free Movement of Persons in Europe*, pp. 481–93. Boston, MA: Martinus Nijhoff.

Appadurai, A. (1993) 'Patriotism and its Futures', *Public Culture* 5: 415–40.

Appadurai, A. (1996) *Modernity at Large: Cultural Dimensions of Globalization*. Minneapolis, MN: University of Minnesota Press.

Aron, R. (1974) 'Is Multinational Citizenship Possible?', *Social Research* 41: 631–43.

Balibar, E. (1991) 'Es Gibt Keinen Staat in Europa: Racism and Politics in Europe Today', *New Left Review* 186: 5–19.

Bermann, G. A. and R. J. Goebel (eds) (1995) *European Community Law — 1995 Supplement to Cases and Materials*. St Paul, MN: West Publishing Co.

Bermann, G. A., R. J. Goebel, W. Davey and E. Fox (eds) (1992) *Cases and Materials on European Community Law*. St Paul, MN: West Publishing Co.

Bhabha, J. (1994) 'European Harmonization of Asylum Policy: A Flawed Process', *Virginia Journal of International Law* 35: 101–114.

Bhabha, J. (1995) 'European Union Asylum and Refugee Policy', *International Practitioner's Notebook* 60: 28–30.

Bhabha, J. (1996) 'Embodied Rights: Gender Persecution, State Sovereignty and Refugees', *Public Culture* 9: 3–32.

Bhabha, J. and G. Coll (eds) (1992) *Asylum Practice in Europe and North America*. Washington, DC: Federal Publications Inc.

Bhabha, J. and S. Shutter (1994) *Women's Movement: Women under Immigration, Nationality and Refugee Law*. Stoke-on-Trent: Trentham Books.

Bunyan, T. (1993a) 'Trevi, Europol and the New European State', in T. Bunyan (ed.) *State-watching the New Europe — A Handbook on the European State*, pp. 27–33. Nottingham: Russell Press.

Bunyan, T. (ed.) (1993b) *Statewatching the New Europe — A Handbook on the European State*. Nottingham: Russell Press.

Burley, A. M. and W. Mattli (1993) 'Europe Before the Court: A Political Theory of Integration', *International Organization* 47: 58–84.

Byrne, R. and A. Shacknove (1996) 'The Safe Country Notion in European Asylum Law', *Harvard Human Rights Journal* 9: 183–204.

Byrnes, A. (1995) 'Toward More Effective Enforcement of Women's Human Rights Through the Use of International Human Rights Law and Procedures', in R. J. Cook (ed.) *Human Rights of Women: National and International Perspectives*, pp. 189–227. Philadelphia, PA: University of Pennsylvania Press.

Clapham, A. (1991) *Human Rights and the European Community: A Critical Overview*. Florence: European University Institute.

Closa, C. (1992) 'The Concept of Citizenship in the Treaty on European Union', *Common Market Law Review* 29: 1137–69.

Cook, R. J. (1990) 'Reservations to the Convention on the Elimination of All Forms of Discrimination Against Women', *Virginia Journal of International Law* 30: 602–70.

Curtin, D. (1993) 'The Constitutional Structure of the European Union: A Europe of Bits and Pieces', *Common Market Law Review* 30: 17–69.

Dehousse, R. (1994) 'Community Competences: Are there Limits to Growth?', in R. Dehousse (ed.) *Europe After Maastricht: An Ever Closer Union?*, pp. 101–22. London: Law Books in Europe.

Detrick, S. (ed.) (1992) *The United Nations Convention on the Rights of the Child.* The Hague, London, Boston, MA: Martinus Nijhoff Publishers.

Emiliou, N. (1995) 'Subsidiarity: Panacea or Fig Leaf?', in D. O'Keefe and P. Twomey (eds) *Legal Issues of the Maastricht Treaty*, pp. 65–83. London: Wiley Chancery.

Falk, R. (1985) 'A New Paradigm for International Legal Studies: Prospects and Proposals', in R. Falk, F. Kratchowil and S. Mendlovitz (eds) *International Law: A Contemporary Perspective*, pp. 651–8. Boulder, CO: Westview Press.

Featherstone, M. and S. Lash (1995) 'Globalization, Modernity and the Spatialization of Social Theory: An Introduction', in M. Featherstone, S. Lash and R. Robertson (eds) *Global Modernities*, pp. 1–24. London: Sage.

Goebel, R. J. (1995) 'The European Union Grows: The Constitutional Impact of the Accession of Austria, Finland and Sweden', *Fordham International Law Journal* 18: 1093–175.

Groenendijk, C. A. (1993) 'Three Questions About Free Movement of Persons and Democracy in Europe', in H. G. Schermers (ed.) *Free Movement of Persons in Europe*, pp. 391–410. Boston, MA: Martinus Nijhoff.

Huntington, Samuel (1996) *The Clash of Civilizations and the Remaking of the World Order.* New York: Simon and Schuster.

Igarashi, A. (1996) 'From Americanization to Japanization in East Asia?'. Paper presented at conference on Globalization and the Construction of Communal Identities, Amsterdam (February).

ILPA and JCWI (1995) *Frontier Law: Why Schengen Isn't Working for Europe's Third Country Nationals.* London: Immigration Law Practitioners Association.

Karliner, J. (1994) 'To Union Carbide life is cheap', *The Nation* 12 December: 725–8.

Meehan, E. (1993) 'Citizenship and the European Community', *Political Quarterly* 64: 172–86.

Meron, T. (1984) *Human Rights in International Law: Legal and Policy Issues.* Oxford: Clarendon Press.

Migration NewsSheet (various issues).

Nederveen Pieterse, Jan (1995) 'Globalization as Hybridization', in M. Featherstone, S. Lash and R. Robertson (eds) *Global Modernities*, pp. 45–68. London: Sage.

Newman, F. and D. Weissbrodt (1990) *International Human Rights.* Cincinnati: Anderson Publishing Company.

O'Keefe, D. (1995) 'The Emergence of a European Immigration Policy', *European Law Review* 20: 21–35.

O'Keefe, D. and P. Twomey (1995) 'Union Citizenship', in D. O'Keefe and P. Twomey (eds) *Legal Issues of the Maastricht Treaty*, pp. 87–107. London: Wiley Chancery Law.

O'Leary, S. (1992) 'Nationality Law and Community Citizenship: A Tale of Two Uneasy Bedfellows' in *Yearbook of European Law, Vol. 12*, pp. 353–75. London: Butterworths.

O'Leary, S. (1996) *European Union Citizenship — Options for Reform.* London: Institute for Public Policy Research.

Peres, S. (1996) 'Towards Equality: Actual and Potential Rights of Third-Country Nationals in the European Union', *Common Market Law Review* 33: 7–38.

Privacy International (1995) *Big Brother Incorporated.* Privacy International.

Robertson, R. (1990) 'Mapping the Global Condition: Globalization as the Central Concept', in M. Featherstone (ed.) *Theory, Culture and Society*, pp. 25–44. London: Sage.

Rouse, R. (1995) 'Thinking Through Transnationalism: Notes on the Cultural Politics of Class Relations in the Contemporary United States', *Public Culture* 7: 353–402.

Sklair, L. (1991) *Sociology of the Global System.* Baltimore, MD: Johns Hopkins University Press.

Snyder, F. (1994) 'Institutional Development in the European Union: Some Implications of the Third Pillar', in J. Monar and R. Morgan (eds) *The Third Pillar of the European Union*, pp. 87–90. Brussels: European Intra University Press and College of Europe.

de Sousa Santos, B. (1995) *Towards a New Common Sense: Law, Science and Politics in the Paradigmatic Transition.* New York: Routledge.

Standing Committee of Experts in International Immigration, Refugee and Criminal Law (1993) *A New Immigration Law for Europe?* Utrecht: Nederlands Centrum Buitenlanders.

Standing Committee of Experts in International Immigration, Refugee and Criminal Law (1994) *Who is a Refugee?* Utrecht: Nederlands Centrum Buitenlanders.

Statewatch (various issues).

Stevens, J. (1992) *The Case Law of the European Convention on Human Rights Relating to Immigration, Asylum and Extradition.* London: The Law Society and the Immigration Law Practitioners' Association.

Van Beuren, G. (1995) *The International Law on the Rights of the Child.* The Hague, London, Boston, MA: Martinus Nijhoff Publishers.

Vincenzi, C. (1994) 'Deportation in Disarray: The Case of EC Nationals', *Criminal Law Review* 163: 156–67.

Weatherill, S. (1995) 'Beyond Preemption? Shared Competence and Constitutional Change in the European Community', in D. O'Keefe and P. Twomey (eds) *Legal Issues of the Maastricht Treaty*, pp. 13–33. London: Wiley Chancery Law.

Weiler, J. H. H. (1988) in discussion: 'Are we Heading for a New Normativity in the International Community?' in A. Cassese and J. H. H. Weiler *Change and Stability in International Law-Making*, pp. 121–46. The Hague: Walter de Gruyter.

Weiler, J. H. H. (1991) 'The Transformation of Europe', *Yale Law Journal* 100: 2403–517.

Small Product, Big Issues: Value Contestations and Cultural Identities in Cross-Border Commodity Networks

Norman Long and Magdalena Villarreal

INTRODUCTION

Much has been written on globalizing processes within international food systems geared to mass consumption markets, but considerably less on the flows of 'ethnic' foods and food-related products that link transnational migrant groups with production sites in their countries of origin. This article contributes to filling that gap by exploring the implications of such commodity networks for understanding the dynamics of global/local relations and cultural identities among Mexicans living on both sides of the Mexico–US border.

The discussion is built around a series of ethnographic accounts aimed at elucidating the social relations, cultural representations and contests of value associated with one such commodity in various production, consumption and commercialization scenarios. This approach contrasts with the theoretical stance adopted by commodity-chain studies that view the sets of relations clustered around any one commodity or category of commodities as forming an integrated sequence of economic value-adding activities (Gereffi and Korzeniewics, 1994; see also Bonanno et al., 1994; Friedman, 1993).[1] While we do not wish to deny the significance of such value-adding processes, our argument owes more to anthropological work on the cultural components of economic transactions and on the construction of the social value of goods (see, for example, Appadurai, 1986; Arce, 1997; Douglas and Isherwood, 1979; Ferguson, 1988; Thomas, 1991) than it does to the political economy of food systems.

Our primary aim is to explore how contrasting meanings, images and practices intersect in the processes by which commodities and their social relations are forged and valorized within an increasingly transnational world. The discussion focuses on the example of maize husks,[2] which is now a growing industry finding its way into markets in the United States, but

---

1. For a critique of these types of model, see Arce and Marsden (1993); Goodman and Watts (1994).
2. Maize husks are the dry leaves that protect the ear of the maize, and which, as we explain below, are used for a variety of purposes, including fodder for cattle, but also the preparation of traditional foods and local craftwork for tourist markets.

which, at the same time, is closely related to Mexican traditional food production and craftwork, and of course to maize, one of Mexico's basic staples. On the basis of recent field research on commoditization, livelihoods and contests of value in western Mexico and California,[3] we examine the moments of value contestation that take place at critical interfaces wherein normative discourses and social interests are defined and negotiated. Hence we do not limit our analysis to predefined 'stages' associated with production, transformation, commercialization and consumption of commodities — where it is generally assumed that major changes in value are realized — but aim to elucidate moments of contestation in which commodity and non-commodity values, but also livelihood concerns, social commitments and cultural identities — often at considerable socio-geographical distance — are constituted.

We argue that commodity forms are defined and/or contested by the actions of specific actors (Long, 1997; Long et al., 1986). Commoditization processes take shape through the actions of diverse sets of interlinked, socially-situated actors, and are composed of specific constellations of interests, values and resources. They have no predetermined or necessary trajectories, except those constructed socio-historically by the parties involved. Commodity forms constitute representations or idioms that actors use to label ongoing social transactions between people, and between people, things, and the market. These relations traverse the various sites of production and consumption and involve social and discursive struggles over livelihoods, economic values and images of 'the market'. As Kopytoff (1986) and Appadurai (1986) have insightfully observed, goods have 'biographies' composed of diverse sets of circumstances, wherein at some points or in some arenas they are accorded the status of commodities (that is, attributed with exchange value, either potential or realized), whilst in other contexts they are not. Commodity biographies, however, have no autonomy of their own, nor do they necessarily share common trajectories: rather they result from the ways in which actors use or interact with the objects in question, thus endowing them with specific meanings and values. The same or different persons may simultaneously confer on an object or relationship both commodity and non-commodity values. Hence, depending on the situation, the signifiers or markers of 'exchange value' as against other kinds of value will vary or be contested.

Commodity and non-commodity issues, then, are matters of contention: they involve actors' differential interpretations of the social significance of particular resources, goods, people, and relationships, and thus point to the

3. The research involves collaboration between the Department of Sociology, Wageningen Agricultural University, and the Centro de Investigaciones y Estudios Superiores en Antropología Social (CIESAS) in Guadalajara, Mexico. This is funded under the WOTRO (Netherlands Foundation for the Advancement of Tropical Research) programme on 'Globalization and the Construction of Communal Identities'.

existence of different, competing 'theories' of value. Such an approach requires the elucidation of alternative actor theories of social value and how they interrelate, rather than the search for some 'new' global theory of value — founded, for example, on Marxist, neoliberal or natural resource based principles.[4] It is important also to recognize that actor-generated value positions crystallize within, and shape and transform, the encounters that take place between particular individual and collective actors.

MULTIPLE USES AND MEANINGS OF MAIZE HUSKS IN MEXICO

In Mexico every part of the maize plant (*milpa*) is utilized in one way or another; nothing is wasted. The most important parts are the kernels of maize which, when made into *masa* (dough), constitute the basic ingredient for making *tortillas*, an essential element of Mexican food — serving similar purposes to those of bread in other parts of the world — and for making a variety of cakes, porridge and drinks. The kernels are also added to meat and other items to make a tasty soup (*pozole*), and the ear of the maize is cut fresh (*elote*) from the plant and cooked as 'corn-on-the-cob'. Ancient civilizations in Mexico used the stem of the maize plant to build the walls of their houses and for fencing, and as an ingredient for organic fertilizer, where it was combined with the leaves and roots of the plant. The latter is still common practice today. The inedible core of the maize ear is used as fuel for household stoves and ovens for baking bread, bricks, and so on. Even a fungus (*huitlacoche*) which grows on the ears of the maize, and the worms that often breed in it, are considered delicacies. The 'hairs' or 'silks' of the ear of the maize make an excellent medicinal tea, especially good, it is said, for the kidneys. The whole plant (with or without the ears and including the husks) is used as fodder for cattle.

Husks (known in pre-Colombian times as *totomoxtle*) — namely, the outer leaves of the ear of the maize — have also been used in a variety of ways: first, they constitute a crucial ingredient for the preparation of *tamales*;[5] until recently it was common practice to dry and use them in the manufacture of handmade cigarettes. They also provide husk strips for tying together bunches of herbs, spices and wild plants and they are an important raw material for handicraft production of dolls and animal replicas, of which the *mulitas de Corpus*, small mules traditionally made for Saint Manuel's day

---

4. Goodin (1992: 22–30) provides an interesting taxonomy of theories of value in his assessment of a 'green' theory of value. Frow (1995) adopts a similar position to ourselves when he criticizes theories of cultural production and circulation based on the notion of a unified and hierarchical system of value.
5. A typical Mexican dish consisting of rolls of maize dough stuffed with meat and savouries, or mixed with cinnamon, sugar, raisins, nuts etc., and wrapped in maize husks for steaming.

and sold in the streets and at fiestas in the central regions of the country, are the best known.

This craftwork, however, bears little resemblance to that which has flourished in recent years, namely, maize husk dolls and flowers that are increasing in importance in tourist markets, where new, creative and colourful ethnic products abound. These include *nacimientos* (dolls representing the nativity scene of Christ) and artificial flowers which range from big sunflowers to lilies, roses, tulips and orchids — varieties which are often totally unfamiliar to the artisans themselves. Their models are frequently taken from American magazines and follow the guidelines suggested by their buyers, who include intermediaries exporting to Europe and the United States.

Maize husk craftwork is a typical product of global processes: Mexican, European and American demand for ethnic products — which fit certain definitions of 'authenticity' (maize being linked to Mexican civilization from ancient times) and at the same time accommodate contemporary tastes and fancies — forge completely new production scenarios, where local artisans reformulate their self identities in accordance with distant (and quite ambiguously defined) consumer expectations.

Such is the case of San Cristóbal, a village located on the shore of Lake Chapala, in the state of Jalisco, Mexico, where the manufacture of dolls and artificial flowers has changed the production scenario of the village.[6] This is especially evident on Wednesday and Saturday evenings, when the streets come alive with whole families carrying huge bundles of colourful husk flowers, to be collected by local traders and commercialized the following day in the Thursday and Sunday tourist markets of Tonalá, a traditional craft centre near Guadalajara.

Luis, who owns a taxi in the village and has become increasingly involved in buying local products to sell to export intermediaries in Mexico City, explains that, although people in the village weave baskets (made out of palm leaves) in their spare time, many fishermen and agricultural producers have turned to the manufacture of flowers. He believes that the trade has taken off because people from San Cristóbal are 'hard workers and like to progress' and that international buyers value the product because it is made by peasant artisans. Luis believes that, even though many villagers know little about their antecedents, their craftwork nevertheless reflects their 'indigenous' origins and heritage.

His mother, on the other hand, cannot understand how husks could turn out to be so valuable. For her, husks are minor items (with no market value) gathered by women when they wish to make *tamales*, or otherwise left in the fields as fodder for the cattle. She told of her surprise when her daughter said that she had received six pesos (approximately US$2 at the time) for a husk doll. 'Six pesos!', she exclaimed; 'but it is only made out of husks!' She

---

6. For a fuller account of the development of maize husk craftwork, see Villarreal (1997).

immediately set off to learn how to make them herself. She claimed that she was too old to learn, but she made progress and earned herself a peso or two. Later her whole family became involved, with her daughter acting as seller. While her daughter-in-law was quietly sitting on a low chair making flowers and her husband cutting wires to help her, the elderly lady proudly showed us two rooms full of multicoloured flowers, some hanging from hooks in the roof, others covering beds, tables, cupboards and the floor.

It was women who first started with this activity in the village. They had learned the trade from outside women engaged in charity work and were later supported by church and government programmes promoting women's activities. The organizers themselves are surprised at the way in which this craft industry has flourished, since it involves a lot of work and investment in special equipment for the cleaning, dyeing, cutting and assembling of the flowers. In the initial stages, men helped their wives with some of the tasks, often behind closed doors; but after the success of the women they too became increasingly involved.

Interestingly, producers do not use husks from their own maize fields for the craft. Although they produce a considerable quantity of husks during harvest times, they do not have the means to store and clean them in order to ensure a continuous supply, and so prefer to purchase husks from packing plants near Guadalajara.

In San Cristóbal, as well as in other parts of the country, maize husks are used to steam vegetables and various meat dishes, and as a natural 'encasement' for honey, *queso de tuna* (tuna-fruit 'cheese'), and a variety of traditional sweets. Their widespread use for making *tamales* can be traced back six centuries to Aztec kitchens. Present-day *tamales* are not very different from those of the Aztecs, although the mode of preparation and the filling varies in the different regions.[7] Nowadays *tamales* are commercialized in the United States in restaurants specializing in 'typical' Mexican food. They are also sold in canned and frozen form in supermarkets, often advertised as authentic Mexican cuisine.

MAIZE HUSKS, LIVELIHOODS AND THE CONSTRUCTION OF SOCIAL VALUE AT THE SITE OF PRODUCTION

The above characterization of the multiple social and cultural significance of maize and maize husks provides a basis for a more detailed exploration of husk production, consumption and marketing. The following account draws on the village of Ayuquila in the Autlán-El Grullo Valley of southern Jalisco.

---

7. Different versions of *tamales* are sheathed in different types of leaves. For example, banana leaves are commonly used in the south of Mexico and in the Central American countries, and the leaves of the maize plant itself instead of just the husk of the cob are used for making what are called *corundas*, a traditional food in central and western Mexico.

The village was slow to enter the process of commercialization of maize husks, but once it began, it brought important changes for many of its inhabitants. The valley is not one of the principal maize husk production areas in Mexico,[8] but the growing market has opened up sources of employment for men and women in the slack agricultural season when there are few other alternatives for wage work. The production process involves not only the maize producers, but also cutters, *cuadrilleros* (labour squad leaders), owners of the packing plants and women workers who are responsible for the cleaning and packaging process. Once they reach the packing plants, the husks are cleaned with a sulphur solution, classified according to quality standards, and packaged.

While in the sphere of consumption, maize husks are attributed with almost mystical qualities pertaining to Mexican identity, 'traditional' cuisine and 'ancestral heritage', at the production site these same products acquire value as 'transmitters of modernity': indeed people in Ayuquila have come to perceive the growth of packing plants as an example of 'modern industry'. In the past only a few of the husks were saved from the maize harvest for making *tamales*, the rest being used as fodder for cattle and for selling in small quantities in local markets, along with other local items such as *nopales* (cacti which grow in the hills or are cultivated in home gardens) or home-made cheese. Nowadays, husks continue to be sold in small packages in local stores and supermarkets, but many local inhabitants express their incredulity at the fact that tons and tons of the product are exported to distant markets.[9] Local belief has it that husks are destined to be transformed in the United States into a special kind of paper used in the manufacture of dollars!

Elena, a woman who now lives in Ayuquila and who worked for a few seasons in a packing plant, visited California for a short period before she was married. There she looked after an elderly lady and also helped her relatives by taking care of their children. Two of her brothers and her sister were working in Pomona for some time. Elena expresses her awe at the way in which the husk industry has grown, explaining that *tamales* are popular among migrants living in the United States and that she herself prepared them during her visit. Still, she does not understand how they can export such large quantities, especially since they are lightweight and a lot of husks go into each kilo. She does not use more than four kilos of husks in a whole year, including those she gives to friends and neighbours. However, she

8. Maize is produced in every region of the country, but the husks are commercialized in at least five regions of the state of Jalisco, where Ayuquila is located. They are also marketed in the neighbouring states of Colima, Nayarit and Michoacán, as well as Oaxaca and Tamaulipas, but Veracruz is considered the major producer.
9. A large proportion of the product is destined for US markets, and the rest is sold within Mexico under the designation 'export quality'.

concludes: 'Americans are peculiar (*los americanos son curiositos*). One never knows what to expect with these modern industries: they even make fancy houses out of cardboard!'. Thus, she and her family are inclined to believe that it is true that Americans make dollars out of maize husks. Such belief is also founded upon an identification of *tamales* as 'poor people's food', belonging to a 'backward' tradition.[10]

Elena now has three adolescent children. A few years ago she worked for one of the packing plants that had set up a small workshop in Ayuquila, where the maize husks were brought in from the surrounding region, after being cleaned with a sulphur solution. A small room was equipped with long boards in front of which the women stood, cutting the ends with scissors, banging the husk clusters on the board or in their hands to shake the hairs out, classifying them and identifying the lower quality ones (*el capote*, those located at the outer part of each cluster that are generally soiled and damaged by insects) for national consumption. The rest were arranged tightly in large frames and repacked.

Working in the packing plants is in many ways a marker of poverty in the region. Only the poorest are willing to toil for long hours under tough conditions for such limited pay. However, it constitutes an important source of employment for women, especially those who have very little schooling. The other alternative is employment as a picker in the tomato fields — which entails shorter working hours and slightly better pay — but women pickers are often stigmatized as 'loose' and liberal women who interact freely with men in the fields. Besides, tomato picking is difficult for those who have small children at home and have to combine household chores with income generating activities. Elena explains that she liked to earn a few pesos and could work for small stretches of time, interrupting the work to go and feed her children, put a pot of beans on the stove or iron clothes. Sometimes she would bring her eldest boy to help put the husks in plastic bags. She claims she was so experienced that one could hardly follow her hand movements as she worked, and that she produced many kilos, thus earning almost as much as other women did working in the tomato fields. However, the smell of sulphur was too strong. It irritated her eyes and made her nose sting. The work is also hard on the hands, because the husks are very rough.

A packing plant was later set up in El Cacalote, a village neighbouring Ayuquila, considered the most impoverished in the region mainly because it has no access to land (see Kreutzer, 1996). Elena maintains that, whereas

---

10. We tried to investigate the rumour of maize husks being used in the manufacture of dollars, and got similar responses. Although people answered with hesitation, they seemed to accept the possibility. We also encountered a parallel rumour concerning the use of maize husk shipments for smuggling marijuana into the United States, since the sulphur used to clean husks masks the smell of the drug when sniffer dogs are used. The 'experts' we consulted said this was not possible, but perhaps both rumours are connected.

women from Ayuquila are now unwilling to engage in these activities, those from El Cacalote are eager to benefit from such work. Here again we encounter a process by which contrasting values *vis-à-vis* maize husk production are framed within local signifiers of wealth and status. Maize husk work is laborious and health-threatening, and is thus attributed a lower status in face of expectations of 'progress' (*el progreso*).

Another issue concerning contests of value — and perhaps a surprising feature of the production process — is that, although maize husks are now a commodity in the markets of Mexico and the United States, at the local level they are not in fact purchased for cash. They are acquired in exchange for labour during the maize harvest, which, it seems, is a convenient arrangement for all parties concerned. The owners of packing plants often work through previous arrangements with *cuadrilleros* (labour squad leaders) who bring together men to harvest maize and strip off the husks. The owner of the field in effect gets his maize harvested for free, the payment being simply the right to appropriate the husks. In addition, if there is much competition for husks because of high market demand or because the quality of the product and/or its plant density is high in a particular field (that is, plenty of large husks that have not been damaged by crop disease), then the *cuadrillero* (in agreement with the packer) will offer the producer free seed for the next season, plus two or three days to hire temporary labour in order to complete the harvesting of the remaining ears of corn (*repepenar*).

Doña Toña administers a packing plant — one of the first to be established in the region — owned by her husband in El Grullo (the capital of the municipality where Ayuquila is located). As she explained:

> They give us the husks — because you should realize that it is a gift, [although] there are people coming from outside, now that the product is scarce, and they come and pay. They pay for the harvesting of maize, so that *parceleros* [owners of a piece of agricultural land] give them the husk. But we have been in this from the beginning. Here the *parceleros* already know us, because we always organize our *cuadrilleros*. We tell them that when they harvest a *parcela* [plot], they have to do a good job so that the owner will look for them again the following year. They come here and look for us. Outsiders coming in don't show concern for the *parcelero*. They don't care whether he likes or dislikes the way the job is done. In the end they will leave. But we live here, and if we want the husks the following year, we don't want them to say that we didn't do a proper job and not give us the husks again.

José is a maize producer (*parcelero* or plotholder in the terminology of packing plant owners, who consider *themselves* to be the producers of maize husks) and small cattle owner who combines these activities with day-labouring. He maintains that he is being 'helped' by the *hojeros* (maize husk traders) to whom he 'gives' the husks in exchange for the labour entailed in the harvesting. He proudly took us on a brief tour around his maize fields during one of the harvesting days. The yield had not been as good as it could have been, he explained, since he had not had enough money to fertilize the whole field, even though the price was higher than last year.[11] We walked towards the centre of the *potrero* (field area), where about ten *cortadores* (those who harvest the maize and cut out the husks) sat under rudimentary 'tents' constructed of old blankets and nylon fertilizer bags held together with branches cut from trees, to protect them from the hot sun. Two of them had their small sons helping them. Beside each tent were the piles of maize each *cortador* had picked, calculated in terms of the amount he knew he could manage to deal with that day. Each pile was covered with cloth or sacks to avoid the maize getting too dry. Harvesting had to be done early in the morning, when the sun was not so strong, and the husks still a bit humid from dew and unlikely to crack when handled. The maize piles had been dampened by sprinkling water over them by mouth. The *cortadores* explained that it was easier to do it this way because they could better control the watering.

The *cortadores* sat astride small wooden benches with perforated disks (José claims they are old tractor disks) at one end. These disks, which served as knives, were held in wooden frames and firmly nailed to the benches. The inside edge was sharpened and the cutter skilfully and quickly passed the ears of maize through it, careful to avoid cutting his fingers. He would then strip off the husk, throw the maize ears in a pile for the owner of the field and the husks in another to be tightly placed in a wooden frame. Once each frame was full, the worker would tie the husks using a special knot and then extract the contents. The knot acts as a kind of signature of the worker so that he can later recognize his bundles at the packing plant.

The workers were obviously fighting against time. They wanted to get as much done as possible in order to maximize their earnings. The young boys were helping their fathers, placing the husks in the frame, sometimes bringing more maize ears, or picking those that had fallen to the ground from the huge baskets the cutters carried on their backs. There is always a degree of competition among cutters: we later discovered that they all know how many kilos the others make each day, and they are envious at the end of the week of any who might have done much better than they have.

Tomasa, José's wife, who often helps her husband in agricultural activities and who had come with us to the field, was busy picking some maize ears that had been left on the maize plants. As we walked towards her, she whispered to her husband that the cutters had done a lousy job, pointing to a number of plants which had not been harvested. José smiled somewhat resignedly, explaining that that was normal. Those were precisely the rows which had not been fertilized, and where the maize was not uniform. The workers did not

---

11. Prices of basic staples in Mexico are set by the government. This, as many authors point out (see Appendini, 1992; Bartra, 1979; Warman, 1988), is a way of subsidizing the urban economy. According to Bartra, this cheapens the price of urban labour, but at the cost of rural production which has been severely decapitalized over the past twenty years.

want to waste time picking one ear here and another there, since this decreases their productivity.

In a way the *hojeros* were doing him a favour, so he could hardly complain. The only way to gain favour with the cutters was to offer them a drink, which is a common practice in the trade. José also complied, bringing a bottle of tequila and some refreshments to keep them happy so that they would show more willingness and harvest his maize properly. 'It's so they can endure (*para el cansancio*)', he explained. 'It is a very heavy job and they have to get up early in the morning and sometimes stay until very late. One doesn't give them a lot of drink: they have to be sober so that they do not cut themselves'. José was spared a lot of costs, since he did not have to pay for the harvesting of maize: he would otherwise have had to pay for at least three workers for two weeks, plus his own labour and that of his two sons, one of whom would give up other income-generating activities to help.[12] Besides, the *cuadrillero* (labour squad leader) had offered to pay for three workers to finish off the harvesting, which José would in fact do himself, thus keeping the money. In addition, the *cuadrillero* arranged, free of charge, to transport the stripped maize to José's house, and offered to deliver it directly to the warehouse for sale. The latter offer was refused, however, since José wanted to de-grain it himself and avoid any further costs. He also planned to keep as much as possible of the harvest for home consumption and animal feed (the household possesses some cattle, two pigs, five horses and a multitude of chickens).

José had also rejected the *cuadrillero*'s offer to provide seed for the next season. He preferred to take advantage of the other offers (such as transporting the maize to his house and paying the extra workers) and he did not want to tie himself to giving his husks to the same *cuadrillero* in the next season. He was already planning to sell the maize as fresh corn the following year; not only is the price higher, but the maize plant also provides better fodder for cattle when it is fresh. These considerations all had to be set against the costs entailed in purchasing animal feed and providing for his dependent mother-in-law.

For the *cuadrillero*, however, offering seed is useful because some varieties are better than others in terms of the size and quality of husks. He also offers money to employ labour for picking the leftovers (*pepenar*) at the end of the harvesting. Normally the amount offered would cover about two or more day's wages, but this is never spoken of in terms of cash payment for husks. This could set a precedent and place the *cuadrillero* in an unfavourable position later when he might be expected to buy the husks instead of exchanging them for favours. This reinforces the point that attributing commodity value to maize husks is to be avoided: this is strategically convenient in economic terms, since the precise exchange value of a favour is subject to

---

12. The common procedure for harvesting is to pick only the ear of the maize, leaving the husk on the plant. Cattle will then be introduced into the field to graze.

change and negotiation, but also because maize husks, apart from constituting an ingredient for animal fodder, are customarily and symbolically associated with the self-provisioning orientation of Mexican peasant households.

On Saturdays, the *cuadrillero*, accompanied by his workers, transports the packs (*pacas*) of husks to the packing plant. Here each pack is weighed, identified by the worker, and registered in a notebook in his name. In this way, each worker has a running total of the number of packs that he has produced. At the end of the week the *cuadrillero* receives payment from the owner of the packing plant according to the number of packs produced by his group and in line with the market price for husks at that time. The *cuadrillero* then arranges to pay each of his workers on the basis of the number of packs each has produced, but making sure that the rate he pays affords him sufficient profit on the deal, usually in the region of 20 per cent.

Cutting husks is a heavy and risky activity and only those that are most desperate for work are willing to undertake it. Alvaro, for example, is the only inhabitant of Ayuquila who works as a cutter. The rest come from El Cacalote or from other neighbouring villages. Alvaro lives on the outskirts of the village, in a new colony formed by day-labourer families who have recently arrived in the region. He explains why so few people want to work as cutters:

> The work is dangerous: the disk is very sharp, like a razor blade. You cut the husk in a quick, circular motion, and if you miscalculate ... well ... I have cut myself several times. Look here, you can see my scars ... it is so sharp you don't even feel it when you have cut yourself. All of a sudden you see a piece of flesh hanging down ... The husk is ruthless. Our fingertips bleed from handling it. When my hands are too sore I have to take two or three days off until I develop calluses. I go fishing or go to the tomato fields if there is work for me there. My wife and son work there during the picking season.

In the tomato fields, however, Alvaro only earns 35 pesos (approximately US$4.60) a day, whilst on husks he can, with the help of his sons, earn more than 100 pesos (approximately US$13.10). The working day is longer; they leave the house at five o'clock in the morning and are not back before six in the evening. Although the maize husk season lasts from three to four months in the region,[13] Alvaro can only endure two months in such work. His wife also insists that he work elsewhere, since 'he complains of pain in his legs and back. They might earn a lot of money in the maize husks, but they end up in pieces!'.

The cutters know in advance in which field they will be working in the days ahead, and although they are not told, they quickly inform themselves about the quality of the harvest in particular fields. Alvaro complains that when his team-mates know that the harvest is poor, they simply do not show up. It is said that this is why many *parceleros* offer them drink as an incentive. This

---

13. Some of the packers continue all year. *Cuadrilleros* travel with their teams of cutters to other places where maize is being harvested.

ensures that they harvest the maize with 'gusto' and do a proper job. Offering drink is also linked to the tradition of celebrating the end of the maize harvest by recognizing all the hard work put into it. Hence cutters have come to expect drink as part of their reimbursement. They speak of *parceleros* or *cuadrilleros* who do not offer drink as stingy, and may not be willing to work with them in the next season. However, cutters themselves have acquired a reputation for being *borrachitos* (drunkards); as they harvest one field after another throughout the season, they start drinking in the fields and may continue at home and in the streets during the weekends. In the eyes of local people, this reinforces their marginal position within the region and serves to mark their activity as of lower status, thus discouraging other day-labourers from engaging in it.

Thus it is not easy to recruit men for this task and there is competition between *cuadrilleros* to secure the best cutters in their squads. *Cuadrilleros* earn a percentage of each kilo of husk delivered to the packing plant, and so are eager to enrol the most experienced men. For example, Don Pedro has been a *cuadrillero* for six years. He makes efforts to keep his men happy. Apart from offering them extra drinks and sometimes aperitifs on Saturdays, he advances them cash when the harvest is almost due. Since harvesting takes place at the end of October and the beginning of November, immediately after the bad months (*los meses malos*) when there are very few possibilities for employment, day-labourers generally welcome the possibility of covering their immediate debts (albeit by acquiring another one). In most cases, the *cuadrillero* will turn to the owner of the packing plant for an advance (to be deducted later from his remuneration) in order to cover these expenses. Owners of packing plants, too, often ask middlemen for an advance to cover their initial expenses.

In this way, a chain of commitments and debts becomes established linking particular producers, cutters, packing plant owners and middlemen. The relationships that form the backbone of this chain are built upon the strategic interplay and handling of cash and non-cash values pertaining to the specific product and involve a series of organizational practices. Similar chains of commitments develop at other points in the itinerary of maize husks. These chains and networks should not be visualized simply as disembodied webs of relations generated by the growing demand for the product in national and transnational markets, but rather as the outcome of a series of 'localized' encounters between various social actors endeavouring to define and pursue their own livelihoods.

CONSUMPTION PRACTICES AND SITUATED VALUES AND MEANINGS IN CALIFORNIA

Let us now consider the consumption end of the commodity chain. This takes us to peripherally-located urban neighbourhoods of Los Angeles,

California. Accompanied by Raul, an illegal immigrant from Ayuquila, we visited the historic centre of Los Angeles. The centre exalts California's heritage as having formed part of Mexico two centuries ago. We sat in a cosy 'typical' restaurant offering 'Mexican' food. The walls were adorned with 'Mexican' *sombreros* and *rebozos* (shawls), and we were entertained by a Mexican musical band composed (we later found out) of a couple of Chicanos[14] and a woman who had travelled from Oaxaca (in the south of Mexico) in search of work and had discovered that she could make a living out of singing with the group.

Raul was visibly uneasy, feeling totally out of place in the midst of a mainly American clientele. He was scandalized by the price of the food, which he claimed was tasteless and in no way resembled Mexican dishes; he told us that he had never seen a *rebozo* of this type before, and that the *sombrero* was actually characteristic only of Jalisco, not the whole of Mexico. We asked for *tamales*. The waitress asked us in Spanish whether we wanted them with a cheese sauce or with a simple one, immediately adding that we should not worry, 'the sauce is not *picante* (hot)'. Raul declined the offer, annoyed at the idea of eating tamales with any sauce — much less a typically American one that was not *picante* but slightly sweet in taste, or topped with cheese! He told us that he could have real *tamales* in Los Angeles whenever he wanted, since his sister-in-law (also an illegal migrant) prepared them in her own kitchen and sold them within their local network.

The *tamales* we were offered then were not only a 'reinvention' of Mexican food, but symbolized a process of re-identification whereby the values and representations associated with particular products are accommodated within specific interpretations of history and folklore. *Tamales* are amongst the most traditional of Mexican dishes, commonly offered at weddings,[15] birthdays, and at religious fiestas celebrating saints' days, All Souls' Day, and Christmas. The Aztecs used *tamales* in wedding ceremonies, where the *casamentera* (matchmaker) would tie the woman's dress (*huipil*) to the man's (*maxtle*), then feed each a *tamal*, and lock them in a room where they would lie together in a *petatl* (or *petate*, a mat usually made with palm leaves). *Tamales* were also used as a main dish for the guests. In this and many other ways, we see how maize and maize products were central to the Aztec and Mayan civilizations. They also cherished myths that linked maize to the origins of man. A Nahuan legend has it that the gods failed several times in their attempt to create man. It was not until they fed him maize that he

---

14. The terms 'Chicanos' and 'Mexican-Americans' refer to people of Mexican origin who live permanently in the United States. The designation 'Chicano', however, is usually applied to persons who exhibit a more militant stance in furtherance of their rights as Mexican-Americans. For a useful overview of the economic, political and cultural dimensions of Mexican-American identities, see de la Garza et al. (1985).

15. Especially in rural areas or within middle and lower class households. Members of élite sectors of the population often take pride in offering European dishes.

became the most perfect living being on earth (see Virginia García Acosta, *Los Señores del Maiz*). This heritage is often exploited by enterprises selling canned or frozen *tamales* that employ Aztec symbols on their labels or refer to some exotic tradition in an effort to create space for their products within specific markets. Restaurants offering Mexican food capitalize on such symbolism.

However, the definition of values attributed to this particular dish, and to Mexican food in general, within different transnational arenas, is reformulated in accordance with specific interests and social relations. This became evident to us when we observed how restaurants specializing in Mexican food in central Los Angeles often advertised themselves as 'Spanish'. Raul explained that this was just another label applied to 'Latinos' — also addressed as 'Hispanics' — but that the dishes offered were similar to those of other 'Americanized' Mexican restaurants, which he would hardly visit anyway. He did not understand the need for different labels. His socialization in California was mainly confined to Mexican migrant networks, mostly originating from his home village, and 'real' Mexican cuisine was only to be found and enjoyed within such networks. In any case, his goal during his stay in the United States was to earn as much money as he could in order to finish building his house in Ayuquila, and to return as soon as possible. To long-term Mexican residents in Los Angeles, however, and particularly to Chicanos, such labelling carries with it significant political connotations. In the context of prevailing discrimination against Mexicans, advertising Mexican food as Spanish entails retrieving that part of history which links California to Europe, thus downplaying the centrality of Mexican history and culture which many Anglos prefer to ignore (Acuña, 1996). Patricia Zavella (1997) explains that, in the state of New Mexico, the term 'Spanish' is used as synonymous for 'Spanish-Americans', which clearly demarcates native-born Americans of Mexican origin from those who had relatively recently migrated from Mexico.

Hence, whatever textbook or so-called authoritative knowledge one might claim to have about the 'true' genealogy of *tamales* and their 'essential' characteristics, they are resignified within local constellations of meaning, and become intertwined in relations that entail political commitments, processes of exclusion and inclusion, and a re-affirmation or reformulation of cultural identities and citizenship. They also point to struggles over the acquisition and legitimacy of certain types of social/ethnic status in California. Clearly, then, food and other products do not carry with them unambiguous, intrinsic sets of values — whether based on market or generalized cultural criteria — but are attributed with localized meanings by particular actors and are shaped by historical circumstances and social commitments.

In order to come to grips with the processes by which such values or clusters of value become fixed, resignified or disowned, we must focus on critical interfaces wherein cultural and social values are negotiated, reformulated or imposed. As described above, labelling and other methods of attaching signifiers to particular products provide an interesting example of how such symbolizations occasion the expression of widely differing opinions and cultural positions, leading in some cases to a direct confrontation of values. Another revealing example concerns the use of modern technologies and modes of preparation for making *tamales* in the United States. As our case material shows, the decision to use these methods entails not merely the possession of a certain know-how but also the claim or belief that certain methods are more 'efficient' and certain recipes more in tune with 'modern' tastes and lifestyles, or contrarily, that they should be avoided in order to preserve Mexican so-called traditions and food preferences. In this way statements about cultural boundaries and social differences are enunciated. The process, of course, is not smooth and clear cut: interwoven through it are not only issues of knowledge, skills, education and political affiliation, but also, as the following example of MaryLou shows, cultural features which are closely related to past experiences, memories, emotions, taste and smell.

Raul, our guide to Los Angeles, lived in Ontario on the edge of the city, with his sister, her husband and their two children. His wife and baby had returned to Mexico a few months earlier. Their neighbour, MaryLou — an Anglo born in the border region — likes to interact with them, since she has no children of her own. She complains, however, that Mexicans do not adapt easily to American ways of life and often feels that, instead of following American norms, they 'flaunt the Mexican flag' in Americans' faces. She also enjoys Mexican food, but *tamales,* for her, are Californian. She has eaten them from the time she was a child, and has since developed new recipes. She taught Raul's sister, Hortensia, how to make them with butter or margarine instead of 'unhealthy' lard, and she loves to include vegetables instead of meat, or pineapple, raisins and coconut in the sweet variety. She explains that Hortensia is a fast learner because she is very young (she is now eighteen) but that most Mexicans make life difficult for themselves by using traditional recipes and methods that require a great deal of time and energy. MaryLou, on the other hand, buys ready-made dough or mixes it herself with an electric mixer and then makes small pancakes which she rolls with the chosen fillings, and wraps in the maize husks. Because making *tamales* can be extremely time consuming, she often prepares large numbers and freezes them. At times she has even used waxed wrapping paper for steaming the tamales instead of maize husks — as is the practice in other Anglo households — although she admits that the taste is not the same.

The procedures MaryLou uses in the preparation of *tamales* highlight cultural markers and social differences. These were pointed out to us by a man known as 'El Cachanilla' (a nickname often applied to citizens from Tijuana, a Mexican city located on the border with California), who owns two supermarkets specializing in Mexican foodstuffs, offering different spices, a wide variety of chillies, meat cut to please his Latino clients, as well as maize husks and flour. Although he did not want to reveal his secret mode of preparation, he assured us that he and his wife make enough *tamales* to supply both their supermarkets. He explained that he learnt the American ways of cutting time in the production process, and complained that many of his compatriots have just never learned:

> Mexicans serve [work for] everybody: *gringos*, Japanese, Chinese and even other Latinos in the United States. Mexicans do the tough work, while others are the entrepreneurs, dealers and tradesmen. This is because the others use their wit to work less and gain more. The Chinese, for example, can speak both Spanish and English after six months in the United States. They need Spanish because most of their clients are Latinos — and they learn it. But Mexicans have been here for many years and we never learn English. Neither do we use our wits to make work more efficient. We come here and learn how to use modern machinery but when back in our country we return to the traditional plough.

He insists that fellow countrymen stick to old-fashioned ideas and never progress. His *tamales*, he added, had exactly the same taste as those prepared at home, since they had the same ingredients, though they were produced differently. Anyway, taste, for him, was all in the mind. To prove his point, he offered us some free of charge, and challenged us to discover any difference in taste.

Having enjoyed homemade *tamales* many times before, we could taste the difference (perhaps it was in our minds, as 'El Cachanilla' claimed) although we had to acknowledge that they were not too bad. Hortensia, however, was not convinced when we took some home for her. Although MaryLou has influenced her own cooking habits — concerning the 'unhealthiness' of lard, for example — she says that sometimes she just goes along with her neighbour to please her and avoid conflicts, but the taste can never be the same. Although 'El Cachanilla's *tamales* might be made with lard, Hortensia could tell them apart from homemade ones. 'Homemade *tamales* are fluffier, they melt in the mouth' she says. 'You can tell the dough is mixed with haste'. She insisted that she would buy some 'real' ones next day, from a Mexican woman who usually peddled them down the street. She explained that it was prohibited to peddle food like that in the United States, but this woman carried them hidden in a cardboard box and only visited the homes of those she could trust. Others had adopted more 'Americanized' procedures, such as taking telephone orders.

In California, Raul and Hortensia interact closely with kin and friends from Ayuquila. Raul works for a construction company and is part of a work team formed by Hortensia's husband, father-in-law and two brothers-in-law and two other relatives from the village. They also gather every Sunday with other compatriots from Ayuquila to play football, after which they eat together at the home of Esther, who is also from Ayuquila. Esther is in her sixties, and she has been living with her sons in California for eight years. She is considered a very generous woman who, in spite of painful varicose veins, is always willing to help fellow Ayuquileños with food and shelter. Her household in Pomona (adjacent to Ontario) includes her half brother and his son, who live in the garage; two nieces; her two sons, one of whom is married with two children; her latest husband, whom she invited to move in a few years after her sons brought her there; and an elderly old man who is not a relative but who lived alone in the village and did odd jobs for her — she took pity on him, and offered him shelter in the United States. The old man now helps her daughter look after the children. Many of Ayuquila's migrants have passed through Esther's household. She also 'adopts' other Mexican migrants who become friends of her sons and who often drop by to eat or spend a few days while they seek work. One of them, a man from the state of Colima, explained to us (in a more than slightly inebriated state) that he very much likes to drink, but he does not dare to do so in the 'cold' American environment. He 'lets go' at Esther's house, however, since he knows he will not be humiliated and made fun of if he falls to the floor or makes a fool of himself. He will be understood and be looked after.

On special occasions, Esther prepares *tamales* for her 'extended' family and guests, especially at Christmas and on 12 December, the Saint's Day of the Virgin of Guadalupe. She enjoys preparing them her own way. As in Mexico, this is frequently a women's collective enterprise: the mixing of the dough (*masa*) — a very heavy task — is done by hand and is usually left to the strongest of the team: several women help spread the *masa* on the maize husks with a spoon, on which the fillings are placed. These are then wrapped and placed carefully in the steamer. Esther says that she enjoys making the *tamales* almost as much as she enjoys the party. It gives her something to do — she does not dance because of her bad legs — and she loves women's talk and the fun of working together. She has invited families from other Mexican regions to these celebrations, and, although she feels obliged to invite the women to help her (and they feel more at home if they contribute to the preparations), she complains that they have different ideas on how to prepare the *tamales*. Once she invited some indigenous women (*inditas*, she says[16]) from Guerrero (in the south of Mexico) who had no one to celebrate Christmas with. They mixed the dough with different varieties of chillies, producing green, red and yellow *tamales*. Esther did not enjoy Christmas so much that year, since it had a different 'flavour'. 'I don't like my *tamales* in colours', she commented. 'Next time I will only invite them to eat.'

Lately, however, Esther has been cutting a few steps in food preparation. She explains that labour is money in the United States, and although she does not have a paid job herself — she is only in charge of cooking, cleaning and paying bills — she has learned to value labour differently. In California she can buy pre-mixed dough in the Mexican supermarket, and thus avoid a lot of work. This would be unthinkable in Mexico, where no one would pay so much money for pre-mixed dough, and no one would think of selling it. She complains that in the United States husks have to be purchased from the

---

16. Strong status differences, based upon ethnic or racial criteria, are prevalent in Mexico. Peasants of so-called indigenous background, who speak poor or no Spanish, are identified as *indios* or *inditos*.

supermarket, and that they are flimsy, torn and expensive. At home in Ayuquila she would go every year and pick the best ears of the maize herself, and thus guarantee good quality husks. She claims, however, that she would never use wrapping paper instead of maize husks: the result would not then be a *tamal*, it would be something else. Nor would she freeze them. 'This is neither necessary nor possible', she says; 'we make *tamales* to celebrate, to eat as much as we please. With my full household, we never have any leftovers. If there are some still in the pot, we continue celebrating!'

In the taste, appearance, and mode of preparation of *tamales*, a wide array of social and cultural tokens mark differences between Anglos, Chicanos, Mexican-Americans and Mexican migrants. Migrants also differentiate among themselves on the basis of various regional and ethnic food preferences. None of these differences, however, are categorical since persons coming from the same general socio-cultural backgrounds may adopt different consumption styles and attribute a variety of meanings to them. As elsewhere, people manage in situations of cultural plurality until events precipitate the need to clear up ambiguities and conflicting normative standards through negotiation and accommodation. Thus, in order to analyse this contestation of values, we must go beyond a consideration of generalized cultural and moral frameworks to examine the organizing and discursive strategies used to accommodate, dispute or ignore, other actors' desires, interests and interpretations. It is in this way that we can achieve a better understanding of the significance of changing food tastes and consumption in an era of increased globalization.[17]

ORGANIZING PRACTICES AND CONTESTS OF VALUE WITHIN TRANSNATIONAL COMMERCIALIZING NETWORKS

Let us now examine the commercial itinerary of maize husks as they make their way towards consumers in the United States. Each stage in the process entails a myriad of negotiations over value and its definition.

Many traders and retailers of maize husks in the United States complain that this commodity is quite profitless in itself. The amount of work required to clean and repack the husks makes it cumbersome and costly, and the price they can ask does not make up for this. This is connected to the fact that in

---

17. It is important to emphasize that we wish to stand back from essentialist and reified interpretations of globalization that stress the uniformity of social change. We also distance ourselves from the 1960s idea of globalization which pictured an emerging world order in terms of 'centre-periphery' or 'metropolis–satellite' relations, thus implying simple asymmetries in economic, political and cultural terms. Instead we view global ordering in terms of a complex and changing pattern of global flows involving movements of people, technology and information, products through commodity markets, images and symbolic representations (Appadurai, 1990), which necessarily contain aspects of homogenization and diversity.

California many consumers are Mexican migrants who come from rural areas where maize husks are traditionally associated with the ideal-typical 'subsistence' orientation of Mexican peasant households in which women's food preparation activities are non-commoditized. Even though husks can be purchased and domestic labour bought, Mexican cultural ideals stress the non-commodified nature of family and domestic life. Whether production takes place on smallholder farms or on large estates, it is customary that, before maize harvesting starts, women from farm-owner and farm-worker households (and by extension their close relatives) are permitted to collect from the crop the best of the ears of maize (that is, the kernels and husks) for use in preparing *tamales*.

Thus migrants are quite unwilling to pay high prices for husks in the United States, but retailers specializing in Mexican spices and foodstuffs need to include them in their sales repertoires in order to keep their customers. 'If we don't offer everything they need for their food preparations, especially in critical periods when they hold national and religious celebrations, they will go elsewhere'.[18] Prices, then, are not unimportant in the appraisal and valuation of products and their consumption, but the interrelations of price and social value cannot be taken for granted. Values entailed in the specification of quality constitute an obvious example of this. Negotiating the precise definition of quality of a particular commodity within specific markets is an everyday issue for traders. It entails dealing with diverse cultural norms and standards and working their way through formal and informal rules and procedures.

For example, Tomás, a maize husk trader and exporter from Monterrey, in northern Mexico, angrily recounts his experiences in the United States, and complains that in their efforts to 'play it safe' Americans simply disqualify their products:

> They use supposedly 'legal' arguments to evaluate our products. In their regulations it is stipulated that if there is ten percent damage in the product it cannot be commercialized in the United States. OK, I can agree with that. But what is the unit? How do they measure the ten percent? Look, it all comes down to the criterion of the inspector. The inspector takes a unit and for him a unit is a husk and he says, this unit has 10 percent damage. Yes, but the unit is not a husk, rather a 20 kilo pack! And so they send you back with all your cargo. They do not touch their heart, they don't know how to show respect as we do. If I make a deal with you, by word only, well we will both comply, I with you and you with me. At least that is what we are used to here in the *Mercado de Abastos* (wholesale market). Not them! For them, everything has to be in writing.

Hence, it is not only the definition of quality that Tomás strongly challenges, but the interpretation of what is regarded as 'proper' social conduct within commercial relations. He complains that arguments about quality are often

---

18. The administrator — a Mexican woman — of El Guapo, a company owned by a Chicano, which distributes maize husks and Mexican spices.

an excuse to back away from agreements that have been reached: if they need the product, the quality is good; if they find that it has not sold well and they have a lot in stock, they refuse it under the pretence of bad quality. A Mexican who believes in prior agreements and has all his documents in order — including payment of import taxes — sees the situation very differently. Often he has no money to return the shipment to Mexico and is charged a fine according to the number of days it remains in the United States. On top of that he will have to pay the costs of destroying the product, which includes paying two inspectors, the use of incinerators plus labour and transport costs. Tomás concludes that the problem is Americans:

> If there were no *gringos* in the United States, we would have no problems. In the first place, they feel superior because they are Americans, you see. They have books that stipulate all sorts of conditions that have to be met, and they expect you to take the product to their shop and surrender to their ways.

The *Mercado de Abastos* of Monterrey where Tomás owns a stall is one of the critical sites for the commercialization of maize husks. Although there are only a few traders specializing in this product, they maintain strategic links to owners of packing plants[19] as well as to intermediaries in the United States and Mexico. Tomás owns a small packing plant himself in the neighbouring state of Tamaulipas, although he is not one of the main maize husk traders. Due to the recent devaluation of the Mexican peso, plus his misfortunes in the United States, he decided to diversify and now combines maize husk trading with other commodities such as spices and lemons.

Manoeuvring his way within the context of Mexican commercial risks and government restrictions is also a trial for Tomás, who needs to access information concerning the ins and outs of tax regulations and other hindrances. Here again, values and definitions are negotiated and contested. For example, the category of goods under which husks will be classified is important, since this will determine the levy imposed on a particular transaction. Because in Mexico the maize husk industry is relatively new and is not sizeable enough to be included in formal trading regulations, Tomás explains that he generally prefers to register his husks as 'rural unprocessed products' (*productos de campo no procesado*). Although husks do pass through a process of cleaning and classifying, he argues that they are not processed, only packaged. Consequently, he does not have to pay Mexican tax on this. On the other hand, when dealing with large supermarkets in Mexico, he registers the transaction under the category 'fruit and vegetables', instead of 'groceries'. Mexican supermarkets generally take no more than two weeks to pay for fruit and vegetables, while for non-perishables they may take up to about three months. Similar considerations have to be taken into account in

---

19. They have strong links with owners of packing plants in El Grullo, close to our main research site, which is why we followed them up.

transactions crossing the Mexico–US border. It depends on the skills of the entrepreneur or intermediary to negotiate the definition of the product and the classification under which it should be regulated and commercialized.

Hence, good relations with bureaucrats and even secretaries are indispensable. Traders engage in complex sets of social relationships comprising not only face-to-face participants but also distant 'acting' components that include individual and organizational actors, relevant technologies, financial and material resources, and media-generated discourses and symbols. Organizing capacity — whether at the level of the individual peasant, migrant or in terms of the co-ordinated actions carried out by a consortium of transnational businesses — necessarily involves these diverse elements. How they are interlocked is what counts in the end.

Maize husks enter the United States through a chain of traders who move the product through several hands to feed into the specialized border intermediaries who are *au fait* with the complicated US frontier import regulations as well as those of Mexico. The traders we interviewed all agreed that the first requisite for exporting is to have good contacts in the United States — 'otherwise they will make you wait, and buy at very low prices'. To make a good deal a trader requires detailed information, not only on clients, prices and costs, but also pertaining to the workings of insurance companies in a foreign country and the criteria for defining quality. Tomás explains:

> In Mexico we have the advantage — or the disadvantage — that the same group of people work in the same shifts everyday at the customs office. You know that your contact person will always be there at certain hours of the day, and in all likelihood will remain there for years, sometimes even a lifetime. Then posts are inherited if the person keeps his networks alive. Contacts are also inherited. My father passed his contacts on to me, and I often pass them on to friends. In the United States it is not like that. Sometimes you are lucky and you get the same person two or three times, but you never know who will be in the customs office.

However angry Tomás was about his recent misfortunes in the United States, he acknowledged that his experiences have not all been negative. He had previously exported maize husks regularly to the United States, but then he had had a good contact — a Mexican-American woman who was in charge of buying foodstuffs for American Airforce bases in different parts of the country. Tomás says that it was a pleasure to do business with her, and that she gave him valuable information. In the end, though, he does not believe her congeniality was due to her Mexican background, since in his experience many Chicanos and Mexican-Americans are even worse than Americans: they take on an air of superiority, but also know how to deal with the schemes and tricks that Mexicans devise to evade American regulations. According to Tomás, although Americans pretend to be very straightlaced, it is also possible to bribe them — but you need the skills to follow through certain tricks, and you need the contacts and the networks. Traders develop modes of operation whereby complex chains are created. These modes of operation often depend heavily on the establishment of close friendship and *compadrazgo* ties which link traders, owners of packing plants and government officials in the customs office. Competition is expected, but certain rules of the game must be observed.

As these transnational networks unfold, traders commercializing maize husks into the United States hinterland must develop ongoing relationships with three other culturally and occupationally distinct groups: Mexicans involved as middlemen; Chicano traders who operate effectively (sometimes with Mexican partners) on both sides of the border; and Americans variously involved in the commercialization, processing and distribution of Mexican processed foods, spices, and often fruit and vegetables. The encounters that take place between these different actors present interesting interface situations wherein values (not only based on commodity notions) are contested and negotiated.

Chicano, Mexican and American traders, for example, negotiate the stereotypical notions of their cultural and ethnic persona and attempt to cross or rework these imagined boundaries and social worlds by building upon differential images of trustworthiness, reciprocity, accountability and entrepreneurship. We were introduced to the owners of a Mexican supermarket located in a Mexican neighbourhood in the Los Angeles area. They were two tall, blond, Anglo-looking brothers who spoke a little Spanish with a heavy Anglo accent but who presented themselves as Mexicans. When we inquired about them, our friends explained that they were of Mexican descent. Their grandfather, who started the enterprise, had been a Mexican. More than that, however, the owners of the supermarket interacted in a very familiar way with their Mexican clients. They had *compadres* among their clientele and they attended beer parties and other celebrations in nearby neighbourhoods. The fact of drinking with Mexicans encouraged sentiments of affiliation which were instrumental in running the business and keeping their clients.

Thus, in addition to the obvious economic interests entailed, such encounters represent cultural interfaces where new social identities are forged and redefined. Furthermore, as Roberts and Spener (1994) suggest, the cross-border area itself becomes an integrated transnational space in which issues of identity are contested on the basis of common historical roots, on the one hand, and everyday social interaction, on the other.

CONCLUSION: BROADER THEORETICAL IMPLICATIONS

Although this article has not ventured to provide a systematic critique of commodity-chain analysis,[20] which attempts to show how systems of

---

20. See the debate between Ben Fine (1995) and others for a comprehensive critical discussion of the underlying theoretical problems raised by commodity-chain and food systems analysis.

production and commercialization are shaped by global consumption, the foregoing case study suggests that such an approach fails to give adequate attention to the multiplicities and ambiguities of social value implicit in the workings of commodity chains and globalization processes. In order to tackle these issues, we need to focus upon processes of value contestation in situated social arenas, wherein the meanings of specific goods, relationships and cultural identities are forged, challenged and reinvented.[21]

Our interest in cross-border commodity flows and the reassembling of cultural meanings in different social locales bears some similarity to Howes' (1996) collection of ethnographic cases on the cross-cultural consumption of goods. Our perspective differs, however, in that we put less emphasis on the issue of how particular cultural frames and contexts transform and 'indigenize' the meanings of goods crossing frontiers, preferring instead to analyse the ways in which the use and meanings of specific products are continuously reassembled and transformed within the livelihoods and social networks of Mexicans who live in a multicultural, transnational world. This helps us to appreciate the plasticity and self-organizing dimensions of cultural and social practices, and thus to analyse the interweaving of the multiple social, cultural and economic values ascribed to specific products, and the organizational practices implicated in their production/consumption.

This, in turn, raises the issue of how ethnic identifications and status differences shape social practices within specific global commodity networks. For example, in the sphere of consumption, ethnic and racial differentiations are implied in the identities associated with *tamales* and their styles of preparation and in the interactions between retailers and consumers; in marketing arenas, entrepreneurial status and nationality differences shape the practice of traders and their capacity to negotiate the passage of maize husks and other products across the international frontier; and in the production sites, social commitments linking producers, cutters, labour squad leaders and packers are procured through the strategic ascription of cash and gift values to the products they dispense. At several junctures in this process, discussions on the cultural 'authenticity' of the product and its handling spill over into more general debates that contrast and evaluate the cultural worth and superiority of 'Mexican' versus 'American' ways of life.

A further implication of this type of analysis is that it highlights how power relations are constituted and sustained through the definitions, attributions and contestations of value. However, power in one locale or part of a commodity network does not automatically determine or guarantee control

---

21. Although the emphasis of this paper has been on commodity values, the study of fiestas and other public rituals offers interesting insights into the processes of value affirmation, confrontation and re-configuration (for an Andean example, see Laite and Long, 1987). Such studies underline the importance of examining the sets of social relations and discursive strategies involved in attempts to fix certain shared values and develop modes of accommodation between opposing moralities and interests.

over the social relations in another. Rather one must visualize the processes involved in terms of a set of interlocking social domains that are cross-cut by commodity flows and social networks wherein relations of status and power are produced, sustained, negotiated, and resisted (see Long and Villarreal, 1994; Villarreal, 1994).

Although this study has focused upon a commodity that is seemingly small in scale and scope — maize husks can hardly be regarded as of paramount interest to Transnational Companies or to the Mexican economy as a whole — it raises questions of a fundamental nature about the valorization and globalization of food and the reproduction of cultural identities and social networks in a transnational world, where the flows of foods and food-related products become increasingly central. It also serves to emphasize, as we have done in previous publications, the critical importance of re-examining processes of commoditization on a global scale from an actor-oriented perspective.

REFERENCES

Acuña, R. (1996) *Anything but Mexican: Chicanos in Contemporary Los Angeles*. London and New York: Verso.

Appadurai, A. (1986) 'Introduction: Commodities and the Politics of Value', in A. Appadurai (ed.) *The Social Life of Things: Commodities in Cultural Perspective*, pp. 3–63. Cambridge: Cambridge University Press.

Appadurai, A. (1990) 'Disjuncture and Difference in the Global Cultural Economy', *Theory, Culture and Society* 7(2–3): 295–310.

Appendini, Kirsten (1992) *De La Milpa a Los Tortibonos. La reestructuración de la política alimentaria en Mexico*. Mexico DF: Colegio de Mexico/UNRISD.

Arce, A. (1997) 'Globalization and Food Objects', in H. de Haan and N. Long (eds) *Images and Realities of Rural Life: Wageningen Perspectives on Rural Transformations*, pp. 178–210. Assen: Van Gorcum.

Arce, A. and T. Marsden (1993) 'The Social Construction of International Food: A New Research Agenda', in *Economic Geography* 69(3): 293–311.

Bartra, A. (1979) *La Explotación del Trabajo Campesino por El Capital*. Mexico DF: Macehual.

Bonanno, A. et al. (1994) *From Colombus to ConAgra: The Globalization of Agriculture and Food*. Lawrence: University Press of Kansas.

Douglas, M. and B. Isherwood (1979) *The World of Goods*. London: Allen Lane.

Ferguson, J. (1988) 'Cultural Exchange: New Developments in the Anthropology of Commodities', *Cultural Anthropology* 3: 489–513.

Fine, B. (1995) 'From Political Economy to Consumption', in D. Miller (ed.), *Acknowledging Consumption: A Review of New Studies*, pp. 127–632. London and New York: Routledge.

Friedmann, H. (1993) 'The Political Economy of Food: A Global Crisis', *New Left Review* 197 (Jan/Feb): 29–57.

Frow, J. (1995) *Cultural Studies and Cultural Value*. Oxford: Clarendon Press.

de la Garza, R. O., F. D. Bean, C. M. Bonjean, R. Romo and R. Alvarez (eds) (1985) *The Mexican American Experience*. Austin: University of Texas Press.

Gereffi, J. and T. Korzeniewicz (eds) (1994) *Global Commodity Chains*. Boulder, CO: Westview Press.

Goodin, R. E. (1992) *Green Political Theory*. Cambridge: Polity Press.

Goodman, D. and J. Watts (1994) 'Reconfiguring the Rural or Fording the Divide? Capitalist Restructuring and Global Agro-food Systems', *Journal of Peasant Studies* 22(1): 1–49.

Howes, D. (ed.) (1996) *Cross-cultural Consumption: Global Markets, Local Realities*. London and New York: Routledge.

Kopytoff, I. (1986) 'The Cultural Biography of Things: Commoditization as Process', in A. Appadurai (ed.) *The Social Life of Things*, pp. 64–91. Cambridge: Cambridge University Press.

Kreutzer, S. (1996) 'El unico seguro que tenemos es el chingadazo'. NOP Report, 'A Socio-economic study on livelihood strategies of inhabitants of El Cacalote, a little village in Jalisco, West Mexico'. Wageningen: CIESAS-WAU.

Laite, A. L and N. Long (1987) 'Fiestas and Uneven Capitalist Development in Central Peru', *Bulletin of Latin American Research* 6(1): 27–53.

Long, N. et al. (1986) *The Commoditization Debate*. Wageningen: Wageningen Agricultural University.

Long, N. (1997) 'Agrarian Change, Neoliberalism and Commoditization: A Perspective on Social Value', in H. de Haan and N. Long (eds) *Images and Realities of Rural Life: Wageningen Perspectives on Rural Transformations*, pp. 226–44. Assen: Van Gorcum.

Long, N. and M. Villarreal (1994) 'The Interweaving of Knowledge and Power', in I. Scoones and J. Thompson (eds) *Beyond Farmer First: Rural Peoples' Knowledge, Agricultural Research and Extension Practice*, pp. 41–52. London: Intermediate Technology Publications.

Roberts B. and D. Spener (1994) 'Social Networks and Trade on the Texas-Mexico Border: The Role of Small-scale Enterprise in the Integration of Transnational Space'. Paper presented at the Latin American Studies Association XVIII International Congress, Atlanta (10–12 March).

Thomas, N. (1991) *Entangled Objects*. Cambridge, MA: Harvard University Press.

Villarreal, M. (1994) 'Wielding and Yielding. Power, Subordination and Gender Identity in the Context of a Mexican Development Project'. PhD Thesis. Wageningen Agricultural University.

Villarreal, M. (1997) 'Las Nuevas Mujeres de Maiz: Acerca de la globalización y los cambios culturales en Jalisco'. Paper presented at the meeting of the Latin America Studies Association, Guadalajara, Mexico (17–19 April).

Warman, A. (1988) *La Historia de un Bastardo: Maíz y Capitalismo*. Mexico DF: Instituto de Investigaciones Sociales UNAM/Fondo de Cultura Económica.

Zavella, P. (1997) 'Reflections on Diversity among Chicanos', in M. Romero, P. Hondagneu-Sotelo and V. Ortiz *Challenging Fronteras: Structuring Latina and Latino Lives in the United States*, pp. 187–94. New York and London: Routledge.

Commodities and the Power of Prayer: Pentecostalist Attitudes Towards Consumption in Contemporary Ghana

Birgit Meyer

In the course of my fieldwork among the Peki, who are part of the Ewe in Southeastern Ghana, I learned several remarkable things. One was that markets and shops are dangerous: they contain goods which one might long for, but alas, once bought, the things may turn against their owner and cause destruction. I was especially warned about the dangers imbued in commodities by a fervent pentecostalist preacher in his early thirties, who told me the following experience. One day he had bought a pair of under-pants at the local market; since the day he started wearing them, he had been harassed by sexual dreams in which he had intercourse with beautiful ladies, although in daily life he was alone. Only after some time did he realize that the dreams were caused by the underpants; having thrown them away, he slept undisturbed by seductive women. Obviously I was not the only person to whom he related this experience: many members of the church in which he used to preach — the Evangelical Presbyterian Church 'of Ghana' — told me his story. Yet he did not stop at warning people about the possible danger inherent in goods, he also offered a remedy to neutralize it: prayer. All church members were called on to say a brief, silent prayer over every purchased commodity in their minds before entering their homes. They were to ask God to 'sanctify' the thing bought, thereby neutralizing any diabolic spirit imbued in it. Only in this way would it be possible to prevent the destructive powers incorporated in the objects from damaging their owners' lives.

As I learned later, this intriguing attitude is not peculiar to pentecostalists in Peki, but is widely shared in Ghanaian pentecostalist circles, both in urban and rural areas. It is especially prevalent among members of classical pentecostal churches such as the Church of Pentecost and the Assemblies of God, as well as among members of prayer groups within mission churches and new pentecostalist churches such as the Evangelical Presbyterian Church

I would like to thank Gerd Baumann, Gosewijn van Beek, Remco Ensel, Peter Geschiere, Peter Pels, Peter van Rooden, Bonno Thoden van Velzen, Marja Spierenburg, Milena Veenis and Jojada Verrips for their comments on earlier versions of this article. It is based on fieldwork carried out in Peki and Accra in 1990, 1991 and 1996. This research would not have been possible without the financial assistance of the Amsterdam School for Social Science Research (ASSR) and the Netherlands Foundation for the Advancement of Tropical Research (WOTRO).

'of Ghana'.[1] Pentecostalism, a pre-eminently global religion (Poewe, 1994), which has been increasing in popularity all over Africa since the late 1980s, offers a peculiar attitude towards the local market, that is, the place from which globally circulated products pass into private homes. It represents commodities offered in the market as animated and, at the same time, provides the means to transform them into mere objects to be used. This article is dedicated to an in-depth examination of this attitude. It focuses on the relationship between religion and consumption in the context of globalization, in other words, on people's (awareness of their) incorporation in global economic, political, social, cultural and religious processes.

While processes of conversion to world religions (for Africa, see for example, Horton, 1971, 1975) and commodification (for example, Appadurai, 1986; Parry and Bloch, 1989; Thomas, 1991) caught the attention of social scientists studying non-Western people's experiences with colonialism and modernization a long time ago (even before globalization became a topic of investigation), the relationship between conversion to Christianity and consumption has been rather neglected. Yet the urge of Ghanaian pentecostalists to purify — or rather, de-fetishize — commodities through prayer suggests that a full understanding of both conversion and consumption requires an investigation of the relationship between the two.

This article provides a sketch of the relationship between Christianity and consumption at the grassroots level. On the basis of a detailed investigation of pentecostalist views and attitudes, it is shown that pentecostalists engage in a dialectic of enchantment and disenchantment. They represent the modern global economy as enchanted and themselves as agents of disenchantment: only through prayer can commodities cease to be fetishes and become mere commodities in the sense commonly accepted by social scientists and economists. I argue that taking for granted the meaning of terms such as 'commodities' and 'consumption' blocks the way for a better understanding of how the global economy is apprehended at the local level, by organizations such as pentecostalist churches. In order to grasp the developments which social scientists circumscribe as globalization, there is a definite need to approach economics as culture (Appadurai, 1986; Gudeman, 1986). The fruitfulness of this approach, which leads us beyond a reification of the economic, is revealed especially through recent anthropological studies of consumption as a cultural practice (see, for instance, Carrier, 1995; Miller, 1987, 1994). Yet in their eagerness to make us 'acknowledge' consumption (Miller, 1995b), proponents of this approach tend to accept the rather instrumental view that in a globalizing world, consumption would serve the construction of modern identities. My research shows that consumption may

---

1. The so-called 'charismatic' churches, which represent a new pentecostalist branch which has become popular since the 1980s among the Ghanaian (aspiring) urban élite, appear to be less concerned with dangers imbued in commodities (albeit on the level of the leaders) and more with gifts (cf. Van Dijk, 1997).

not necessarily serve this positive goal; as commodities are considered able to impose their will on their owners, their consumption may also threaten to dissolve identity. Rather than assuming a knowledge of what consumption is and does, our investigations make us wonder how the people we study themselves view and deal with consumption. Only an anthropology which is prepared to keep on wondering about the meaning of its own vocabulary may claim to grasp what is going on in a globalizing world.[2]

CHRISTIANITY AND CONSUMPTION

Before looking at current pentecostalist attitudes towards prosperity, the global market and the consumption of foreign commodities, it is necessary to place pentecostalism in its proper historical perspective, by examining how nineteenth-century Ewe converts to Christianity appropriated the missionary stance towards goods that was communicated to them through both the sermons and material culture of the German Pietist missionaries of the Norddeutsche Missionsgesellschaft (NMG). This section briefly traces the history of the introduction of Western consumer goods as part and parcel of missionization and examines Ewe Christians' attitudes towards Western commodities.

In the course of the seventeenth century, the Ewe settled in the area lying between the rivers Volta and Mono and stretching from the coast some 200 km inland.[3] Through slave trade and the concomitant presence of European traders on the coast, the Ewe were part of a global system of trade; this entailed among other things that Western goods found their way far into the hinterland. Yet the more frequent consumption of Western goods on a day-to-day basis only occurred in the last decades of the nineteenth century in the course of the incorporation of the Ewe area into British Gold Coast and German Togo, when an increasing number of Ewe engaged in wage labour or the production of cash crops.

In this process mission societies played a crucial role. For the NMG, a German Pietist mission society which was active among the Ewe from 1847 onwards, the spread of the Gospel and world trade clearly belonged together. Unlike other Protestant mission societies such as the Basler Mission, which was active among the neighbouring Asante, the NMG did not run stores of

---

2. I fully agree with Appiah's argument that understanding what happens in the world as a whole presupposes actual intercultural discussion. His statement concerning the understanding of modernity also applies to the understanding of 'globalization': 'the question what it is to *be* modern is one that Africans and Westerners may ask together. And, as I shall suggest, neither of us will understand what modernity is until we understand each other' (Appiah, 1992: 107, emphasis in original).

3. On Ewe history, see for example Amenumey (1964, 1986); Asare (1973); Spieth (1906); Wilks (1975); also my own brief overview (Meyer, 1995a: 49ff).

its own. However, both at home and in the mission field it co-operated closely with the trading company Vietor which was owned by a Pietist trader (see Ustorf, 1986). The NMG and Vietor company often settled at the same places and, at least for the local population, their association was evident, despite the usual disclaimers of NMG-missionaries who desperately tried to keep Christianity at a distance from worldly matters such as stores. While the Vietor company bought crops such as cotton and, from the turn of the century onwards, cocoa from the Ewe and, at the same time, offered European goods for sale, the NMG promoted paid labour through its educational system, including teachers, clerks, cash crop farmers and artisans.[4] Interestingly, the NMG did not favour converts' adoption of trade as a profession. Trade was to remain a European monopoly and the role of Africans was merely to sell raw materials to, and buy commodities from, Western trading companies.[5]

This promotion of work for money, and the subsequent incorporation of people into world trade, either as producers of raw materials or as consumers of Western commodities, was part and parcel of the propagation of a new Christian lifestyle. For the most visible characteristic feature of Christians was their material culture: the traditional compound housing the extended family was to be exchanged for a house for the nuclear family, which contained Western furniture, china-ware, all sorts of iron kitchen utensils, books and European cookies; Christians were expected to wear clothes which were either imported from Europe (black coat and tie for the men) or made from European materials (dresses in Western or African styles for women). To both the missionaries and the Ewe converts, the possession of Western goods was a self-evident feature of Christian life and their lack was regarded as a sign of 'savagery'. Yet it seems that their ideas about consumption differed considerably.

The NMG held a complicated stance towards consumption. Although the mission considered trade a civilizing strategy by which Africans could be lifted up from their 'heathen' life conditions, and thus favoured the *use* of Western goods in Africa, it associated the *pleasures* of consumption with an indulgence in worldly matters which would prevent eternal salvation. In line with the popular lithograph depicting the well-known image of 'The broad and the narrow path',[6] the missionaries associated pleasures such as

---

4. The NMG stimulated men much more than women to take up paid labour. Young women could only work as 'housegirls' at the mission posts or as childcare attendants in the kindergarten, and after marriage they were expected to devote themselves fully to their families. Against the wishes of the mission, however, many married women engaged in trade.
5. Ewe mission workers were not allowed to supplement their small incomes through trading activities. The only thing they were expected to do besides their job was to grow their own food.
6. For a detailed analysis of this lithograph, see Meyer (1995a: 25ff).

entertainment, beautiful clothes and good food and drinks with the 'broad path', which would eventually end in hellfire, and abstinence from these pleasures and indulgence in charity with the 'narrow path', which would lead to salvation in the heavenly Jerusalem. As I have shown elsewhere (Meyer, 1995a: 24ff), the Pietist NMG-missionaries were true exponents of Weber's innerworldly ascesis (1984/1920); that is, they promoted an ethic which favoured the virtue of production above the pleasure of consumption. This, at least, was their stance in their home base, Württemberg in southern Germany. The missionaries from this area were highly suspicious of industrialization, urbanization and the new possibilities offered by mass consumption, and the dream of the good, old, rural way of life encouraged many of them to go to Africa (Jenkins, 1978). Yet ironically, once there, they contributed to sparking off the very same processes from which they wanted to escape at home.

The attitudes of Ewe Christians towards consumption have to be deduced from missionary sources. From the missionaries' frequent complaints it becomes clear that for the Ewe, the mission was a road towards 'civilization', that is, a state of opened eyes (*nku vu*) which implied the (striving for) possession of Western goods.[7] The missionaries were especially critical about Ewe staying on the coast near the commercial and administrative centres, who actively traded with Europeans and who were wealthy enough to furnish themselves and their homes with all sorts of new things (Ustorf, 1989: 241ff). Yet things that were ordinary, taken-for granted objects of use for the missionaries, were new (and often luxury) goods to the Ewe. These goods not only symbolized 'civilization', but also contributed to turning upside down existing societal and familial structures. Western goods either replaced other home-made things (in the case of clothes, for instance) or contributed to transforming customs and habits, as in the case of nuclear family houses which had an impact on traditional patterns of production and distribution; Western-styled furniture contributed to the transformation of eating habits, and European clothes undermined existing patterns of co-operation between husbands and wives.[8]

The mission's emphasis on individual salvation and a certain material standard of living were interrelated and contributed to the emergence of a group of people for whom consumption became a practice to emphasize individuality at the expense of forms of identity based on lineages or clans and the patterns of production, distribution and consumption related to them. Clearly, to Ewe converts Western goods were building blocks of a new

---

7. Elsewhere, I have dealt with the Ewe's striving for civilization through the consumption of Western commodities in more detail; see Meyer (1997b).
8. In pre-colonial times there had existed a peculiar division of labour in the production of clothes between husband and wife. While spinning was the exclusive task of women, weaving was done only by men. In this way husband and wife had to co-operate in order to make clothes (Spieth, 1906: 356).

type of lifestyle, by which they could distinguish themselves from other people in society, for instance the traditional élites. This is not to say that Ewe converts' consumption of Western goods is to be explained merely in terms of conspicuous consumption à la Veblen. Rather, Western goods offered new 'means of objectification' (Miller, 1987) by which Ewe converts could construct a new, modern identity — modern not only in the sense that they possessed hitherto unknown things, but, above all, in the sense of a change of notions of selfhood. They identified themselves as modern consumers, that is, persons with a 'consciousness that one is living through objects and images not of one's own creation' (Miller, 1995a: 1). This meant that they wanted to go beyond mere subsistence, to enjoy things which they had not produced by themselves or in their surroundings, and to confine consumption to the nuclear family.

The mission represented those indulging in the pleasures of consumption as 'Halbgebildete' (semi-educated), that is, people who were merely imitating Western ways, which was attributed to superficiality and a lack of profound character.[9] Although the mission did indeed regard Western goods as a necessary ingredient of a Christian lifestyle, it expected converts to view material matters as subordinate to the 'true content' of the Christian message, and consumption as subordinate to production. Christians were expected to work hard and walk humbly on the 'narrow path', abstaining from 'worldly' pleasures. The mission's allegedly anti-materialistic stance also came to the fore in its feverish fight against the Ewe's materialist outlook in traditional religious matters and the denunciation of their worship as 'fetishistic'. The missionaries preached continuously that by worshipping rivers, stones and other objects, the Ewe were truly worshipping Satan (Meyer, 1992, 1994, 1995a). Associating these 'fetishes' with the Devil, the missionaries asked the Ewe to burn all objects related to their old religion and adopt a much more spiritualistic and self-conscious attitude towards the divine. Converts were no longer to allow 'fetishes' to possess them, thereby drawing a strict boundary between people and things. A good Christian was to subject the object world to his or her own will and strive after higher, immaterial values.

Of course, by representing missionary Pietism as a non-materialistic form of worship and, at the same time, expecting converts to adopt a Western lifestyle, the mission mystified its own actions. Ewe converts' attitudes towards consumption were so disturbing to the mission because they laid bare a characteristic feature of the Pietist mission: the fact that conversion to Christianity required Western commodities. Rather than merely enabling people to buy commodities, Christianity itself was produced through consumption.

Until the 1940s, the lives of Ewe converts proved the association of Christianity and the ability to buy and consume Western goods to be valid.

---

9. On the NMG's use of the pejorative term 'Halbgebildete' see Meyer (1997a).

In Peki, for instance, people became increasingly involved in the cultivation of cocoa. The popular nickname people gave to this crop, black gold, testifies to the relative ease by which cocoa farming yielded money. While the men planted the seeds and looked after the plants, women were responsible for the transport of the fruits to the cocoa merchants, from whom they then bought all sorts of Western goods in return. In this way, women had money at their disposal which they could invest in trade; they thus became to some extent independent from subsistence production and contributed to the further spread of more and more Western goods until even in the remotest village global commodities became accessible.

Although cocoa cultivation and trade were practised by Christians and non-Christians alike, for all those earning money in this way (or through other activities) it was relatively profitable to identify themselves as Christians. While traditionally, farming was organized by the patrilineal lineages and members were expected to share their wealth with their extended family, the mission emphasized the nuclear family as the unit of production and distribution and consumption. To the dismay of the missionaries, many people took up this emphasis for other reasons than intended by the mission, and converted because they thought 'that being Christians all their properties will be saved' (the Ewe teacher E. Buama, quoted in Meyer, 1995a: 79). The implications of this remark become evident if one considers that among the Ewe there existed a fear that wealthy people might fall victim to witchcraft (*adze*) attacks inflicted upon them by poorer, envious relatives. This fear of witchcraft was part and parcel of an ethic which condemned a crude accumulation of wealth by individuals and which called for sharing one's gain with members of the extended family (Meyer, 1995a: 135–6). Of course, rich people existed none the less, but they needed to protect themselves against destructive attacks, for instance by *dzo* (medicine, or 'magic'). By offering a way out of established patterns of production, distribution and consumption, missionary Pietism clearly undermined the previous moral order.

Even during the cocoa boom people occasionally experienced their dependence upon the world market in negative terms (for instance, when cocoa prices fell), but it was only during World War II that the disastrous aspects of this dependency become fully apparent. As a result of the war, European demand for cocoa slumped; Ghanaian producers were stuck with their products and were thus unable to continue buying Western goods. After 1945, the situation improved in the colony as a whole, but not in Peki. As a result of an outbreak of the devastating cocoa disease 'swollen shoot', in the course of the 1950s cocoa cultivation ceased in the Peki area. Since there was no alternative cash crop to be cultivated for the world market, people had to either migrate to other parts of the colony or return to subsistence production, which, of course, severely limited their ability to buy Western goods. Not surprisingly, this went along with a revaluation of the extended family and related ethics, at least by those at the poor end of the scale. Thus, after the decline of cocoa cultivation, migration became virtually the only way to make money. Those who stayed at home permanently — above all married women, children, and the elderly — were comparatively poor; they had enough to eat, but were more or less dependent on their richer relatives for cash. No longer linked to the world market as producers, villagers were severely limited in their possibilities for consumption.

Western goods continued to be available in Ghana, albeit only to a small élite. Especially as a result of the Structural Adjustment Programme of the late 1980s and early 1990s, goods from the global market became increasingly common in shops and markets. Yet to the majority of people, these goods remained unaffordable, only stimulating dreams of a better life. By the time of my fieldwork in Peki in 1991/2, the consumption of foreign goods had become highly problematic. Those who were old enough remembered the first half of the twentieth century as Peki's Golden Age, that is, as a time when they could enjoy Western drinks, cigarettes and sweets, buy beautiful Western furniture and wear modern clothes made from imported materials. Now poverty and the concomitant inability to consume in accordance with their desires were the rule. Women's trade really was 'petty' and revolved mainly around American wheat flour for home baking; items such as sweets, mostly imported from Holland; cheap jewellery, mirrors, and batteries from Asian countries; powders, perfumes and soap from Europe, USA or neighbouring African countries; as well as sugar, cigarettes, candles and milk powder, and small items of clothing such as the underpants which brought such problems to the pentecostalist preacher.

Since for most people a whole kilo of sugar, a whole packet of cigarettes, or a whole tin of milk powder was too expensive, traders usually divided imported food items into affordable amounts. Through this peculiar division, petty trade thus played a crucial role in making available foreign goods to people who were unable to purchase a product as a whole, but who still longed to consume other things than those produced locally. Evidently, the purchase of a small sachet of sugar, a Dutch 'toffee' or a cheap pair of pants or bra were symbols of a longed-for lifestyle which asserted people's consumptive desires even more strongly. In a situation of scarcity, the presence of such articles in stores, as well as on films shown in video-cinemas or broadcast on TV (TVs being found in virtually every pub since the early 1990s), fed desire without ever granting satisfaction. To most people, the markers of 'civilization', which had played such a crucial role in the definition and production of Christian identity, were no longer part of real life but only the stuff of dreams.

PENTECOSTALISM

In Ghana economic decline was paralleled by the rise of new churches. These so-called Spiritual churches, which promised their members not only salvation but also material well-being in this world, became increasingly appealing to mission church members after Independence in 1958. From the 1980s onwards (a disastrous period in Ghanaian socio-economic history which was marked by severe starvation), pentecostalist churches became increasingly popular.[10] This development also took place in Peki. The pentecostalist churches which I encountered there[11] are mostly attended by young educated people (a group which is worrying about the future and at the same time experiencing a great gap between dreams and actual possibilities), and middle-aged women, who are often thrown back upon themselves and have to take care of their children without receiving much assistance from their (absent) husbands. Socially speaking, the churches are most attractive to people who are relatively powerless in the male-oriented gerontocratic power structure which still prevails in Ewe society, and who attempt to move upward economically, mainly by business and trade. While in most cases the immediate reason for a person to join a pentecostalist church is an experience of affliction, the experience of healing as such cannot account for continued church membership. Rather, in these churches people find a perspective from which to look at the changing world and to address both modernity's malcontents and its attraction (Meyer, 1995a).

Pentecostalism is not organized in one single association, but rather consists of a plethora of different, sometimes rival, churches, founded by different prophets who have seen the light.[12] All the same, I believe it is appropriate to speak of a pentecostalist complex because these churches have so much in common. Interestingly, the pentecostalist churches place much more emphasis on Christianity being a 'world religion' than the former mission churches whose theologians currently attempt to Africanize Christianity.[13] The pentecostalist churches have little interest in typically African forms of expressing faith and rather organize services and prayer sessions according to established pentecostalist forms which are similar in, for instance, Sweden (Coleman, 1996), Belgium (Roelofs, 1994), America (Lindermaier, 1995) and Ghana. There are frequent contacts with European and American

---

10. Between 1987 and 1992 the number of Pentecostal churches grew by as much as 43 per cent, the African Independent Churches by only 16 per cent. Growth rates of other types of churches also remained far below the growth rate of the Pentecostal churches (Survey of the 'Ghana Evangelism Committee', 1993).

11. I conducted research in the Lord's Pentecostal Church (*Agbelengor*) and the Evangelical Presbyterian Church 'of Ghana'. These two churches split away from the Evangelical Presbyterian Church, the church resulting from the NMG, in 1961 and 1991 respectively. For the history of these secessions see Meyer (1995a: 184ff).

12. Only a restricted number of pentecostalist churches has been accepted into the Ghanaian Pentecostal Council. By pentecostalist churches, I mean all those churches within and outside this council which share the features outlined below.

13. The attempts of the Moderator N. K. Dzobo to Africanize the form and content of the Christian message in the Evangelical Presbyterian Church met so much resistance by a pentecostalist prayer group in the church that it split away from the mother church and became independent as the Evangelical Presbyterian Church of Ghana. On this conflict, see Meyer (1992).

pentecostalist associations, who assist in the setting up of so-called Bible Schools, where pentecostalist preachers are trained. Preachers such as the German Reinhard Bonnke or the American Morris Cerullo are well known in Ghana, and in many houses in Peki I saw posters advertising past 'crusades'.

The pentecostalist churches present themselves as representatives of global Christianity — some even have 'international', 'world' or 'global' in their name — and claim to be able to provide correct knowledge about the state of the world. People attending these churches are taken beyond the scope of local culture, which is denounced as limited, and provided with revelations about what is going on beneath the surface of the global political economy. The idea circulates — stimulated by the book of Revelation — that the end of the world has come near and that Satan is trying to prevent people from following God and being saved. There is, as it were, a worldwide conspiracy in which everybody on earth has become entangled, if only unconsciously. Since Satan can operate on a worldwide scale only by making use of local agents, local pentecostalist churches are to engage in the struggle against Satan's particular representatives. The global war against the Devil is to be fought everywhere.

The way the Ghanaian pentecostalist churches present themselves is in marked contrast to the established mission churches, which are criticized for failing to help their members to retain health and wealth, and to the Spiritual churches, which are accused of doing so by making clandestine use of traditional spirits, that is, Satan's demons. The pentecostalist churches claim to rely solely on the Word, which is thought to be able to both invoke and represent the Holy Spirit, and vehemently oppose reliance on objects such as amulets, candles and incense in healing practices. Representing the world in terms of an opposition between God and the Devil, they offer their members an elaborate discourse about evil spirits, which includes a whole range of local spiritual entities such as old deities, ancestor spirits, witchcraft, native medicines (*dzo*, a term translated as both 'magic' or 'juju' in popular discourse), as well as 'modern' magical powers derived from India or from the bottom of the ocean. All these entities are said to be servants of Satan whose worship will make a person's spirit and body accessible to his evil machinations, which will eventually result in destruction and death.

The obsession with demonology is one of the most salient features of the new pentecostalist churches (Gifford, 1994; Meyer, 1992, 1994). Although the belief in the existence of the Devil is central to many Ewe Christians irrespective of the church they attend, it is the pentecostalist churches which continuously dwell on the boundary between Christianity and 'heathendom'. In contrast to the mission churches they find it important to keep on fighting Satan, who is held to operate in the guise of evil spirits, and therefore offer their members rituals of exorcism which are to do away with poverty and sickness.

Pentecostalists distinguish between the realm of 'the physical' (in Ewe: *le nutilame*), that is, the visible world, and 'the spiritual' (in Ewe: *le gbogbome*), that is, the invisible world, and contend that the latter determines the former. Consequently, sickness and mishaps are understood to be a result of evil spirits intruding into a person's spirit and body. In their view, there is a spiritual war going on between God and the Devil, and this is taking place both in the world as a whole and within a person's individual spirit. Pentecostalist preachers claim to be able to penetrate the invisible and to bring about physical healing and improvement of material conditions by fighting a spiritual battle against demons.

During prayer meetings members are protected against possible intrusions of evil spirits, so that they cannot be harmed by, for instance, *adze* or *dzo* which envious family members and neighbours may wish to inflict upon them. People experiencing bodily and spiritual weaknesses are called forward separately and if they are found to be possessed, attempts are made to deliver them from the powers of darkness which are disturbing them and to fill them with the Holy Spirit.[14] Deliverance is to ensure that a person is severed from all previous ties with spiritual entities, as well as from the social relations they imply. In the end, prayers create individuals whose spirits are fully possessed by the Holy Spirit and separated from the complex for which the Devil stands.[15] Significantly, demonic possession is not confined to the individuals experiencing it, but rather is a matter of public interest. The exorcism of demons takes place in front of the congregation, and pentecostalist churches offer their members the possibility to listen to testimonies from people who were involved with evil spirits in the past.

Pentecostalist Attitudes Towards the Market and Consumption

Prosperity

One of the great concerns of the members of pentecostalist churches is to be successful in life. In the face of inflation and economic decline, pentecostalists seek divine protection to carry on and, if possible, progress. It will not come

---

14.   Each exorcist attends to one person upon whom he lays his hand. In doing so the exorcists attempt to continue Jesus's work on earth, who also liberated people from evil spirits. As long as the afflicted person remains calm under the exorcist's hand, he or she is considered as being filled with God's Spirit. But if a person starts moving, this is attributed to the presence of evil spirits who feel disturbed by the power of the Holy Spirit touching the person through the mediation of the preacher. Once this occurs, the exorcist calls upon his colleagues to drive out the demon who is considered to harm the afflicted person (for a detailed account of this see Meyer, 1995a: Ch. 9 and 10).

15.   Significantly, this contrasts sharply with traditional healing practices which aim at the restoration of social ties (on traditional Ewe religion see, for example, Rivière 1981; Spieth, 1906, 1911; Surgy, 1988). Pentecostalism's remedy against mishaps and sickness clearly is individualization. Elsewhere I have demonstrated this in more detail (1995a: 247–9). On deliverance, see also Meyer (1998).

as a surprise, therefore, that money and goods are important themes in pentecostalist discourse.[16] Several authors have pointed out that all over the world pentecostalists embrace a so-called prosperity gospel (for example, Coleman, 1996; Gifford, 1994) which teaches that God will bless true 'born again' Christians with prosperity. During my fieldwork I saw how successful preachers proudly attributed their wealth to God, a claim which certainly attracted people into their churches.[17]

Most of the persons attending a 'National Deliverance Meeting' organized by The Lord's Pentecostal Church in April 1992 in its 'healing station' at Tokokoe,[18] were traders seeking success in business. In a fasting service organized by the same church in Peki Blengo I heard the pastor ask all members to rise, close their eyes and fill in a cheque in their minds which was then sent up to heaven; the people were assured that God would sign this cheque and that they would, in the future, receive the money requested — if only they believed. Afterwards a woman stood up and gave testimony that she had sent such an invisible cheque to the Almighty some time ago and that shortly afterwards a relative in Europe had sent her the very same amount for which she had asked, thereby implying that God had used the relative as his tool. One could hear similar testimonies in other pentecostalist churches whose congregations would all offer special prayers for success in business.

The contribution of pentecostalist churches to their members' financial efforts is above all symbolic. Unlike the NMG in the early days, pentecostalist churches do not actively support members in matters of production and do not run trading companies. It is emphasized that people should try to earn their money through hard work, and there are prayers in order to make these efforts successful; by just sitting down and praying one will not progress (though prayers may play an important part). In the sphere of accumulation and distribution the pentecostalist churches also play an important, although again symbolic, role. By offering protection for a person's individual business and by cutting symbolically the blood ties connecting a person with his or her family, pentecostalist churches promote economic individualism. In this way they lead people beyond the confines of their family, or accommodate those who already find themselves thrown back upon themselves, thereby translating the burden of being let down into the virtue of individual responsibility. In symbolic terms pentecostalist churches thus promote an ethics supporting the

---

16. Although not necessarily in a solely positive sense: on pentecostalist ideas about satanic riches (money achieved in exchange for sacrificing a beloved close relative) see Meyer (1995b).
17. In turn, an increase of members will make those running a church richer.
18. Like many other pentecostalist churches, this church runs a 'healing station' or 'prayer camp' because its leaders believe that in severe cases of possession persons can only be exorcised if they are taken out of their family's reach of influence. In this station, exorcism prayers are offered once a week. These prayers attract not only residents but also people from the surrounding area. Occasionally, the church organizes prayer sessions on a national scale.

'spirit of capitalism'. This, however, is of little consequence for the life conditions of the majority of the members. Pentecostalist churches cannot offer efficient remedies against economic misery on a large scale and most members definitely are not rich. Rather, pentecostalism provides an imaginary space in which people may address their longing for a modern, individual and prosperous way of life.

Yet, this positive attitude towards prosperity is only one aspect of pentecostalists' stance towards trade and consumption. Recalling the account of the sexy underpants with which we started, we may assume that goods also have a dark side; this side, which has been neglected in the literature on African Pentecostalism at least, will occupy us in the remainder of this section.

The Dangers of the Market

As already noted, many women in pentecostalist churches engage in trade. They share the widespread fear of strange things going on in the market which would not meet the eye but which might have very severe consequences 'in the physical'. This links to the idea that, next to the visible, there is also an invisible witch market going on, in which meat is sold. This meat is taken 'spiritually' from human beings who are eventually 'eaten up' by witches until they fall sick and die. Of course, one has to take great care that one does not fall victim to these witches who are, above all, motivated by envy and seek to do away with successful traders or to prevent business women from ever prospering. Pentecostalists regard the Holy Spirit as the sole entity able to protect them against being eaten by witches and to provide at least some of them with the much-desired 'spirit of discernment', that is, the ability to peep into the otherwise invisible realm.

Another dangerous aspect of the market is the presence of successful trading women who are suspected of having made a deal with occult powers. There is, for instance, a rumour according to which certain traders carry a snake in their vagina which will make them rich in exchange for abstaining from having children (see Meyer, 1995b: 245). Another rumour has it that certain women have a snake lying at the bottom of their pot from which they sell food, in order to make it taste so good that customers will become addicted and always return. Some of these cheats are said to have been exposed by brave pentecostalist preachers whose prayers have made the snake (a representative of the Devil, of course) appear at the surface of the pot; all customers ran away. Many women also complain that traders use other types of *juju* in order to attract customers; why otherwise would certain women prosper whereas others, who sell the very same items, do not?

Inquiring why pentecostalists are against this type of trade *dzo*, which after all works so well, I learned that the danger with the purchase of trade *dzo* is that the trader will be required to observe certain taboos and to humble himself or herself before the *dzo*'s spirit. The problem is that, once the traders are rich, they will forget these requirements, for this is how prosperous people are. As a result, the *dzo* that made them rich will turn against them and make them poor or mad. Against this background it is not surprising that pentecostalism is attractive to traders: by offering prayers for the progress of business it provides assistance which is in many respects complementary to popular trade magic while, at the same time, it does not involve a pact with a destructive power.

These types of rumours, which focus on the traders themselves, have circulated since cocoa cultivation was taken up on a massive scale and cocoa farmers became increasingly indebted to traders who offered them goods in advance for the forthcoming season's crop. Debrunner (1961: 71) reported that traders were regarded as people who made money through magical means and were therefore able to wield power over less rich and less influential people. In contrast to the mission churches, which discard such ideas as superstitions and propagate a secular view of the market, pentecostalist churches take the widespread fear of the market as a magical place as a point of departure, thereby engaging actively in the enchantment of the economy. By representing the market as a domain of possible activities of Satan's agents, and themselves as capable of providing adequate protection against these powers, they confirm people's fear that trade is a dangerous and insecure affair — a fear which is, of course, very much to the point since global trade works according to laws which are not transparent from a local perspective, but which nevertheless have very real (and often negative) consequences for one's own business. Next to the rumours about the dangers of the market there are nowadays an increasing number of narratives focusing on the dangers imbued in the commodities themselves. In this way, not only trade, but also consumption itself is represented as a dangerous matter.

The Dangers of Consumption

In pentecostalist circles many stories dealing with the dangers imbued in goods are spread through popular magazines, movies and songs, public sermons and confessions, and by way of gossip. In this context the realm of the sea is a matter of great importance. According to popular imagination, the bottom of the ocean is the dwelling place of *Mami Water*, that is, mermaids and mermen who may appear on earth in the shape of beautiful people and entice human beings to become their spouses. Once married to a *Mami Water* spirit, a person is no longer allowed to marry a human being and cannot have children, but in exchange for sacrificing the capability of sexual reproduction one will receive riches derived from the bottom of the ocean. This narrative, which circulates along the entire African coast (Drewal, 1988; Fabian, 1978; Wendl, 1991; Wicker, n.d.), has recently been taken up by pentecostalists who have incorporated it in their imagination of the satanic and claim that *Mami Water* spirits are agents of the Devil.[19]

The confession laid down by the Nigerian Emmanuel Eni in his booklet 'Delivered from the Powers of Darkness' (1988) is extremely popular in Ghanaian pentecostalist circles and even in the West African diaspora in Europe, because it is considered a first-hand account of the realm of darkness — Eni only became a 'born again' Christian after having a serious involvement with Satan.[20] In this confession, which I have examined in some detail elsewhere (Meyer, 1995b; see also Marshall, 1993: 227; Wicker n.d.: 19), Eni makes some revealing remarks about the relationship between the Devil and consumption. Recounting his arrival in the realm of the *Mami Water* spirits at the bottom of the sea, which, as everybody knows, abounds with goods, he tells his readers that he even went into the scientific laboratory where scientists and psychiatrists joined forces to design 'flashy cars', the 'latest weapons', 'cloth, perfumes and assorted types of cosmetics', 'electronics, computers and alarms' (Eni, 1988: 18). Eni does not tire of warning people that the Devil has told him 'that since man likes flashy and fanciful things he would continue to manufacture these things and make sure man has no time for his God . . .' (ibid: 22). Since one of the areas where the Devil would win souls was in secondary schools, he would make sure to send satanic agents there who would tempt schoolgirls with 'cosmetics, dresses, underwear, books, provisions and money' (ibid: 32) to forget about God. Eni also warns his readers about the dangers of the market: 'The market is one of the major areas of operations . . . Certain fanciful products sold in the market e.g. necklaces, lipsticks, perfumes and food items such as sardines "queen of the coast" etc. have strange origin' (ibid: 54).

Eni is not very clear about how these objects 'of strange origin' work upon their owners: do they simply distract people's minds from God or do they connect people to Satan in a more active way? Put differently, do the fanciful things have a power of their own by which they can make their owner behave in a way in which he or she would not behave without them? Answers to these questions can be gained by a closer investigation of pentecostalist praxis. For, all over the country, pentecostalists not only read Eni's account, but also supplement it with similar experiences.

That there is a constant need to be suspicious about (fanciful) goods was one of the most important messages of the prayer sessions I encountered in Pekị. During one prayer session I witnessed a preacher calling forward a seventeen-year-old girl who was wearing a Western dress with a flowered design, a belt with a lock in the form of a butterfly, a necklace with a coloured

---

19. The confessions of two pentecostalist girls about their involvement with Mami Water spirits inspired the Ghanaian script writer and film producer Socrate Safo to make 'Women in Love I and II' (released by Movie Africa Productions in 1997).

20. The fact that I once saw a person reading this pamphlet in a bus in Amsterdam testifies to the global spread of this account.

heart and earrings in the shape of strawberries. According to the preacher she was related, through these adornments, to *Mami Water* spirits who would make her indulge in 'flirting' and spend money on fanciful things. Therefore he asked her to do away with these things; a request which she, however, refused to meet. The preacher warned the people present that by adorning themselves young women would risk devoting themselves to *Mami Water* spirits and thus forego marriage and childbirth in their future adult life. Clearly, for pentecostalist preachers the possession of fashionable jewellery amounts to more than mere distraction from God. It rather implies a state of being possessed by satanic powers.

In the same vein, during my stay in Ghana in 1996, pentecostalist preachers kept on warning female members to be very careful about Rasta-hair, through which they would be linked to *Mami Water* spirits. Hair-dressers told me that while many customers would at least pray over the artificial hair before it was woven into their own hair, others would refrain from wearing it altogether. During deliverance services, too, preachers used to command women whom they suspected of being possessed by marine spirits to take off their Rasta look.

Pentecostalist discourse on consumption not only describes fashionable adornments as dangerous, but also targets other goods that are regarded as solid prestige items which many people aspire to possess. In Peki Avetile I heard a young man confess in public about his engagement with the powers of darkness prior to his conversion (for an elaborate presentation and discussion of this case see Meyer, 1995c: 55ff). Among other things he said that a demon had taught him to make appear before his mind's eye any place he wanted to see. He often gazed at shops in America and Europe which were filled with commodities such as bicycles, watches and TV sets — goods he longed for but did not possess in real life. The demon told him how 'to convert these goods into the demonic world', that is, to bring them under satanic control, by sprinkling lavender water on the ground in every shop he saw, thereby making sure that anybody buying any of these items would be tied to the Devil. Therefore the items would exert a destructive influence on their owners and could only be used to 'glorify' Satan. This implied that nothing productive could be done with these commodities, they would spoil easily, and eventually their owner would end up poor. He said that virtually nobody could ever be aware of what he had done to these objects because he operated in the 'spiritual realm' into which only those few people who 'were in the Holy Spirit' could penetrate.

Since the young man made his confession in public, many people were able to share his experiences and relate them to their own lives. Many were shocked to learn that Western commodities with a commonly accepted use value such as watches, bicycles or TV-sets — objects which pentecostalists also desired and which meant much more than certain types of cosmetics and jewellery 'from under the sea' — were also possible tools of Satan. In addition, the young preacher's account of what happened to him through his underpants made clear that consumption of objects 'converted to the Devil' or 'of strange origin' could also be dangerous for Christians. Thus, even 'born again' Christians were not safe and ran the risk of being subjected to Satan through consumption, even without being aware of it. I noticed a certain eagerness regarding revelations of the realm of darkness which were considered to be of great help for one's conduct in the world. In this way the world became increasingly insecure day by day, but at the same time pentecostalism offered appropriate remedies to ward off Satan's intrusive attempts. Hence the advice to abstain from the purchase of certain fashionable things and to purify all other commodities ranging from food items to electronic articles through prayer, that is, by predicating God's spirit upon the object.

De-fetishizing Commodities

At first sight, the pentecostalist discourse on consumption may appear to be a misrepresentation of global economic facts and be dismissed as a product of fantasy which blurs the boundary between people and things. This is not a fruitful perspective, however: a closer look at the pentecostalist poetics of consumption can offer insight into people's experience and view of globalization.

Perhaps the most salient feature of the pentecostalist discourse on consumption is the emphasis laid on the possibly 'strange origin' of Western commodities. It is due to this origin that a commodity may be dangerous. By pointing out that, since there is a gap between a commodity's creation and its appearance on the local market, each commodity encapsulates its origin and 'biography' (Kopytoff, 1986), pentecostalist discourse problematizes the alienation which consumers experience *vis-à-vis* foreign commodities. The point here is not so much that under the condition of global capitalism people only have a very limited, partial view on the process in the course of which commodities are produced, marketed and consumed (Appadurai, 1986: 54), but rather that they are unable to control this process. In short, the problem is not the inability to understand the market, but rather the inability to fully control it. This holds especially true in a country such as Ghana, where the value of imported foreign goods far outweighs that of exported raw materials, and where virtually all commodities (except locally produced foodstuff) are encountered only in a phase in which they are offered (and desired) as consumer goods, not in the phase of production.

By stressing that commodities may be dangerous because of their past, pentecostalism suggests that the appropriation of Western goods through consumption is problematic and involves consumers in the danger zone of inverted possession: rather than possessing the commodity, the owner risks being possessed by the commodity. The commodity can thus not be properly possessed because it has itself become a thing which is directed by powers outside a person's own will and which exercises control over his or her body at certain moments, thereby defying the modern ideal of the autonomous self — a fetish (cf. Pietz, 1985: 10ff). This modern fetish is, ironically, similar to the religious objects burned by the missionaries earlier on. Fetishism, having shifted from the shrine to the market, strikes back. In both cases the fetish clearly is a material fixation of historical cross-cultural encounters which occupies a new space between the known and the unknown (Pietz, 1985). Both are expressions of a tension between the striving for proprietorship of one's self and the notion that a person is to a large extent 'operated' through spiritual powers. Whereas the representation of local gods as fetishes criticizes the local religion for failing to let people own themselves (the main project of Western missionary societies and their local converts), the representation of commodities as fetishes is a critique on capitalist consumption. In this way, the very means by which local converts were to achieve Christian identity (and thus proprietorship of the self) are suspected of making people lose this identity.

In order to grasp the pentecostalist notion of the animated commodity it is useful to turn briefly to the Marxist notion of commodity fetishism. I do not intend to discuss this in any detail (but see Carver, 1987; Pietz, 1993; Taussig, 1980), but will merely summarize those aspects which are of immediate relevance to our comparison. Marxist theory regards commodity fetishism as the appearance of the products of human labour as autonomous entities and explains this 'false consciousness' as being based on an objective illusion which conceals a commodity's origin in exploitative social relations. Marx used the concept of fetishism primarily in order to reveal the true nature of commodities as a product of labour from which its producers have become alienated and which they are unable to appropriate. Here, making visible the exploitation from which a commodity originates destroys — or at least lays bare — its fetishistic appearance.

By contrast, pentecostalists actively fetishize commodities by referring to their unknown and hidden origin. Here awareness of the commodity's origin does not drive away the fetish, but rather makes it. By exposing the past, hitherto hidden life of the commodity, pentecostalist preachers claim to inform people about its true nature. In this view, commodities as they are found in the market truly are fetishes; the problem is that most people are not aware of this, and regard them as harmless goods. Fetishism here is not an illusory product of false consciousness, but an awareness which is able to explain, and eventually overcome, alienation. Only a commodity stripped of its past and embedded firmly in the present through prayer is a commodity in the sense of current economic discourse.

Of course, the origin referred to by pentecostalists is not the one which Marx had in mind, but a more spiritual one which is beyond the visible (albeit distanced) processes of production and marketing. For pentecostalists commodities become fetishes because the Devil appropriated them before they appeared in the market (or at the time when they are exposed in shops).

Through the supposedly innocent act of buying, the consumer is linked with Satan. Entering into a relationship with the diabolic, owners lose their own will and identity, their spirits and bodies are reduced to signs which refer to, and even 'glorify', the power of the Devil. Consumption thus threatens to turn people into powerless signs — metonyms of the satanic — and in order to prevent this, one has to be aware of the fetish-aspect of commodities and prevent them from conquering one's spirit.

What is interesting here is the close association of Satan with the global market as the source and target of desire. It is through this circularity that people are drawn into its reach and come to adopt what Campbell (1987: 89) called the 'spirit of modern consumerism', that is, modern people's continuously frustrated hedonistic expectation that the purchase of the latest fashion would yield enduring pleasure. Pentecostalist preachers clearly leave no doubt that the Devil makes use of, above all, fanciful, designed goods which follow fashion and which are usually employed to attract the attention of the opposite sex. By allowing themselves to be charmed by such objects, people spend all their time feeding their desire for the new things which continually appear on the market. The true fetish, then, is the lust for pleasure and luxury which subverts a person's own individual will and locks him or her in the circularity of the market as the source and target of desire. Pentecostalists warn young people especially that their own (sexual) desire may eventually turn against them and make them forget and forego what really matters in life: instead of preparing themselves for marriage and childbirth they live in a dreamworld in which they are subordinated to spirits, bereft of a personality of their own.

With this warning, the pentecostalist stance towards consumption resembles that of the nineteenth-century Pietist missionaries. Contemporary pentecostalists' 'broad path', from which they struggle to stay away, is the splendid realm under the sea. As in the case of the missionaries, this puritan critique of fashion (and of sex as a means to acquire these prestigious commodities)[21] does not, of course, mean a general abstinence from consumption of Western goods in practice. Rather, it signals that consumption is a dangerous matter which requires highly self-conscious consumers who should not keep running after everything new and who should rather control their desire.

Significantly, the pentecostalist discourse on consumption does not stop at exposing the dangers of commodities. It also claims to have the power to provide a safe alley towards consumption. By turning church members into vessels of the Holy Spirit, who are capable of fighting Satan and his demons through prayer, pentecostalism empowers believers to transform commodities into mere objects. It provides them with a ritual able 'to plumb the magicalities of modernity' (Comaroff and Comaroff, 1993: xxx). By invoking God's power over every commodity bought, they perform 'exit rites' for the commodity,

---

21. According to this Puritan view, sex should be used for reproductive, not consumptive ends.

through which it is purified from its polluting past in the global market — in short, it is de-fetishized. Stripped of its history, it is safe to carry into its owner's house. Through this process, the object is subordinated to its owner; now it can no longer act as a fetish nor turn its owner into a satanic sign. Only through the act of prayer — the predication of the Word upon a thing — an owner thus truly becomes an owner, that is, a person able to overcome the alienating gap between a commodity's origin and its appearance on the local market, and to appropriate it through consumption.

Of course, this is not a linear project which results in the creation of self-determined persons who have for ever escaped the danger of inverted possession. It would be a regrettable omission to reduce the pentecostalist discourse on consumption to the successful construction of modern notions of selfhood and identity, firmly rooted beyond the powers of darkness which defy these notions. As I stated earlier, revelations about the realm of darkness, which bring about the, albeit imaginary, transgression into the forbidden zone of excessive sexual indulgence and waste of money and things, are extremely popular among pentecostalists. What is appealing here is 'the unspeakable mystique of the excessive, the abrogation of the useful, and the sensuous no less than logical intimacy binding overabundance to transgression in a forwards and backwards movement that is difficult to put in words' (Taussig, 1995: 395). The pentecostalist discourse on consumption clearly addresses not only the dangers and possibilities of consumption, but also offers a virtual space — a dreamland located at the bottom of the ocean — to dream about its forbidden pleasures which defy any rational, utilitarian stance. It takes seriously people's wildest dreams in which they lose themselves in their desires, and offers them the possibility to claim ownership over things: a dialectic of being possessed and possessing.[22]

CONCLUSION

For obvious reasons, the study of consumption has recently been placed high on the anthropological agenda. Since it seems that people confront the global to a large extent through foreign commodities, consumption has become a privileged field in the study of the interaction between the local and the global. Advocating the 'acknowledgement' of consumption as a cultural practice which is located in time and space (Miller, 1995b), these studies oppose the still common notion that mass consumption of global products would destroy cultural authenticity at the expense of homogenization.[23] Yet

---

22. Thus, pentecostalist discourse clearly goes further than the local rumours about devil-contracts described by Taussig. It not only permits transgression into a virtual realm of abundance and excess, but also enables people to consume without losing themselves.
23. For a critique of anthropologists' search for 'authentic culture' see especially Thomas (1991).

it is undeniable that in the context of globalization people increasingly consume resources which were not created in their own society — which are thus not 'authentic' — and, as Miller (1994) argues, have to be appropriated through mass consumption. In other words, consumption — and not, as Marx thought, production — entails the possibility of overcoming alienation and creating local identity.[24]

I agree that consumption may have the capacity to create identity at certain times and places (as, for instance, in the initial phase of missionization among the Ewe), but there is more to consumption than this constructive aspect. Our examination of the Ghanaian pentecostalist discourse on consumption reveals that the appropriation of commodities may be highly problematic. Yet until now, this aspect of consumption has hardly been an object of ethnography. Somehow the assumption prevails that globalization and the desire for Western commodities go hand-in-hand,[25] and it looks as if the main problem which people face in the field of consumption is the unequal distribution of money to buy Western commodities. While the witchcraft accusations and suspicions that may result from asymmetrical power relations and unequal consumptive possibilities have recently become an object of increased anthropological investigation,[26] consumption as a practice has not yet received the attention it probably deserves.

While not denying that people may strongly desire foreign goods, this article has concentrated on the problematic aspects of their consumption. It has shown that in order to retain control over Western goods, a person has to strip them of their fetishistic properties, thereby making use of religion in order to produce them as commodities in the sense of Western economists' prose. Here consumption does not merely entail a practice of appropriating objects, but also a highly complex reflection on the culturally specific nature of commodities in which anti-materialist and hedonistic inclinations are in conflict with each other — an interplay of anxiety and desire (cf. Taussig, 1995). Rather than simply providing building blocks for the construction of identity and selfhood (Friedman, 1994),[27] consumption entails the risk

---

24. Although Miller emphasizes consumption's constructive aspects, he is aware that consumption may be problematic. He defines commodities which a person is unable to appropriate through consumption as fetishes (Miller, 1990).

25. This may, of course, be so in particular cases. See for instance Gandalou (1989) on 'la Sape'; i.e. the struggle of young inhabitants of Brazzaville to accumulate famous designer clothes from France and Italy (cf. also Friedman, 1994: 105ff).

26. See, for instance, the work of Geschiere (for example, 1995) and Thoden van Velzen and Van Wetering (for example, 1988).

27. Friedman (1994: 104) views consumption as 'an aspect of a more general strategy or set of strategies for the establishment and/or maintenance of selfhood'. I disagree with this view not only because it leaves behind all too easily the problematic aspects of consumption to which I have tried to draw attention in this paper, but also because Friedman neglects the materiality of things by subsuming consumption under identity construction.

(or, perhaps, the temptation) of losing, rather than gaining, one's self (and hence one's Christian identity).[28]

Another important aspect of consumption which has not yet gained sufficient attention is its imaginary dimension in a situation of scarcity (but see Veenis, 1994), as well as the capacity of religious organizations to take up the dreams arising in such a situation and control the consumptive practices of their adherents. As we saw, Christian missions successfully converted the Ewe into consumers of Western goods which became not only symbols of 'civilization' but played an active part in the subversion of traditional patterns of production, distribution and consumption. While the desire for Western goods, which was generated from the beginnings of missionization, remained, actual life conditions changed in such a way that Christians have become to a large extent unable to realize in practice the 'civilized' way of life which Christianity is supposed to entail. In a situation of material scarcity and bereft of their consumptive possibilities, Christians are forced into an extreme form of 'innerworldly ascesis' which does not even allow them to re-produce themselves as Christians in real life any longer. Hence many are virtually taken away into a dream world under the sea, where the things one's heart desires abound.

Pentecostalism helps people, albeit temporarily, out of this dream; not because it regards the *Mami Water* imagery as just fancy, but exactly because it confirms the spiritual reality of this imagery and maintains that *Mami Water* spirits may have effects on anybody, not only those who involve themselves in a spiritual marriage with these beings. By pointing out that the Devil may not only appropriate the abodes of local deities but also commodities as fetishes, the taken-for-granted association of Western goods with Christian civilization is opened up (and this, of course, follows the actual state of things). Now it is possible to not only demonize local African religion, but also the global capitalist economy to which many people in Ghana — at least those who do not (or no longer) engage in cocoa cultiva-tion — are basically linked as consumers.[29]

By representing commodities from the global market as enchanted by Satan's demons, and consumption as the major battlefield where the war between him and God takes place, pentecostalism in Ghana elaborates upon,

---

28. I strongly agree with the plea of Rouse (1995), not to regard identity construction as a universal concern of all cultures but rather to understand the globally occurring quest for identity as part and parcel of Western bourgeois hegemonic projects. The pentecostalist concern with the fetish (both in the form of the local god and the Western commodity) clearly testifies to a struggle for modern personhood without ever attaining it once and for all.

29. Given that people in this area are linked to the global market above all as consumers, not as producers, it is not surprising that consumption, not production, is represented as a field of satanic activity. Here lies the main difference between the present paper and studies such as the one by Taussig (1980) which focused on Columbian plantation workers' and Bolivian mineworkers' fantasies of devil contracts.

and confirms, people's suspicions about the global market. Yet significantly, there is no advice to believers to abstain from the consumption of all imported goods (only from a very few things — a sort of symbolic abstinence). In pentecostalist discourse, no value judgement is predicated upon globalization. This is not a question of good or bad, but a matter of danger and control.[30] Pentecostalist discourse emphasizes the dangers imbued in commodities and, at the same time, presents itself as the sole instance which is truly able to help people *handle* globalization. It claims to connect people with a global community of 'born again' Christians whose form of worship follows more or less the same pattern (Johannesen, 1994) and to offer true revelations about the state of the world. Local circumstances are understood in the light of this knowledge. Pentecostalist churches thus clearly offer people a scope of identification far beyond local culture. At the same time, the incorporation of the local into the global is problematized. The message is that people need pentecostalism in order to disenchant commodities and that neither the state nor the former mission churches would be able to achieve this; only through pentecostalism can people be connected with the 'world' without running the risk of being overrun. I contend that this version of Christianity is so successful in Ghana because it takes as a point of departure both the desire to have access to the world *and* existing fears about the nature of the global market and one's connection with it. Affirming that the market is an abode of invisible satanic forces, adherents can claim that a pentecostal religion is needed in order to profit from, rather than fall victim to, globalization.

REFERENCES

Amenumey, D. E. K. (1964) 'The Ewe People and the Coming of European Rule, 1850–1914'. MA thesis, University of London.

Amenumey, D. E. K. (1986) *The Ewe in Pre-Colonial Times. A Political History with Special Emphasis on the Anlo, Ge and Krepi.* Ho: E. P. Church Press.

Appadurai, Arjun (1986) 'Introduction: Commodities and the Politics of Value', in A. Appadurai (ed.) *The Social Life of Things. Commodities in Cultural Perspective,* pp. 3–63. Cambridge: Cambridge University Press.

Appiah, Kwame Anthony (1992) *In My Father's House: Africa in the Philosophy of Culture.* New York and Oxford: Oxford University Press.

Asare, E. B. (1973) 'Akwamu-Peki Relations in the Eighteenth and Nineteenth Centuries'. MA thesis, University of Ghana.

---

30. Comaroff and Comaroff (1993: xxx) have aptly caught the irony of 'modernity' (as 'a Eurocentric vision of universal teleology') in their statement that 'the more rationalistic and disenchanted the terms in which it [modernity] is presented to "others", the more magical, impenetrable, inscrutable, uncontrollable, darkly dangerous seem its signs, commodities, and practices'. Yet I do not agree with their view that it is necessarily 'malcontent' which gathers 'in this fissure between assertive rationalities and perceived magicalities' (ibid). As this paper shows people may also be striving to appropriate modernity because they find certain aspects very attractive.

Campbell, Colin (1987) *The Romantic Ethic and the Spirit of Modern Consumerism*. Oxford: Basil Blackwell.

Carrier, James C. (1995) *Gifts and Commodities. Exchange and Western Capitalism since 1700*. London and New York: Routledge.

Carver, Terrell (1987) *A Marx Dictionary*. Cambridge: Polity Press.

Comaroff, Jean and John Comaroff (eds) (1993) *Modernity and Its Malcontents. Ritual and Power in Postcolonial Africa*. Chicago, IL: The University of Chicago Press.

Coleman, Simon (1996) 'All-Consuming Faith. Language, Material Culture and World-Transformation Among Protestant Evangelicals', *Etnofoor* IX(1): 26–47.

Debrunner, Hans W. (1961) *Witchcraft in Ghana. A Study of the Belief in Destructive Witches and its Effect on the Akan Tribe*. Kumasi: Presbyterian Book Depot.

Drewal, Henry John (1988) 'Performing the Other. *Mami Wata* Worship in Africa', *The Drama Review* 32(2): 160–85.

Eni, Emmanuel (1988) *Delivered from the Powers of Darkness* (2nd edn.). Ibadan: Scripture Union.

Fabian, Johannes (1978) 'Popular Culture in Africa: Findings and Conjectures', *Africa* 48(4): 315–34.

Friedman, Jonathan (1994) *Cultural Identity and Global Process*. London: Sage Publications.

Gandoulou, J. D. (1989) *Au coeur de la sape: moeurs et aventures des Congolais à Paris*. Paris: L'Harmattan.

Geschiere, Peter (1995) *Sorcellerie et politique en Afrique. La viande des autres*. Paris: Karthala.

Ghana Evangelism Committee (1993) *National Church Survey. 1993 Update. Facing the Unfinished Task of the Church in Ghana*. Accra: Assemblies of God Literature Centre.

Gifford, Paul (1994) 'Ghana's Charismatic Churches', *Journal of Religion in Africa* 64(3): 241–65.

Gudeman, Stephen (1986) *Economics as Culture. Models and Metaphors of Livelihood*. London: Routledge & Kegan Paul.

Horton, R. (1971) 'African Conversion', *Africa* 41(2): 86–108.

Horton, R. (1975) 'On the Rationality of Conversion. Part I & II', *Africa* 45(3): 219–35, 373–99.

Jenkins, Paul (1978) 'Towards a Definition of the Pietism of Württemberg as a Missionary Movement'. Paper prepared for African Studies Association of the United Kingdom Conference 'Whites in Africa — Whites as Missionaries', Oxford.

Johannesen, Stanley (1994) 'Third Generation Pentecostal Language: Continuity and Change in Collective Perceptions', in K. Poewe (ed.) *Charismatic Christianity as a Global Culture*, pp. 176–99. Columbia, SC: University of South Carolina Press.

Kopytoff, Igor (1986) 'The Cultural Biography of Things: Commoditization as Process', in A. Appadurai (ed.) *The Social Life of Things. Commodities in Cultural Perspective*, pp. 64–91. Cambridge: Cambridge University Press.

Lindermaier, Orestis (1995) ' "The Beast of the Revelation". American Fundamentalist Christianity and the European Union', *Etnofoor* 7(1): 27–46.

Marshall, Ruth (1993) ' "Power in the Name of Jesus": Social Transformation and Pentecostalism in Western Nigeria "Revisited" ', in T. Ranger and O. Vaughan (eds) *Legitimacy and the State in Twentieth Century Africa*, pp. 213–46. Basingstoke: Macmillan.

Meyer, Birgit (1992) ' "If You Are a Devil You Are a Witch and, If You Are a Witch You Are a Devil". The Integration of "Pagan" Ideas into the Conceptual Universe of Ewe Christians in Southeastern Ghana', *The Journal of Religion in Africa* 22(2): 98–132.

Meyer, Birgit (1994) 'Beyond Syncretism: Translation and Diabolization in the Appropriation of Protestantism in Africa', in Ch. Stewart and R. Shaw (eds) *Syncretism/Anti-syncretism. The Politics of Religious Synthesis*, pp. 45–67. London: Routledge.

Meyer, Birgit (1995a) 'Translating the Devil. An African Appropriation of Pietist Protestantism. The Case of the Peki Ewe, 1847–1992'. PhD thesis, University of Amsterdam.

Meyer, Birgit (1995b) ' "Delivered from the Powers of Darkness". Confessions about Satanic Riches in Christian Ghana', *Africa* 65(2): 236–55.

Meyer, Birgit (1995c) 'Magic, Mermaids and Modernity. The Attraction of Pentecostalism in Africa', *Etnofoor* 8(2): 47–67.

Meyer, Birgit (1997a) 'Christianity and the Ewe Nation. On the Encounter Between German Pietist Missionaries and Ewe Mission Workers'. Paper presented at the Conference 'Identity in Africa', University of Leiden (22–3 May).

Meyer, Birgit (1997b) 'Christian Mind and Worldly Matters. Religion and Materiality in Nineteenth-century Gold Coast', *Journal of Material Culture* 2(3): 311–37.

Meyer, Birgit (1998) ' "Make a complete break with the past". Memory and Post-colonial Modernity in Ghanaian Pentecostalist discourse', *Journal of Religion in Africa* 28(3), forthcoming.

Miller, Daniel (1987) *Material Culture and Mass Consumption*. New York: Basil Blackwell.

Miller, Daniel (1990) 'Persons and Blue Jeans. Beyond Fetishism', *Etnofoor* 3(1): 97–111.

Miller, Daniel (1994) *Modernity. An Ethnographic Approach. Dualism and Mass Consumption in Trinidad*. Oxford: Berg.

Miller, Daniel (1995a) 'Introduction: Anthropology, Modernity and Consumption', in D. Miller (ed.) *Worlds Apart. Modernity through the Prism of the Local*, pp. 1–22. London and New York: Routledge.

Miller, Daniel (1995b) 'Consumption as the Vanguard of History', in D. Miller (ed.) *Acknowledging Consumption*, pp. 1–57. London and New York: Routledge.

Parry, J. and M. Bloch (eds) (1989) *Money and the Morality of Exchange*. Cambridge: Cambridge University Press.

Pietz, William (1985) 'The Problem of the Fetish, I', *Res* 9: 5–17.

Pietz, William (1993) 'Fetishism and Materialism: The Limits of Theory in Marx', in E. Apter and W. Pietz (eds) *Fetishism as Cultural Discourse*, pp. 119–51. Ithaca and London: Cornell University Press.

Poewe, Karla (ed.) (1994) *Charismatic Christianity as a Global Culture*. Columbia, SC: University of South Carolina Press.

Rivière, Claude (1981) *Anthropologie réligieuse des Evé du Togo*. Lomé: Les Nouvelles Éditions Africaines.

Roelofs, Gerard (1994) 'Charismatic Christian Thought. Experience, Metonomy, and Routinization', in K. Poewe (ed.) *Charismatic Christianity as a Global Culture*, pp. 217–33. Columbia, SC: University of South Carolina Press.

Rouse, Roger (1995) 'Questions of Identity. Personhood and Collectivity in Transnational Migration to the United States', *Critique of Anthropology* 15(4): 351–80.

Spieth, Jacob (1906) *Die Ewe-Stämme. Material zur Kunde des Ewe-Volkes in Deutsch-Togo*. Berlin: Dietrich Reimer.

Spieth, Jacob (1911) *Die Religion der Eweer in Süd-Togo*. Leipzig: Dietersche Verlagsbuchhandlung.

de Surgy, Albert (1988) *Le système religieux des Évhé*. Paris: Éditions L'Harmattan.

Taussig, Michael T. (1980) *The Devil and Commodity Fetishism in South America*. Chapel Hill, NC: The University of North Carolina Press.

Taussig, Michael T. (1995) 'The Sun Gives Without Receiving: An Old Story', *Comparative Studies in Society and History* 37(2): 368–98.

Thoden van Velzen, H. U. E. and W. Van Wetering (1988) *The Great Father and the Danger. Religious Cults, Material Forces, and Collective Fantasies in the World of the Surinamese Maroons*. Dordrecht: Foris Publications.

Thomas, Nicolas (1991) *Entangled Objects. Exchange, Material Culture, and Colonialism in the Pacific*. Cambridge, MA: Harvard University Press.

Ustorf, Werner (Hg.) (1986) *Mission im Kontext. Beiträge zur Sozialgeschichte der Norddeutschen Missionsgesellschaft im 19. Jahrhundert*. Bremen: Übersee-Museum.

Ustorf, Werner (1989) *Die Missionsmethode Franz Michael Zahns und der Aufbau kirchlicher Strukturen in Westafrika (1862–1900). Eine missionsgeschichtliche Untersuchung*. Erlangen: Verlag der Ev.-Luth. Mission.

Van Dijk, Rijk (1997) 'The Pentecostal Gift: Ghanaian Charismatic Churches and the Moral Innocence of the Global Economy'. Paper Presented at the 13th Satterthwaite Colloquium on African Religion and Ritual (19–22 April).

Veenis, Milena (1994) ' "Only because of the Bananas ..." Western Consumer Goods in East Germany', *Focaal* 24: 55–69.

Weber, Max (1984/1920) *Die protestantische Ethik I. Eine Aufsatzsammlung*. Herausgegeben von Johannes Winckelmann. Gütersloh: Gütersloher Verlagshaus.

Wendl, Tobias (1991) *Mami Wata oder ein Kult zwischen den Kulturen*. Münster: Lit Verlag.

Wicker, Kathleen O'Brien (n.d.) 'Mami Water in African Religion and Spirituality', in J. K. Olupona and Ch. H. Long (eds) *African Spirituality*, Crossroad Press: forthcoming.

Wilks, Ivor (1975) *Asante in the Nineteenth Century. The Structure and Evolution of a Political Order*. London: Cambridge University Press.

Domesticating Diamonds and Dollars: Identity, Expenditure and Sharing in Southwestern Zaire (1984–1997)

Filip De Boeck

Magi na biso ekomi combien?	*What does our magic amount to?*
Dollard!	*Dollars*
Bongo courant na biso?	*And our electricity [energy]?*
Dollard!	*Dollars*
Kaka oyo ya Inga?	*Our electricity of Inga?*[1]
Dollard!	*Dollars*
Bafonctionnaires ba yei milayi	*But why, then, have our civil servants*
mpo na nini?	*become so thin [lit. so long]?*
Nzala!	*Because they are hungry!*

(Street vendor's song, Lemba zone, Kinshasa, September 1995)

Lorsqu'un diamant a dans un rêve une signification excrémentielle, il ne s'agit pas seulement d'association par contraste: dans l'inconscient, les bijoux comme les excréments sont des matières qui coulent d'une blessure, des parties de soi-même destinées à un sacrifice ostensible (ils servent en fait à des cadeaux somptueux chargés d'amour sexuel). (Bataille, 1967: 27)

INTRODUCTION

Since the beginning of the 1980s, the zones of Kahemba and Kasongo-Lunda, two administrative units in the southern corner of the Kwaango (a subregion of the *région* or province of Bandundu), have been the scene of an increasing traffic in diamonds, which for the most part come from Angola, and are 'smuggled' across the Angolan–Zairean border by *pincheurs*, petty diamond traders from various corners of Zaire. More recently, Zairean *garimpeiros* have started to settle in Angola and sell their diamonds on the spot to UNITA *comptoirs* in return for dollars.[2] The transborder traffic into Zaire accounts for a significant proportion of this country's (unofficial) exports (an estimated $500 billion in 1994). A large part of these smuggling activities take place on what is traditionally considered as Luunda land, a

---

1. *Inga* is a reference to the Inga barrage on the Zaire river, which feeds the electricity line to Shaba; for a history of the Inga–Shaba project, see Willame (1986).
2. Although the term 'smuggle' implies by definition an aspect of illegality, it must be stressed that none of those involved in the transborder diamond smuggling consider their activities to be illegal or to constitute a criminal offence.

vast and sparsely populated territory referred to as *mabeet*, which extends
along both sides of the border and is mainly inhabited by Luunda and
Chokwe populations. Most of the diamonds entering the Zairean side of the
mabeet are sold to expatriate or Zairean diamond traders who operate
through *comptoirs* in the local market-towns of Kahemba, Tembo and (to a
lesser extent) Kulindji and Kimwangala. With the exception of Kulindji, all
of these towns are located at the fringe of the Luunda territory.[3]

This article intends to explore the impact of the recent diamond traffic on
both rural and urban life in southwestern Zaire, in an attempt at a 'multi-
sited' ethnography (Marcus, 1995) of the circulation of cultural meanings,
commodities, money and identities in an increasingly diffuse time-space, in
which the standard dichotomies between rural and urban worlds, lived world
and system, traditional and modern, or precapitalist and capitalist realities
have lost much of their explanatory strength (cf. De Boeck, 1996). I will
consider the widespread phenomenon of the *bana Lunda*, 'the children of
Lunda', young Zairean urbanites who travel from all over Bandundu to the
Angolan province of Lunda Norte in order to dig for diamonds. I will
investigate the changes brought about by the diamond trade and by the influx
of these urban youngsters in the rural border area, as well as the impact of the
accompanying monetization, called *dollarization*, on the daily life of the
villagers in southwestern Zaire.

In 1994 and 1995, I spent some time conducting research amongst groups
of *bana Lunda* along the Zairean–Angolan border and in the city of Kikwit
(subregion Kwilu).[4] At first, what interested me most was how, upon their
return, they spent the money they had earned in Angola. It turned out that in
many, if not most, cases the money — made at great risk after months of
suffering in Angola in the context of an ongoing civil war (referred to as 'the
war of Lunda' [*epaka Lunda*]) — was spent in a very short span of time on
women and on items such as beer, gold chains, clothes and transistor radios.
This article analyses the collective habitus as well as local notions of
autonomous male identity and personhood informing this ostentatious
spending or *potlach* behaviour. At the same time, it examines complementary
aspects of male personhood which give rise to simultaneous but alternative
distributive attitudes which stress an ethics of sharing. It also looks into the

---

3. While the towns of Kahemba and especially Tembo (the only place in the Zairean
    Kwaango where diamonds are found on a large scale, in the river Kwaango itself) continue
    to grow in importance, the trading activities in Kulindji and Kimwangala almost
    completely disappeared after 1991, due to the changing nature of the diamond traffic.
    Some of the *comptoirs* that were active in these towns before have moved to Angola and
    continue to operate from Luanda.

4. This formed part of more extensive field research (1987–89, 1991, 1994) among the
    Luunda of the Upper Kwaango (region of Bandundu, subregion Kwaango, zone of
    Kahemba), and in Kinshasa (1992, 1994) and Kikwit (1995, 1996), where a small but
    diverse Luunda and Cokwe 'diaspora', more or less successfully connected with the
    diamond trade or derived trading activities, has settled.

relationship between this ambivalent spending and sharing behaviour and the passionate register of the imaginary concerning diamonds, dollars, and local economies of desire in relation to the city, to modernity and to the West and the (white) Other.

Much of the literature concerning economic patterns of production, consumption and accumulation in relation to issues of modernization and development reflects the dictates of first-world imperatives and moralities. In varying degrees, moral economy theories confirm this tendency by the importance given to social solidarities based on kinship and 'affection' (Gudeman and Rivera, 1990; Hyden, 1980; Taussig, 1980) and the capacity of moral economies to elude, defy and, in more extreme 'soft state' theories, even penetrate and pervert the rationality of the capitalist market and the state (cf. Hyden, 1983). In contrast to such an interpretation which erects an overly-simplistic binary opposition between a 'rational' market economy and an 'irrational' 'economy of affection', I do not consider the smugglers' excessive consumption behaviour as a failure or an incapacity to acculturate to the capitalist ideology and practice of accumulation and profit-making.[5] At the same time, I would also argue against a one-sided interpretation of the diamond trade as destructive of local forms and logics of solidarity and reciprocity. I contend, on the contrary, that current urban Zairean practices related to the accumulation and the consumption of diamonds and dollars in a globalized economy are underpinned and shaped by local rural modes, conceptions and categories of wealth, accumulation, expenditure, physical and social reproduction and well-being which originate in (pre)colonial moral matrixes, attitudes, practices and beliefs, in particular in relation to hunting ritual and the historical realities of the ivory, rubber and slave trades. To illustrate this, I will predominantly draw on Luunda data. Although the *bana Lunda* category is a multi-ethnic one, in which the aLuund have become a minority, most of these non-aLuund (including Yaka, Chokwe, Pende, Yansi, Mbala, Suku) share a common socio-cultural universe with their Luunda neighbours and hold similar notions of hunting and male personhood. Historically, most peoples of the southern Zairean savannah belt owe a great deal of their ritual and political institutions to the Luunda sphere of influence. The Luunda ethnography in this chapter should thus be taken as short-hand for the much broader cultural horizon of southern Zaire.

Diamonds and dollars allow people to negotiate, discursively or otherwise, between different realities and identities. They offer the possibility of negotiation and recomposition of identity in a process, not only of 'self-realization' and promotion of social status (through excessive expenditure and consumerism, for example), but also of 'self-making', that is, as the process of capturing and 'fixing' the non-steady state of selfhood and of one's own

---

5. For recent criticisms of Hyden's concept of the 'economy of affection' see Bernal (1994); Geschiere (1992); Lemarchand (1989); Scott (1995).

identity in different cultural situations (cf. Battaglia, 1995). Diamonds trigger the imagination which, as an 'organized field of social practices' (Appadurai, 1990), draws from different sources of the imaginary such as the hunt, sexuality, initiation, and political leadership. As such, acquiring diamonds and spending dollars allows for a (discursive) appropriation and transformation of modern capitalism as the dominant figure of hegemonic power in the global system, providing people with a possibility to think, negotiate and reinvent in practice the relationship between one's own past and identity and the legacy of colonialist modernity and its ideology of 'progress', in new and in many respects (at least from a subaltern point of view) more advantageous ways. At the same time the conclusion of this article points to the existence of common moral discourses in which current spending and consumption patterns come under attack. It is my argument that these criticisms, which generate strong but often inapplicable or inaccessible moralities, take root in far less discursive or politicized fields of praxis, in which excess and heterogeneity are dealt with in reference to practical definitions of relations of commensality and solidarity.

A SHORT HISTORY OF DIAMOND TRAFFIC IN THE *MABEET*, 1980–95

The Luunda area in Kahemba zone is situated along the Zairean border with Angola, and extends well into the Angolan province of Lunda Norte. Traditionally, the political and ritual authority of the paramount Luunda titleholder, who resides in Zaire, extends over a large territory on both sides of the border, including the strategically important diamond mining town of Cafunfo (Kafunfu), a good two days' walk from the Zairean Luunda royal village. According to a recent census (1989) the total Luunda population on the Zairean side of the Luunda territory numbers some 37,000 (30,000 in 1974), whereas the total population of the zone of Kahemba, an area of some 20,000 kms^2 which includes Luunda land, is estimated at 170,000 (94,000 in 1974). The huge growth in the population of Kahemba may be explained by the post-1980 boom in Zairean–Angolan diamond smuggling. Most of the newcomers have been concentrated in the trading town of Kahemba, some 250 km northeast from the heart of Luunda land. Elsewhere in the zone of Kahemba the population has only slightly increased, as the numbers given for the Luunda area attest.

The aLuund of the *mabeet*, and the neighbouring Chokwe and Suku, were formerly part of a larger regional 'traditional' trading system which predated the colonial period and which hinged on the trade of such commodities as wax, rubber, ivory, guns and slaves, but also of 'power' objects and masks that aLuund purchased from their neighbours (see De Boeck, 1993). In the 1980s, diamond trade, the modes of commerce and barter, the use of caravans to carry goods into Angola, even the trade routes themselves, did not differ drastically from their (pre)colonial counterparts. Nevertheless, the

Luunda communities of the southern Kwaango were ill prepared to play a major role in the regional diamond traffic that came into existence along the border in the early 1980s. Colonization had brought an end to the previous long-distance trade into Angola. The Belgians never invested much in Kahemba's local economies. Outside the administrative centre of Kahemba itself, the area's economic activities have never gone beyond the subsistence level, with no agricultural surplus for export, and a yield that is often not even sufficient to satisfy local demands (De Boeck, 1994a). Apart from the poor quality of the roads and transport facilities and more generally the geographical isolation of the area, this lack of interest in Kahemba on the part of the colonial, and later the Congolese and Zairean authorities, was primarily due to the absence of large quantities of resources such as rubber. Rather, the colonial administration saw the Upper Kwaango as a reservoir of the cheap labour forces needed for maintaining the level of the more profitable palm oil, rubber and sugar production in the large plantations of the Kwilu and the Lower Congo. Throughout the colonial period, much like today, the main source of income for the local population consisted of the sale of wax in the Mikondo, and caterpillars elsewhere (Nange, 1981: 41). Until recently, the caterpillars were sold to travelling traders from Kikwit and Kinshasa. Prior to the advent of the diamond trade, this trade provided the villagers' sole source of cash income. However, due to the general deterioration of the roads (accelerated by the influx of the *comptoirs*' four wheel drive vehicles), the devaluation of the Zairean currency and the shortage of fuel, this long-distance trade by truck has almost completely disappeared in the *mabeet* today. Basically, then, except for the relative growth of cash-flow due to increased diamond smuggling, the economic situation has not improved much over the years.

Although most of the diamond trade was and still is to a large extent controlled by financially stronger outsiders, the prospect of making a quick profit has lured many young villagers into the trade. aLuund from both Angola and Zaire cross the border almost daily, and thus play a prominent role in the Angolan–Zairean diamond smuggling trade (De Boeck, 1996). This trade came into existence in 1979/80; throughout the 1980s, businessmen and diamond traders of all sorts travelled back and forth between Kinshasa, or older and more established diamond centres in the Kasai such as Tshikapa or Mbuji Mayi, and the border town of Kahemba. From there, they sent goods to Angola in exchange for diamonds from the Angolan Cafunfo mine and other neighbouring mines along the Kwaango river.[6] In

---

6. Losamba, another major diamond mining site, is located some 40 km from Cafunfo. Before independence, both mines were exploited by the Portuguese company DIAMANG. Together, these two mines are estimated to cover 60 per cent of Angolan diamond production. Experts estimate that the Losamba diamond sites are probably earning UNITA $300 m–$350 m a year (*Financial Times*, 3 May 1996). The remaining 40 per cent of diamond production mainly derives from the area around Dundo-Lukapa, to the east.

this way, diamonds were acquired directly from the mines, from individual diggers (*creuseurs*) and divers (*plongeurs*), or from middlemen (*cocseurs*) who buy and resell diamonds on the spot.[7] A person involved in selling goods in Angola is called *kandongueur*. The goods (such as wax cloths, cigarettes, whisky, radios, batteries, soap, sardines and dried salted fish) were carried across the border by *pincheurs*. These carriers either worked for their own account — individually, or as members of a small group or ring (*écurie*, literally: 'stable') which is usually based on kin and/or ethnic ties, or even contiguity (youngsters from the same neighbourhood in Kinshasa or Kikwit) — or in association with financially stronger traders or a diamond *comptoir*, to whom one is often obliged through debt. The flow of these goods into Angola coincided with a severe shortage of consumer goods in Angola itself in the 1980s (Azam, Collier and Cravinho, 1993). Throughout the 1980s most of the local involvement in the trade was limited to being a carrier, guide or scout. Crossing the Zairean–Angolan border, which is officially closed, was (and still is) a dangerous venture. Frequently, people were killed by land-mines or shot by Angolan government troops, locally referred to as *faapul* (from FAPLA, the armed forces of the Movimento Popular de Libertaçao de Angola, MPLA), who controlled Cafunfo and the greater part of the province of Lunda Norte, the 'African Klondike', throughout the 1980s.[8] Returning to Zaire was just as hazardous an undertaking, not only because taking diamonds out of Angola was declared illegal by the MPLA, but also because, on the other side, Zairean soldiers patrolled the border, officially to defend Zairean territory from MPLA attacks and to arrest trespassing 'Angolans' (mostly local aLuund, for whom the border and an Angolan or Zairean national identity are of little importance), but basically to loot and extort money (a practice known as *raka-raka*, literally: 'fast')

The Angolan government estimates that the $5 m or $6 m a month of officially declared production is less than a tenth of the total Angolan output. In recent years, many smaller 'wild' open mining sites have developed nearby Cafunfo, along the river Kwaango. For a full account of the history of the (recent) exploration of the diamond sedimentary deposits in the Kwaango basin see Fieremans (1977). For a comprehensive view of the evolution of the more established diamond exploitation and its social repercussions in the Zairean Kasai province, see Kambayi and Mudinga (1991), Tshibanza and Tshimanga (1985), and Tshibanza (1986). For a beautiful description of the diamond exploitation and the rubber trade between aLuund and the Portuguese *comptoirs* in Northern Angola in the early twentieth century, see Soromenho's novel *Camaxilo* (1956), originally published in 1948 in a Portuguese version as *Terra Morta*.

7. Amongst the diamond divers one distinguishes two groups: the *plongeurs* who possess the necessary equipment to breathe and stay under water, and the *kazabuleurs* or *zolo-zolo* who dive without the help of engines and air tubes. *Mwetistes* are those who keep the small rubber boats (*ndingi*) on the same spot in the water with long poles, and who help the divers to pull the sacks of sand and rock-waste (*mutsanga*) out of the water. The *mutsanga* is then sifted by the *tamiseurs*.

8. In 1981 and 1984 UNITA unsuccessfully tried to take Cafunfo and drive the MPLA out.

from returning diamond traders. For a short while during 1991, with the introduction of the multi-party system in Zaire, Zaireans entering Angola, especially those suspected of having UDPS (Union pour la Démocratie et le Progrès Social — Zaire's main opposition party) sympathies, were also tortured or killed by the fighters of UNITA (Uniao Nacional para la Independencia Total de Angola), who thereby took revenge for the fact that Zaire had turned its back on Mobutu, longstanding friend and ally of Savimbi and UNITA.

Since the early 1990s, the nature of the diamond trade has changed considerably. In December 1992, after refusing to recognize the outcome of the presidential elections, UNITA attacked the town of Cafunfo, which they had been sharing with MPLA during the period of the peace treaty. UNITA thus gained control over the diamond mines, which had until then constituted one of the main sources of income for the MPLA. During the following months, the town of Cafunfo was attacked and bombed extensively by the MPLA. In October of 1994, the MPLA again took control of Cafunfo, but failed to stop the parallel digging activities along the Kwaango. In November 1994, UNITA and MPLA signed a new peace treaty in Lusaka, and with Savimbi's subsequent agreement to act as Angola's vice-president, a period of renewed co-habitation in Lunda Norte seemed to have set in. Since early 1995, Cafunfo has been under MPLA control, while the mining sites along the Kwaango are for the most part, and despite strong MPLA pressure, under the control of UNITA.

Under the UNITA occupation of Cafunfo, bartering virtually came to an end. Since the end of 1992, the diamond trade has been monetized: all the diamonds are paid for in US dollars, giving rise to a monetary economy that functions independently from, or has replaced, the 'official' Zairean and Angolan money markets. The changed nature of the trade also put a stop to the import of Zairean goods into Angola. As a result, the whole Zairean–Angolan diamond activity became more sedentary. When UNITA occupied Cafunfo, Zaireans were allowed to settle in the mining sites along the Kwaango to dig up diamonds. As a consequence, the former *pincheurs* and diamond traders (*kamangistes*) were supplanted by numerous 'children of Lunda' (*bana Lunda*), penniless Zairean youngsters from all over southern Zaire and Kinshasa, who walk hundreds of miles to the Southern Kwaango in order to cross the border and try their luck in Angola. In the first half of 1994, an estimated 25,000 to 30,000 Zairean *garimpeiros* or illegal diggers were permanently living in and around Cafunfo, digging diamonds under the harsh control of UNITA, which ensured that it received a large percentage of all the diamonds thus produced.[9] UNITA has also imposed forced manual

---

9. In return for permission to dig, UNITA claims up to 50 per cent of the diamonds found. Through local diamond *comptoirs* UNITA buys a significant proportion of the remaining diamonds.

labour on the Zaireans working in these mines. Every morning, before starting to work in the mines, the diggers are forced by UNITA troops to help build dams and other constructions, a practice known as *la parade*.[10] In this way, UNITA has basically used cheap Zairean labour to help sponsor its war and rebuild its infrastructure in the post-war era (see also Misser, 1994; Wrong, 1996).

The increasing trans-border diamond smuggling has had far-reaching effects on the economies of both rural and urban sites in southwestern Zaire. It has led to the rapid 'dollarization' of local economies. In cities such as Kikwit and Kinshasa, even school fees are now paid in dollars rather than in the local Zairean currency. The whole of Southwest Zaire has thus entered a vicious circle: the more the diamond trade injects dollars into the local economic system, the more dollars replace national Zairean and Angolan currencies, the greater the need for dollars therefore becomes, and the more people are drawn into the diamond-smuggle, which provides the unique source of dollars for most Zaireans.

MONEY, WEALTH, AND HUNTING

In Luunda land new sources and forms of material wealth, introduced from the outside in the form of new commodities as well as money, have always been incorporated into a wider notion of fecundity in terms of physical health and social and physical reproduction (in relation to agriculture, hunting and reproductive sexuality). For example, to dream about diamonds, money, or gold is considered a good omen in exactly the same way as is dreaming about palm or banana trees (their rich regimes suggest fertility and plenty), white people, a house with a roof of corrugated iron (sign of material wealth and access to the whites' riches), people covered with cassava flour (also a reference to the 'whiteness' of the ancestors), baskets of cassava roots, and termites (again a marker of rich fecundity and plenty).

A semantic analysis of Luunda terms with regard to money and wealth through goods and people reveals more clearly the parallels between these various sources of wealth. The aLuund use several notions to denote money. The most recent term is *nfalaang*, derived from the French *franc*. A much older, probably precolonial, notion that applies to money is that of *(m)uhaamb*, which establishes a link between money and the more encompassing, spiritual notion of fecundity as used in the *mahaamb* institutions.[11]

---

10. Many diggers try to 'do the *choc*', that is, dig for diamonds outside the official working hours supervised by UNITA troops. If captured by UNITA while 'working *choc*', the clandestine diggers (*choqueurs*) are usually executed on the spot.
11. The Luunda ritual horizon hinges predominantly on the existence of ritual institutions devoted to non-ancestral spiritual agencies or *mahaamb* (sing.: *haamb*). Even today, among the aLuund, ritual institutions exist for more that twenty-five named *mahaamb*, although

A third term for money, *mboong*, which is sometimes used by aLuund, is borrowed from kiKoongo *mbongo*. Using a pidginized kiKoongo vernacular, youngsters of Kikwit will for example speak of Angola as 'the land of *mbongo*' (*pays ya mbongo*). The notion of *mbongo* again links money to other sources of wealth and more in general to 'fertility'. In his classic Koongo dictionary, Bittremieux glosses *mbongo* as 'cloths', 'value', 'payment', 'money', 'riches', and wealth in people (*muana mbongo*: 'slave [bought child]'), but also as 'seed', 'fruit', 'young' and 'fertile land' (*ntoto mbongo*) (Bittremieux, 1923: 383). A fourth, more specifically Luunda notion is that of *ubit* or its more common variant *dipit*, money, wealth, riches. A wealthy or 'rich' man is referred to as *mpich*, and the verb *-pit* means 'to become rich', 'to earn'.

What is interesting about this fourth notion is that it does not so much make the link to agriculture as to the domain of hunting and notions of manhood. Not only does the verb *-pit* mean 'to tame', the stem *-pit* also recurs in the word *mupit*, a hunter's trap. Furthermore, the verb *-pit* also means: 'to outsmart someone', 'to cheat someone', as in the expression *iiny wanpit manaangw*, 'who has outsmarted me' (literally: 'who has trapped/ captured my wisdom?'). The notion of wisdom (*manaangw*) is a core notion in relation to the way in which aLuund conceptualize male personhood. I will deal with notions of wisdom in relation to male person- and elderhood below. For the time being, however, let us concentrate on the relationship that exists between money/wealth and hunting. Clearly, in the (masculine) Luunda view, wealth, money and material riches have to be hunted, tracked down, trapped and 'tamed' in the same way as game. Zairean French and kiKoongo vocabularies illustrate the parallels well: one 'tracks' and 'captures' wealth, which in the present context translates as dollars and diamonds (kiKoongo: *kusosa mbongo*, to search for money; *kuzwa/kubaka mbongo*, 'to capture

---

their importance has considerably diminished since the 1960s. While particular forms of disease and misfortune are associated with particular *mahaamb*, these spiritual agencies can also be invoked to obtain fertility, wealth, and well-being. *Mahaamb* may thus be either benevolent or malevolent; they possess a positive as well as a negative side. As such, they are capable of promoting someone's well-being and luck, but also of provoking diseases of all kinds, death and misfortune, especially when they have been 'neglected', that is, when their ritual installation has not taken place for some time. To install a *haamb* is to appease its anger. One of the most important *haamb* cults with regard to material wealth is the *haamb dia santu*, a longstanding cargo-cult vehiculated through statues of the Virgin Mary and other catholic saints, such as Saint Anthony (see Bastin, 1988; de Castro Henriques, 1993, 1995; Lima, 1971). The *santu* cult metonymically evokes the (white) outsider's world: objects playing an important role in the cult are, for example, bread and potatoes (the white man's food), forks, knives, spoons and white plates (evoking the white man's eating habits), but also soap, dollar notes and other currencies. These commodities and goods, as well as the *haamb* statues (catholic saints or white people) themselves, allow the aLuund to bring the white man's world into their own ritual universe and to attract his sources of wealth as well as to domesticate or dominate objects of wealth from this different world.

money'; French: *attraper l'argent, attraper le doll(ar), attraper le diam*), in the same way as one 'captures' game (*attraper le gibier*). In other words: wealth behaves unpredictably, especially the wealth that comes from outside and is connected with the world of the white man, such as dollars and diamonds. These are sources of wealth that are like wild and dangerous animals; they need to be captured, trapped, snared, tamed (*-pit*) and appeased before they can be domesticated and integrated into the known realms of the village life or, for that matter, the order of the *cité*, which thereby become empowered.[12]

For most Luunda villagers, as well as for the *bana Lunda*, dollars and diamonds are like wild animals and indeed behave in unpredictable and irrational ways. First of all, the market value of neither diamonds nor dollars is fixed. Due to hyperinflation, speculation, and the different living conditions in Zaire and Angola, the worth of the dollar may vary a lot and can never be predicted. The decline of the Zairean and Angolan economies has accelerated dramatically over the past years. In Zaire, before 1991, inflation oscillated around a level of 50 to 100 per cent per year. In 1992, 1993 and 1994 inflation reached levels of 3000 per cent, 8300 per cent and 6000 per cent respectively. Although in 1995 the inflation rate dropped to 700 per cent, it then went up again, leading to the introduction in late 1996 of new banknotes, in denominations of 100,000 to 1,000,000 zaires.[13]

In such a context, it is not surprising that dollars and diamonds are interpreted as being wild and undomesticated items. They are, in a Maussian sense, animated, sometimes even individualized living objects, that behave in irrational and even 'demonic' or 'satanic' ways, and according to rules that

---

12. The bush and the forest are, in many respects, the — as yet untamed — sources of wealth and well-being. The hunter strengthens the inside, the village and the household, by domesticating and bringing home these forces from the outside. For a detailed example, see De Boeck (1996), dealing with the empowering of the royal courtyard through the ritual domestication of the leopard's skin. On somewhat similar notions of 'capturing' the untamed among the neighbouring Yaka, see Devisch (1993: 86ff).

13. In a desperate attempt to curb rampant inflation and as a stop-gap measure to find sufficient banknotes to pay the regular army and secure the diamond trade, the Birindwa government introduced a new currency on 21 October 1993. The *nouveau zaire* or *zaire lourd*, as the new currency is referred to, had the same value as 3 million old zaires. The NZ was not accepted for political reasons in the diamond-producing areas in the central Kasai region, nor is it accepted by smugglers bringing stones from Angola. In October 1995, in another bid to stabilize the NZ, the Kengo government unsuccessfully tried to introduce new rules for diamond buyers to fight the increasing dollarization of the economy, requiring that 50 per cent of the traders' hard currency be lodged with the central bank, and that diamond deals take place in NZ only. Dealers estimated that diamond purchases fell by as much as 70 per cent in October 1995 after the new rules had been introduced. Since diamonds are one of the few sources of hard currency available, the Kengo government was very quick in announcing modifications to the new rules, allowing purchasers to buy diamonds in hard currency once again.

are mainly controlled by *ayimbaadi*, persons belonging to another, foreign and far-away world.[14]

In Angola too, money behaves unpredictably. Many *bana Lunda* in Angola see their dollars evaporate before they can even make it back to the Zairean border. As one youngster in Kikwit explained upon his return from Angola in September, 1995:

> For me the dollar is like the *nouveau zaire*, because in Angola, the dollar is worthless. We exchange it for Kwanza [Angolan currency], which we call *bakwanzumba*. $100 equals 10,000,000 Kwanza. In order to survive one needs dollars, but in Angola one spends an amount like that in an hour on food only. Over there, twelve bottles of beer easily cost $150. With cigarettes and the expenses for the kitchen one spends almost $300 every day. A kilo of manioc flour already costs 5,000,000 Kwanza, and the Lebanese traders sell a can of sardines for 2,500,000 Kwanza. Therefore we have started to drink the water from the river Kwaango, and eat raw manioc. That is how we get yellow fever, malaria, and bloody diarrhoea. That is also why people have started saying: *bana Lunda dollard pamba-pamba* [bana Lunda worthless dollar].

Another youngster comments:

> The day the Americans will arrive in Angola, they will weep when they see what people have done to their money, the dollar. In Angola, dollars are worthless. If you sell a diamond of ten carats, you will spend almost all the money you made on food alone.

Just like wild animals, diamonds and dollars are potentially dangerous: they may take possession of one. As *bana Lunda* state: 'money makes you confused and with your head in the clouds', 'you can no longer see or think straight', 'it takes hold of you and drags you down'. In the words of one *mwana Lunda*:

> When you are not yet in possession of diamonds, you think of all kinds of good and valid projects. But as soon as you capture a diamond you forget about all your projects. You forget that you are there for *ntsingi*: you forget all the difficulties in Angola and at home and you start making debts even before you have sold your diamond or know its worth.

Like animals, diamonds and dollars may even devour and consume a person. This is taken quite literally by the *bana Lunda* themselves. It is, for example, widely assumed that when one is the victim of *mpiaka*, that is, when one does not dig up some diamonds after a certain period of time, one has been cursed or 'pursued' by bad luck. In order to lift this curse, one 'sells a

---

14. The word *chimbaadi* is not only used to denote the white man, but is also applied to everyone who lives like a white person and who does not belong to the village, such as people from the Zairean administration, civil authorities, or traders from Kinshasa. For most aLuund, the ways of the *chimbaadi* and the goods he brings along are a constant source of amazement, wonder and awe. The concept *chimbaadi*, while holding material promises of wealth and plenty, thus also evokes 'strangeness' and feelings of unease and discomfort.

finger' (Lingala: *koteka misapi*), a tooth (*koteka minu*), an eye (*koteka miso*), or one's vertebral column, by which is meant sperm (Lingala: *koteka mokongo*). Although I have personally met a number of people who had one of their fingers amputated or a tooth pulled out, and therefore have no reason to doubt the *bana Lunda*'s claims that these practices do 'really' occur, it seems to me that their importance does not primarily situate itself on this literal level. These practices and discourses are first and foremost significant on the level of a collective imaginary, desire and discourse which reflects the deeply felt *angst* experienced by the subaltern in a social reality that escapes or crushes him and that no longer seems to make sense. In using a discourse of the 'senses' in which the actual boundaries of individual human bodies are dismembered and severed through cannibalism (see below), violence, maiming and torture, the *bana Lunda* express their more general experience (all too real in the Angolan and Zairean contexts) of a maimed culture, and of an agonizing society in which the production and reproduction of social memory and meaningful habitus is jeopardized, and in which they themselves are under a constant threat of dispossession and dislocation of Self.

The 'selling' of one's vertebral column or sperm refers to a specific practice known to all who dig for diamonds in Lunda Norte. Near the town of Luremo, on the Kwaango's right bank, lives an old woman. In order to assure success in the search for diamonds, one has to spend the night with her (sell one's backbone). Afterwards diamonds will find their way easily to one. The first diamond that is subsequently 'captured' is given to the woman by way of compensation. Other informants mention incest between mother and son, or the sacrifice of the lives of one's parents, as successful ways of lifting the curse that prevents one from 'capturing' diamonds and dollars:

A friend of mine, by the name of Mundelembongo [literally: 'white man's money'], was told by a female sorcerer in Mwana Kafunfu, Angola: 'If you want to make a lot of money, you should spend the night with your mother. Afterwards, come back to me and I will give you all the money and diamonds you need'. Mundelembongo returned to Zaire and explained his problem to his mother, who fled and never returned to her home. Because his mother was no longer available, he returned to Angola, where he sacrificed the life of his child. The child died suddenly in Kikwit, without having been ill.

In return for diamonds, the sorcerer will tell you to sacrifice your mother and father. If you can't do this right away, he will give you dollars and tell you: 'Give this money to your father [By accepting it the father will die]. If your father refuses to take the money because he is a sorcerer himself, then buy a loincloth for your mother, that way, we will grab her life easily'.

Diamonds and dollars, in other words, take possession of one and, as diamond traders repeatedly state, make one 'mad'. Diamonds are consequently described as 'demons'.[15] In a movement of dispossession and disappropriation, they reduce the *mwana Lunda*, dominate and fragment him

---

15.   On the image of satan in relation to diamonds, see also Prioul (1995).

in the body, and thereby make him abdicate responsibility for his body and his acts, firmly locking him up in the world of the imaginary. As such, diamonds and dollars have a terrible effect on people: they make a person lose all sense of self-determination; they turn a person into a thief, a cheat and a liar; they 'eat' or destroy people, for in return for stones one sacrifices one's manhood (symbolized by the tooth, the eye and the backbone, three key elements in the conceptualization of male personhood — see below); they cause one to become an animal or a sorcerer (*mukishi mwana Lunda*), both of which are characterized by disruptive, incestuous or cannibalistic behaviour, breaking down the normal boundaries that characterize the cultural order of life in the village, given form in the relationships between the generations, or between genitor/genitrix and offspring. By sleeping with an old woman, who, being post-menopausal, is structurally not considered a woman anymore, or by 'eating' one's mother and father — and thus one's own life-source — or one's child, the *mwana Lunda*, like a sorcerer, thus inverts the natural flow of the life-stream from ascendants to descendants.

In return for diamonds, one not only sacrifices one's own work power and productivity (finger), one's youth, strength and beauty (tooth) and one's fertility and sexual prowess (backbone), but diamonds even make one 'sell' one's friends (Lingala: *alekisi baninga na ye*) or family members; they totally isolate one and invert the normal ties of solidarity and reciprocity into the destructive internal mechanisms of redistribution by sorcery. The longing or hunger for dollars and diamonds is, informants state in a Bataille-esque turn of phrase, like an incurable festering sore which re-opens every time one runs out of money.

In Zaire, the postcolonial relationship to modern capitalism and the West (that is, as an imagined topos, iconically represented by the dollar bill) is increasingly expressed metonymically, in a relation of the greatest possible contiguity. In 1996, a popular wax print in southwestern Zaire depicted dollar bills; one could thus literally wear dollars (or their images) on one's skin. These dollar representations blur the boundaries between the signifying 'real' and the representational 'imaginary'; by means of a principle of magic through contiguity they attract the wealth of the outside world of the *chimbaadi* and thus the universe of modernity and the city. At the same time, seductive as it is, the world of 'modernity' is also an unpredictable and, from a subaltern point of view, often irrational one; it is a world in which different rules apply. To some extent, Zaire's city-life, the stage on which the relationship with modernity is most fully played out, has always been a night-life, enacted in the oneiric environment of the bar and the *nganda*, where dollars are most ostentatiously spent in an economy of ejaculation (cf. below). In order to dominate and 'tame' dollars, they have to be brought out of the 'nocturnal' realm (of sorcery, but, as will be argued below, also of the bar) into the realm of the day and the established order of the village world, where the clientelism that is characteristic of the bar (and of sorcery) does not apply, but where the order is defined by life-giving reciprocity between hunter and family, husband and wife, between living and dead, and between the generations.

The idiom of sorcery, itself indissolubly connected to kinship as its necessary shadow-side, reveals to what extent capitalism and kinship inter-penetrate. The examples given above suggest that, in the Zairean imaginary, the capitalist logic of buying and selling easily adapts to and even exemplifies the nocturnal logic of sorcery. As Mauss has shown, within the logic of reciprocity, closedness, or blockage of flow is seen as socially negative (see also Taylor, 1992). This blockage, with the conflicts and violence it entails, is often expressed in terms of sorcery or witchcraft. In the Zairean populist understanding of the capitalist logic, blockage is understood to be necessary to make profits and maximize capital. In this interpretation, capitalism indeed becomes an 'economy of constipation' (Bataille, 1967) in which southwestern Zairean notions of '*kula*-like' circularity and personalized reciprocity of the gift (De Boeck, 1994a) seem to be transformed into a linear and exclusive, negative model of transaction to which access is much more restricted. Here, the figure of the accumulating, non-sharing individual, the successful PDG, entrepreneur or diamond trader coincides with the figure of the sorcerer or the witch. For a certain urban élite, for example, the regime's *dinosaures* for a long time exemplified and provided a role-model of this ideal entrepreneurship. However, when one tunes in to *radio trottoir*, the *cité*'s pulsating heartbeat and the window on the popular imagination, it becomes clear to what extent this collective imagination views the successful entre-preneur and politician, or the rich person, in powerful images of witchcraft and cannibalism, for example in connection with the figure of the satan (cf. Meyer, 1995), the *ndoki*, or the *mami wata* who provides money in return for the lives of one's own offspring, thus embodying the ultimate blockage and reversal of the life-flow (see also Fabian, 1978; Fisiy and Geschiere, 1991; Geschiere, 1995; Warnier, 1993).

The logic of self-interested profit-making, although viewed as problematic, easily pervades rural ties of kin-based solidarity. The recent increase of sorcery accusations in Luunda land testifies to the permeability of the two spheres. Sorcery accusations are increasingly linked to money and diamond matters. Disputes over access to wealth in people, elephant tusks, guns, tributes, first crops and meat from the hunt, have by no means disappeared, but to some extent they have been overshadowed by conflicts over carats and money. These conflicts are usually due to a failure to share the profits and benefits from successful diamond deals. This in itself is not a new develop-ment: the failure to share has always been a common source of conflict. Luunda proverbs illustrate this, but simultaneously stress the strength of kin-based ties: 'When we quarrel it is about wealth, but never about kinship'. What has changed undeniably with the coming of the diamond trade, is the fact that sorcery is increasingly disconnected from kinship. In common Luunda practices of sorcery, referred to as 'the elders' sorcery' (*ulaj wa amaleemb*) an attack is usually 'provoked' by the victim himself, because of his disregard of basic principles of respect, reciprocity and solidarity in his relation with the attacker, who feels wronged (De Boeck, 1991a). In this type of sorcery both the attack and the retaliation are always firmly situated within one's own lineage or clan group, and characteristically result from a collective decision by the lineage elders themselves. In recent years, however, one witnesses the spread of 'wild sorcery' (*ulaj wa chisakasak*), in which a person may become the victim of a total stranger's evil intentions or greed. The penetration of kin-based systems of exchange by a capitalist logic, based on self-interest and profit, is gradually changing the idioms of sorcery themselves. These are increasingly conceptualized in terms of the vocabulary of marketing and commodification. In the early 1990s, throughout Luunda land, people commented on the development of *chikeend*, a new form of sorcery which supposedly originated among the neigbouring Yaka people, and in which sorcerers are believed not simply to exchange, but actually to buy and sell human flesh from and to one another.[16]

In the same way that disaffection and affection, or witchcraft and kinship, are indissolubly linked together in local systems of reciprocity and exchange, so the monetized market economy is marked both by constructive and destructive tendencies. The fact that the aLuund establish the link between hunting and the trapping or 'capturing' of diamonds is no coincidence: hunting, as ideology and practice vehiculated through the *uyaang* hunting cults (De Boeck, 1991b: Ch. 7), may itself be used constructively or destructively. This shows most clearly in the ambivalences revealed in gendered processes of reciprocity and exchange that mark the practice of hunting. For example, Luunda men commonly associate female regenerative powers with death and the realm of sorcery on the one hand, and with food on the other. This connection is also revealed in the structural similarity between penetrating a woman and 'giving away one's blood', that is, sperm (*-pan mash*) (cf. the practice of 'selling one's backbone' in the diamond smuggling context), and dying because of a sorcerer's attack (*-pan mooy kudi alaj*, 'giving away vital life-force [*mooy*] to the sorcerers'), for 'blood is the fat of those who eat me, it is the sorcerer's happiness'. For a Luunda man, therefore, the analogy between a sorcerer feeding on the 'fat' of his victims, and a woman's growing and fattening by male blood-substance is obvious.[17]

Practices and discourses of sorcery thus also blend in with the hunter's universe, and bring out fundamental ambivalences inherent in the hunting practice. In some respects, the hunter's solitary and autonomous character

---

16. Significantly, the transaction underlying the acquiring of diamonds and dollars by means of ritual power objects and sorcery is also glossed as 'selling' by the *bana Lunda*. As has been illustrated by Geschiere (1992, 1995), traditional, 'irrational' concepts of witchcraft thus easily translate into a 'modern', 'rational', vocabulary inspired by capitalist transactions.

17. Birthgiving, in a way, is the female equivalent of hunting: a woman 'captures' a pregnancy ('*attrape une grossesse*'), and the image of the trap is used to convey this: the female vagina 'traps' male life-force and captures the pregnancy.

likens him to the sorcerer. Hunting, in all its aspects from the shooting of an animal to the cutting up and the distribution of its parts, is therefore also viewed as a model that refers to the anti-order of sorcery. The aLuund consider that a hunter's gun may itself become an 'abscess that attacks the wrong place', thereby killing rather than feeding the hunter's relatives. To assure a successful hunt, for example, some *uyaang* rituals are believed to initiate the hunter in the nocturnal knowledge concerning the ritual killing of his relatives and the use of their blood (especially from affines, such as one's own wife, or the wife's brother or his children, as well as from those of the hunter's mother's side, such as his own mother's brother or his children). Both sorcerer and hunter, also referred to as 'the sorcerer of the animals', are engaged in actions of killing, trapping, and shooting (for the sorcerer hits his victims with his 'guns of the night'). Both are engaged in deviant practices, such as *kabwiidi*, the ability to disappear and reappear at another place. Both are characterized by heightened sensory (and especially visual and olfactory) capacities: hunters, like sorcerers, diviners and political title-holders, subject themselves to rituals to 'open up' or 'unlock' their eyes, and both possess a canine smelling capacity which, in the hunter's case, is represented by two small wooden dog figures, tied to his gun. The same blood-red colour that characterizes the sorcerer's eyes, is also linked to the blood of the hunt, symbolized by the red feathers of the tauraco (*ndjuw*, musophaga rossae) that are worn by the hunter (and the warrior).

CAPTURE, EXPENDITURE AND THE CONSTRUCTION OF MALE IDENTITY

Hunting epitomizes, of course, masculine sexuality and male identity. Similarly, the *mwana Lunda*, in capturing and spending diamonds and dollars, becomes 'a person' and acquires an identity as man. I believe the construction of masculinity and male identity expressed by the *bana Lunda* to be modelled upon a whole habitus of male person- and elderhood that is deeply rooted in longstanding moral matrixes and practices that are also exemplified by the hunter. As such, the past is sedimented (although in a transformed way) in the bodies and the praxis of the contemporary diamond hunters.

In the world of the diamond trade, lavish spending and excessive consumerism has become the major marker of success. One of the aspects people associate most with the successful diamond trader is his inexhaustible financial capacity to buy bottled beer, a sign of luxury, for his friends and acquaintances. As Pepe Kalle, a popular Zairean star, sings about the *mwana Lunda* in one of his songs: 'let those who want to drink, drink, let those who want to get drunk, get drunk; I have sold stones!' (Pepe Kalle and L'Orchestre Empire Bakuba, 1993). One bar in Kikwit is named: 'What is 10 million [to us]?', implying: to us, the 'diamond hunters', it is just a small amount of money. The successful *mwana Lunda* has 'hands that spend easily'; he 'spends dollars as if they were peanuts'. This spending behaviour is referred to as *la boum, dijigunda, dijibunda*. The *boumeur* or *dijibundeur* knows how to turn life into a party — *loyenge*. Many speak in this respect of 'savoir vivre'. The realization of this economy of desire and the sense of a good life is not only associated with bottled beer, with access to western consumer goods (most clearly exemplified by the ghetto blaster — the louder the more prestigious!), and the capacity to contract large debts in bars and nightclubs, but also with the conspicuous consumption, the 'eating' of women: 'When you have a lot of dollars, your "savoir vivre" in Angola shows in the quantity of booze and women you can handle' say the *bana Lunda*. Spending money also shows one's worth and importance. As such, it has nothing to do with principles of 'affection'. As Mauss already noted, to give is to manifest one's superiority; it establishes social hierarchies. In this sense, the *mwana Lunda*'s dollar really is *renommiergeld* (Mauss, 1985/1950: 221):

> To make oneself known, one has to distribute money. Everybody has to know that you have money, the women, the friends. If you have US$40,000, it is very easy to spend $3000 or even $4000 on a woman in one night. And you are not going to court just one woman. The women have to be numerous so that everybody will know you. Your friends have to know that they are dealing with a real *patron*. The *bana Lunda* love to be called *patron*. I am *patron*! You frequent all the bars, and even the soldiers have to recognize your importance. If they pass you by in the street, you might give them $50 each for their *matembele* (their 'vegetables', their food) in the evening. In Zaire, if you want to be considered in Zaire, you got to have money!

Another man adds: 'you need money to be considered in the eyes of God, for God only recognizes the rich'. The capacity to spend lavishly, or, to use Bataille's image, to spend in an excremental way, creates a seductive image of oneself, makes one visible, and is a sign of strength: 'we are strong', *bana Lunda* say, 'we can behave "au taux du jour" ', that is, we have the financial means, the possibilities. Of such a person it is said that he is 'planted like a pole', assuming a central and straight position, seen and heard by everyone; in short, be a real *patron* or *chef*, recognized by God, by the state (here personified by the military), and even by the white man. Imagine my surprise when, walking in Kikwit's main market, a man totally unknown to me ran up to give me $50 'to buy cigarettes for myself'.

Given the analogy between hunting game and capturing diamonds, one easily sees how the ostentatious distribution of dollars, and the voracious and frenzied consumption of beer and women as a means to acquire prestige, provide people with an urbanized version of the hunter's distribution of meat as a strategy not only to increase one's potency but also to acquire a valued social status. The substructure of this easily discernible parallel is formed by a whole register of values that echoes more traditional notions of male personhood and identity. Among the aLuund, for example, undifferentiated experiences of body, mind and emotion underly the gradual growth towards social personhood.[18] One's self-awareness of the growing, living body as physical expanse in time and space (*mujiimbw*) also underpins and determines one's 'becoming a person'. It is in and through his body, and as he grows older, that an individual incorporates the social realm and externalizes his self-identity, in a gradual process of growing towards personhood, which, for the aLuund, involves a twofold, dialectical, process of growing towards one's social role: firstly, the realization of one's individual self-identity, autonomy and responsibility, implying volition, intentionality, individual ambition and self-consciousness, and secondly a gradual body-centred insertion (through speech, listening, seeing) into the lives of other individuals. This insertion also implies a growing responsibility. The more one becomes the focus of the social life of the kin group, the more one is given respect, but the more, also, one becomes responsible for the redistribution and sharing of the goods that circulate in the kin group.

With regard to the first aspect, Luunda men view the ideal male body-self as a self-contained, relatively autonomous entity. This ideal is embodied in varying degrees by the hunter, the elder, the family or lineage head and, in the most exemplary way, by the paramount title-holder. In growing towards the status of elder, a man 'becomes a person', that is, someone who is courageous, firm and brave, who has self-restraint and shows perseverance, strong will, character, courage, and a sense of responsibility. The progressive acquiring of 'personality' (*wuuntw*), metaphorically expressed through cosmological images of verticality and 'uprightness' (*nteendeend*), implies an increasing bodily verticality, autonomy and containment, and sets a man apart from the others. A man has to be 'hard as a bullet'. Such hardness is also expressed through the image of the tooth. Furthermore, the teeth also refer to a man's capacity at manipulating the word (see also Weiss, 1992 on the connection between teeth, speech and agency). A true man is 'like a drum' and raises his voice to treat the problems of the family unit, the lineage or the village.

The hunter shares all of the sensory capacities characterizing the senior man, the elder, the judge, the lineage head, all those 'who may carry a belt', the sign of masculine individuation and autonomy. All of these character-istics of masculinity are also highlighted in *uyaang*, an elaborate complex of hunting rituals. *Uyaang* may alternatively be referred to as *kangoong*, which is also the name of a species of mouse with a black line on its back. The same name is given to the vertical tattoo scar which aLuund apply between the eyebrows as a sign of beauty and to signify the hunter's erectness and strong backbone. Similarly, teeth play an enormously important role in *uyaang* hunting ritual. It is the human tooth that symbolizes hunting power and is focused upon in *uyaang* hunting ritual.[19]

---

18. For a more detailed account of Luunda elderhood, see also De Boeck (1994b).
19. For example, a major part of a senior hunter's burial ritual deals with the extraction of one of his molars. This tooth will be incorporated in ritual hunting objects which will be inherited by a young hunter to whom the deceased acted as 'hunting father'. On *uyaang*

It is easy to see how many of the connotations and qualities of 'traditional' Luunda notions of male personhood and identity also surface in the *bana Lunda*'s construction of manhood. The *bana Lunda*'s explicit preference for beer (as opposed to the lemonades or *sucré* drunk by women) parallels Luunda men's preference for strong and bitter palmwine, as opposed to the freshly tapped sweet wine favoured by women. The gold chain has replaced the belt as marker of male importance, and the ghetto blaster is the *bana Lunda*'s version of 'being like a drum'. Less superficially, the acts of 'selling' one's backbone, or tooth, for example, clearly highlight important corporeal indicators of male personhood that are also stressed in traditional notions of Luunda manhood and virile health (*ngol*). The same goes for the 'selling of one's eyesight'. 'Seeing' (*-tal*) or 'fixed, intense staring' (*-tal ne*), marks the attitude of the elder, in contrast with the sideways look of women (*-tal nkeew*).

The physical and moral qualities attributed to the 'true man' who is 'firm in the heart' are also part and parcel of the *bana Lunda*'s discourse. They stress the importance of autonomy and self-sufficiency: one has to be *cascadeur*, someone who can look after himself. The quality of 'courage' is stressed time and again: in order to survive in Angola and face hunger, illness, imprisonment, torture, forced labour, beatings, and war, one has to be courageous and 'hard', one has to know how to endure pain, hardships and suffering: 'a man must know how to suffer like we suffer in Angola'. One has to show stamina, and be able to 'take a beating' (*supporter le coup*). Another quality which is invariably stressed is the capacity to 'control', to be 'on top of the situation', to be 'calm' and 'patient'.

Overall, then, the suffering experienced in Angola is the Zairean youngsters' new rite of passage into manhood. Not only do the hardships of digging for diamonds evoke the hardships of hunting (sleeping in the open, spending weeks in the bush, facing dangers), but youngsters also explicitly compare the passage in Angola to the hardships of life in the *mukanda*, the old circumcision bush camp, where one is circumcised, learns the skills of hunting and drumming, and is (often quite literally) beaten into manhood and 'erectness'.

As in *mukanda*, the boys who exit Angola have been initiated, they have been transformed, and have (nominally, at least) acquired a new identity and social status as adult man. The *bana Lunda* proudly display the marks of this initiation, grafted onto their bodies: the marks of whiplashes, bullet wounds, beatings and shell-splinters, the missing ears, cut off by UNITA fighters or MPLA troops, or the stumps which remain as a reminder of the limbs that had to be amputated after having stepped on a landmine or a booby trap. In a very

---

among the Ndembu, see also V. Turner (1953: 37–46; 1967: 280–98). E. Turner (1992: 165ff) stresses the importance of the human tooth in Ndembu hunting ritual. See also Bastin (1978; 1988: 17–21; 1990) and Lima (1971) on *uyaang* hunting practices among the Angolan Chokwe.

real sense, the hardships of digging diamonds echo the hardships of hunting or circumcision. Their passage in Angola turns them into 'hunters', and in the same way as a hunter's catch 'makes the clans grow and multiply' (*kavudish yikaand*), the captured diamonds and dollars may bring wealth and fertility to one's family. In this respect, it is also interesting to note that the analogy made by hunters between the shot animal and the female body is echoed in their general attitude towards diamonds and dollars. Invariably, hunters refer to game in strongly sexual terms, comparing, for example, the smell of the wounded animal's blood to the 'vaginal odours of a bitch'. Hunting discourse therefore often conceptualizes shooting as an act of penetration, as the hunter's ejaculation. Popular Zairean urban discourse reflects these views: women are taken possession of on the *champs-de-tir*, and male ejaculation is referred to as 'shooting the bullet' [Lingala: *kobeta cartouche*]. As such, the relationship between hunter and game is structurally similar to that between a husband and his wife. Like game, therefore, diamonds and dollars are talked about in female terms: dollars are affectionately called *dolls*, while women are spoken of as diamonds to be captured. In the Zairean songs of the moment, sweethearts are given names such as *diamante* and in one of the songs of a famous Zairean crooner, Koffi Olomide, a girl, upon being asked her name, replies: 'my first name is "money" (*motete*) and my family name is "wealth" (*mosolo*)'. One could say that here analogy ends to make place for an inversion of gender roles, in which youngsters and women become more powerful than elders and men (on the theme of money in popular Zairean music see Tshonga-Onyumbe, 1983).

DIAMOND HUNTING AND THE (RE)MAKING OF MORALITY

In a seminal essay, Guyer (1993) focuses on nineteenth-century African notions of accumulation. As she rightly points out:

> ... the development of currency in Equatorial Africa may be associated with the relatively great importance of *capture* [emphasis added] as a source, and destruction or immobilizations as destinations; that is, with what Gregory (1982) terms 'alienation'. In accordance with the principle of self-realization, the assets were not things at all, but the singular persons who harnessed sources and controlled fates. (Guyer, 1993: 256–7)

Viewed as such, the process of capturing and subsequently spending (in other words, destroying) diamonds and dollars thus becomes a process of self-realization through appropriation: it singularizes the successful *mwana Lunda*, who thereby realizes one major aspect of the Luunda notion of male personhood, that of a strong and autonomous person. As Guyer, para-phrasing Gregory, remarks, this process of self-realization can subsequently 'promote a dynamic of growth' (Guyer, 1993: 257). When applied to the *bana Lunda* phenomenon this observation helps us to understand how the appropriation, the 'capturing' of one's identity (see the notion of 'trapping wisdom' below), cast in terms of the autonomous and singularized hunter, the 'true man' and the 'patron', sets in motion a process of growth which leads to the realization of a second, complementary aspect of male person- and elderhood: that of a growing sense of insertion into and responsibility for the lives of other members of one's kin-group. Gradually a man becomes the fixed centre of the group for which he is responsible. The elder ideally forms the middle of the relationships that are being knotted around him and of which he becomes the constituting focal point and nexus. Of a family head it is said that 'he sits in the middle'. This process of growing toward the status of senior man, and thus toward the acquiring of erectness, goes together with the acquiring of 'wisdom' (*manaangw*). It requires a process of learning (*manaangw ma kwileej*) in order to 'complete one's wisdom'. Mature adult men are said to have 'trapped' this wisdom (*-pit manaangw*). The elder thus has 'acquired wisdom' and becomes a 'wise man' (*kakwaand*), rooted in 'ancestral wisdom' and knowledge (*mabaanz ma ukuluump*). This wisdom covers outstanding male capacities such as alertness, perspicacity, sagacity and judgement, firmness, discretion and longsightedness.

The construction of male identity is ambivalent insofar as it evolves around two opposing aspects — that of singularized, autonomous manhood, a model which seems to be idealized by many youngsters — and a second aspect of social responsibility, highlighting the elder's capacity to weave the social network and give a tangible form to ties of reciprocity and solidarity. In the context of ongoing diamond smuggling, stress is often put on both aspects simultaneously. With regard to the second aspect, for example, diamond smugglers organize themselves in *écuries*, new units organized around existing or newly invented kin ties, ethnic affiliation or shared locales, in which redefined rules of solidarity, mutual reciprocity and distribution of wealth apply. One also sees how a sense of responsibility towards one's immediate family members is often foregrounded.

The first generation of diamond smugglers is rapidly disappearing: many of them have died in Angola, and of those who survived the war, many have died of AIDS as a result of their 'savoir vivre'. In September 1995 I attended the funeral of one of them, a renowned Kikwit diamond smuggler, who for many personified the ideal and much admired version of the *boumeur*. Simultaneously, however, people also criticize irresponsible *potlach* beha- viour, to praise instead the 'wisdom' of those youngsters who invest their money in more lasting things such as a parcel of land or some cattle, or who construct a house for their parents.

The social critique on the 'wild' spending or destroying of wealth is exemplified, for example, in the commentary provided by 'Brother Musaka', a Kikwit shopkeeper who sells cassava flour. On a blackboard which he uses to advertise his goods in front of his shop, he has drawn a man, sitting on a chair with his head in his hands. Under this little scene is written: 'Too bad for this brother who travelled with Air Kasai [who took the plane to the

diamond mining town of Tembo, along the Zairean-Angolan border]'. Next
to it is written the following text in kiKoongo:

> ONE DOESN'T JOKE WITH FOOD! All the money that I brought with me from Tembo
> was spent on beer, cigarettes and women. I have done nothing good with it. What should I do
> now? Ah, in the name of my mother! It is my friend, who entertained me in the bars, who is
> to blame for this. Will Brother Musaka still give me cassava flour?

The moralizing criticism of 'wild' patterns of spending, destruction and
consumption is again connected to traditional moralities which strongly
condemn 'destructive' hunting practices. When constructed in terms of
sorcery, the act of hunting does not feed or enhance the well-being of the
hunter's kin-group: the hunter uses his powers to his own ends by 'eating'
affines and offspring, those he is supposed to feed. Such a hunter is no longer
in control of his own hunting powers; he is, on the contrary, controlled by
them. Similarly, the diamond hunter who selfishly spends his dollars, does
not master the powers residing in them, has not domesticated or trapped
them properly; rather his 'wisdom' has been trapped by them. It is in this
light that the existing criticism of money acquired through sorcery should be
viewed. It is widely believed that money obtained by those deviant means
does not last long and is quickly spent. Although, to my knowledge, there is
no equivalent term in either uLuund, Lingala or kiKoongo, such money is, in
a very real sense, what the Luo would term 'bitter' or ill-gotten money
(Shipton, 1989). The owners of such money have no control over it and 'eat'
(spend) their money 'like idiots'. There are, therefore, many accounts of
sorcery money that caused its owner to go crazy. Some of these tales relate
how ill-gotten dollars and diamonds turn into worthless paper or stones
upon returning from Angola. Other tales circulated by *radio-trottoir* tell how
'bitter' dollars, hidden inside their owner's house, start to multiply so rapidly
that they fill the whole house. Trapped within the house, the owner cannot
escape in time and is suffocated or crushed by tons of dollars.[20] 'Bitter'
money inverts the trapping logic, revealing the dialectics of possessing and
being possessed: the dollars (game) trap the hunter in his house. Such money,
in other words, is dangerous to its holder and the holder's family; it refuses to
be spent wisely, just as meat from hunting sorcery does not feed. It is,
however, precisely this 'feeding' capacity which marks the difference between
honest (diamond) hunter and sorcerer: whereas a sorcerer undermines, 'eats'
and corrupts the social order, the hunter or the 'wise' diamond smuggler
contributes to its maintenance. Through elaborate rules of distribution of
meat from the hunt, hunting enables Luunda men to transcend endogamous
sorcery as a destructive internal mechanism of redistribution (that is, it
counters the sorcerers' distribution of their victims' meat amongst them-

---

20. For similar stories with regard to money obtained in the 1991 Kinshasa lootings, see Yoka
    (1994a, 1994b).

selves), and to transform this negative reciprocity into a life-giving means of extended social reciprocity. Similarly, the 'wise' spending of dollars benefits the whole kin-group. As such, people not only stress the aspects of autonomy and self-containment inherent in notions of male person- and elderhood but also stress its complementary aspect: that of responsibility and moral uprightness. As one *mwana Lunda* explained to me: 'Diamonds are something saintly. To capture a valuable diamond and return with it to Zaire, one has to come from a family of saints, and one has to be like a saint oneself: always behave honestly, don't be tempted by your neighbour's diamonds'.[21]

All of this illustrates that the practices surrounding diamonds and dollars are also accompanied by a moral critique of some aspects of the diamond smuggling economy that are interpreted as immoral. It is not so much the act of ostentatious spending *as such* that is immoral, but expenditure that does not correspond to accepted patterns of self-realization, that is, spending which is not domesticated or tamed, and which deteriorates into an uncontrolled and wild flow of money and commodities.

DIAMONDS, DOLLARS AND THE INVERSION OF TERRITORIALIZATION

What the above makes clear, in my mind, is that the impact of diamonds and dollars is not solely negative, as is so often claimed in development studies and sociological analyses, which usually tend to echo Marx's or Simmel's more general views on money as destructive of kinship bonds and solidary communities (cf. Kambayi and Mudinga, 1991: 99ff; for an insightful discussion of Marx and Simmel on money see Bloch and Parry, 1989). Of course, the transborder diamond smuggling has produced negative effects: at the level of the household and the lineage, for example, it has indeed had a severe impact on the structuring of gerontocratic relations of authority and respect as well as on labour divisions and other gendered relationships (see above). Disregarding the advice of their fathers, brothers and husbands, many women now travel to Angola, often for considerable periods of time, earning money in prostitution. Such women are considered to be 'dogs that break the leash'. However, given the extremely harsh circumstances in which most Zaireans live (in town, but also in rural areas such as the southern Kwaango), it becomes increasingly difficult for these women's husbands to refuse their wives' money upon their return, or indeed to divorce them altogether. Moreover, diamonds have not only drastically altered the structuration of social relationships on the micro-level, they have also caused

---

21. This comment also illustrates the way in which the qualities of sainthood are no longer mediated through the *santu* sculpture as in a former period, but are being projected onto and interiorized by the diamond hunters themselves.

an acceleration of the spread of AIDS in the countryside. More generally, the diamonds have given rise to a general sense of growing insecurity, banditry and violence. I certainly do not want to deny or downplay these disruptive effects occasioned by the neocolonial intrusion and the brutal mercantilism of the diamond *comptoir* economy, or by the criminal maintenance of inflation and dollarization. However, unequivocally putting the stress on the negative impact of diamond trading activities links in too much with the longstanding and deeply romantic idea that the introduction of modernity, linked to a cash economy, is bound to have a thoroughly negative impact on an authentic, 'traditional' village life, thereby conveying a sense of lost cultural virginity and authenticity (and nostalgia is indeed the inevitable flip side of globalization; see Robertson, 1992).

This is not to deny the ruptures and fragmentations caused by such an imbrication. Many popular Zairean songs bemoan the 'lack of a place to which one fully belongs' (*kozanga esika*), thereby indicating a deeply felt rupture with one's lived world (cf. Ngandu, 1992), which has been fragmented and torn apart by the manifold processes of (de-, neo-, post-)colonization, by the manifest brutalities of the postcolonial state, as well as by more covert and subtle forms of social, economic and symbolic violence. The diffuse sense of place no longer allows one to draw the dividing line between urban and rural realities, 'modern' and 'traditional' worlds, or the level of the local and the global, in a self-evident way. In many ways, 'city' and 'village', then, have become states of mind, rather than spatial realities. In Africa, commodity relations, based on monetary transactions, have always formed the key metaphor for the structuring of relationships in the urban contexts. Central to this development of the African city has been the functioning of the *comptoir* economy. The political economy of the *comptoir*, which today characterizes the diamond trade in Angola and Zaire, has always been essentially colonial. It was used by the colonizer as a forceful means to transform and, above all, urbanize the African material and mental landscape (Sinou, 1993). Undoubtedly, in the late 1980s and the early 1990s, the *comptoir* economy in Bandundu and Angola contributed considerably to the urbanization of places such as Kahemba or Tembo in the Kwaango, or the mining settlements in Angola. Dollars are no longer generated in the city, but in the rural hinterland. As in the times of the precolonial slave and ivory trade in which the aLuund were deeply involved, the 'periphery' has thus regained centrality in the economic dynamics. At the same time, the economy and the social life of the existing Zairean urban space (and the city of Kikwit is an obvious example here; see Mpuru, 1993) is marked by an accelerating ruralization and increasingly depends on the economic activities of the former periphery. This process of *villagization* of the city (see also Devisch, 1995) goes hand in hand with growing social barriers and an increasing polarization and segregation of the urban space, between, on the one hand, the commercial and 'European' centre of cities such as Kinshasa and Kikwit, urbanized by the Belgians before independence, and now taken over by those who have access to diamond dollars, and, on the other hand, the endless 'peripheral cities', *la cité* (La Fontaine, 1970; Nzuzi, 1992) where an increasing number of city-dwellers — the vast majority of Zaireans who do not have access to diamond dollars and no longer participate in a failing system of commodity market exchange — try to survive.

The contemporary diamond *comptoir* economy has thus occasioned an 'urbanization' of the rural locale. At the same time it has contributed to a mental (rather than, or alongside, a material) ruralization of the urban sites, in that it has allowed people, through the medium of diamonds, to introduce and reinvent older notions, mentalities, practices, and moralities within that urban space. Above I have discussed the ways in which the *bana Lunda*'s identity constructions are deeply rooted in longstanding moral matrixes and habituses. As such, the reality of the *bana Lunda* phenomenon and the diamond trade in the Kwaango and the Angolan plateau of Lunda Norte is not only geographically that of the frontier: the 'frontier' is also socio-cultural and economical, in a pot-pourri between 'rural' and 'urban', local and global, 'traditional' and 'modern' categories, practices, mentalities, relationships and belief systems. For those involved at the local level, diamonds and dollars, in other words, facilitate a negotiation between different realities and identities. Like language, money carries meaning and constitutes a form by means of which the contents of the relationships between self and other may be defined. I argue, therefore, that diamonds and dollars offer the possibility of negotiation and recomposition of identity, in a process, not only of self-realization and promotion of social status in the terms proposed by Guyer (Guyer, 1993; Guyer and Eno, 1995; see also Barber, 1995) but also of a more encompassing 'self-making', in the sense given to it by Battaglia (1995), that is, as the process of capturing and 'fixing' the non-steady state of selfhood and of one's own identity in different and increasingly diffuse cultural situations and locales. In this way, by way of paraphrasing Kopytoff (1987), the frontier, *in casu* the universe of the Zairean diamond 'frontier', as intermediate spatial reality and as mentality, reinvents and hence (re-)presents and reproduces certain aspects of 'traditional' African society in the postcolonial context, introducing local moralities in innovative ways onto the translocal and the global scene. More precisely, the traffic, the smuggle and the sale of diamonds offers the possibility to bridge the gap between different socio-cultural contexts and, to use Hyden's otherwise questionable image, to capture modernity while (partly) remaining uncaptured or 'untrapped' oneself. Therefore, diamonds are not unidimensionally to be seen as the source of ecological destruction, or as the tools of social disjunction, introducing prostitution, alcoholism, violence and exploitation into the rural space; to as important an extent the acquisition of diamonds and the spending of dollars also mobilizes a social capital and forms a forceful means of social transformation of the modern, the (post)colonial and the city in terms of the 'traditional', the precolonial and the countryside.

Let me illustrate this with one last example. In the city of Kikwit, one finds large boards along the streets advertising Tembo, a dark Zairean beer. The publicity for this bottled beer is combined with an advertisement for Benda, a brand of soap. Both the bottled beer and the soap function as powerful icons, conjuring up the world of modernity, the luxurious life-style of the West, named Putu, Miguel, or Mikili, geared towards progress. The brewer's slogan (in kiKoongo) is: *Tembo kuntwala!* (Tembo is the future!). However, the beer's trade-name is not only the kiSwahili gloss for 'elephant', Tembo is also the name of a booming diamond-mining town along the Zairean–Angolan border. In consequence, the *bana Lunda* have appropriated the brewery's slogan to point out where their future lies: in Angola. In other words, the *bana Lunda* have created their own, 'indigenous' version of modernity and of Europe, and thereby engage in a 'reinvention' of capitalism (Bayart, 1994) in their own terms. As Pepe Kalle sings in one of his popular songs: 'They went to Europe, but had to land in the desert'. The phrase not only refers to the hardships of the Zairean diaspora in Europe, which turns out to be a desert for those who have to live there, it also indicates that the world of modernity, defined in terms of the West, has become inaccessible to most Zaireans. Modernity, with its tempting promises, embedded in a vision of an expansive capitalism in service of the nation-state, has become the fool's paradise in which the Zairean nation is no longer capable of living. The *bana Lunda*'s response lies in the invention of an Africanized Occident of the little man, reterritorializing the West and its pathways of accumulation. Traditionally, one of these pathways into modernity's sources of wealth was western-style education, often in combination with that second colonizing tool, a religious, seminary-style training (Mudimbe, 1994). Quite literally, a student visa is one of the most likely roads of access to Europe (Mayoyo, 1995). It must be mentioned here that, ironically, a crude stone sculpture of a hunter battling with a wild animal symbolizes the victory of education over savagery at Kinshasa's university campus. However, many diamond hunters tend to turn away from schooling and education, and thus from a politics that disciplines and domesticates persons, space and time along the lines of western models already outlined in the colonial library. I often heard the remark that in Angola, 'diamonds seem to flee intellectuals'. Similarly, *bana Lunda* would argue that 'French is not money', that those who have gone to school 'have no money, only French', or that 'French cannot be eaten' (again, language and money are used to mark and define the relationship between other and self, the West and the rest). The fact that many school teachers and students have become diamond smugglers only proves their point.[22]

---

22. The same attitude is echoed in a song called *olingi mwasi kaka mbongo* (To love a woman one needs money), sung by Koffi Olomide: 'Those who have no means, lead a life of philosophizing, a life filled with words, but a woman does not eat words'.

Diamond digging and smuggling offers access to 'savoir vivre' to those for whom the privileged worlds of western education are not accessible. Those who cannot afford a SABENA or Air France ticket to Europe (and the 'Boeing' or *bwingi* is another powerful icon of modernity), walk, or take the small aircraft carriers of Air Kasai, Malou Aviation or Air Excellence(!), to Tembo, Kahemba and Angola, that is, to their own, accessible, version of 'Terra Nova' (the name of a 'diamond' bar in Kikwit), where modernity is redefined along lines that leave room for a continuity with one's own social reality and past. As such, the diamond diggers' 'taming' of diamonds and dollars is not (exclusively) related to notions or practices of resistance against 'modernity' (that is, to taming as strategy for diluting the potential destructive effects of monetary exchange and of commodities; see Miller 1995a: 145; 1995b: 6). Rather, 'taming' is presented here as a form of action to appropriate and transform 'modernity', and, perhaps more importantly, introduce, or, with a less imperialist term, *infuse* (trans)local moralities onto the global scene. In this way, diamonds and dollars allow people to draw a 'rhizomatic' map, to use the botanical image developed by Deleuze and Guattari (1980) in their reflections on capitalism and schizophrenia, and which they use to describe the operations of capitalism (which also include processes of colonization and acculturation, disrupting and reinscribing local cultural territories and spaces and domesticating the foreign). The rhizomatic dynamics, however, may also apply to the cartography of the *mwana Lunda* who, by turning the periphery–centre division inside out, dissociates himself from representations imposed from outside and from above. As such the *bana Lunda* reconstitute static and closed conceptions of the unidirectional relationship between modernity and tradition, city and countryside, the West and its offshoot, Africa, in terms of shifting lines of partial (translocal as well as local–global) connections and patterns of de- and reterritorialization, offering the possibility of inverting the colonial experience from 'Terra Morta' (cf. Soromenho, 1956: footnote 6, above) to 'Terra Nova', as well as inverting the process of the globalization of the local.[23]

CONCLUSION

Diamonds and dollars allow the *bana Lunda* to engage in processes of inverted territorialization which enable the active 'taming' of the urban space, of modernity and of the world of the white Other. These motions of de- and reterritorialization are part of a creative and dynamic process that reaches far beyond the passive and mimetic reproduction and representation of modernity as evoked by Mudimbe (1988), for whom the intermediate

---

23. See also Bayart (1989) and Brydon (1988) on the usefulness of the model of the rhizome for an analysis of the postcolonial situation.

space between 'so-called African tradition and the projected modernity of colonialism' is designated by marginality and reveals the strong tension between a modernity that often is an illusion of development, and a tradition that sometimes reflects a poor image of the past. If anything, the *bana Lunda* phenomenon shows that postcolonial studies often tend to be far too one-sided in their focus on patterns of passive consumption. The 'intermediate space' is not only defined by marginality or by colonial palimpsestual inscription. That, again, is a one-sided, marginalizing interpretation from a first-world perspective. I have endeavoured to illustrate how my analysis leads away from Mudimbe's understanding of the intermediate space towards a reality that has more in common, perhaps, with Bhabha's *inter* or in-between 'Third Space' (Bhabha, 1994); how the colonizer's invention of Africa is mirrored and answered by the colonized's displacement and spatial relocation of a reinvented Europe; and finally how, through processual transformations, local actors are actively engaged in defining the content and architecture of the intermediate space-time in which they find and indeed 'make' themselves. I have also illustrated how this translocal architecture very often takes on forms that are strongly rooted in local pasts, even if this past is signified and thereby transformed in the present. The critical point here is that former responses to specific, historically contextualized forms of mercantilism are carried into the present in an attempt to get a grip on an economic and mercantile landscape that shares multiple characteristics with the trading practices from the past, but which is also significantly different in other respects. Futile as this attempt may therefore seem from the outside, the 'taming' in the *bana Lunda*'s practice of 'taming' or 'domesticating' diamonds and dollars should not be understood as a practice of passive consumption, or as a particular form of resistance against the realities of a penetrating capitalism, but, on the contrary, as a form of active capturing, of the urban space, for example (in the same way as the *sapeurs* of Brazzaville and Kinshasa appropriated the West in the early 1980s by their appropriation of French designer fashions in a political economy of elegance, thereby refashioning the West in their own terms; see Friedman, 1990; Gandoulou, 1989; Yoka, 1991). It would be interesting in this respect to further analyse the influence on Zairean urban youth subcultures of western images of hunting and the frontier, as circulated through westerns and action movies. For example, Kinshasa's youngsters' argot, known as *hindoubill* (a mixture of Lingala, French and local vernacular languages), has its roots in a movement called *billism*, which originated between 1957 and 1959 and could be found all over the city of Léopoldville, but not in the 'white' zones of Ngaliema, Léopoldville and Limete (Kolonga, 1979). This movement grouped various competing youth gangs (such as the 'Yankies of Ngiri-Ngiri'), music bands (some of which are still performing today) and ludic groups of young urban 'terrorists', more generally known as 'The Spongers of the Far West' (*Les Ecumeurs du Far West*). Each of these groups had their own rituals of initiation. These consisted, for example, of a period of seclusion in the bush, where one was trained into a specific style of combat, called *bilayi*. The movement mainly found its inspiration in American westerns, to which Kinshasa's urban young had access by way of the various movie theatres that had started to spring up in the urban zones of Kintambo, Lingwala, Kinshasa and Barumbu in the second half of the 1950s. As such, *billism* captured and transformed the image of the cowboy-hunter, and in particular of the culture-heroes Buffalo Bill and Pecos Bill, to make it its own. The *Billies* also renamed various areas, markets, schools, bars and other public spaces of Léopoldville, bestowing upon them such names as 'Texas' or 'Dallas', in a moment of reterritorialization which almost certainly implied a criticism of the Belgians' insufficient and segregationist urbanization of a too-rapidly expanding city. Undoubtedly, the *Billies'* practice of reclaiming and renaming parodied the colonizer's imperialist obsession with mapping and labelling, while at the same time playfully commenting upon the claims of the emergent nationalist movements. More recently, the way in which western action movie 'hunters' and warriors have been captured and localized can also be observed in the Angolan context. In 1992, for example, the 'Ninja's', a special anti-terrorist task force, made their entrance on the Angolan scene (Antonio, 1995). Similarly, Rambo-style or Kung Fu dress is preferred by diamond digging youth on the Liberia–Sierra Leone border (Richards, 1996). Like the cowboy, the images of the Ninja, Rambo and other Exterminators have been used by the *bana Lunda* themselves as further elaborations of their own images of the hunter.

The moral and social economies that are given shape in the hunting of diamonds and the spending of dollars form an attempt at bridging the ruptures that indeed characterize the lived worlds of many in contemporary Zaire's intermediate spaces, and provide people with a possibility to realize and actively (re)make their own identity, to introduce longstanding local moralities in new contexts, and to think, negotiate, reinvent and define the relationships between one's own past and identity on the one hand, and the colonial legacy, the *mundele*, the west, 'modernity' and 'progress', on the other. From the *bana Lunda's* point of view, the negotiation (rather than negation) between these two realms takes place on their own terms, in imaginative and — in their eyes — more advantageous and less marginal ways, which challenge the incomprehensible logic of a monetary economy while simultaneously providing access to the benefits of modernity. The image of the diamond 'hunter' has a strongly epistemic power, offering the possibility to remake identity and place and generate — to some extent — a socially viable environment for those within the diamond scene. The examples which I have provided clearly show that part of this remaking and reclaiming of identities is strongly discursive. I have stressed, however, that there is also another dimension at play: a deeply rooted habitus, a past, a bedrock of moral matrixes that is embodied by and externalized (although often in fragmented and strongly transformed ways) in the practices of the *bana Lunda*. It is perhaps this dimension rather than the discursive one which ultimately forms the source for the regeneration of identity, for a new or renewed generative order and for newly defined modes of dealing with excess and heterogeneity in the urban locale. In this evolution, the generational aspect seems to be of foremost importance. The moralizing criticism of uncontrolled prodigality entails in effect a shift in emphasis from the socio-logics of the hunter to that of the elder and, by extension, the family unit. As the example of Brother Musaka's statement (in kiKoongo!) shows, this also means that the masculine figure of the hunter (and hunting praxis as such) is itself recaptured and thereby rescued from the field of a disappropriative imaginary as exemplified in sorcery, to be brought back home (quite literally) by other forces. These spring from different sources, from much more feminine fields and spaces which mediate more than they are intermediate: the female domains of the household and, most importantly, the kitchen, the fireplace and the cauldron. This field is far more basal than any Bhabhaesque 'in-between'. In it the significance and the rhythms of reciprocity, com-mensality, conjugality and gender relations are most fully explored and defined. The reappropriation of male body and sexuality takes place in and through this intimate domain of the household, and as such forms the necessary complement of, and precondition for, any successful and lasting outward (social, political, economic) reappropriation or diversion of space. But that will have to be developed further in a future paper.

ACKNOWLEDGEMENTS

Field research has been made possible by grants from the Research Fund of the Catholic University of Leuven, the 'Vlaamse Leergangen', and the Belgian National Fund for Scientific Research (NFWO). Preliminary versions of this article have been presented at the conference on 'Globalization and the Construction of Communal Identities', Amsterdam (March 1996), the Twelfth Satterthwaite Colloquium on African Ritual and Religion (April 1996), and the conference 'Argent, feuille morte?', Leuven (June 1996). I would like to thank Birgit Meyer for her editorial remarks, as well as R. Devisch and the other participants at the Doctoral Seminar of the Africa Research Centre (ARC) of the Catholic University of Leuven for their stimulating comments and criticisms on an earlier version.

REFERENCES

Antonio Africano, M. (1995) *L'Unita et la deuxième guerre civile angolaise*. Paris: L'Harmattan.
Appadurai, A. (1990) 'Disjuncture and Difference in the Global Cultural Economy', *Public Culture* 2(2): 1–24.
Azam, J. P., P. Collier and A. Cravinho (1993) 'Crop Sales, Shortages and Peasant Portfolio Behaviour: An Analysis of Angola', *The Journal of Development Studies* 30(2): 361–79.
Barber, K. (1995) 'Money, Self-realization, and the Person in Yoruba Texts', in J. Guyer (ed.) *Money Matters. Instability, Values and Social Payments in the Modern History of West African Communities*, pp. 204–24. Portsmouth, NH: Heinemann; London: James Currey.

Bastin, M.-L. (1978) *Statuettes Tshokwe du héros civilisateur 'Tshibinda Ilunga'*. Arnouville: Arts d'Afrique Noire.

Bastin, M.-L. (1988) *Entités spirituelles des Tshokwe (Angola)*. (Quaderni Poro 5.) Milan: Stampa Sipiel.

Bastin, M.-L. (1990) 'Die Bruderschaft der Berufsjäger *mayanga* bei den Tshokwe (Angola)', in G. Völger and K. v. Welck (eds) *Männerbande Männerbunde. Zur Rolle des Mannes im Kulturvergleich*, pp. 327–30. Köln: Rautenstrauch-Joest-Museums (*Ethnologica* 15.1)

Bataille, G. (1967) *La Part maudite, précédé de La Notion de dépense*. Paris: Minuit.

Battaglia, D. (1995) 'Problematising the Self: A Thematic Introduction', in D. Battaglia (ed.) *Rhetorics of Self-Making*, pp. 1–15. Berkeley, CA: University of California Press.

Bayart, J.-F. (1989) *L'État en Afrique. La politique du ventre*. Paris: Fayard.

Bayart, J.-F. (ed.) (1994) *La réinvention du capitalisme*. Paris: Karthala.

Bernal, V. (1994) 'Peasants, Capitalism and (Ir)rationality', *American Ethnologist* 21(4): 792–810.

Bhabha, H. (1994) *The Location of Culture*. London and New York: Routledge.

Bittremieux, L. (1923) *Mayombsch Idioticon*. Gent: Erasmus.

Bloch, M. and J. Parry (1989) 'Introduction', in J. Parry and M. Bloch (eds) *Money and the Morality of Exchange*, pp. 1–32. Cambridge: Cambridge University Press.

De Boeck, F. (1991a) 'Therapeutic Efficacy and Consensus among the aLuund of SW Zaire', *Africa* 61: 37–71.

De Boeck, F. (1991b) 'The Art of Hunting, The Art of Child-Bearing: Uyaang Hunting Ritual and Therapeutic Fertility Cults', in F. De Boeck 'From Knots to Web. Fertility, Life-transmission, Health and Well-being among the aLuund of SW Zaire', pp. 339–428. Doctoral thesis. University of Leuven.

De Boeck, F. (1993) 'Symbolic and Diachronic Study of Intercultural Therapeutic and Divinatory Roles among aLuund and Chokwe in the Upper Kwaango', in K. Schilder and W. van Binsbergen (eds) *Ethnicity in Africa*, pp. 73–104. (Thematic issue of *Afrika Focus* 9.1–2)

De Boeck, F. (1994a) ' "When Hunger Goes around the Land": Hunger and Food among the aLuund of Zaire', *Man* 29(2): 257–82.

De Boeck, F. (1994b) 'Of Trees and Kings: Politics and Metaphor among the aLuund of Southwestern Zaire', *American Ethnologist* 21(3): 451–73.

De Boeck, F. (1996) 'Postcolonialism, Power and Identity: Local and Global Perspectives from Zaire', in R. Werbner and T. Ranger (eds) *Postcolonial Identities in Africa*, pp. 75–106. London: Zed Books.

Brydon, D. (1988) 'Troppo Agitato: Reading and Writing Cultures in Randolph Stow's *Visitants* and Rudy Wiebe's *The Temptation of Big Bear*', *Ariel* 19(1): 13–32.

de Castro Henriques, I. (1993) 'Interférence du religieux dans l'organisation du commerce en Angola au XIXe siècle', in J.-P. Chrétien (ed.) *L'invention religieuse en Afrique. Histoire et religion en Afrique noire*, pp. 133–51. Paris: ACCT/Karthala.

de Castro Henriques, I. (1995) *Commerce et changement en Angola au XIXième siècle. Imbangala et Tshokwe face à la modernité*. Paris: L'Harmattan.

Deleuze, G. and F. Guattari (1980) *Mille plateaux. Capitalisme et schizophrénie 2*. Paris: Minuit.

Devisch, R. (1993) *Weaving the Threads of Life. The Khita Gyn-Eco-Logical Healing Cult among the Yaka*. Chicago, IL: The University of Chicago Press.

Devisch, R. (1995) 'Frenzy, Violence, and Ethical Renewal in Kinshasa', *Public Culture* 7(3): 593–629.

Fabian, J. (1978) 'Popular Culture in Africa: Findings and Conjectures', *Africa* 48: 315–34.

Fieremans, C. (1977) *Het voorkomen van diamant langsheen de Kwango-rivier in Angola en Zaïre*. Brussels: Académie Royale des Sciences d'Outre-Mer.

Fisiy, C. and P. Geschiere (1991) 'Sorcery, Witchcraft and Accumulation: Regional Variations in South and West Cameroon', *Critique of Anthropology* 11(3): 251–78.

Friedman, J. (1990) 'The Political Economy of Elegance', *Cultural History* 7: 101–22.

Gandoulou, J. D. (1989) *Au coeur de la sape: moeurs et aventures des Congolais à Paris*. Paris: L'Harmattan.

Geschiere, P. (1992) 'Kinship, Witchcraft and "the Market". Hybrid Patterns in Cameroonian Societies', in R. Dilley (ed.) *Contesting Markets. Analyses of Ideology, Discourse and Practice*, pp. 159–79. Edinburgh: Edinburgh University Press.

Geschiere, P. (1995) *Sorcellerie et politique en Afrique. La viande des autres*. Paris: Karthala.

Gregory, C. (1982) *Gifts and Commodities*. Cambridge: Cambridge University Press.

Gudeman, S. and A. Rivera (1990) *Conversations in Columbia*. Cambridge: Cambridge University Press.

Guyer, J. (1993) 'Wealth in People and Self-realization in Equatorial Africa', *Man* 28(2): 243–65.

Guyer, J. and S. M. Eno Belinga (1995) 'Wealth in People as Wealth in Knowledge: Accumulation and Composition in Equatorial Africa', *Journal of African History* 36: 91–120.

Hyden, G. (1980) *Beyond Ujamaa in Tanzania: Underdevelopment and an Uncaptured Peasantry*. Berkeley, CA: University of California Press.

Hyden, G. (1983) *No Shortcuts to Progress: African Development Management in Perspective*. Berkeley, CA: University of California Press.

Kambayi Bwatshia and Mudinga Mukendi (1991) *Le 'citancisme'. Au coeur de l'évolution de la société Luba-Kasai. Sens et non sens d'une mentalité*. Kinshasa: Saint Paul.

Kolonga Molei (1979) *Kinshasa, ce village d'hier*. Kinshasa: Sodimca.

Kopytoff, I. (ed.) (1987) *The African Frontier. The Reproduction of Traditional African Societies*. Bloomington, IN: Indiana University Press.

La Fontaine, J. S. (1970) *City Politics. A Study of Léopoldville 1962–1963*. Cambridge: Cambridge University Press.

Lemarchand, R. (1989) 'African Peasantries, Reciprocity and the Market. The Economy of Affection Reconsidered', *Cahiers d'Études Africaines* 113: 33–67.

Lima, M. (1971) *Fonctions sociologiques des figurines de culte Hamba dans la société et dans la culture Tshokwé (Angola)*. Luanda: Instituto de Investigaçao Cientifica de Angola.

Marcus, G. E. (1995) 'Ethnography in/of the World System: The Emergence of Multi-Sited Ethnography', *Annual Review of Anthropology* 24: 95–117.

Mauss, M. (1985/1950) 'Essai sur le don. Forme et raison de l'échange dans les sociétés archaïques', in M. Mauss *Sociologie et anthropologie*, pp. 145–279. Paris: Quadrige/Presses Universitaires de France.

Mayoyo Bitumba Tipo-Tipo (1995) *Migration Sud/Nord. Levier ou obstacle. Les Zaïrois en Belgique*. Brussels: Institut Africain-CEDAF; Paris: L'Harmattan.

Meyer, B. (1995) ' "Delivered from the Powers of Darkness". Confessions of Satanic Riches in Christian Ghana', *Africa* 65(2): 236–55.

Miller, D. (1995a) 'Consumption and Commodities', *Annual Review of Anthropology* 24: 141–61.

Miller, D. (1995b) 'Introduction: Anthropology, Modernity and Consumption', in D. Miller (ed.) *Worlds Apart. Modernity through the Prism of the Local*, pp. 1–22. London: Routledge.

Misser, F. (1994) 'Les diams, nerfs de la guerre d'Angola', *Croissance* 370: 28.

Mpuru Mazembe Bias (1993) 'Approvisionnement vivrier immédiat de Kikwit: aperçu préliminaire', *Géokin* 4(1): 37–48.

Mudimbe, V. Y. (1988) 'Discourse of Power and Knowledge of Otherness', in V. Y. Mudimbe *The Invention of Africa. Gnosis, Philosophy, and the Order of Knowledge*, pp. 1–23. London: James Currey.

Mudimbe, V. Y. (1994) 'Domestication and the Conflict of Memories', in V. Y. Mudimbe *The Idea of Africa*, pp. 105–52. Bloomington, IN: Indiana University Press; London: James Currey.

Nange Kudita wa Sesemba (1981) 'L'homme et la femme dans la société et la culture Cokwe'. Doctoral thesis. Louvain-la-Neuve: Université Catholique de Louvain.

Ngandu Kashama, P. (1992) 'La chanson de la rupture dans la musique zaïroise moderne', in M. Quaeghebeur and E. Van Balberghe (eds) *Papier blanc, encre noir. Cent ans de culture francophone en Afrique centrale (Zaïre, Rwanda et Burundi)*, pp. 477–89. Brussels: Labor.

Nzuzi Lelo (1992) 'Gestion foncière et production de l'habitat urbain au Zaïre', *Géokin* 3(2): 241–63.

Pepe Kalle and Orchestre Empire Bakuba (1993) *Poto Malili: Kinshasa Moto! Moto! Moto!*. Brussels: Musicanova. [Sabam recording reference: Mus 1003].

Prioul, C. (1995) ' "La pierre du diable". Témoignage Gbaya-Kara sur le diamant centrafricain (1967–1970)', in P. Claval and Singaravelou (eds) *Ethnogéographies*, pp. 337–62. Paris: L'Harmattan.

Richards, P. (1996) 'Chimpanzees, Diamonds and War: The Discourses of Global Environmental Change and Local Violence on the Liberia-Sierra Leone Border', in H. L. Moore (ed.) *The Future of Anthropological Knowledge*, pp. 139–55. London and New York: Routledge.

Robertson, R. (1992) 'Globalization and the Nostalgic Paradigm', in R. Robertson *Globalization. Social Theory and Global Culture*, pp. 146–63. London: Sage.

Scott, C. V. (1995) *Gender and Development. Rethinking Modernization and Dependency Theory*. Boulder, CO: Lynne Rienner.

Shipton, P. (1989) *Bitter Money. Cultural Economy and Some African Meanings of Forbidden Commodities*. (American Ethnological Society Monograph Series no. 1) Washington, DC: American Anthropological Association.

Sinou, A. (1993) *Comptoirs et villes coloniales du Sénégal. Saint-Louis, Gorée, Dakar*. Paris: Karthala/Orstom.

Soromenho, C. (1956) *Camaxilo [Terra Morta]*. Paris: Présence Africaine.

Taussig, M. (1980) *The Devil and Commodity Fetishism in South America*. Chapel Hill, NC: University of North Carolina Press.

Taylor, C. C. (1992) *Milk, Honey and Money. Changing Concepts in Rwandan Healing*. Washington, DC: Smithsonian Institution Press.

Tshibanza Monji (1986) 'Le phénomène creuseurs et ses paradoxes', *Zaïre-Afrique* 206: 341–55.

Tshibanza Monji and Tshimanga Mulangula (1985) 'Matières précieuses et libéralisation: esquisse d'un bilan provisoire', *Zaïre-Afrique* 196: 337–47.

Tshonga-Onyumbe (1983) 'Le thème de l'argent dans la musique zaïroise moderne de 1960 à 1981', *Zaïre-Afrique* 172: 97–111.

Turner, E. (1992) *Experiencing Ritual. A New Interpretation of African Healing*. Philadelphia, PA: University of Pennsylvania Press.

Turner, V. (1953) *Lunda Rites and Ceremonies*. Livingstone: Rhodes-Livingstone Museum.

Turner, V. (1967) *The Forest of Symbols. Aspects of Ndembu Ritual*. Ithaca, NY: Cornell University Press.

Warnier, J.-P. (1993) 'L'économie politique de la sorcellerie en Afrique Centrale', in G. Gosselin (ed.) *Les nouveaux enjeux de l'anthropologie. Autour de Georges Balandier*, pp. 259–71. Paris: L'Harmattan.

Weiss, B. L. (1992) 'Plastic Teeth Extraction: The Iconography of Haya Gastro-Sexual Affliction', *American Ethnologist* 19(3): 538–52.

Willame, J.-C. (1986) *L'épopée d'Inga. Chronique d'une prédation industrielle*. Paris: L'Harmattan.

Wrong, M. (1996) 'Angola's Peace now Hangs on Who Gets the Diamonds', *Financial Times* 3 May 1996.

Yoka Lye Mudaba, A. (1991) 'Système de la mode à Kinshasa: culte du paraître', in Mashin Mazinga (ed.) *La ville africaine et ses urgences vitales*, pp. 31–7. Kinshasa: Facultés Catholiques de Kinshasa.

Yoka Lye Mudaba, A. (1994a) 'Mythologie de la violence à Kinshasa', *Zaïre-Afrique* XXXIV 282: 83–8.

Yoka Lye Mudaba, A. (1994b) 'Profession: Sandrumeur', in C. Djungu-Simba Kamatenda (ed.) *Sandruma on demon-cratise! Receuil de nouvelles*, pp. 149–58. Kinshasa: Les Editions du Trottoir.

Globalization and the Power of Indeterminate Meaning: Witchcraft and Spirit Cults in Africa and East Asia

Peter Geschiere

Why is there such a strong tendency in many parts of post-colonial Africa for people to interpret modern processes of change in terms of 'witchcraft'? Notions like 'witchcraft', 'sorcery' or *sorcellerie* seem to be omnipresent: in the newspapers, in *radio trottoir*, on TV. Witchcraft seems to be in the open — probably much more so than a few decades ago. It is hardly possible to discuss issues of 'globalization' and 'identity' without stumbling on these notions.[1] As Comaroff and Comaroff (1993: xxix) put it in their introduction to one of the first books to address this close link between modernity and witchcraft: 'Witches ... embody all the contradictions of the experience of modernity itself, of its inescapable enticements, its self-consuming passions, its discriminatory tactics, its devastating social costs'. The question as to why this is so is an urgent one. Throughout the continent, there seems to be a growing panic about a supposed proliferation of witchcraft, especially in the more modern sectors. The idea that witchcraft 'is running wild' triggers panicky and sometimes extremely violent witch-hunts by ambitious *nganga* (witch-doctors) but also by State judges and *gendarmes*. The new forms of wealth to which so few people have access but which evoke wild fantasies among the many are a central focus in all this.

The question of why this close conceptual link between modernity and witchcraft exists in Africa is also an extremely tricky one. The very fact that notions like witchcraft, sorcery, *sorcellerie* — or whatever term people

With many thanks to Jean Comaroff, Prasenjit Duara, Cyprian Fisiy, Birgit Meyer, Francis Nyamnjoh, Peter Pels, Rafael Sanchez and Peter van der Veer for their suggestions.

1. It is all the more surprising that anthropologists, despite their long-standing interest in the topic of witchcraft as such, neglected for so long its modern dynamics in relation to politics, new forms of entrepreneurship, and so on (see Geschiere, 1997: Ch. 8). This changed abruptly in the early 1990s when a sudden spate of articles and books on the modern dynamics of witchcraft discourses and practices began to appear (see, for instance, Ashforth, 1996; Bastian, 1993; Comaroff and Comaroff, 1993, and forthcoming; Fisiy and Geschiere, 1990, 1991; Offiong, 1991; Niehaus, 1993; Shaw, forthcoming; see also earlier contributions by Geschiere, 1988; Rowlands and Warnier, 1988; and, from the margins of anthropology, Desjeux, 1987; and especially de Rosny, 1981, 1992; cf. also a fascinating and quite frightening series of interviews by Chenuaud, 1995, of *Radio France Culture* on recent developments in Brazzaville).

use[2] — have become so current suggests a conceptual continuity: the use of these terms seems to indicate that people try to relate modern changes to a 'traditional' discourse on occult forces. This apparent continuity might, however, be deceptive. The notions concerned prove to be highly dynamic and often quite unsystematic concepts, subject to constant re-interpretations and shifts of meaning. This raises the question of change under an apparent continuity: to what extent are these notions being re-interpreted in new circumstances; and how do these re-interpretations affect their role in daily life?

Discussing this relation between witchcraft and modernity is tricky for another reason as well. It seems to provide the umpteenth proof of Africa's Otherness — not to say its backwardness. At the conference on 'Globalization and the Construction of Identity' on which this volume is based, all three presentations on Africa (by De Boeck, Meyer and myself) related the conference theme to witchcraft. This made another of the participants (Peter van der Veer) wonder with some suspicion whether it is not a sign that Africa is still 'anthropology-land'? The threatening equation of Africa with witchcraft — and anthropologists' role in this equation — is certainly problematic. When making a brief lecture tour through India with two African colleagues, I was quite embarrassed to have to discuss witchcraft in present-day Africa with Indian audiences: no matter how I approached the subject, it was quite clear that, to many in the audience, I was confirming the worst stereotypes about Africa's primitiveness. Since many still see modernization as basically a process of disenchantment, the resilience of witchcraft in Africa seems to be a blatant sign of the continent's backwardness.[3]

It is, therefore, important to insist that in a more general perspective Africa is not so special in this respect (as in many others). Africans are certainly not the only ones to succumb to modernity's enchantment. It might be even more

---

2. I will come back to the considerable terminological problems raised by these terms. Here a brief note on the terminology used in this article must suffice. Western notions like 'witchcraft', 'sorcery' or *sorcellerie* are no doubt unfortunate translations of African terms which often have a far broader meaning. In many cases, a more neutral and less pejorative translation, like 'occult forces', would be preferable. The problem is, however, that terms like 'witchcraft' or 'sorcery' have been generally appropriated by Africans. They are widely used, not only in the rumour machine of *radio trottoir*, but also in newspapers, on the radio or on TV. It is in these terms that public debates are waged. Social scientists can therefore hardly avoid these terms since they have become part of the issues raised by the dynamics of these discourses. Moreover, I do not follow Evans-Pritchard's distinction between 'sorcery' and 'witchcraft' (see, for example, Evans-Pritchard, 1937) which — despite a long series of criticisms — has made it into many textbooks on anthropology, since it is difficult to apply in the changing circumstances of modern Africa.

3. But see Obeysekere (1977), who already emphasized then that the increase of spirit cults and sorcery in especially the more modern sectors of society in Sri Lanka did not at all agree with the Weberian equation of 'modernization' and 'disenchantment' (cf. also Kapferer, 1983, 1997). This indicates, moreover, that in Asia too the obsession with witchcraft/sorcery can be strong. It is also a recurrent element in European stereotypes about Asia (see, for example, Couperus, 1900/92).

important to point out that parallel examples come not only from capital-ism's periphery,[4] but also from its core-countries, both the old-timers and the newly emergent ones. In a seminal paper, soon to be published, Jean Comaroff (forthcoming), following Hacking (1991a, 1991b), explores striking parallels between witchcraft in modern Africa and the increasing obsession with child abuse — especially at the hands of parents, child-minders or other intimates — in the West.[5] She recognizes that it is too easy to just qualify the increasingly aggressive attempts to unmask child abusers in our midst as modern forms of witch-hunts — the procedures are very different — but at a deeper level there are important correspondences. Both stem from a confusing mixture of intimacy (the enemy is supposed to come from within) and a frightening vision of vast, open-ended networks of Satan worshippers or witches that are, moreover, of a highly commercial nature. Both obsessions — with witchcraft and with child abuse — are 'products of moral perplexity ... ways of phrasing local interventions in global histories' (Comaroff, forthcoming).[6] In such a broader perspective, it becomes hard indeed to see the connection of witchcraft and modernity as just another sign of Africa's Otherness.

In earlier publications (Fisiy and Geschiere, 1991, 1996; see also Geschiere, 1997), I have tried to explain the modernizing capacities of witchcraft discourses in present-day Africa by emphasizing their surprising ambiva-lence. 'Witchcraft' is supposedly used as a levelling force, undermining inequalities in wealth and power, but the same force is often supposed to be indispensable for the accumulation of such wealth and power. Witchcraft is both jealousy and success. It is used to kill but also to heal. It is evil but it can be controlled and used in a positive way; and so forth.

---

4. See, for particularly vivid examples, Taussig's studies of the role of shamans and ideas on the devil in Columbia, in direct relation with economic changes (Taussig, 1980, 1987).

5. See also La Fontaine (1992) and other contributions in two special issues of *Etnofoor* on 'Evil' (*Etnofoor* 1992 [1/2]) and 'The Enchanted World' (*Etnofoor* 1995 [1]). One of the reasons for La Fontaine and Comaroff to draw a parallel between witchcraft in Africa and the obsession with child abuse in the West is that both seem to epitomize Evil in its most basic form. However, I have attempted elsewhere (Geschiere, 1997), to show that the tendency of many anthropologists to equate witchcraft and evil too easily has been a stumbling block for understanding the modernizing capacities of these ideas. The African notions, now translated by witchcraft, often exhibit a staggering ambivalence in nearly all respects, but especially in relation to an opposition between good and bad; this ambivalence is particularly important to the modern dynamics of these discourses. In this article, I focus on another aspect of Comaroff's comparison between witchcraft and the fear of child abuse, which to me was most enlightening — namely the idea that both express people's worries about globalization's threatening encroachment on intimate spheres of life.

6. There is a striking parallel here with Orestis Lindermayer's (1995) analysis of the perception, quite current among present-day American fundamentalist Christians, of the European Community as 'the Beast of Revelation' announcing the end of time.

In this article I want to focus on a comparison with Weller's recent study (1994) of an upsurge of ghost worship in Taiwan, closely linked to the impressive economic development of this 'Asian tiger'. While the economic context is thus quite different from the present situation on the African continent, there is none the less a similar tendency to associate the new forms of wealth, highly suspect but at the same time very seductive, to occult forces; and there is the same confusing mixture of intimacy and bewilderingly wide horizons. Moreover, in Weller's interpretation there is a similar emphasis on ambivalence or 'indeterminate meaning' as he calls it. He vividly illustrates the staggering riches of meaning compressed in ghost worship, full of inconsistencies but brimming with associations and alternative interpretations. In his view, it is their '(over)saturated meaning' that gives these cults their strength and their broad appeal. On the other hand, he stresses that this 'messy exuberance' also makes the struggle for 'interpretative control' by those who try to get a grip on it, both inside and outside the cult, so difficult.

The parallels with the modernity of witchcraft in Africa are indeed striking. Here too, there is a staggering production of meaning, highly unsystematic and contradictory but, precisely because of this, extremely powerful: witchcraft discourses — like the Taiwanese spirit cults — allow for so many interpretations that they can explain any course of events and are, therefore, impossible to falsify. This exuberance of meaning excludes any essentialist interpretation, pinning witchcraft down to a fixed essence. Yet, a comparison with Weller's examples can serve also to raise the question as to the specific implications of interpreting modernity in witchcraft terms (rather than, for instance, in terms of Chinese ghost worship). Whatever witchcraft is, and no matter how exuberant a production of meaning it inspires, there are certain basic characteristics: it refers to hidden aggression by human actors, often acting from close by, from within one's intimacy. To what extent does this idea affect people's perceptions of modernity, their struggles to control its destructive aspects or to gain access to the prizes it offers?

DIGRESSION: 'GLOBALIZATION' AND 'IDENTITY'

Jean Comaroff (forthcoming) also highlights (with her usual, enviable force) the broader interest of this topic to debates on globalization and identity. She warns that globalization seems to make anthropology lose its bearings: the problem becomes how to relate visions of global change to the daily realities of people, the discipline's familiar study matter. Thus, recently fashionable notions — not only 'globalization', but also 'identity' and the general postmodern tide — seem to dissolve anthropologists' trusted topics. We were accustomed to accepting that the local — the old anthropological refuge — could only be understood in relation to the State. At the end of the 1960s, for instance, the launching of the notion of 'Local Level Politics', the idea that local politics had to be related to supra-local agencies like the State (cf. Swartz, 1968), was heralded as an important new beginning. Such new beacons were rapidly superseded, however, by the realization that 'the' nation-State was only an abstraction which, moreover, seemed to be dissolving under the impact of wider, globalizing tendencies. These increasingly widening perspectives opened up fascinating insights, but they seemed to do some sort of vanishing trick with the anthropologists' topics of research which appeared to be melting away in a world in which everything is in constant flux.[7] Comaroff (forthcoming) has a surprisingly concrete answer to the danger of losing our bearings in ever broader abstractions and wider spaces:

> Indeed, if we wish to get beyond banal generalizations and formal abstractions to a richer sense of the lived conundrums of late African modernity — of the shifting engagement of local and global, the paradoxical role of the state, or the taunting lure of commodities — one could do little better than explore the practical poetics of witchcraft.

The gist of her paper is that this does not apply to Africa only. Witchcraft and the parallel moral concerns which Comaroff discusses from other parts of the world have in common this surprising capacity to relate 'the local' and 'the global' in highly imaginative ways.

Indeed, one of the main questions raised by the remarkable resilience of witchcraft in postcolonial Africa is how a discourse, grafted upon the local realities of family and home, can so easily incorporate the ever widening circles of change under the impact of global processes. It is this remarkable capacity which makes witchcraft a strategic, concrete entrance point — unfortunately all too real in the grip it has on people's minds — for studying how globalization is lived in day-to-day life. It can help also to overcome easy distinctions between 'the' local and 'the' global. Witchcraft discourses highlight the intricate and often confusing or even frightening articulations of the two. In this sense they run clearly parallel to popular discourses on the hidden side of modernity elsewhere in the modern world.[8]

In such a perspective, concepts like 'globalization' or 'identity' have a clear but limited usefulness. They have served as some sort of a revival to anthropological witchcraft studies, forcing them out of the isolation of village and tradition. Indeed, one of the main reasons for anthropologists to become interested in witchcraft again (see note 1 above) was its enigmatic capacities of fusing the local and the global and its central role in efforts to clarify shifting identities.

---

7. Cf. Appadurai (1990) with his notion of various open-ended '-scapes' (ethnoscapes, ideoscapes, finance scapes etc.), overlapping and crosscutting each other. See also Hannerz (1992).
8. Cf. Jean Comaroff (forthcoming): 'as global processes play ever more pervasively into African worlds, they engage in complex, evanescent ways with local social forms, crystallizing in distinctive institutions and modes of practice. Witchcraft cuts across the fault-lines of these junctures'. See also Austen (1993); Geschiere (1995); Meyer (1995).

Yet, it is also clear that these notions have a strong tendency towards abstraction — they can easily become a kind of vanishing box, in which 'everything that is solid melts into air' (to use Marx's familiar dictum in another context). The main merit of the term 'globalization' might be that it continues to defy all attempts to tie it to an empirical core. The same applies to 'identity' which seems to be just as elusive a notion.[9] Both terms are, at most, sensitizing concepts. However, the combination of the two abstractions might have quite specific implications. As indicated in the Introduction to this volume, this combination can serve to bring to the fore the tension between, on the one hand, open-ended processes of change — penetrating local realities so deeply that any distinction between the local and the global becomes highly precarious — and, on the other, the need to define clearly outlined beacons.[10] Thus, the paradoxical combination between, on the one hand, 'globalization' with its connotations of open-endedness and unboundedness, and, on the other, 'identity' which seems to require definition and clarification, can help us to understand why 'witchcraft' or related moral concerns play such a prominent part in people's perceptions of modernity.

There is a worrying parallel between witchcraft discourses and Arjun Appadurai's interpretation, elsewhere in this volume, of ethnic violence as stemming from 'a radical uncertainty about self and other', and at the same time as 'the most ghastly technique for the establishment of certainty ... about identities'. Witchcraft discourses also express a basic uncertainty: anybody can be a witch, especially those who are involved with new ways of life. Yet the same discourses also indicate drastic means (accusations, ordeals) for trying to clarify at least temporarily the identities of the others, especially those in the immediate surroundings.

Witchcraft can be seen as one possible discourse to solve this tension between the fascination with open-ended processes of globalization and the need for boundaries and clarification about our own and others' identities. Comparing different ways — different discourses — by which people try to solve this dilemma can help to counter the abstracting tenor of broad notions like globalization or identity. It can also help to highlight different trajectories in the ways in which people try to deal with modernity's dreams and threats. Different notions are invoked to solve modernity's dilemmas. The question is, again: what are the specific implications of, for instance, witchcraft discourses for the ways in which people experience modernity?

---

9. The very fact that it was some sort of a discovery for many social scientists that most people have 'multiple identities' illustrates how far this notion is abstracted from daily experiences.

10. Cf. Bayart (1996), in which he shows with great perspicacity and a wealth of examples how 'globalization' always seems to go together with *clôture culturelle*. See also Bayart (1994: 9–46).

GHOST WORSHIP IN TAIWAN: SATURATED MEANING AND PROBLEMS OF INTERPRETATIVE CONTROL

For Taiwan, the 1970s were not only the years when economic development definitively 'took off'; they were also the years of an abrupt upsurge of popular religion, notably ghost worship. Weller (1994) studies the powerful example of the temple of the Eighteen Lords, which became one of the most successful in this branch. He describes it as a somewhat scandalous cult, and uses evocative terms to highlight the riches of its imaginary: 'saturated meaning', 'murky origins', 'piling on too much meaning', 'messy exuberance ... teeming with possible interpretations, most of them incompatible but co-existing'. He opposes this rich but chaotic mixture to the struggle for 'interpretative control', intrinsic to any striving for hegemony (or counter-hegemony), whether by outsiders, such as the nation's politicians, or insiders, like the family who controls the temple. In his view, the exuberance of the cult — a 'free space', full of 'indeterminate meaning' — is the real secret of its power and its broad appeal. It allows the cult to integrate effortlessly rapid processes of social change, but it also makes the cult impervious to any attempt towards a 'unification of meaning' or a forging of 'a strong interpretative community'. Although it brims with subversion it does not develop into a direct challenge to the dominant political order. Weller could just as well have been writing about witchcraft in Africa.

In the early 1970s, the temple of the Eighteen Lords was just 'a simple roadside shrine for unidentified bones' on a remote part of the island's coast — 'the sort that sits untended and almost unnoticed all over the countryside' (Weller, 1994: 125). Shrines like this — places where people worship ghosts in the hope of getting their support for some precarious endeavour — are abundant throughout the Chinese cultural area. Like all these shrines, the Eighteen Lords had their own founding myth: a somewhat vague story, of which different versions circulated, about a fishing boat washing ashore with seventeen dead men aboard, and a dog. The dog is the true hero of the story: he was still alive but insisted on being buried with his seventeen masters; thus, he became the eighteenth Lord. Dog statues play a central role in the cult.

The upsurge of the cult began when the government launched a plan to build a nuclear power plant on the spot of the grave which would, therefore, have to be demolished. This threat proved to be a boost to the cult. After a series of protests, accompanied by ominous accidents (several injuries and even a few deaths among the workers; one of the building cranes 'freezing' just above the grave, and so on), the government withdrew its plan and even constructed a new temple on the place of the already damaged shrine. In the 1980s, this temple became one of the most frequented in the entire island: 'hot and noisy', as a Chinese place of popular worship should be, 'a carnivalesque extreme', which brought huge profits to the committee that ran the place.

Weller emphasizes the subversive particularities of the cult. In the hierarchy of the Chinese spiritual world, ghosts are at the lowest level, well below gods and ancestors. He equates gods to bureaucrats, ancestors to kinsmen, but ghosts to 'the unincorporated dead', and to 'beggars, bandits and strangers who fall into no proper social category: they are asocial and individual' (ibid: 130). However, the temple building by itself shows that the Eighteen Lords do not respect this hierarchy. Weller describes it as a kind of post-modernist avalanche of styles and meanings. The building flaunts its origins as just a ghost shrine by various spatial arrangements, but its incongruously large scale makes it rather like a temple for a god; in fact, it has now included a small statue for an earth god, in order to affirm its higher pretensions. There are other confusing and unusual aspects: worshipping the Eighteen Lords is supposed to be most effective in the night or in the early hours of the morning (and not during the day as in most other cults); people's offerings, too, are somewhat bizarre, burning cigarettes next to incense. The worship is focused on the grave and two large dog statues that have to be touched and rubbed by the suppliants. This rubbing — again most unusual — reinforces the messy, even sexual atmosphere of the cult.

From Weller's description (ibid: 127) it is clear that the temple is a highly chaotic and even dangerous place. People arrive in cars and buses during the night. Since the place is very crowded, especially at this time, one has to park at a considerable distance, then walk in the dark through an unruly area, full of hawkers, pickpockets and rickety shacks, where all sorts of junk is sold, to arrive finally at the temple where people are pushing and jostling in order to get to the dog statues and the grave.

Weller (ibid: 143) relates the popularity of the cult to the economic climate of the 1980s in Taiwan: a boom period which was at the same time full of uncertainty. The cult is especially linked to 'the rapid development of small-scale entrepreneurial capitalism and of a kind of "gambling mentality" ' (ibid: 148). These were also the years when there was a flowering of illegal lotteries and a surprisingly widespread interest in playing the stock market, with housewives lining up to buy shares. One of the recurrent requests to the Eighteen Lords is for success at such hazardous ways of making a fortune. Most interestingly, Weller sees a direct link between the upsurge of these cults and people's increasing worries about the lack of productive investment possibilities in Taiwan itself, creating a kind of superabundance of capital and encouraging ever more adventurous forms of investment. The stock market crash of 1990 had a sobering effect on all this. It also lost the Eighteen Lords an important part of its clientele (ibid: 149–51).

The cult itself celebrates accumulation of wealth in all its modes and gradations. As is typical for ghost worshipping, it is a highly individualistic cult, with a strong a-moral undercurrent. Indeed, in Weller's view, one reason for its success in Taiwan, especially in the 1980s, was its ability to reflect 'a world of individualistic, utilitarian and amoral competition' (ibid: 129).

Weller's analysis of ghost worship during Taiwan's boom is part of a broader, comparative study, also including an analysis of the Taipeng rebellion in the middle of the nineteenth century and a study of the recent student protests on Tiananmen square in Beijing (the latter as an example of the scope for counteraction under totalitarian regimes). He uses this comparison to go beyond the conceptual opposition — which in his view paralyses current analysis of social movements — between opposition and accommodation: between the tendency to explain any form of deviant behaviour as resistance, and the view that most resistance remains within the terms of the hegemonical regime and thus reinforces existing relations of power (ibid: 9). Weller tries to show that both analytical frameworks imply that social scientists seem to be intent, in their own way, on imposing a 'unification of meaning' which severely distorts the abundance of meanings generated by such movements (ibid: 16). In his three examples there is a highly creative 'accumulation of meaning'. However, this does not necessarily lead to 'precipitation' — that is, to the crystallization of some sort of counter-hegemonic project. On the contrary, 'precipitation' requires a laborious and concerted effort towards simplification and interpretative unification — this time by potential leaders — which is made all the more difficult because of the superabundance of meaning accumulated by such movements, this very superabundance being the essence of their appeal. Weller emphasizes that the success or failure of such attempts towards interpretative unification do not so much depend on the meanings involved, but rather on the 'organizational solutions' forged by potential leaders (ibid: 27). His example for this is the Taipeng rebellion which, after a period of chaotic blossoming of an enormous array of meanings, succeeded in restricting this richness and concentrating it into a clear attempt to wrest hegemony from the ruling Manchu dynasty. One of the conclusions of his comparison is, therefore, that 'the Taipeng succeeded where the Taiwanese ghosts failed' (ibid: 182).

One may wonder whether, at least in this particular conclusion, Weller does not allow himself to become imprisoned in a resistance-accommodation dichotomy. The riches of his analysis of the Eighteen Lords rather suggests that in this case the issue of resistance is hardly at stake. His evocative sketch of the 'messy exuberance' of the cult demonstrates clearly that it has such an enormous appeal precisely because it remains a 'free space' in which all sorts of meanings can be accommodated: this is probably exactly what the people who run the temple are striving for.[11] Weller's study shows that such a 'free

---

11. Cf. Weller (1994: 142) on the Eighteen Lords: 'As a set, these possibilities offer no obvious and consistent message, nor are they meant to'. Actually, it is somewhat surprising that Weller pays so little attention to the people behind the Eighteen Lords. It is clear that the sudden upsurge of the cult cannot be reduced to the planned action of some shrewd entrepreneurs. Weller is, therefore, no doubt right in trying to avoid the dangers of a limited actor approach. But it is striking that actors are completely absent from his

space' full of 'indeterminate meaning' is not only appealing in contexts of economic decline and pressing scarcity (as in present-day Africa). Apparently, the imponderables of a boom period — when people have to deal with potentialities that appear to be highly promising but at the same time impossible to control and, moreover, highly mysterious in their unpredictability — also make the messy exuberance of such occult *imaginaires* highly attractive.

'WITCHCRAFT' IN AFRICA: PARALLELS AND DIFFERENCES

Exuberant production of meaning and a difficult struggle for interpretative control: such ideas also apply very well to the dynamics of witchcraft discourses in postcolonial Africa and their intertwinement with people's perceptions of a modern way of life.

However, it may be important to stress that this link between witchcraft and modernity is neither self-evident nor constant. In the 1960s, in the first years of Independence, there was rather a tendency — certainly among the new élite — to oppose witchcraft to modernity, or in any case to separate them conceptually. In those days, people preferred not to talk too much about witchcraft: that seemed to be somewhat old-fashioned or even anti-modern. This changed with increasing rapidity in the 1970s. In many respects, witchcraft came out into the open: it became a public issue, much discussed in newspapers, on the radio and at all sorts of meetings. An important indication of this change was that the State became more and more willing to take the issue seriously. Shortly after Independence, civil servants, in their wish to be modern, tended to follow the example of their colonial predecessors, ignoring witchcraft as much as possible, at least in public. In later years, governments in many African countries became increasingly sensitive to the popular pressure that something had to be done against the proliferation of witchcraft. In 1971, during my first period of field-work in Cameroon, a friend of mine from the East province — at the time an ambitious young politician — told me: 'I know that you white people do not believe in witchcraft. That is why the colonial State protected the witches. But now the State is in the hands of Cameroonians who know

---

chapters on the Eighteen Lords (in contrast to his Taipeng study where the central actors figure prominently, despite considerable historical distance). The question is whether more attention to, for instance, the committee responsible for maintaining the Eighteen Lords temple — apparently the people who are profiting most from its success — would some-what qualify Weller's emphasis on the superabundance and indeterminacy of meaning in the cult. After all, these managers must have some idea in mind when accepting certain additions to the cult and refusing others. This question is especially interesting in comparison with the role of witchcraft in, for instance, Africa. In witchcraft, actors are by definition hard to trace which makes the flow of meaning all the more difficult to control.

that witchcraft is all too real. Soon the law will be changed so that we can deal with witchcraft'.

Another indicator of this change was the emergence, throughout Africa, of a new type of modern 'traditional healer' (still called 'witch-doctors' or *féticheurs* by many people). The *nganga* (healers) I knew in the 1970s were still 'traditional' figures, mostly without any schooling, living in modest mud houses, often at the outskirts of the villages. They kept a low profile. They had good reason to do so since the State — throughout the colonial period but also in the first years after Independence — looked upon them with some suspicion, regularly persecuting them for defamation or breach of the peace.

In the 1980s, however, a new type of *nganga* came to the fore: emphatically modern figures with sunglasses, speaking fluent French, armed with a wide array of books on magic (especially Indian occult knowledge) and mixing all sorts of modern elements — from Christian rituals but also from medical knowledge — with their therapies. These specialists do everything to make themselves conspicuous. They often live in large houses with big signs, announcing their profession and their special skills ('astrologist', 'Rosecrucian' and so on). Many have an aggressive way of addressing potential clients, frightening them with warnings and not hesitating to direct open accusations at people in their close surroundings. They particularly try to enhance their status by boasting about the important people — civil servants, politicians, Ministers — whom they have among their clientele. The most important change is no doubt that some of them indeed succeed in getting some sort of official recognition: in some areas of the country *nganga*, rather than being persecuted by the State Courts as in the past, now appear as expert witnesses to help the judges solve the problem of how to establish evidence against witches.

There are also important innovations in the contents of people's witchcraft notions. A striking example is the rapid spread throughout southern and western Cameroon of the belief in a novel type of witchcraft, associated with the new forms of wealth. I have published extensively on this topic, together with my Cameroonian co-author Cyprian Fisiy:[12] here a brief sketch must suffice. It is particularly interesting that similar notions have very different effects in the various regions of southern and western Cameroon, depending on the socio-economic context and more specifically on the institutional means by which people try to impose control and interpretative clarity on these frightening innovations in the occult world.

In these parts of Cameroon, people use different names for this new type of witchcraft — *ekong, nyongo, famla, kupe* — but the basic notions are the

---

12. See Fisiy and Geschiere (1991, 1993); cf. Fisiy (1990) and Geschiere (1997). See also the fascinating books by de Rosny (1981, 1992) on his initiation as *nganga* (healer) and on the struggle of his *nganga* colleagues against *ekong*.

same.[13] *Ekong* is explicitly contrasted with older forms of witchcraft that make people eat their victims. Instead, *ekong* witches turn their victims into some sort of zombies which are put to work on 'invisible plantations'. *Ekong* witches are to be recognized by their possession of the much coveted new items of wealth: sumptuous houses with tin roofs, refrigerators and other electrical equipment, cars. Indeed, it is *ekong* which makes these witches so rich through the illicit exploitation of the labour of their zombie-victims.

In other respects, *ekong* does relate to older ideas on witchcraft. It is, for instance, striking that even this modern form of witchcraft is in all sorts of ways related to kinship. Just as with older forms of witchcraft, it is only by sacrificing a close relative (even your own mother) that one gets access to an *ekong* coven. De Rosny (1981) emphasizes, moreover, that even in the highly urbanized context of Duala, *nganga* always invoke the co-operation of the family when trying to cure an *ekong* victim; if the family is not willing to collaborate, the *nganga* are powerless since it is from internal tensions that *ekong* has emerged. However, when discussing *ekong*, people tend to stress its modern aspects: its close relation to new forms of consumption and new modes of accumulation. De Rosny understands *ekong* as a popular way of addressing the mysteries of the modern market economy: the vagaries of prices and employment possibilities, the staggering enrichment of the few and the misery of the many (ibid).

Ekong is capable of addressing these wider problems because it introduces its own geography, marked by a constant increase of scale. Characteristically, most inland groups point to Duala, historically the main port through which European trade penetrated this whole area, as the place of origin of *ekong*. However, its central point is Mount Kupe, a wooded mountain 100 miles to the North of Duala, which is often identified — also by groups living much further inland — as the main 'market of sorcery'. It is on this mountain that the invisible plantations where the zombies are supposedly put to work are generally located. *Nganga* who try to cure victims are supposed to leave on a hazardous nightly journey to Kupe in order to retrieve the 'souls' of their clients. This mountain has become a national symbol for illicit but much coveted wealth: booklets with Mt. Kupe on the cover are selling very well in the main Cameroonian cities since they are supposed to contain secret information on how to get rich. However, *ekong*'s geography seems to have become increasingly transnational in its scope. In 1995, several informants from both the southern and the western parts of the country told me that Mount Kupe had become a relay station for the trafficking of *ekong* witches throughout the world. People now often relate *ekong* to the mafia or other global networks of crime.

---

13. Indeed, similar notions seem to have emerged with considerable force throughout West Africa, especially in the postcolonial period; cf. van der Drift (1992) on Guinea-Bissau; Meyer (1995) on Ghana; Offiong (1991) on East Nigeria.

Another novelty, which clearly demarcates *ekong* from older witchcraft notions, and which moreover point to its specific historical backgrounds, is the sinister role that whites are supposed to play in the trafficking of *ekong* victims. Bureau (1962), de Rosny (1981) and others point out that the *ekong* fantasies — people dream that they are being led away to the Ocean, unable to see their captors' faces and with their hands tied behind their backs — clearly reflect old traumas of the slave trade. Other elements, such as the idea that *ekong* victims are transported 'in lorries' to 'large labour camps' on Mt. Kupe, rather recall experiences of forced labour during colonial times.

Ekong has also its own history, which clearly indicates its varying impact, depending on the socio-economic context. For nineteenth century Duala — at the height of the commercial success of the great Duala entrepreneurs — de Rosny (1981: 91) describes *ekong* as a secret association of chiefs and notables; feared but also respected, it represented 'the class of the wealthy'. In present-day Duala, however, *ekong* 'has been democratized; it is no longer the privilege of the rich, but within reach of all people. Its generalization has made it all the more menacing' (ibid, my translation).

In the 1950s, Ardener witnessed the outbreak and subsequent containment of a true panic among the Bakweri living on Mt. Cameroon, 40 miles to the northwest of Duala, because of the supposed spread of *ekong* (here more often called *nyongo*). Apparently the panic was triggered by fear of a new type of house with a tin roof. As elsewhere, such a modern house was the new status symbol par excellence, but in this area it was also seen as a sure sign that the owner was a *nyongo* witch. The fear among the Bakweri of these new forms of wealth could only be vanquished by inviting a powerful *juju* from the Banyangi (100 miles inland) who exorcised *nyongo* and thus liberated the new prestige goods — at least for the time being — from their stigma (Ardener, 1970).

The spread of *ekong* further inland, into the Grassfields (present-day West and Northwest Provinces) and the forest areas of the Centre and South provinces, seems to have followed somewhat later, especially after Independence. Characteristically, it coincided with the rapid rise of a new elite due to decolonization. In these areas, *ekong* seems to address especially the difficult relation of these new élites — whose wealth by far surpasses traditional bounds — to their village of origin. However, in this context too, very different patterns appear to be possible. The hierarchical societies of the West appear to have organizational solutions for incorporating, at least to a certain extent, these *nouveaux riches* and their new forms of wealth and power; here the chiefs act as some sort of crystallization point, 'whitewashing' the suspect new forms of wealth and thus containing popular fears of *ekong*. By contrast, in the forest societies — highly segmentary in character and marked by strong levelling tendencies — the new forms of wealth still seem to constitute an unresolved problem. Here, the general concern about a proliferation of new forms of witchcraft leads to a frantic search for new sanctions with quite dramatic consequences.

The Forest Area: Indeterminate Meaning

One of the most disconcerting changes in the East Province (the part of the forest area where I have been doing field-work since 1971) occurred quite abruptly, at the end of the 1970s. Completely unexpectedly (certainly to me), State Courts began to condemn witches. This constituted a dramatic reversal of the jurisprudence until then, under which people accused of witchcraft could only be condemned when there was 'tangible evidence' of physical aggression. Since 1980, however, all Courts in this Province have been regularly convicting witches to heavy jail sentences (up to ten years) and fines, without clear empirical proof — all that is required is the declaration of a *nganga* (healer/witch-doctor) who has 'seen' that the accused left their bodies at night to engage in destructive practices (see Fisiy and Geschiere, 1990; Geschiere, 1997). As noted, this also constitutes a complete reversal of the Courts' attitude to the *nganga*, who used to be regarded with suspicion and regularly convicted of defamation. Now their expertise seems to be indispensable to the judges trying to find proof against supposed witches.

Clearly, the Courts' willingness to persecute people accused of witchcraft reflects the private opinion of the judges, who often characterize the East as an area ridden with witchcraft (and therefore even dangerous to the civil servants who have to work there). However, it is just as clear that the Courts are under heavy popular pressure to intervene. There seems to be a general concern in the region (as in other parts of the forest area) that local institutions are no longer capable of dealing with the proliferation of witchcraft. This inspires a panicky search for outside institutions able to deal with novel witchcraft threats. It is not only the State which is under heavy pressure to intervene: people have also turned for help to the established Churches, and, more recently, especially to the Pentecostalists and kindred movements.

This general disarray is related to the institutional profile of the forest societies (highly segmentary and lacking clear-cut institutions to deal with witchcraft threats) and also to the diffuse character of their witchcraft discourses. The central notions, *evu* among the Beti or *djambe* among the Maka, are extremely broad and therefore all-pervasive in character. The deep ambiguity of these notions is striking. In principle, *evu* or *djambe* are very evil powers. They force people — that is those who are willing to develop the *djambe* or *evu* in their belly — to participate in the nightly witches' encounters, where they offer their own kin to their acolytes to be eaten during communal cannibalistic banquets. Yet these same forces are indispensable to any form of success: prominent elders, chiefs, rich people and indeed all persons with leadership aspirations are invariably associated in one form or another with these secret powers. Discourses on *evu* and *djambe* have a strikingly circular character: for instance, the *nganga* — the obvious persons to provide protection against witchcraft attacks — are only able to do so because they are supposed themselves to be 'super-witches' who have developed their *evu* to an extraordinary degree. The main protection against witchcraft is to be found within the realm of witchcraft itself. In daily life, such notions create a kind of catch-22 situation.

Philippe Laburthe-Tolra, one of the main ethnographers of the Beti in Central-South Cameroon, offers a vivid example of this circularity. He recounts how he tried to interview a number of Beti elders in one of the villages where he was working. However, his efforts were suddenly interrupted when one of the elders began to cross-examine him:

> Why was he asking all these questions? How could they be sure that he and his assistant did not have a dangerous *evu* in their belly?' The other elders agreed and only wanted to continue the interview if Laburthe and his assistant submitted themselves to an oracle which would determine whether they had or had not the *evu*. After some reluctance they accepted. They had to choose between two horns and they were utterly relieved when it turned out that they had chosen the empty horn — that is, they had no *evu*.
>
> However, they were in for a new surprise. As Laburthe describes it in his flowery style: 'At the very moment of triumph, to my great surprise, the elders were taken with consternation and distress: "But if you have nothing, if you have no *evu*, what can you understand? We cannot tell you anything: you are children ..." Thus, we found ourselves discredited as "failures" because we had nothing in the belly ...' (Laburthe-Tolra, 1977: 1027; my translation)

Laburthe finally concludes that even though *evu* is basically an evil force, it is at the same time seen as indispensable to the functioning of society.

The imaginary of *evu* or *djambe* is strongly reminiscent of Weller's emphasis on 'saturated meaning' and 'messy exuberance.' Indeed, it is the very diffuseness of these notions that makes them so all-pervasive. In any situation they allow for a broad array of interpretations and it is precisely this indeterminacy — *evu* can explain the dominance of the powerful but it can also be the secret reason of their downfall — which makes them impossible to falsify or to break away from. It is the same quality which allows them to integrate so easily all sorts of changes and innovations. Here too, this 'messy exuberance' makes any attempt — whether by local leaders, missionaries, or State officials — at a 'unification of meaning' and 'the imposition of interpretative control', to quote Weller once again, extremely difficult.

Life in Beti or Maka villages and townships is punctuated by constant rumours about witchcraft. However, people's interpretations of the events referred to differ widely. Indeed, people often switch from one interpretation to another, depending on the context. Does a particular event prove that Mr So-and-So is really a witch? Or did he use his occult powers to protect the community? Or does the course of events prove, in fact, that he is really an 'innocent' who has been set up by other witches? People can engage in endless debates on such questions and it seems to be impossible to arrive at a definitive interpretation. Precisely because the imaginary of *evu* or *djambe* exhibits a 'messy exuberance' of meaning, it is hard to come to a decisive evaluation of a person's identity, especially of those very near to you. Anyone can turn out to be an evil witch.

The openness of the discourse on *djambe* or *evu* closely corresponds, of course, to the extremely flexible institutional profiles of these societies. Prior

to the colonial conquest (around 1900), these societies consisted of small
patrilineal units of shifting character, constantly splitting up and fusing with
other units. There was no authority above these family hamlets and even
inside the communities, the elders' authority was circumscribed by strong
levelling forces (of which witchcraft was and remains an important one).
Chieftainship was mainly a colonial creation which hardly took root. Today,
the *chefs de village* and even more the *chefs supérieurs* are still mainly
administrative figures who have no special role to play in the containment of
witchcraft. The obvious figures to turn to in such matters are the *nganga*, the
'traditional healers' but, as already noted, these are highly ambiguous
figures. Like other witches, they are supposed to have sacrificed a close kin
before being initiated by their 'professor'. Nowadays, many people say that
the *nganga* themselves have been corrupted by *kong* (the local term for the
zombie witchcraft of the new rich). So how could they be of any value for
containing this novel threat?

It might be characteristic that there is hardly any attempt in these societies
to localize witchcraft, in the sense of tying it to specific locations or arenas.
Just like the witches, who are supposed to meet 'somewhere' at night — but
people will never specify exactly where — the *nganga* has no clearly localized
moorings. Successful *nganga* may be visited by their clients in their courtyard — and, more recently, a new type of 'modern' *nganga* try to convert
their homesteads into formal 'hospitals' — but they are basically wandering
figures, constantly on the road, visiting their clients or trying to recruit new
ones. In many respects, *nganga* are outsiders to the local communities;
indeed, the very fact of their being initiated raises the suspicion that they have
betrayed the bonds of kinship. For the Kako in the eastern part of the
country, Copet-Rougier (1986: 87) states that a *ngan* (the Kako equivalent of
the *nganga*) should not stay too long in his own village, as that would be too
dangerous for his own people.

This institutional context can explain why people are ready to turn even to
the State — despite its heavy authoritarianism and people's deep fear of the
gendarmes — for protection against the proliferation of witchcraft. The
State, with its judicial apparatus and its *gendarmes*, does offer a specific locus
(the Courts) and formal procedures for dealing with this threat. The judges
do not hesitate to impose a 'unified meaning' on the cases brought before
them and they mete out harsh punishments (up to ten years in prison and
high fines) to those whom they convict as 'witches'.

The effects of this judicial offensive against witchcraft are highly problematic, and there are good reasons to doubt whether the State is really equipped
to deal with such occult threats (see Fisiy and Geschiere, 1990). The judges
base their convictions on article 251 of the Cameroonian *Code pénal*, which
seems to be borrowed from the French *Code* and offers quite a shaky basis
for such convictions. One particular problem is that the law asks for tangible
evidence (*des preuves tangibles*) which is often difficult to establish in occult
cases. The judges try to solve this problem of evidence by invoking the help of

the *nganga* and their 'expertise', but in many respects the *nganga* seem to be some sort of Trojan horse, corrupting the Courts' efforts towards 'unification of meaning' from the inside.

In several of the cases on which we could consult the Court files, the *nganga*, when called upon to give his testimony, presented himself as 'Mr So-and-So, *sorcier* (sorcerer/witch)'. This is completely in line with the local discourse in which the *nganga* is indeed a 'super-witch': however, in the official discourse, imposed by the Courts, anybody who confesses to be a witch should be convicted. Indeed, an accused who dares to call himself *sorcier* is sure to be put into jail. Yet the *nganga* does so without any further reaction from the judges. Apparently the latter recognize that there are different types of *sorciers*, some of which have to punished, while others (the *nganga*) are valuable allies in the struggle against *la sorcellerie*.

This terminological confusion has deeper implications. Officially, the State and its servants condemn witchcraft as an evil, to be eradicated altogether. Privately, however, many civil servants (judges included) are deeply involved with witchcraft, enlisting the services of *nganga* to protect them or even to attack their rivals. The murderous competition for posts and promotion in the public service is a hotbed for witchcraft rumours and machinations.

Small wonder, then, that the practical results of the judicial offensive against witchcraft have been disappointing and even counter-productive. A crucial problem is that the sanctions applied by the State do not really solve the issue of witchcraft. Putting witches into jail does not take away their supposed occult powers. On the contrary, in jail one is supposed to meet really dangerous witches from whom one can learn all sorts of new secrets. The consequence is that convicted 'witches', once released from jail, are even more feared by their environment. The *nganga* are supposed to be able to neutralize people's occult powers — if somebody confesses, the *nganga* can take away his evil *evu* — but people certainly do not believe that putting someone in jail or making him pay a heavy fine will have such healing effects. Moreover, the involvement of the *nganga* with the State's judicial offensive might undermine their healing powers. *Nganga* who regularly appear as witnesses before the Courts seem to become punitive figures who see it as their task to deliver 'witches' to the *gendarmes* instead of trying to cure them.

These confused and in the end counter-productive interventions by the State confirm how difficult it is to impose 'interpretative control' over the 'messy exuberance' of witchcraft beliefs in these societies. Clearly, the State cannot offer the organizational solutions that can make such an effort towards 'unification of meaning' successful. Informants from other areas, notably the western Grassfields, often express amazement that 'these' forest people are so eager to put their witchcraft affairs before the State courts. In the view of these informants this is simply further proof of the backwardness of the forest societies and their lack of organization. How can they expect the State to resolve such questions? Do they not have their own ways of dealing with such matters?

The Western Grassfields: Interpretative Control by the Chief

It is striking that the spread of the same set of ideas on new forms of witchcraft and wealth has had very different effects in the Grassfields in the West and Northwest Provinces of Cameroon.[14] Here too, these ideas focused on the emergence of new urban élites, especially since the end of the 1950s, and on their precarious relation to the home area. However, people tried to deal with these suspicions in a different way.

There were good reasons for the rapid spread of notions of *ekong* (here often called *famla*) into this particular area: it is from here that, especially in postcolonial times, a new bourgeoisie of successful entrepreneurs emerged who are now supposed to play a dominant role in the national economy of Cameroon. In his fascinating study of *L'Esprit d'entreprise au Cameroon* which focuses especially on Bamileke entrepreneurs, Warnier (1993) states that many of these entrepreneurs are the subject of recurrent *famla* rumours. However, Warnier adds, quite surprisingly, that these rumours hardly seem to affect the position of these entrepreneurs.

The new forms of wealth are, apparently, as suspect in the Grassfields as in the forest areas, and people relate them directly to the feared *famla*. The difference is that in the Grassfields this novel witchcraft threat seems to be under control, at least to a certain degree. Rumours about *famla* lead less often than in the forest societies to a general panic or a frantic search for new sanctions in order to contain this threat.

A series of case-studies from this area, presented by Mbunwe-Samba (1996) and Fisiy (in Fisiy and Geschiere, 1991), highlight a recurrent pattern. People react sharply against *famla* when it is supposed to be active within the village. Then the *fon* (chief) will mobilize the associations of his Court to chase suspected *famla* witches from the village. However, when a successful entrepreneur returns to the village and dedicates his new wealth to the *fon* — by offering him an important present or buying a title at his court — he is accepted; in several of these cases this even included persons who only a few years earlier had been chased out of the village. In Fisiy's words: the chief still has the power to 'whitewash' the suspected wealth of the new rich and the occult powers behind it. He can still act as a crystallization point for reintegrating his successful 'sons' abroad into the structures of the chieftaincy. The *fon* is still credited with the moral authority to neutralize the dangerous

---

14. This area straddles the border between former British and former French Cameroon (respectively the present-day West and Northwest Provinces). Nowadays, people make a distinction between the Bamenda, living in the anglophone Northwest Province, and the Bamileke in the francophone West Province, but in geographical, historical and socio-cultural respects, the whole area is more or less uniform. See, for different trajectories of the *ekong* beliefs in other areas (among the Bakweri and Bakossi of the Southwest, and the Duala of the Littoral), Geschiere (1995, 1997).

powers of the new rich and thus allay fears about the proliferation of new witchcraft threats (in Fisiy and Geschiere, 1991: 270).

The broader institutional setting of these societies is indeed very different from that of the forest area. The Grassfields societies have a strong hierarchical tradition. The *fon* (or *fo*) is the centre of social life in all respects. Around his court are organized a number of more or less secret associations, the most important being a kind of police society, often called *kwifoyn*. Connected to these associations is a complex system of graded titles controlled, again, by the *fon*. Warnier (1985) emphasizes the importance of long-distance trade and the accumulation of wealth abroad for people's status in these societies, also in the precolonial period. However, individual success in trade was only acceptable if it was backed by the authority of the *fon*. Indeed, the strict control of the *fon* over outside relations and wealth was the very basis of his power. This model proved to be highly resilient in colonial times. The active role in post-colonial times of the chiefs and their associations in containing *famla* rumours and in re-integrating the new urban élites into the local structures continues this tradition.

This central position of the chiefs goes together with another interesting difference *vis-à-vis* the forest societies: the strong tendency to try to 'compartmentalize' the witchcraft discourse. Many elements in this discourse are the same as in the forest: witchcraft is supposed to reside in someone's belly, witches are supposed to fly away at night to betray and devour their kin during nocturnal banquets. However, in the Grassfields societies there seems to be a conscious effort to overcome the ambiguity and the circularity of this discourse, and to institutionalize clear-cut distinctions, especially between permitted and illegitimate uses of the occult forces. Predictably, the *fon* play a crucial role in this. Just as in the forest area, the chiefs themselves are closely associated with the occult. However, in the Grassfields, there is a heavy emphasis on all sorts of institutional boundaries between the chief and the evil expressions of occult power. In principle, it is the chief who decides whether these powers are used in an acceptable or unacceptable way. If someone is suspected of having access to sources of occult power without the blessing of the *fon*, this is automatically seen as a-social and therefore marked as 'witchcraft'. The *kwifoyn*, the chief's secret police association, is supposed to deal with it in its own secret ways. However, the pursuit of wealth by a subject who has the blessing of the chief can never be witchcraft. On the contrary, this is supposed to strengthen the chief and thus the community as a whole.[15] To put it in simpler terms: in the last instance it is the chief who

---

15. For a detailed treatment of the complex relation between the *fon* and *sem* (occult power, in some contexts equated with witchcraft, but never so in relation to the *fon*), see Goheen's (1996) study on Nso (Northwest Cameroon), especially her nuanced analysis of the role of such ideas in the precarious pact of the *fon* with the new élite.

decides who is a witch and who is not. He has the moral authority to clarify someone's true identity. Despite all the ambiguities which mark the witchcraft discourse, even in the Grassfields, the chief has enough 'interpretative control' to impose a final 'unification of meaning'.[16]

However, as one might expect when witchcraft is at stake, this last conclusion must be nuanced. It is, for instance, a moot point whether the Grassfields chiefs will retain enough moral authority to exercise this kind of 'interpretative control' in the future. The eagerness with which many chiefs try to share in the wealth of their successful subjects — by creating all sorts of pseudo-traditional titles at their courts which the *nouveaux riches* can buy, but also by privatizing and selling their customary land rights — raises the question of whether the chief still controls the new élite or whether the roles are reversed (see also Fisiy, 1992). Warnier (1993) characterizes the Bamileke chieftaincy as a 'shell' which is emptied and refilled by the new élites. Goheen (1996: 145, 161) evokes a very powerful image expressing the doubts of the people of Nso (one of the largest Northwestern chiefdoms) about the collaboration of their chiefs with the new élites. People wonder whether these *nouveaux riches* will be 'the chief's new leopards' who, like the notables of former days, will accompany him at night when, transformed as a lion, he prowls the country in order to protect it against evil. Or will they prove to be 'sorcerers of the night' who corrupt his court from the inside?[17] In the Grassfields too, the chiefs' 'interpretative control' threatens to be submerged by the 'indeterminate meaning' and the 'messy exuberance' of witchcraft.

---

16. These efforts towards an unequivocal compartmentalization of the witchcraft discourse seem to go together with a trend towards 'localizing' the discourse (in the sense of tying it to certain places). The topography of witchcraft itself also remains fairly vague in the Grassfields (witches are supposed to be active in the most unexpected places) but the struggle against it is at least linked to specific and more or less sacred places: the chief's court and the shrines of the *kwifoyn*. Moreover, the *ngankang* (the equivalent of the *nganga*) is also more or less integrated with the community through his/her relations to the *fon* (cf. Pradelles de Latour, 1991).

17. See also the interesting text by Basile Ndjio (1995) on a recent series of performances of the *Ngru*, a Bamileke purification ritual. Apparently, in 1994 this old ritual was suddenly revived simultaneously in several rural chieftaincies in the West Province but also in the Bamileke quarter in the city of Duala. Ndjio interprets the staging of the ritual as a somewhat desperate attempt by the chiefs to restore their authority, severely undermined by their close collaboration with the regime. Typically, the chiefs were strongly supported in organizing this ritual by the 'external élites' and the administrative authorities. Equally typical is the ambiguous role of the *nganga* as a kind of broker between these groups. A year later, Ndjio returned to these places and found that, although the chiefs and some notables were still satisfied with having staged the ritual, the people in general were more sceptical. Many talked about it as a swindle that served only to enrich the chiefs and the *nganga*.

CONCLUSIONS

What is the value of comparisons such as those presented here? To what extent can they help to answer our original question as to why, in Africa, reasonings in terms of witchcraft are so central to people's speculations about modernity?

A comparative perspective shows in any case that this is not particular to Africa. Elsewhere too, and not only in the poorer parts of the global economy, global processes of change create 'intermediary spaces' filled with an 'indeterminate but exuberant production of meaning', to use Weller's terms. For Sri Lanka, for instance, Obeysekere (1975, 1977) relates an increase of spirit cults and sorcery back in the 1970s especially to the preoccupations of more or less modern elements of the 'lower middle class'. In Africa, this 'intermediary space' seems to be filled with a wide array of discourses and practices — Islam, Christianity (lately especially in the form of Pentecostalism), ideologies of 'authenticity', and so on — but witchcraft seems to dominate, effortlessly articulating itself with other principles and ideas.

One way of explaining this linking of witchcraft and modernity is to see it as a product of globalization processes as such. This is especially relevant if one focuses on the terms used, their provenance and their impact. It is clear that 'witchcraft', 'sorcery' and *sorcellerie* are Western terms and as such quite distorting translations of local notions which often have much broader and more ambivalent meanings. Indeed, the general acceptance of these Western terms throughout Africa can be seen as proof of how deeply globalization processes have penetrated African culture. It is clear also that the borrowing of these terms has had special effects, which are part of a much broader process of pejoration of African notions and beliefs. The general use of notions like 'witchcraft' now reduces older cosmologies in which all men's surroundings are animated to an ugly core: the horrible image of the witches feasting on each others' relatives. In this sense, the resilience of 'witchcraft' in postcolonial Africa, despite all 'modern' changes, can be seen as the very effect of globalization and the impact of modernity.[18]

Indeed, for Mudimbe (1988), 'witchcraft' and 'sorcery' are among the more important terms which Africans borrowed from the 'colonial library' — that

---

18. A different but very intriguing attempt to explain witchcraft as the result of globalization itself — in this case especially early globalization processes — is to be found in Austen (1993). He tries to show that the different trajectories of witchcraft beliefs in Europe and Africa can only be understood against the background of the evolving historical relation between the two continents. He relates the witchcraft craze in sixteenth and seventeenth century Europe to the anti-consumption ethos of early capitalism ('the European version of zero-sum economics') and the later abandonment of witchcraft beliefs to the increasing abundance of consumption goods. However, this abundance depended on low-cost import from the South — for Africa notably through the slave trade. In this continent it is precisely the slave trade which is still 'the major historical reference to the equation of capital accumulation, zero-sum economics ... and witchcraft' (Austen, 1993: 103).

is, from Western anthropologists, missionaries and civil servants. He is no doubt right that the borrowing of these terms was not gratuitous. Yet, as I have tried to show elsewhere (1996: 178), precisely in the field of the occult forces, there is a danger of overrating the colonial influence.

> A telling example is the one quoted above of the Cameroonian judges who in the recent witchcraft trials try to impose an unambiguous discourse on witchcraft in which a *sorcier* is always evil and has to be punished. However, they have to rely on the expertise of the *nganga* ('traditional healer') who introduces himself as a *sorcier* when called upon to deliver his testimony. The local discourse with all its ambiguities — the *nganga* can only heal precisely because he is a witch — corrupts the clear-cut Western discourse on witchcraft propagated by the judges (at least in their formal capacity).

The apparently well-defined terms from the colonial library seem to be corrupted by the powerful ambiguities of older discourses on the agency of spirits animating men's surroundings which can be both good and evil but are always directly related to human actors (cf. Appiah, 1992). Thus, these ambiguities come to mark people's perceptions of modernity as well.

The comparison with Weller's interpretation of the upsurge of spirit cults in Taiwan — their 'overflow' of 'indeterminate meaning' defying 'interpretative unification' — can also help to explore the specific meaning of expressing modernity's enchantment especially in terms of witchcraft, as is done in many parts of Africa. There are certainly correspondences with Weller's examples, yet the reference to witchcraft does have its own implications.

Weller describes his spirit cults — hot and noisy — in line with general characteristics of Chinese popular religion. In the same vein, discourses on witchcraft, despite all dynamics and variations, do embroider on certain general principles which affect people's experiences of modernity in special ways. A basic notion is that of an omnipresent hidden aggression by human actors from within one's close surroundings — in Africa especially from within one's family.[19] The new notions of witchcraft quoted above, such as the *ekong* or *famla* of the *nouveaux riches* in Cameroon, relate this local reference point to broader horizons. They introduce novel definitions of the self and the other. They imply that witches see their fellow men no longer as meat to be eaten — one could say also, as life to feed upon in order to strengthen one's own life force — but rather as labourers to be exploited. Moreover, these zombie-labourers have to circulate in ever wider, apparently open-ended circuits. These new circuits of wealth are frightening but also extremely exciting. Yet these same notions, despite all their novelty and increase of scale, remain closely linked to kinship and the house. It is too

---

19. Cf. Geschiere (1997: 11): '[Witchcraft] expresses the frightening realization that aggression threatens from within the intimacy of the family — that is from the very space where complete solidarity and trust should reign'. In many parts of Africa witches are supposed to have special powers over their close relatives while the most dangerous witchcraft comes 'from within the house'. See also de Rosny (1981), Meyer (1995), Niehaus (1993, 1995).

simple to interpret them as just some sort of capitalist version of witchcraft. They also refer to family tensions and aggression from within the home: one has to sacrifice a close parent in order to have access to them; any form of therapy requires primarily a coming together of the family.[20]

This ambivalence makes witchcraft highly relevant for the dilemma, mentioned at the beginning of this article, between open-ended globalization and the need to outline well-defined identities.[21] *Ekong*, and witchcraft in general, is about the horrors *and* the enticements of new circuits of people and goods which seem to be open-ended. It is also an attempt to definitively clarify the true identity of people within one's close surroundings.[22]

The relation between witchcraft discourses and globalization is further complicated by the elusive character of these discourses, notably their paradoxical relation to locality. It is clear that witchcraft has a local tenor: it refers to intimacy, in Africa notably to the family and 'the house'. Yet from the examples above it is also clear that these discourses have a peculiar, non-localized character: they are not clearly linked to well-defined places. The stories about the witches and their nocturnal conspiracies refer at most to imaginary places, not visible to ordinary mortals. In the forest societies of Cameroon, discussed above, not even the *nganga* (witch-doctor) is clearly anchored in one place. In the more hierarchical societies of West Cameroon, the efforts towards compartmentalization of the witchcraft discourse, towards fixing boundaries and distinguishing more destructive and more constructive uses of these forces, go together with a further localization. Even here, however, the attempts at compartmentalization and localization remain highly precarious. Witchcraft basically seems to defy localization. Witches are everywhere. The omnipresent association with flying emphasizes their staggering mobility. Indeed, witches are now commonly supposed to fly all over the globe in one night.

There is an interesting contrast here with Weller's examples of Chinese spirit cults. These spirits have a mobility of their own, but at least their cult is clearly fixed in the Temple. By contrast, witchcraft has no localized cult, no

---

20. Does this reference to kinship, the old anthropological hobby-horse, offer another proof that Africa is still 'anthropology-land'? I do not think it does. It is certainly regrettable that anthropologists have tended to reify kinship, thus freezing a highly dynamic principle of organization (see Geschiere, 1994). However, this should not make us turn away from the subject as such. The ideology of kinship remains crucial for constructing social security in many parts of Africa. Kinship proves to be as dynamic and resilient as witchcraft. Indeed, in Africa, witchcraft constitutes in many respects the dark side of kinship. Elsewhere (Geschiere, 1997: 214), I tried to show that it is the stretching of kinship — people still trying to bridge new inequalities between city and village, between élite and population, in terms of the kinship ideology — that constitutes the context for the exuberance of witchcraft fantasies.

21. See the Introduction to this volume; see also Bayart (1996).

22. Cf. Appadurai's interpretation, in this volume, of ethnic violence as a definitive fixing of people's identity.

fixed place in which it can be *encadré* (to use a term of which French officials and their francophone successors are so fond). It is clear that this non-localized nature of witchcraft makes it all the more difficult to impose interpretative control — even more difficult than in Weller's examples. The futile attempts, discussed above, of the Cameroon State to get a grip on the supposed proliferation of witchcraft is a good illustration of these difficulties.[23]

Witchcraft's paradoxical relation to locality can explain why people associate these discourses so easily to globalization processes. For outside observers, it may seem more or less self-evident that witchcraft epitomizes 'the local' in opposition to 'the global'. However, things are more complicated than this. Witchcraft is so fascinating precisely because it seems to surpass effortlessly any boundary and any form of localization. Ever since colonial times, the mobility and fluidity of African societies was seen as a basic problem by the representatives of the new State, in their strenuous efforts to impose boundaries and fix the population.[24] There are intriguing convergences here with the new forms of global mobility that, according to some, spell the end of the territorial nation-State as the main organizing principle of global society (see, for instance, Appadurai, 1996). Seen in this light, it is clear that the association of witchcraft and modernity is more than an exotic peculiarity. It is about converging visions of open space, both frightening and enticing.

REFERENCES

Appadurai, Arjun (1990) 'Disjuncture and Difference in the Global Cultural Economy', *Public Culture* 2(2): 1–25.

23. See also Meyer's seminal explanation of why Pentecostalists recently have been much more successful in their struggle against witchcraft throughout Africa. Instead of denying witchcraft (as many official churches do, to a certain degree), Pentecostalism offers a well-defined location — the church during the service — where people can 'act out' their witchcraft dreams and then be purified (see Meyer, 1995). Apparently the Pentecostalists succeeded in creating an arena, a ritual space, for combating witchcraft that is much more effective than the arenas the State can provide. The Courts with their disciplinary apparatus of fines and prison terms are hardly capable of getting to the heart of witchcraft, while the Pentecostalists' exorcisms do, at least in the eyes of the population. See also Mbembe (1992).

24. For a challenging treatment of this issue, see Roitman's recent thesis on North Cameroon (1996). She sketches an ongoing struggle between two opposing modes of organization: the Fulbe order based on circulation and mobility, and the colonial one based on territorialization. The consequence of this opposition was that the control over *la population flottante* (another key-term in the jargon of French or francophone civil servants throughout Africa) became a crucial issue in State formation, both colonial and post-colonial. Roitman relates the recent collapse of borders in this part of Africa, creating a truly transnational economy, to an upsurge of *la population flottante* breaking once more through the very principles of modern State formation in the area.

Appadurai, Arjun (1996) *Modernity at Large: Cultural Dimensions of Globalization.* Minneapolis, MN: University of Minnesota Press.

Appiah, Kwame A. (1992) *In My Father's House, What Does It Mean to Be an African Today?* London: Methuen.

Ardener, Edwin (1970) 'Witchcraft, Economics and the Continuity of Belief', in Mary Douglas (ed.) *Witchcraft Confessions and Accusations*, pp. 141–60. London: Tavistock.

Ashforth, Adam (1996) 'Of Secrecy and Commonplace: Witchcraft in Soweto', *Social Research* 63(4): 1183–234.

Austen, Ralph (1993) 'The Moral Economy of Witchcraft: An Essay in Comparative History', in Jean Comaroff and John Comaroff (eds) *Modernity and Its Malcontents: Ritual and Power in Postcolonial Africa*, pp. 89–110. Chicago, IL: University of Chicago Press.

Bastian, Misty L. (1993) ' "Bloodhounds Who Have No Friends": Witchcraft and Locality in the Nigerian Popular Press', in Jean Comaroff and John Comaroff (eds) *Modernity and Its Malcontents: Ritual and Power in Postcolonial Africa*, pp. 129–66. Chicago, IL: University of Chicago Press.

Bayart, Jean-François (forthcoming) (1994) *La réinvention du capitalisme.* Paris: Fayard.

Bayart, Jean-François (1996) *L'illusion identitaire*, Paris: Fayard.

Bureau, René (1962) *Ethno-sociologie religieuse des Douala et apparentés.* Recherches et études camerounaises 7/8. Yaounde: IRCAM.

Chenuaud, Bernard (1995) *Congo: La guerre des âges.* Paris: Radio France, France Culture. November 1996 (on tape).

Comaroff, Jean (forthcoming) 'Consuming Passions: Child Abuse, Fetishism, and "The New World Order" ', *Culture.*

Comaroff, Jean and John Comaroff (eds) (1993) *Modernity and Its Malcontents: Ritual and Power in Postcolonial Africa.* Chicago, IL: University of Chicago Press.

Comaroff, Jean and John Comaroff (forthcoming) 'Occult Economies and the Violence of Abstraction', *American Ethnologist.*

Copet-Rougier, Elisabeth (1986) 'Catégories d'ordres et réponses aux désordres chez les Mkako du Cameroun', *Droit et Cultures* 11: 79–88.

Couperus, L. (1900/92) *The Hidden Force.* London: Quartet Books.

Desjeux, Dominique (1987) *Stratégies paysannes en Afrique noire: Le Congo — Essai sur la gestion de l'incertitude.* Paris: L'Harmattan.

van der Drift, Roy (1992) *Arbeid en Alcohol: De Dynamiek van de Rijstverbouw en het Gezag van de Oudsten bij de Balanta Brassa in Guinee Bissau.* Leiden: CNWS.

Evans-Pritchard, E.E. (1937) *Witchcraft, Oracles and Magic among the Azande.* Oxford: Clarendon Press.

Fisiy, Cyprian F. (1990) 'Le monopole juridictionnel de l'État et le règlement des affaires de sorcellerie au Cameroun', *Politique africaine* 40: 60–72.

Fisiy, Cyprian F. (1992) *Power and Privilege in the Administration of Law: Land Law Reforms and Social Differentiation in Cameroon.* Leiden: African Studies Centre.

Fisiy, Cyprian F. and Peter Geschiere (1990) 'Judges and Witches, or how is the State to deal with Witchcraft? Examples from Southeastern Cameroon', *Cahiers d'études africaines* 118: 135–56.

Fisiy, Cyprian F. and Peter Geschiere (1991) 'Sorcery, Witchcraft and Accumulation: Regional Variations in South and West Cameroon', *Critique of Anthropology* 11(3): 251–78.

Fisiy, Cyprian F. and Peter Geschiere (1993) 'Sorcellerie et accumulation', in Peter Geschiere and Piet Konings (eds) *Les itinéraires d'accumulation au Cameroun/Pathways to Accumulation in Cameroon*, pp. 99–131. Paris: Karthala; Leiden: African Studies Centre.

Fisiy, Cyprian F. and Peter Geschiere (1996) 'Witchcraft, Violence and Identity: Different Trajectories in Postcolonial Cameroon', in Richard Werbner and Terence Ranger (eds) *Postcolonial Identities in Africa*, pp. 193–222. London: Zed Books.

Geschiere, Peter (1988) 'Sorcery and the State in Cameroon', *Critique of Anthropology* 8(1): 35–63.

Geschiere, Peter (1994) 'Parenté et argent dans une société lignagère', in Jean-François Bayart (ed.) *La réinvention du capitalisme*, pp. 87–113. Paris: Fayard.

Geschiere, Peter (1995) *Sorcellerie et politique en Afrique. La viande des autres*. Paris: Karthala.
Geschiere, Peter (1996) 'Local Knowledge and Imported Knowledge — Witchcraft, Healing and New Forms of Accumulation', in Peter Meyns (ed.) *Staat und Gesellschaft in Afrika: Erosions- und Reformprozesse*, pp. 170–80. Hamburg: LitVerlag.
Geschiere, Peter (1997) *The Modernity of Witchcraft, Politics and the Occult in Postcolonial Africa*. Charlottesville, VA: University of Virginia Press.
Goheen, Mitzi (1996) *Men Own the Fields, Women Own the Crops: Gender and Power in the Cameroon Highlands*. Madison, WI: The University of Wisconsin Press.
Hacking, Ian (1991a) 'The Making and Molding of Child Abuse', *Critical Inquiry* 17(2): 253–88
Hacking, Ian (1991b) 'Two Souls in One Body', *Critical Inquiry* 17(4): 838–67.
Hannerz, Ulf (1992) *Cultural Complexity: Studies in the Social Organization of Meaning*. New York: Columbia University Press.
Kapferer, Bruce (1983) *A Celebration of Demons*. Bloomington, IN: Indiana University Press.
Kapferer, Bruce (1997) *The Feast of the Sorcerer: Practices of Consciousness and Power*. Chicago, IL: University of Chicago Press.
Laburthe-Tolra, Philippe (1977) *Minlaaba, histoire et société traditionnelle chez les Bëti du Sud Cameroun*. Paris: Champion (also published as: 1981, *Les seigneurs de la forêt*, Paris: Publications de la Sorbonne; and 1988, *Initiations et sociétés secrètes au Cameroun*, Paris: Karthala).
La Fontaine, Jean S. (1992) 'Concepts of Evil, Witchcraft and the Sexual Abuse of Children in Modern England', *Etnofoor* V(1/2): 6–21.
Lindermayer, Orestis (1995) ' "The Beast of Revelation", American Fundamentalist Christianity and the European Union', *Etnofoor* VII(1): 27–47.
Mbembe, Achille (1992) 'Provisional Notes on the Postcolony', *Africa* 62(1): 3–38.
Mbunwe-Samba, Patrick (1996) *Witchcraft, Magic and Divination — A Personal Testimony*. Bamenda: Phyllis Kaberry Centre; Leiden: African Studies Centre.
Meyer, Birgit (1995) 'Translating the Devil: An African Appropriation of Pietist Protestantism: The Case of the Peki Ewe in Southeastern Ghana, 1847–1992'. PhD Thesis, University of Amsterdam.
Mudimbe, Valentin Y. (1988) *The Invention of Africa: Gnosis, Philosophy and the Order of Knowledge*. Bloomington, IN: Indiana University Press.
Ndjio, Basile (1995) 'Sorcellerie, pouvoir et accumulation en pays bamiléké: Cas du *Ngru*'. Yaoundé (mimeo).
Niehaus, Isaac A. (1993) 'Witch-Hunting and Political Legitimacy: Continuity and Change in Green Valley, Lebowa, 1930–1991', *Africa* 63(4): 498–529.
Niehaus, Isaac A. (1995) 'Witches of the Transvaal Lowveld and their Familiars: Conceptions of Duality, Power and Desire', *Cahiers d'études africaines* XXV(2–3): 513–41.
Obeysekere, Gananath (1975) 'Sorcery, Premeditated Murder and the Canalization of Aggression on Sri Lanka', *Ethnology* XIV: 1–23.
Obeysekere, Gananath (1977) 'Social Change and the Deities: Rise of Kataragama Cult in Modern Sri Lanka', *Man (n.s.)* 12(3/4): 377–96.
Offiong, Daniel A. (1991) *Witchcraft, Sorcery, Magic and Social Order among the Ibibio of Nigeria*. Enugu: Fourth Dimension Publishing.
Pradelles de Latour, Charles-Henry (1991) *Ethnopsychanalyse en pays bamiléké*. Paris: EPEL.
Roitman, Janet (1996) 'Objects of the Economy and the Language of Politics in Northern Cameroon'. PhD Thesis, University of Pennsylvania (Dept. of Political Science).
de Rosny, Eric (1981) *Les yeux de ma chèvre: Sur les pas des maîtres de la nuit en pays douala*. Paris: Plon.
de Rosny (1992) *L'Afrique des guérisons*. Paris: Karthala.
Rowlands, Michael and Jean-Pierre Warnier (1988) 'Sorcery, Power and the Modern State in Cameroon', *Man (n.s.)* 23: 118–32.
Shaw, Rosalind (forthcoming) *The Dangers of Temne Divination: Ritual Memories of the Slave Trade in West Africa*. Chicago, IL: University of Chicago Press.
Swartz, Marc J. (ed.) (1968) *Local Level Politics*. Chicago: Aldine.

Taussig, Michael (1980) *The Devil and Commodity Fetishism in S. America*. Chapel Hill, NC: University of Carolina Press.

Taussig, Michael (1987) *Shamanism, Colonialism and the Wild Man, A Study of Terror and Healing*. Chicago, IL: University of Chicago Press.

Warnier, Jean-Pierre (1985) *Echanges, développement et hiérarchies dans le Bamenda précolonial (Cameroun)*. Stuttgart: Steiner.

Warnier, Jean-Pierre (1993) *L'Esprit d'entreprise au Cameroun*. Paris: Karthala.

Weller, Robert P. (1994) *Resistance, Chaos and Control in China*. London: Macmillan.

Time and the Global: Against the Homogeneous, Empty Communities in Contemporary Social Theory

John D. Kelly

> In short, *geopolitics* has its ideological foundations in *chronopolitics*.
> Johannes Fabian (1983: 144)

> Comparison of others' attempts to setting off on a sea voyage in which the ships are drawn off course by the magnetic north pole. Discover *that* North Pole. What for others are deviations, for me are data by which to set my course. I base my reckoning on the differentia of time that disturb the 'main lines' of the investigation for others.
> Walter Benjamin (1989: 43)

Discourse on 'globalization' is itself globalizing, from roots that are deeper in business and policy journalism than in the academy, and toward multiple futures trackable from no one vantage. As far as I can tell, its authors (now including me) tend to address it with an almost antinomic mixture of respect and aggression — respect for its sublime enormity and ubiquity, but also a sense of moral and political urgency to its specification, as two recent US journalistic examples will illustrate:

> Because this phenomenon we call 'globalization' — the integration of markets, trade, finance, information and corporate ownership around the globe — is actually a very American phenomenon: it wears Mickey Mouse ears, eats Big Macs, drinks Coke ... countries that plug into globalization are really plugging into a high degree of Americanization (Friedman, 1996: A27).

> How do you define the uniformity of thought prevailing in our societies? ... My arrogance does not go so far as to offer a program to a movement that, anyhow, needs a vision, not a blueprint. But I am brave enough to suggest four points, four taboos that the movement will have to smash if it is not to be blocked by the diversions of official propaganda. The first is the assumption that the form the internationalization of the economy has taken — so-called globalization — is a natural and inevitable result of technological progress. Actually, it is the outcome of a deliberate policy: the extraordinary expansion of international transactions has more to do with the decision to free capital movements than with the invention of computers and modems. (Singer, 1996: 22)

Here I am more interested in what is similar about these texts than their differences. For Friedman, the 'Foreign Affairs' columnist for *The New York Times* newspaper, 'The only answer is multi-localism', not Singer's movement; both 'multi-localism' and 'Americanization' are precisely the sorts of thing that Singer, Europe correspondent for *The Nation*, sought to dismiss as diversions. Yet both Friedman and Singer invoked not globalization but something someone was 'calling' globalization, both relied on synecdochal icons (mouse ears, modems) to concretize vast process, and both gave the underlying process two definitions, what it is and what it really is: first the globalization definition (Friedman's 'the integration of . . .', Singer's 'the form the internationalization of the economy has taken'), and then the discernment of true underlying form: 'Americanization', or 'the decision to free capital movements'.

I am not interested in dismissing globalization as a false front, false consciousness, mere surface or even partial truth (though at times, as you will see, I feel all these ways about 'identity'). I am more interested in what globalization is, than in what it really is, more interested in its implications for theory and method in social and cultural scholarship, than in playing the hero finding the secret core (though one cannot avoid both roles when things get serious). We will reconsider arguments akin to those of Friedman and Singer: Friedman's is anticipated in theories of 'Westernization', and perspicaciously criticized by Ulf Hannerz; Singer's outrage against premises about natural and inevitable progress is anticipated by Walter Benjamin's. We are well advised by both Friedman and Singer to remember, even when we focus on matters of culture and cultural globalization, that it all obviously has something to do with corporations and capital. But let us return to what globalization is, now not any alleged underlying thing called 'globalization', but the theory, in the context of social theory.

Globalization theory, as I see it, distinguishes itself in social theory with an important premise, a new solution to the long-standing 'units problem' for comparative social science.[1] Against presumption that societies, cultures, nation-states or other units exist, that they are bounded, separate, discrete and/or autonomous, the premise of globalization theory is that, at least at present, there are no absolute political, social or cultural boundaries un- breached by global flows. Comparison, generalization, or any other modes of social theorizing, whether about economics, religion, kinship or politics, must then address not separate examples or discrete cases, but rather

---

1. To be clearer about this premise, the concept of globalization clearly refers to an ongoing process, and so also implies both that there was a time when the globe was less global, and that it is getting increasingly unitary as time passes. The units problem, recently renewed in anthropology by Wolf's critique (1982) of ethnographic method and theory, perhaps first emerged in late nineteenth century efforts to defend ambitious, evolutionary comparative methods in anthropology and other social sciences against increasing numbers of sceptics. As Stocking (1987: 318) shows, the issue was raised by Galton against Tylor in 1888 and became known as 'Galton's problem': when Tylor cited multiple cases of similar social phenomena, which were truly independent and which connected, or at least derived from a common source? Where Galton's scepticism of the separateness of social fields interrupted Tylor's effort to document a general theory of social evolution, and fed directly into Boas's increasingly radical scepticism of general ethnological theories, Wolf's scepticism of separateness served his effort to resituate ethnology in a 'new, historical political economy', an ultimate science of what really is, perceiving not just breaching, connecting and unifying flows, but an underlying 'manifold' of social relations, a different global metaphor which I will not examine here.

phenomena that are densely and dynamically interconnected. So, now what? As Hannerz (1992: 267) has put it, the problem now is 'grasp of the flux'.

Against the absurd prospect of writing the world, the search is on for conceptions of social realities that are supple enough to handle this flowing and flowed-at mode of being. If we neglect, here, deliberately reductionistic approaches claiming foreknowledge of the real social foundations, common current tools for grasping the flows include concepts of identity, ethnicity, and nation as imagined community. Richard Fardon, for example, has recently argued that the conceptions of culture and society have come to seem 'innocent dupes of the political triad' of nation, ethnicity and identity, that representations of the very existence of cultures or societies are 'a derivative fact', complicit in 'the historical plots' of nationality, ethnicity or identity, and the agents possessing and possessed by them (Fardon, 1995: 7–8). Fardon's description certainly captures the trend of contemporary scholarship, but the problem has not been solved. No matter how earnestly the new names avoid innocence by emphasizing explicit and implicit political interests, nothing, it seems to me, is less likely to solve the problem of 'grasping the flux' than allowing new names to revitalize the old units, and keep us operating as if the world is first of all a collection of nameable groups.

This essay will address the limits I perceive to reliance on conceptions of identity, ethnicity, nation and other forms of 'imagined community' as a solution to the problem of describing either 'local' or 'flowing' social dynamics in an already globalized social field. It will proceed mainly by a critical rereading of *Imagined Communities*, Benedict Anderson's remarkable, now classic reflection on nations and nationalism, with particular attention to the story of global history as Anderson tells it, and to Anderson's use of Walter Benjamin's concept of 'homogeneous, empty time'.[2] Not to put too fine a point on it, it will be a polemic against Anderson's understanding of Benjamin's concept and its implications, and thereby an argument against an aspiration for global symmetries that I perceive as an unpromising feature of much current scholarship. Before turning to Anderson's now famous arguments and images, however, I will offer a few more comments about space–time premises and the scholarly place of globalization theory itself: both the place globalization theory finds in genealogies of social theory, and the place globalization theory offers scholars in its world.

---

2. I will also discuss other theoretical works, and make references especially to Fiji and India, my two more particular area interests as a scholar. This is a theoretical essay, however, oriented further by the premise that theory can be approached by way of critical engagement with the images, metaphors, and other touchstones that can be so useful, but also so fettering. If theory in social science is not sheer abstraction — and I think it rarely or never is — the point is rather that its tropes are not grounded in the first instance, none are safe, and all merit their moment of conscious, critical examination.

THE PLACE, SPACE AND TIME OF GLOBALIZATION

More than fifteen years ago, Carl Pletsch published a powerful description and critique of the division of labour in the (Western) social sciences circa 1950 to 1975. His main point was that modernization theory organized social science research in the West, and did so even though scholars were sceptical from the outset of the very idea of modernizing. Modernization theory informed the idea of first, second and third worlds, 'the most primitive system of classification in our social scientific discourse' (Pletsch, 1981: 565), and justified the allocation of different kinds of scholarship to each — economists to the first, for instance, area specialists to the second and anthropologists to the third. General laws of human behaviour were thought to be visible especially in the first world, where things and people were most developed and unconstrained by either ideology (as in the second world) or tradition or culture (as in the third). The third world was destined to modernize, and become either more like the first world, or entrapped in ideology by the second. Or so went the theory.

Pletsch argued persuasively that one could not simply 'cast aside this conceptual ordering of social scientific labor', entrenched as it was in the research programmes of disciplines. He called instead for criticism 'in the Kantian, Hegelian, and Marxist sense': not only acknowledgement that the modernization theory and its three-worlds scheme was imbricated with the politics of the Cold War — that much was obvious, he showed, to everyone from the outset — but criticism that would 'finally transcend it by devising another conceptual umbrella for social science that will serve all the useful purposes that the three worlds notion served, without its obvious defects' (ibid: 588). Whether or not social history actually follows a Hegelian dialectic, something I doubt, Pletsch is surely right that social theory does.

In 1981 Pletsch predicted that a revolution against the paradigm was in preparation. I would argue that since then, not one but two alternative conceptual umbrellas have been proposed with both the potential breadth of reference and the conceptual simplicity (or 'primitivity') necessary to be new transdisciplinary paradigms. Both are imbricated with changes in the social world, including the end of the cold war, but neither, as yet, has been established institutionally: I refer of course to postmodernism on the one hand, and globalization theory on the other.

The topic here being globalization, I will not inquire very far into the unique history of postmodern social theory. Its history has already been written, always already, by postmodernists themselves. In fact, postmodernism has narrated its own story continually, self-consciously, and even obsessively. Drawn forth especially when both third world hopes and second world threats grew increasingly dubious, postmodernism has offered the drama of its own arrival as the concept capable of overcoming the drama of modernization. For this reason, despite real commitment to anti-essentialism and non-foundational theorizing, it has trouble abiding without seeming at least as final, at least as much a claim to being the end of history itself.

The three worlds of modernization, as a classification scheme, presented first of all a geography. It was a geography connected to a history, but first of all, a simple image or 'primitive classification' of space. Postmodernism subsumed the spaces of modernization in a three stage scheme of time, encompassing the dramas of modernization as a mere prelude to the creative destruction of the modern by the postmodern. Now, globalization returns us to space — finds in space a way out of the end of time.

To be clear here, all three of these 'conceptual umbrellas' for social science are chronotopic (Bakhtin's term), conceptions that establish space–time possibilities. All project premises about both space and time, the configuration of human places and their possibilities past, present and future. None the less, what they distinguish, count and name in the foreground varies extremely, an alternation with a clear dialogic. In a globe of blurring cold war boundaries, a time scheme projecting a radically new future enabled subsumption of modernization's three worlds into the past; precisely as that future failed to objectify itself as a real and present new society, arose calls for new kinds of observation of social relations in space. It has been fair for scholars to ask of postmodernism, what were its premises about allegedly 'other' societies in space, about cultural difference and colonial history (see, for example, Chow, 1993; Kaplan, 1995a; Spivak, 1994; Stoler, 1995). It strikes me as equally fair, and more interesting, to ask now, what theories of time and history are possible within the premises of globalization. This, and not either deconstruction or defence of anyone's nation or identity, seems to me the intrinsic task for cultural scholarship in a globalizing world.

TO THE ANGEL OF HISTORY, THE NATION IS NOT AN IMAGINED COMMUNITY

So now we turn to Anderson's *Imagined Communities* in pursuit of the theory of global time and history that, I think, makes this text so very popular among scholars. In Anderson's now famous formulations, the nation is a community constituted by imagined rather than face-to-face relationships, especially by a sensibility of 'deep, horizontal comradeship' (Anderson, 1983, 1991: 7), feelings fostered by print capitalism, especially novels and news-papers. 'Print-language is what invents nationalism' (1991: 134) and, in turn, 'nations inspire love, and often profoundly self-sacrificing love' (ibid: 141). Thus Anderson argues, nations and nationalism are 'cultural artefacts of a particular kind' (ibid: 4), born in the break-away self-consciousness of the 'creole pioneers', that is, the European colonies in the new world, then 'awakened' in Europe and pirated into being elsewhere, a 'modular' kind of cultural artefact, 'capable of being transplanted' (ibid: 4), 'available for pirating' in the early nineteenth century (ibid: 81), and 'everywhere modularly imagined' after World War II (ibid: 113). What we have here is not only a cultural theory of the nation but also a story of an emergently modularized global culture, a story of capital-driven print languages rendering the world into synchronized, symmetrical units of imagined, communal self-love.

In order to put Anderson's theory of the nation into bold relief, let us carry with us three other depictions of what distinguishes nations among human groups.

> So what, we may ask, is the just basis for a nation's claim to independence? Must a people first wander the wilderness for 2,000 years, suffer repeated persecution, humiliation and genocide in order to qualify? Until now, history's answer to the question has been pragmatic and brutal: a nation is a people tough enough to grab the land it wants and hang onto it. Period.

This version of 'history's' definition of the nation, from an op-ed newspaper essay by novelist John LeCarré (1994), is refreshingly uninterested in cognition, sensibilities, and experiences, and refreshingly interested in the will, of the typical, active nation. Recalling, next, Ernest Renan's now classic discussion (1990/1882) of the nation as definable not by shared race, language, antiquity or territory, but by shared memory and will, LeCarré's definition poses an interesting challenge to the scholarly tradition now following Benedict Anderson. Anderson's discussion of the nation has sent recent scholarship in search of nationalism as a style of memory, imagination and community, in search of expressions and elicitations of 'deep, horizontal comradeship' and so on. As if nationalism was adequately understood as some kind of search for, realization and enactment of some kind of identity. Is there more to matters of will, especially the importance of organized, instituted will, than is imagined in our current philosophies of identity?

Max Weber put a similar insight more practically:

> Time and again we find that the concept 'nation' directs us to political power. Hence, the concept seems to refer — if it refers at all to a uniform phenomenon — to a specific kind of pathos which is linked to the idea of a powerful political community of people who share a common language, or religion, or common customs, or political memories; such a state may already exist or it may be desired. (Weber, 1978: 393–4)

In this brief and far less celebrated comment on the nation as a type of social group, Weber singled it out for a specific emotion, 'this pathetic pride in the power of one's own community, or this longing for it', group obsession with seeking, having and revealing power and privilege.[3]

---

3. The quote is from the 1978 edition of *Economy and Society*, in which Guenther Roth and Claus Wittich revised all previous translations, in this case that of Ferdinand Kolegar. I am told, authoritatively, that 'pathos' and 'pathetic' here are lexically-literalist bad

The estrangement of the nation as a social form is accomplished differently by this trio, Renan, Weber and LeCarré, than it is by Anderson. If we understand the nation to be a collective, let alone collected, will to power, then we can expect far more from its praxis than the quiescent being of community, and similarly we have different questions about its poetics, the chronopolitical imaginaries that might collect and direct the wills. Quite concretely, we might inquire more into imaginations of the present and future as well as shared forgettings and memories. As scholars try to describe a globalizing world, to grasp the flows, we should not be naïve about what historical imagery is for. Especially if we seek to understand the poetics and praxis of people in these flows, colonizers, migrants, and other diasporic peoples, and if we seek to accomplish practical things with these under-standings — as I think we should — then we might admit that by trying to grasp this flow, and to lead others to a general consciousness of it, we are also trying to interrupt other narratives of history, in Prasenjit Duara's phrase 'rescuing history from the nation'.

In this sense grasping the flow, finding and communicating present realities that transgress nation-state imaginaries, resembles what Walter Benjamin (1968: 255) depicted as seizing a flash in a moment of danger, a praxis for historians. The real task of the historian, Benjamin insisted, was not to relive the past by empathy, not to set the present aside in order to recover (in a naïve sense) the way it really was, and certainly not to locate and portray with a judicious even-handedness the same number of details about each unit of time across equal units of space, as if human history was a story of progress across 'homogeneous, empty time' (ibid: 261). Instead, Benjamin called upon historians to be cognizant of debts and danger, debts owed to the dead who struggled and sacrificed and danger in the present. This historian realizes that '*even the dead* will not be safe' (ibid: 255) without historians' active inter-vention, that memory of losses and sacrifices will be lost or distorted in the interests of the presently powerful, and most importantly, that memories of past struggles, the flashes seized, can become inspiration for political movements in the present and future.

---

translations, creating in English an overtone of dismissive pity, where 'emotion' and 'emotional' would better convey Weber's point. To provide the fuller form, Weber's comment, in his short chapter on 'Ethnic Groups' in *Economy and Society*, continues as follows:

> The more power is emphasized, the closer appears to be the link between nation and state. This pathetic pride in the power of one's own community, or this longing for it, may be much more widespread in relatively small language groups such as the Hungarians, Czechs or Greeks than in a similar but much larger community such as the Germans 150 year ago, when they were essentially a language group without pretensions to national power.

For clarifying this translation issue, thanks to participants at the Conference on Global-ization in Amsterdam (3 March 1996) and to Patrick Eisenlohr.

Benedict Anderson relies on Walter Benjamin, and specifically on imagery from Benjamin's 'Theses on the Philosophy of History', to provide much of the mood and some of the substance of his study of *Imagined Communities*.[4] Tracking the different moods and meanings that Anderson attaches to Benjamin's images will enable us to trace how far Benjamin's ideas actually orient the theorizing of Benedict Anderson, and to spot, quite vividly, the chronopolitical vectors that are specifically Anderson's. In particular, to state my own thesis, Anderson's theory of the peculiarity of the nation as an 'imagined community' depends upon his use of Benjamin's image of 'homogeneous, empty time' (1968: 261, 264): but Anderson insists upon acceptance of the reality of this chronotope, which to Benjamin was precisely the image of history that had to be refused.

We shall twice return to 'homogeneous, empty time', but to open questions about mood and purpose let us begin with the 'angel of history', another image from Benjamin (1968), with which Anderson concluded the first edition (1983) of *Imagined Communities*:

> In all of this, China, Vietnam, and Cambodia are not in the least unique. This is why there are small grounds for hope that the precedents they have set for inter-socialist wars will not be followed ... nothing can usefully be done to limit or prevent such wars unless we abandon fictions like 'Marxists as such are not nationalists', or 'nationalism is the pathology of modern developmental history', and instead, do our slow best to learn the real, and imagined, experience of the past.
>   Of the Angel of History, Walter Benjamin wrote that:
> 'His face is turned towards the past. Where we perceive a chain of events, he sees one single catastrophe which keeps piling wreckage upon wreckage and hurls it in front of his feet. The angel would like to stay, awaken the dead, and make whole what has been smashed. But a storm is blowing from Paradise; it has got caught in his wings with such a violence that the angel can no longer close them. The storm irresistibly propels him into the future to which his back is turned, while the pile of debris before him grows skyward. The storm is what we call progress' [Illuminations 257–8].
> But this angel is immortal, and our faces are turned towards the obscurity ahead.

To sense some tension between Anderson's own tropics and Benjamin's, consider the progressivism of Anderson's forward facing scholar doing his or her 'slow best', who hopes to do something eventually useful 'to limit or prevent wars', and the scholar-heroes envisioned in Benjamin's thesis, seizing flashes in moments of danger, 'man enough to blast open the continuum of history' (Benjamin, 1968: 262). Anderson asks in the first line of the Preface to the second edition, 'Who would have thought that the storm blows harder the

---

4.   Anderson claims a close relationship. The first line of the acknowledgments in *Imagined Communities* is: 'As will be apparent to the reader, my thinking about nationalism has been deeply affected by the writings of Erich Auerbach, Walter Benjamin, and Victor Turner'. Much connects these authors to Anderson: their interest in the transporting powers of literature (cf. novels, print capitalism), their studies of world views and what supports and overturns them (cf. the national language, the bureaucratic pilgrimage), and possibly also their searches for aesthetic solutions to political questions.

farther it leaves Paradise behind?' I think Benjamin would have, the Benjamin who announced that 'it is our task to bring about a real state of emergency' (Benjamin, 1968: 257). Where Anderson (1991: xi) declares himself 'haunted by the prospect of further full-scale wars between the socialist states', Benjamin seems haunted, instead, not by active nationalists or indeed by the fascists, but by the spectre of quiescence among the exploited. What, then, is Benjamin's hopelessly aware angel of history doing for Anderson's text?

Clearly, a pathos of nationalism is located especially, for Anderson, in socialist nations. Anderson's text began and ended with the wars in Indo-China, wars 'of world historical importance' because the belligerents were 'revolutionary' states engaging without plausible denial in 'conventional' war (Anderson, 1991: 1). Anderson sees and measures out nationalism — strange and important to notice — first of all, neither, for example, as an anticolonial civil force, nor a pressure of a United Nations world-spirit, not as a bourgeois ideograph nor a modern necessity, but instead as the demon responsible for derailing 'regimes whose independence and revolutionary credentials are undeniable' (ibid: 1), derailers of world history. The nation first commands Anderson's attention as the killer of a utopian political aesthetic.

Thus while pathos abounds, we find quite different foundational resentments directed at nationalism by Anderson than, for example, LeCarré. The assignment of pathos in LeCarré's plain tale is the more easily accounted for (and I hope not caricatured, for it cuts close to my own commitments) in the Nietzschian template for ('slave') philosophies based on resentment: the politically-weak intellectual, morally sympathetic with the weak of the world, will tend to find ordinary political quests for power not good but evil, especially when they succeed. Anderson, more complexly, blames nationalism for the collapse of a political dream revealed as a fantasy, the virtuous revolutionary state, and yet locates nations first of all in the social imaginary and the explosion of the fantasy in 'world history' (cf. 'world historical' quoted above). He then refuses Tom Nairn's depiction (quoted in Anderson, 1991: 5) of nationalism as the modern pathology, favouring instead this 'slow best' research into the nation as experienced. The result is a fascinated delineating of the real effects of the nationalist imaginary, a delineation now undertaken by an army of scholars, and still overarched with a vast sense of disappointment and disillusionment.

Benjamin's own pathos finds a third vector, not directed at the nation or nationalism. Benjamin, the most flamboyant in his resentments, attacks especially (not Fascists but) Social Democrats, for their narcotic doctrines of gradualist progress:

> The concept of the historical progress of mankind cannot be sundered from the concept of its progression through a homogeneous, empty time ...
>
> History is the subject of a structure whose site is not homogeneous, empty time, but time filled by the presence of the now. Thus, to Robespierre ancient Rome was a past charged with the time of the now which he blasted out of the continuum of history. The French Revolution viewed itself as Rome reincarnate ...

The awareness that they are about to make the continuum of history explode is characteristic of the revolutionary classes at the moment of their action ...

We know that the Jews were prohibited from investigating the future. The Torah and the prayers instruct them in remembrance, however. This stripped the future of its magic, to which all those succumb who turn to the soothsayers for enlightenment. This does not imply, however, that for the Jews the future turned into homogeneous, empty time. For every second of time was the strait gate through which the Messiah might enter. (Benjamin, 1968: 261, 264).

For Benjamin, the idea of living in homogeneous, empty time is pathetic, and the agents promoting it were evil. The pathos of the angel, unable to intervene, awaken the dead, make whole what is smashed, is not his final word. Tellingly, the angel appeared far closer to the final word of Anderson's essay than he did in Benjamin's theses. Benjamin ended here with the Messiah, and allied the historian not with the angel (not doing 'our slow best to learn the real, and imagined, experience of the past', Anderson, 1991: 161) but with the Messiah, shaping 'a conception of the present as the "time of the now" which is shot through with chips of Messianic time' (Benjamin, 1968: 263). What exactly it means to figure the agent of revolution as the Messiah is something the Benjamin scholars might never settle[5] but Benjamin's scorn is palpable for this conception of homogeneous, empty time, the Benjaminian image that, above all, Benedict Anderson found useful.[6]

---

5. For a good introduction to the issues involved in sorting out Benjamin's Judaism and Marxism see Rabinbach (1989) or the biography by Witte (1991). The crucial texts for the assertion of a Judaism deeper than and alien to his Marxism are those of his friend Gershom Scholem (1976, 1981). The literature privileging his Marxism is vast; important works include Buck-Morss (1989) and Tiedemann (1988, 1989). My own view — offered to help you understand me, not as an authority — is with those who see Benjamin as irreducibly both Marxist and Jewish, like other Marxists committed to class struggle as the real story in history but much unlike most other Marxists, believing in revelation and redemption as actual events: revelation, to those who can seize it, from actually existing things themselves, and redemption when victories add meaning to all prior sacrifices in struggle. Thus Scholem was insightful when he described Benjamin as a 'theologian marooned in the realm of the profane', and when he emphasized that Benjamin's search for revelation and redemption, and his 'Holy Writ' writing style, set him utterly apart from the analytical and critical style of most other twentieth century writers (Scholem, 1976: 187, 193, 198). Benjamin's own answer to Scholem's vision of historical materialism as an alien, entrapping limit to his thought is clear in his perception of the theology in Marx's own Holy Writ, as the 'Theses on the Philosophy of History' famously argue.

6. In fairness to Anderson and his affiliation of the angel and the historian, I should note that Benjamin certainly, in complex and changing ways over the course of his life, saw *himself* connected to the 'Angelus Novus', the 'new angel', a Paul Klee painting that was one of Benjamin's favourite possessions, and was the direct inspiration of his description of this angel of history. Scholem (1976) traces Benjamin's changing interpretations of the angel in relationship to himself as a success and failure. Finally, in this connection, note that while Benjamin affiliated good historians with the Messiah, this does not mean he saw any such success in his own works. Benjamin's biographer Witte connects Benjamin's self-affiliation with the angel of history with Benjamin's commentary on Kafka's sense of hope: 'Thus as Kafka puts it, there is an infinite amount of hope, but not for us. This statement really

GATES THROUGH TIME AND SPACE

So Benjamin offers us, as the antidote to the Social Democrats' 'homogeneous, empty time' of slow progress and deep, horizontal symmetries, an image of intellectually fostered, but class-based, anti-evolutionary Messianic moments. When the French Revolution exploded the continuum of history by viewing itself as Rome reincarnate, this 'tiger's leap into the past ... this same leap into the open air of history is the dialectical one, which is how Marx understood the revolution' (Benjamin, 1968: 261). Recalling that, for Anderson, the scandal of ordinary war among purportedly 'revolutionary' states marked the end of utopian illusions, perhaps we should reluctantly agree with Anderson as a rewriting of Benjamin, into the deeper pathos in which the homogeneous and empty is the real, and historian intellectuals can only partner with the angel. Or can we find things between the theological and the null? Even if we don't want to rely on Messiahs, revolutions or dialectical tiger's leaps, can we still find gates through time and space, and space-times neither homogenized nor emptied? Probably almost everywhere; but let us content ourselves, in the confines of an essay, with two descriptions of diasporic people, by intellectuals themselves enmeshed in the histories of movement.[7] Both concern the configuration of space and time in the British empire, the first chosen, perhaps perversely, as an example of a failed effort to homogenize and empty a history of human labour flow, the second, a return to one of Anderson's paradigmatic figures.

Benedict Anderson's reflections on nationalism focused on shared memory, and he added a chapter to the second edition (1991) on the strangeness of the obliged amnesias that stabilize national narratives. In my work in the Fiji Islands, I find a striking instance of an amnesiac recollection of diasporic passage which was a literal effort to orient a national memory. Could anyone narrate the colonial exploitation of labour diaspora within the frame of inevitable gradual progress? Yes, of course; and doing so — to transpose Benjamin's objection to the tactics of the Social Democrats — can lead the diasporic population (like 'the working class') to 'forget both its hatred and its spirit of sacrifice, for both are nourished by the image of enslaved ancestors rather than that of liberated grandchildren' (Benjamin,

---

contains Kafka's hope; it is the source of his radiant serenity' (Scholem, 1989: 225; cf. Witte, 1991: 203).

7. For readers who would rather that critique of Anderson's theory be conducted by way of a fuller ethnographic treatment of a particular national history, see Kelly (1988, 1991, 1995), Kaplan (1995b), Kaplan and Kelly (1994), and especially Kaplan and Kelly (forthcoming), a book in progress concerning colonial law and postcolonial politics. For a sympathetic but devastating critique of Benjamin's 'political Messianism' and dialectical tiger's leaps, see Tiedemann (1989, esp. 200–1). Regarding 'Probably almost everywhere', apologies to James Boon (cf. Boon, 1984: 157). On the question whether the ubiquity of 'gates', sites of flow after all, is itself the homogenizing, emptying force, see the conclusion of this essay.

1968: 260). This message was published by the Hon. Vivekanand Sharma, member of Fiji's Parliament, in a supplement to *The Fiji Times* (12 May 1979), Fiji's leading English-language (and simply, leading) newspaper. The supplement commemorated the centenary of the first arrival of indentured South Asians to Fiji, where their descendants have become half the population. One would never know, from Sharma's tone, that politicians among the ethnic Fijians, the other half of Fiji's population, were already increasingly encouraging of ethnic Fijian nativism and resentments against 'Indians' or Indo-Fijians. The first of Fiji's pro-ethnic Fijian, anti-Indo-Fijian military coups was five years and two days away.

> Pioneering has always been a major element in the development of resources for the good of mankind and there are numerous examples of this in history. The Christian Bible tells of how the prophet Moses led his people out of Egypt into the promised land across the Nile where today after decades of toil flourishes the land of Israel.
>
> In the History of India itself there were mass migrations of people from Asia Minor to North India and from North India to the Deccan Plateau. In recent history there have been pioneering movements from India to Mauritius, Trinidad, South Africa, British Guyana, Surinam and Fiji.
>
> All of these movements have been in search for a better opportunity to enjoy life in its fullest sense. In many cases it has involved hardships that have been conquered and those of us who are living in Fiji now are reaping the fruits of the efforts of our forefathers. Our chosen land is a land of peace, of freedom, of religion, and of opportunities. It is our duty today to continue with the good work done by those whose memory we treasure so much to ensure that our children and all those who follow them will have the same opportunities that were created for us.

People who move inherit the earth. All they have to do is keep up the good work, 'in search for a better opportunity'. If Benjamin would find pathos in the pleasure taken in the present and expected in the future as an arrival across a continuous progress, and if Anderson might find pathos in the simultaneous, purposeful remembrance and forgetting of past hardship and (here displaced) conquest, I fight a virtual anger at the mildness of this political will. We should fight such anger, in the interests of a clearer understanding. In Fiji, after the Indo-Fijians forced independence onto both the British and the ethnic Fijians, and before the coups interrupted all stories of evolving constitutional democracy in Fiji, Indo-Fijian politicians had persistently tried to shape the nation in this romance of development (see also Kelly, 1988). Abandoning all grievances and pleading for community and future prosperity, abjuring their hatred for their intimate enemies the British, the Indo-Fijians had hoped to evade the hatred of the ethnic Fijians. It didn't work; few, among the ethnic Fijians, have yet come to see themselves as partners with immigrants in a world of flows in search of better opportunity and continuous progress, and one hears fewer serious efforts, in recent years, to tell the story this way.

Benjamin underestimated the Fascists in his attack on the Social Democrats, as much as Sharma underestimated the Fijian nationalists in his nervous triumphalism about Fiji's freedoms. Of course, there is a sense in which the

Indo-Fijians have maintained 'the same opportunities' for their children, even in post-coups Fiji, since Indo-Fijians had almost as little actual political power in 1979 as they do at present. None the less, something very odd is going on, not only in Fiji but in many other places in the world, in the willed forgetting of the exploitation and violence of colonial labour history in some narrations of diaspora, in diaspora narratives of 'opportunity' and 'progress' that abandon the power of memories of sacrifice. There are many varieties of transnational, diasporic pathos, not only willed forgetting but also remembering, for example remembering a 'promised land' across intervening millennia. Dilemmas in the representation of diasporic flows cannot be understood, I suspect, except in relation to dilemmas in the collecting of political will. For now, though, what has been demonstrated is that homogenizing and emptying the diasporic passage, the assertion of a shared, evolving, prosperity-world, can be a desperate and even doomed tactic in some localities, even if it draws upon the tropics of the European Social Democrats that Benjamin hated and Anderson thought already universal.

What we shall seek next are the means to imagine transformations taking place as things 'flow' that do not fit any Hegelian script: changes that are not merely progressive, arrested, or regressive, not merely gradual or revolutionary, not merely big or small movements in one field, but rather, other kinds of interruptions, eruptions, and especially, connections, of social time and space. In this search we shall be well served by other tools to measure and describe. Thus I defer our second diasporic self-narrative, a British one, until after we develop a new descriptive concept.

SEA CHANGES

Both Ruth Benedict and Ranajit Guha resort to a Shakespearean allegory, the 'sea-change', to characterize transformations that they find particularly significant. First, Ruth Benedict, in her World War II ethnography of Japan, *The Chrysanthemum and the Sword*:

> I found that once I had seen where my Occidental assumptions did not fit into their view of life and had got some idea of the categories and symbols they used, many contradictions Westerners are accustomed to see in Japanese behavior were no longer contradictions ... Virtue and vice as the Occident understands them had undergone a sea-change. The system was singular. It was not Buddhism and it was not Confucianism. It was Japanese — the strength and the weakness of Japan. (Benedict, 1946: 19)

Benedict also uses other metaphors for the same process of change.[8] More interesting for us, she connects these breaks in the flow of translation, these

---

8. Two other examples: 'Americans, in order to understand ordinary self-disciplinary practices in Japan, therefore, have to do a kind of surgical operation on our idea of "self-discipline"' (Benedict, 1946: 233). 'Special Japanese meanings of this word "sincerity"

'sea-changes' experienced by anthropologists and others, to the larger and longer history of cultural flows and change that Benedict, Boas and most of the Boasians were interested in:

> A tribe may share ninety per cent of its formal observances with its neighbors and yet it may have revamped them to fit a way of life and a set of values which it does not share with any surrounding peoples. In the process it may have had to reject some fundamental arrangements which, however small in proportion to the whole, turn its future course of development in a unique direction. (Benedict, 1946: 9)

Anything that flows across cultural boundaries can undergo a sea-change as it is fit into a different way of life and set of values. The process itself can turn future courses of development in unique directions.

To me this sounds much like the global process Ulf Hannerz has labelled creolization. Of course Benedict, more than most of the Boasians, had a commitment to the unity of a cultural pattern that puts her work out of step with commitments in globalization studies to privilege heterogeneity, to imagine all boundaries porous, and to render locality more complexly and contingently. Few would now follow her lead in privileging the whole culture as a unitary agent, and I do not doubt that the premises of globalization oversimplify the world less than hers did. Equally, however, it would be wrong to accuse her of seeing cultures as either ahistoric or hermetically sealed; in fact the evidence is ample that she, like her teacher Boas, was fundamentally interested in this process of sea-change, in which transcoursing values both get changed, and make changes, without one grid for their history or vector to their 'development'.

The Shakespearean source of the 'sea-change' metaphor is *The Tempest* I.2:

> Full fathom five thy father lies,
>   Of his bones are coral made,
> Those are pearls that were his eyes.
>   Nothing of him that doth fade
> But doth suffer a sea-change
> Into something rich and strange.

---

have already been referred to in passing. *Makoto* does not mean what sincerity does in English usage. It means both far less and far more ... Once one has accepted the fact that "sincerity" does not have the American meaning it is a most useful word to note in all Japanese texts. For it almost unfailingly identifies those positive virtues the Japanese actually stress' (ibid: 215, 218).

Davidsonians can whine as they like about the perils of wilful bad translation in ethnography. Benedict's clear, amply documented claim is that there is no simply good translation across cultural boundaries, that even closely comparable conceptions, those that cross-language dictionaries consociate, undergo a 'sea-change' as they change contexts.

Things rich and strange, made by their refashioning after transcursion into a new context. Bruno Latour, among more recent social theorists, is fascinated by the way objects brought into being for a purpose, with their function inscribed into their form, can then gain a life of their own, new functions which further affect their form; subjects too. Full cognizance of this fundamental similarity, in fact, undermines the absolute separation of subjects and objects, Latour argues. If indeed one abandons anchors — if one resents nautical play, 'grounding' is also an adequate, slightly more abstract image — like Benedict's presumption of the always ongoing whole culture, then, following Latour, one finds a world in which all similarity and difference is made, negotiated, renegotiable, a world both multiply ordered and orderable, and inexhaustibly chaotic as well. A world without stability in functions or telos even for well-made subjects and objects, without one direction for progress. Rich and strange indeed (though some might argue that Weber already described it).

Let us counterpose this supercreolizing sea-change world, which could in its own kaleidoscopic way be homogenized and in some sense empty, with a different scholar's 'sea change'. Hannerz's classic contrast of global process pitted 'creolization' as a world pattern against 'westernization', the sort of world vision ambiguously promoted by Benedict Anderson in his conceptualizations of modal, pirated nationality and nationalism, 'cultural artifacts' with 'formal universality' (Anderson, 1991: 4–5). Anderson does open the door to a more creolizing reading. He carefully insists that 'once created, they became 'modular', capable of being transplanted, with varying degrees of self-consciousness, to a great variety of social terrains, to merge and be merged with a correspondingly wide variety of political and ideological constellations' (ibid: 4). Depending upon how we imagine these mergers, then, we would seem to place the world proliferation of nationalism and nationality somewhere on a westernization–creolization spectrum, and somewhere between stable modules of form, and merger mush.

'Merging and being merged with' does not quite get us to the kinds of rejections and contentions observable in Fiji and elsewhere. Ranajit Guha observed a different sea-change when the British devised the so-called 'Permanent Settlement', a land tenure rule for a conquered territory, Bengal:

By tracing the intellectual ancestry of the Permanent Settlement to the very beginnings of Political Economy, it also helps to throw some light on the latter as it moves along an important, if obscure, part of its trajectory. Physiocratic thought, the precursor of Political Economy, was an implacable critique of feudalism in its native habitat and proved to be a real force in undermining the *ancien régime*. Ironically, however, while being grafted to India by the most advanced capitalist power of that age, it became instrumental in building a neo-feudal organization of landed property and in the absorption and reproduction of pre-capitalist elements in a colonial regime. In other words, a typically bourgeois form of knowledge was bent backwards to adjust itself to the relations of power in a semi-feudal society ...

Political Economy was not the only body of knowledge to have suffered a sea change under conditions of colonialism. There were other systems of thought too which the western bourgeoisie had relentlessly used in their struggle against feudalism during the period of their ascendancy in their own societies but which they modified and compromised all too readily in order to find a social base for their power in the conquered lands of the Asian continent. Capitalism which had built up its hegemony in Europe by using the sharp end of Reason found it convenient to subjugate the peoples of the East by wielding the blunt head. (Guha, 1981: 6–7)

A 'sea change under conditions of colonialism' involves something more than merging or even creolizing. It involves a reconsideration of its tools according to new needs by a transcoursing agency. Under the Permanent Settlement Bengal gets endowed with a tradition suited to the needs of new rulers and foisted as continuous with an alleged despotic oriental past, a land tenure system of 'permanent' rights and duties. The terms and descriptions of political economists are deployed to distil a legal feudalism for Bengal, even while, in Europe, this new discourse on political economy is a vital tool in the deliberate dismantling of 'unfree' feudal regimes.

Bengal was fixed in a tradition by a modern-minded colonizer, and not its own tradition, but a useful tradition, an almost caricatured feudalism as remembered by those who were its implacable foes in Europe, and a feudalism improved to stabilize both colonial relations and company incomes.[9] Regardless how much actual bad faith there was in the colonizers' construction of a legal memory of the past of the colonized, clearly a variable in actual colonial history, there was omnipresent a will to make the colonial law work efficiently, and to that end, to match up found law in some workable way with the needs of the colonizers' present. Further, Guha's main point, the retooling also most radically affected the most radical of the new political discourses of the colonizers' home social order. The growing range of enlightenment freedoms, let alone the deepening formal horizontality of democratic comradeship, were precisely what the conquered societies could not be 'ready for', without negating the manifest reality of conquest, sedimented in the new old institutions. In British Bengal the idea of a 'permanent' settlement was perhaps most extremely articulated, but in a larger sense, it was clearly not unique to Bengal. In Fiji, another colonial permanent settlement still lives: proponents of the paramountcy of Fijian

---

9. Guha's observation of the sea change suffered by political economy in empire resembles, in some ways, many other depictions of colonial social relations. It is not novel in observing that colonial practices made real the premise of 'comparative method' scholarship that differences in space could be mapped as difference in time, an argument available in versions ranging from 'underdevelopment' theory to the critique of Orientalism (see also discussion of Fabian's version below). An important aspect of Guha's account is that he does not argue that the British *had* to do it this way. Unlike arguments, notably Said's, that seek to precipitate imposed inferiority as a logical necessity, as if the West intrinsically depended upon the maintenance of inferior difference of the 'Other', Guha finds not that Europe needed India to be different, but simply that the permanent settlement and its sea change political economy created easy channels for the exercise of colonial power.

chiefs, an aristocracy deliberately made by British administered customary law, still continually refit horizontality, plurality, and even democracy into service to their hierarchy, but not without struggle.

So, we have here a specific kind of sea change, a sea change worked by colonial agency, that does not fit onto the westernization–creolization continuum. It is a change that neither fits the local into the procrustean bed of a universal nor is a creole localization, is not merely a reproduction of the modal form nor merely a reformulation of it by admixture with local forms, materials and agencies. It is a change worked on imported tools to meet the new needs of a transcoursing political will, Europe finding modernity in and for itself while also finding feudalism elsewhere. Almost needless to say, this is precisely the sort of process that makes the connected global space–time of European world rule in the eighteenth and nineteenth century something quite other than a homogenizing, emptying force. Here, reconsidering another argument of Anderson's will help clarify.

In his chapter on 'Official Nationalism and Imperialism', Anderson describes Thomas Macaulay's Minute on education, its aspiration to use education to create 'a class of persons, Indian in blood and colour, but English in taste, in opinion, in morals and in intellect' (Anderson, 1991: 91). Anderson concludes, 'it can be safely said that from this point on, all over the expanding empire, if at different speeds, Macaulayism was pursued' (ibid). Flatly not true. In the wake of the 1857 Sepoy Rebellion, that is, the 'Mutiny' and its threats, the British Raj massively backed away from the goal of Anglicizing India (see especially Cohn, 1983). In many later colonies, such as Fiji, paternalist planning never contemplated an effort to eradicate difference between indigenous Fijians or Indian so-called 'coolies' and British culture and sentiments. Fiji's Indians, in particular, built most of their own schools, and impelled the government to support the English curriculum. To Anderson, the official nationalisms of the world failed inevitably because they were contradictory amalgams of two different types of structures, nation-states with their deep, horizontal communities and dynastic realms with their hierarchy, foundering in practice on the career limits placed upon civil servants among the colonized. Macaulay, then, must have been confused? Disingenuous? This brings us to Macaulay, our second narrator of global chronopolitics, himself enmeshed in a diaspora.

GATES THROUGH TIME AND SPACE, AND THE WILL TO USE THEM

It is telling, to begin with a coda, that in Anderson's account, the fact that Macaulay was a Whig need never come up. The England toward which Macaulay sought to Anglicize India, insofar as Anglicizing India was really his goal, was far from the 'deep, horizontal comradeship' of Anderson's imagination. Deep comradeship, perhaps, but in the minds of the Whigs, let alone the Tories, hardly horizontal.

Anderson trolls the history of the late eighteenth and early nineteenth century fishing for the emergent liberal democrats. Referring to the American Declaration of Independence and to the new calendars of the French Revolution, Anderson toys with the idea that time itself was absolutely punctuated, directly invoking Benjamin: 'A profound feeling that a radical break with the past was occurring — a "blasting open of the continuum of history"? — spread rapidly' (Anderson, 1991: 193). It is certainly true, to focus on England, that 'the Liberal creed' (to use Karl Polanyi's phrase) rode with the new science of political economy to an extraordinary popularity and influence in early nineteenth century England (see, for example, Polanyi, 1944; Semmel, 1970). Many liberal texts became famous, such as James Mill's 'Essay on Government', a highly abstract, modularizable argument for deeply horizontal democracy. But so too did the responses of worthy opponents, in an England that never gave up either Lords or Crown.

Writing in 1829, a year after Mill, Macaulay was derisive about much in Mill's now classic liberal argument. He began by attacking the utilitarian audience celebrating it:

> in general, ordinary men, with narrow understandings, and little information. The contempt which they express for elegant literature is evidently the contempt of ignorance. We apprehend that many of them are persons who, having read little or nothing, are delighted to be rescued from the sense of their own inferiority, by some teacher who assures them that the studies which they have neglected are of no value ... smatterers, whose attainments just suffice to elevate them from the insignificance of dunces to the dignity of bores (Macaulay, 1860/1829: 670).

This derision of the liberal audience fit the context of rivalrous Whig versus Liberal journals of opinion, but it also pointed directly toward the core of the critique Macaulay then developed. Macaulay, the soon to be great historian, was as aware as Benedict Anderson that the Liberal argued for a radical break with the past, its literature and wisdom, in the light of a new dawn.[10] Where Mill tried something impossible, to 'deduce the science of government from the principles of human nature' (ibid: 681) Macaulay argued instead for actual research into the past and present in line with the methods of science.

> Proceeding thus — patiently, diligently, candidly — we may hope to form a system as far inferior in pretensions to that which we have been examining, and as far superior in real

---

10. Or as Macaulay (1860/1829: 681) put it: 'And such is this philosophy, for which the experience of three thousand years is to be discarded; this philosophy, the professors of which speak as if it had guided the world to the knowledge of navigation and alphabetical writing; as if, before its dawn, the inhabitants of Europe had lived in caverns and eaten each other! We are sick, it seems, like the children of Israel, of the objects of our old and legitimate worship. We pine for a new idolatry. All that is costly and all that is ornamental in our intellectual treasures must be delivered up, and cast into the furnace — and there comes out this calf!'.

utility, as the prescriptions of a great physician, varying with every stage of every malady, and with the constitution of every patient, to the pill of the advertising quack, which is to cure all human beings, in all climates, of all diseases. (ibid: 683)

Macaulay was not, as he pointed out vigorously, arguing in favour of monarchy or aristocracy because he was attacking Mill's argument for democracy. If two conceptions could summarize what he did seek to favour, I think they would be civilization and liberty, the classic Whig commitment being that each produced the other. Macaulay insisted: 'civilized men, pursuing their own happiness in a social state, are not Yahoos fighting for carrion' (ibid: 678), and to know their interests and thus their motives we have to know their civilization, not merely their human nature.

It now gets particularly interesting for those of us well-read in our Anderson. Let us recall that Macaulay's civilization of literature and liberty was doomed, in Anderson's model, to either naïvely or disingenuously dangle the prospect of horizontal community across imperial spaces actually determined by hierarchy. We discover, reading Macaulay, that he was actually quite impatient with Mill's conception of *community*, for its naïvety about value and time. Mill had announced a solution, democracy with frequent elections, for the problem of rendering the interests of government identical with those of the community. On these terms, Macaulay observed:

we are rather inclined to think that it would, on the whole, be for the interest of the majority to plunder the rich ... we have to notice one most important distinction which Mr. Mill has altogether overlooked. Throughout his Essay, he confounds the community with the species. He talks of the greatest happiness of the greatest number; but when we examine his reasonings, we find that he thinks only of the greatest number of a single generation. (ibid: 679)

To Macaulay, the government either served or threatened not merely the community of the present but also the past and future, either improving or undoing 'the work of so many ages of wisdom and glory', 'taste, literature, science, commerce, manufactures' (ibid: 680). In that light, horizontality would invite disaster. Macaulay concluded:

the higher and middling orders are the natural representatives of the human race. Their interest may be opposed, in some things, to that of their poorer contemporaries, but it is identical with that of the innumerable generations which are to follow. (ibid: 680)

We could inquire into the affinities between Macaulay's vision and the principles of Maastricht and of America's New Democrats — scepticism of redistributive government, commitment to protect private wealth in the alleged interest of future generations — the politics of such interest to Singer, as quoted at the outset. But let us keep Macaulay, and his imagined civilization, in his own time, and follow him into India. What exactly was the education plan?

The line quoted by Anderson is the one widely remembered, but let us put it in its context. As Vishwanathan (1989) has recently detailed, the debate in India not only concerned whether to teach vernacular texts or English ones, but also whether to teach the classics and the Bible as sources for Indian improvement, to use them in Indian schools as they were used in European schools. The solution advocated by Macaulay and others was to teach English texts, in order that England could play the civilizing role for India, that Greece, Rome, and ancient Israel played for post-Renaissance Europe. Teach them to whom? The crucial, neglected context couldn't be clearer:

> it is impossible for us, with our limited means, to attempt to educate the body of the people. We must at present do our best to form a class who may be interpreters between us and the millions whom we govern; a class of persons, Indian in blood and colour, but English in taste, in opinions, in morals, and in intellect. To that class we may leave it to refine the vernacular dialects of the country, to enrich those dialects with terms of science borrowed from the Western nomenclature, and to render them by degrees fit vehicles for conveying knowledge to the great mass of the population. (Macaulay, 1972/1835: 249)

To Macaulay, Anglicization was not the end, but the means, the most convenient way to produce fit vehicles for conveying knowledge. The target was not to make all or any of India into something like or part of Britain, but rather to lead the Indian upper class to become guardians and fomenters of a civilizing process. Was Macaulay disingenuous, or naïve, about what outcome would follow from success in such a process? He professed not to be, in his speech on the East India Company charter in 1833:

> It may be that the public mind of India may expand under our system until it has outgrown that system; ... that, having become instructed in European knowledge, they may, in some future age, demand European institutions ... it will be the proudest day in English history. To have found a great people sunk in the lowest depths of slavery and superstition, to have so ruled them as to have made them desirous and capable of all the privileges of citizens, would indeed be a title to a glory all our own. (Macaulay, 1910/1833: 192)

Glory. Exactly what was Macaulay's vision of the nation, and why was it not a good idea to teach those students in India everything the English knew and loved about Rome?

For all his commitment to teaching English 'taste, opinion, morals, and intellect', Macaulay could not have wanted the Indians to become English in essential ambition, English in political will. In a less celebrated Macaulay speech, concerning war with China in 1840, Macaulay describes vividly what the English seize at a moment of colonial danger:

> I was much touched ... by a passage in one of Captain Elliot's despatches. I mean that passage in which he describes his arrival at the factory in the moment of extreme danger. As soon as he landed he was surrounded by his countrymen, all in an agony of distress and despair. The first thing he did was to order the British flag to be brought from his boat and planted in the balcony. The sight immediately revived the hearts of those who had a minute before given themselves up for lost. It was natural that they should look up with hope and

confidence to that victorious flag. For it reminded them that they belonged to a country unaccustomed to defeat, to submission, or to shame; to a country which had exacted such reparation for the wrongs of her children as had made the ears of all who heard of it tingle; to a country which had made the Dey of Algiers humble himself to the dust before her insulted Consul; to a country which had avenged the victims of the Black Hole on the field of Plassey; to a country which had not degenerated since the great Protector vowed that he would make the name of Englishmen as much respected as ever had been the name of Roman citizen. (Macaulay, 1910/1840: 267–8)

Obviously, aspiring to be Rome could only be modular in a world doomed to extraordinary frustration. It is hardly clear, pace Anderson, that Macaulay was simply the modular Englishman. More has been written than can be rehearsed here, about conflict in British imagination between Athens and Sparta, and between remaking Jerusalem and reincarnating Rome. Let us simply note that whether it was an effect or a cause, regardless of how it fit into the sea changes of Empire, this England, living up to the vow of the Protector, seeking the legacy of Rome, this imagined England was no mere community. There is a geopolitical will here, an image of the past that is more than the story of community origins and an image of the future that is more than making home secure. There is, to borrow again the term from Johannes Fabian, an arrogant chronopolitics directly informing the imperial agents, reproduced and ramified in their work upon their intellectual and institutional tools. No doubt, in the many European empires across time there were actually several varieties intertwined, with differences and tensions, for example, between those remaking Jerusalem and Rome having multiple possible outcomes, even before the creolizing impact of various 'local' interests and powers. In short, the point for globalization theory so far is, that European colonial empires not only increased and channelled global flows, but also worked temporal sea changes widely across the globe. Now, what about those 'others', those 'locals'?

CHRONOPOLITICS, SCHOLARLY

Here Johannes Fabian's 1983 critique of temporal premises in anthropology, *Time and the Other*, can help us name some cardinal dilemmas in the tracing both of global chronopolitics and of the place of new scholarship in it. These days, one more often hears about the 'local' than 'the Other'. One hears even about 'local people', people awkwardly, implicitly contrasted with some other kind of people, usually unnamed, but obviously including the writer and reader. If not 'Global people', perhaps 'transnational'. All this may be the transformation, into spatial coordinates, of the practices in scholarly time reckoning critiqued by Fabian, making his argument well worth attention even if it might, itself, have to suffer a certain sea change when we consider scholars in relation not to 'the Other' but to the global.

The thesis of *Time and the Other* was that anthropology, to Fabian's day, was guilty of what he calls allochronism, complicit with and legitimizing of colonial and neo-colonial global relations. Allochronism means denial of coevalness, and by 'coevalness', in turn, Fabian meant 'a common, active "occupation", or sharing of time' (Fabian, 1983: 31). He sought, in short, 'ways to meet the Other on the same ground, in the same Time' (ibid: 165), a meeting that should be confrontational and ultimately dialectical; thus his final gloss on 'coevalness': 'a dialectical concept of Time' (ibid: 182). At least as much a new Hegelian as Pletsch, Fabian sought a praxis for scholars to make the ground of coevalness, on which in turn the confrontation of Europeans and others could produce a new synthesis. 'Anthropology as the study of cultural difference can be productive only if difference is drawn into the arena of dialectical contradiction' (ibid: 164).

In Benedict, Fabian correctly perceived a champion for a style of analysis he condemned, a cultivator of 'Gardens of Culture'.[11] This, interestingly, led him to a misrepresentation of her politics, cloaked in his own explicit allochronism: in Benedict's 1946 *Chrysanthemum and the Sword*, we are told, 'The spirit of the times is aptly expressed'. Benedict, wrote Fabian, does not question 'the legitimacy of "being American to the hilt" ', and aided unreflectively in a national effort 'to bring the enemy down and, soon after, establish effective control and assure transformation of these values toward the model of the anthropologist's society' (Fabian, 1983: 47–8). Fabian is right that Benedict (and Mead, Bateson and many others; see Yans-McGlaughlin, 1986) sought, during World War II, to help bring the enemy down, but his characterization of her goals in 1946 (though fairer as estimations of some of the other Boasians he depicts) underestimates her intentions and self-consciousness in ways of interest to us here. In fact, Benedict sharply criticized plans to Americanize Japan.

> What the United States cannot do — what no outside nation could do — is to create by fiat a free, democratic Japan. It has never worked in any dominated country. No foreigner can decree, for a people who have not his habits and assumptions, a manner of life after his own image. The Japanese cannot be legislated into accepting the authority of elected persons and ignoring 'proper station' as it is set up in their hierarchical system. They cannot be legislated into adopting the free and easy human contacts to which we are accustomed in the United States, the imperative demand to be independent, the passion each individual has to choose his own mate, his own job, the house he will live in and the obligations he will assume. (Benedict, 1946: 314)

---

11. The phrase, intentionally derisive, is from Ernst Bloch's critique of Spengler, quoted by Fabian and justifiably connected to his own critique of Benedict (Fabian, 1983: 44–8). Though Fabian does not note it, Benedict is explicit in connecting her own thought to Spengler's, in *Patterns of Culture* and elsewhere. I doubt the conclusion that relativism is always allochronic, and wonder whether it would be fairer as a claim against Marxists and other Hegelians. In any case, I hope one need not be Hegelian in order not to be conservative.

This argument is central to her book. Where most anthropological writings, including Fabian's, presume a transnational audience of students and scholars, Benedict wrote for (and reached — her book was a bestseller) a different specific audience: the US government and public. Acutely self-conscious that her audience in the US was wielding enormous global power, Benedict sought to bring that audience to self-consciousness about the very existence of a specifically American culture. In order to demonstrate the contingent, cultural foundations of things that Americans took for nature or good sense, she used contrasts with Japan didactically — 'The idea that the pursuit of happiness is a serious goal of life is to them an amazing and immoral doctrine' (ibid: 192). She wrote against 'protagonists of One World' — in fact, 'As Americans they urge our favorite tenets on all nations' (ibid: 14, 16; note the way 'our' binds both author and readers to a non-universalist, non-privileged, but shared cultural commitment). She put her politics into a phrase, 'making the world safe for difference'. Here we come to her specific commitment, criticized by Fabian, that Americans can be Americans 'to the hilt':

> The tough-minded are content that differences should exist. They respect differences. Their goal is a world made safe for differences, where the United States may be American to the hilt without threatening the peace of the world, and France may be France, and Japan may be Japan on the same conditions. (ibid: 14)

Pace Fabian, Benedict's commitment is neither unreflective nor unreflexive. Her Americans can be American to the hilt only if they put away both their swords and their self-satisfaction.

Let us set aside the allochronic dismissal of Benedict's arguments as 'the spirit of the times' and compare Fabian and Benedict as if contemporary, thereby constituting the kind of arena for dialectical confrontation that scholars are actually capable of producing. Fabian correctly observed that the holism in Benedict's theory of culture has little in common with 'the emphasis on totality that originates in dialectical thought', that in dialectical thought, Fabian's approach, the 'constituting acts are *negations* of cultural distance', and that this difference was connected to Benedicts's 'tough-minded acceptance of radical cultural difference', against what she saw as 'soft sentiments about One World and Universal Brotherhood' (Fabian, 1983: 47). However, Fabian is less observant about the more practical difference between the politics of his own and Benedict's essays. Like Fabian, Benedict was conscious of a global politics to her book, and like Fabian, she sought to use scholarship to reshape the ground of group dialogues. Where the new Hegelian sought to shock scholars, via critique, into realization of their allochronism, thereby to lead them to prepare a new ground for coeval self and other dialectics, the student of Boas sought to shock the American public, via sea changes wrought upon their own key conceptions, into consciousness of American culture as one among many, thereby to lead them *away* from forcing their time and space onto others. 'The world must be made safe for democracy', US President Woodrow Wilson had announced to the US Congress on 2 April 1917, when seeking the declaration of war that put the USA into the First World War. Benedict's 'world made safe for differences' was unmistakably a challenge to this classic official foreign policy pronouncement; but to what end?

Built into genre in Fabian's text, and also in this one, but not in Benedict's, is at worst a premise that reforms of scholarly consciousness and praxis somehow intrinsically reshape world history, or at best a lack of explicit plans for intervention beyond academic arenas. At the core of Benedict's text, and research programme, is engagement with actual power and thus 'complicity' with it (as is so often said with a Pontius Pilate shudder). What, from Fabian's and Benedict's dynamic scholarly projects, might now flash up to address the dangers intrinsic to our contemporary globalization discourse? Should we be seeking a world safe for differences, or negation of distance in vigorous dialogues 'on the same ground, in the same Time', or what?

Benedict's intervention into actual politics was both a strength and a limitation to her anthropology, precisely because all actual politics are in some sense local. While fully respecting her effort to thwart American triumphalism, we should note that this was, no matter how globally relevant, a locally-directed political move that she made, a book designed to reshape American sensibilities. The idea of a 'world made safe for differences' has other implications, much in the service of contemporary power élites, if it is to be globally applied as a general ethical standard. The same respect for differences that would limit the goals of American intervention could justify repression of many other forms of change, as for example when the military coup in Fiji that overturned an elected government was justified as protection for an endangered indigenous culture.

What then of Fabian's dialectical imaginary? A highly promising site to re-enter his argument, in search of a means to address a world of global–local links and flows, is another of his citations of Ernst Bloch, an aphorism with which he began his chapter including the critique of Benedict: 'At any rate, the primacy of space over time is an infallible sign of reactionary language'. If indeed the temporal promise of postmodernism, the overcoming of the telos of the modern, increasingly appears a dead end, is there a danger that the scholarly turn to globalization-style spatial reckoning will cover over important temporal processes, real and potential? Is 'coevalness' or something like it the key to conceiving the temporal politics of globalization?

There is actually an important ambivalence in Fabian's imagery, between space and time and also thereby between symmetry and asymmetry, an outcome I believe of his effort to have his Hegelian dialectic and reflexivity too. His main arguments reveal asymmetries beneath the apparent symmetries of others, especially allochronism within structuralism, function-alism and relativism. His dialectical dream is both *symmetric* and *spatial*: a shared ground, same plane, coeval confrontation of self and other in an 'arena of dialectical contradiction'. He spots scholars making, remaking and hiding asymmetries in time and power, and he wishes to stop them. But just so, when addressing realities of ethnography in context, Fabian shows that 'the other' cannot abide as a partner in symmetric, dialogic fantasy, but is, rather, an object manufactured by use and neglect of *asymmetric* realities, a real history of power. The critique insists on revealing realities of asymmetry, but the utopia is still a symmetry.

It seems to me that most scholars seek and privilege symmetries, on deep aesthetic and ethical grounds, leading notably to the great current satisfaction with the concept of identity. The virtues of symmetry are currently debated explicitly in science studies. Bruno Latour is a forceful advocate for a research method radically privileging symmetry, and there is much to be said for his vision of symmetry. According to Latour, a scholar should work hard to avoid privileging the truth or power either of his or her own conceptions, or those of one side, agency or context in an actuality studied, in order, instead, to simply follow actual interdefinition of actors and chains of translations:

> The analyst does not need to know more than they; he has only to begin at any point, by recording what each actor says of the others. He should not try to be reasonable and to impose some predetermined sociology on the sometimes bizarre interdefinition offered by the writers studied. (Latour, 1988: 11)

Latour carries to a new extreme an attractive aspiration not to succumb to the insistent claims of Western knowledge and power, one that refuses either ethnocentrism or allochronism. Yet there is a problem.

The Latourian scholar, suspending his own arrogance and commitments of culture and knowledge, is also neglecting specific dimensions of what Talal Asad (1993: 179) has called 'translation as a process of power', specifically the existing pattern of flows to translation. Asad's critique of Ernest Gellner's essay on anthropological relativism could also apply to the otherwise quite different arguments of Latour:

> he fails to consider what cultural translation might involve when it is considered as institutionalized practice, given the wider relationship of unequal societies. For it is not the abstract logic of what individual Western anthropologists say in their ethnographies, but the concrete logic of what their countries (and perhaps they themselves) do in their relations with the third world that should form the starting point for this particular discussion. The dilemmas of relativism appear differently depending on whether we think of abstracted understanding or of historically situated practices. (ibid)

We could literally construct, if we focus as Asad would have us, maps of the flows of translation and translation skills in the globalizing world. The dynamic asymmetries in the weather patterns of discourse, the pressure systems of language and genre, would provide different images of globalization than would symmetric discovery of everyone's identity. If one path for scholarship on time and the global would lead from respect for differences through quest for symmetry to the reconfiguration of all history as confrontations over assertions and narrations of identity, quite a different direction opens here. What happens if we recast Fabian's argument without its symmetric, dialectical dream, within, instead, these strictures of Asad? Fabian's dialectic, in the Marxist branch, is already clear in its preference for critique over utopia, and with his emphasis on attending to actually existing power asymmetries he would surely align here with Asad rather than Latour. What then for 'coevalness', if we give up dialectical dreams and no longer grasp it for our telos? Rather than building a new common ground, or finding a null point, Asad would have us begin with 'political confrontations already in place ... in an asymmetrically structured political terrain' (ibid: 273). Let us reconsider time, and coevalness, in this terrain.

Recalling Fabian's first definition of coevalness, 'a common, active "occupation" or sharing of time', let us banish all utopian, symmetric or dialectical 'common ground', and seek the temporality within the 'political confrontations already in place'. What are the actual terms of trade in temporal consociality? Who controls what they share with whom, at what price? Is common occupation of a space–time always a matter of sharing? Consider not only buying and selling, but also imposition, and Anderson's 'pirating'. Actual forms of active occupation? How about that by Britain of Bengal in 1757, and that by the US of Japan in 1946? In sum, if not transplanted into abstract dialectical arenas, actual histories of negation of temporal distance and construction of common memory are likely to be rife with asymmetries of translation and institution.

This leads to the most important question about time and the global for contemporary globalization scholarship: exactly when, and why, did who decide to share homogeneous, empty space–time, and the nation-state as a political form, with a globe full of Others? Who turned Others into 'communities' of 'locals', and why?

HOMOGENEOUS, EMPTY TIME

To paraphrase my frontispiece quotation from Walter Benjamin, I am convinced that other scholars setting off to explore and chart globalization have been far too attracted by the magnetic forces of nationalism, identity and community. Whence the force in this attraction? 'Discover *that* North Pole', Benjamin advised. Find 'the differentia of time that disturb the "main lines" of the investigation for others'. Let us summarize a bit, both the disturbances I have spotted and the 'main lines' I hope to lead you to doubt.

Disturbances: in Fiji, a living aristocracy of Fijian chiefs retain the power not to be impressed by arguments concerning progress, equity, or horizontality. As the most influential Fijian chief of the twentieth century, Ratu Sir Lala Sukuna, put it in his Annual Report as Secretary for Fijian Affairs in 1950, Fijian affairs were 'based not on contract and freedom but on consanguinity and status' (quoted in Lal, 1992: 135). Assertions of rightful hierarchy are omnipresent in the discourse of ethnic Fijian nationalism, and any good account of their roots would have to emphasize not only creolizing reassertion of indigenous hierarchy, but also this happy redeployment of *gemeinschaft* theory. If anything is an imagined *community*, this surely is. Guha has laid out the precise logic of such redeployment, the sea-change redeployment of European narratives of modernity, the careful construction of an imagined European past as colonial present and future and the reasons for it. Finally, with Macaulay, in empire midstream, we find not a self-contradicting modernizer but a creolizing Whig with a civilizing mission, a self-conscious promoter of the glory of an empire folding both liberal political economy and Tory conservatism into new places in a Whig conception of an élitist, scientific, Rome-like civilization. In short, common active occupation of colonies by colonizers led to a civilization shared at a price: cognizance of its temporal hierarchy and your place in it. What happened to *that* time, in theory and reality?

Main lines, in theory: What happened to 'homogeneous, empty time' in Anderson's custody? What general history is Anderson conveying? To recall, for Benjamin the idea of a general tide or flow of progress was the pathology, the crucial, narcotic delusion. 'Nothing has corrupted the German working class so much as the notion that it was moving with the current' (Benjamin, 1968: 258). In turn, 'the concept of the historical progress of mankind cannot be sundered from the concept of its progression through a homogeneous, empty time' (ibid: 261). In contrast, *Imagined Communities* begins with profound disillusionment about Marxist revolutionary time, yet, as noted above, suggests that another revolutionary moment, that of the French and American Revolutions, was an actual 'radical break', a 'blasting open of the continuum of history'. Let us look more closely at Anderson's depiction of this radical break.

Anderson quotes Auerbach on a medieval Christian consciousness of a transtemporal kind of simultaneity in the connections between distant events existing eternally in Divine Providence, 'something close to what Benjamin calls Messianic time' (Anderson, 1991: 24). Christian, Jewish, we could quibble, but let us follow Anderson to the main point: that 'the very possibility of imagining the nation only arose historically when, and where, three fundamental cultural conceptions [this was the third], all of great antiquity, lost their axiomatic grip on men's minds' (ibid: 36). Benjamin's hopes are Anderson's antiquity. 'What has come to take the place of the medieval conception of simultaneity-along-time is, to borrow again from Benjamin, an idea of "homogeneous, empty time" in which simultaneity is, as it were, transverse, cross time, marked not by prefiguring and fulfillment, but by temporal coincidence, and measured by clock and calendar' (ibid: 24). Borrowing an image from Benjamin like a book from a library, Anderson has put to new use what Latour would call an entelechy, an item made real inscribed with its original purpose, but capable of various translation and transformations by future actions. Benjamin, aware that *'even the dead* will not be safe' (1968: 255), can do nothing to save his imagery from transformation into the marker of the triumph of the Social Democratic utopia. Benjamin suffers a sea-change.

Anderson reglosses the crucial time conception as 'horizontal-secular, transverse-time', a locution that has not come to rival Benjamin's original, but one that points better to important Andersonian claims: that nations imagine themselves among each other horizontally, across one clock moment existing simultaneously and evenly, symmetrically. There is an abstraction, in Asad's terms, to Anderson's treatment, an interest in 'the very possibility of imagining the nation':

> The slow, uneven decline of these interlinked certainties, first in Western Europe, later elsewhere, under the impact of economic change, 'discoveries' (social and scientific), and the development of increasingly rapid communications, drove a harsh wedge between cosmology and history. No surprise then that the search was on, so to speak, for a new way of linking fraternity, power and time meaningfully together. (Anderson, 1991: 36)

Now, let us remember Macaulay again. Macaulay's England was no mere nation among many figured transversely, symmetrically across time. It was, indeed, a prefigured fulfilment, living up to the Protector's vow to rival Rome, and recognizing and reconfiguring an extraordinary amount of the rest of the world while doing so.

Where and when, exactly, was global space–time imagined to be homogeneous and empty?

Anderson's time duplex, ancient and modern, skips the crucial moment of colonial empires, empires whose sea changes made real, inscribed into social institutions, the temporal hierarchies of enlightenment evolutionism. As much recent research makes clear (see, for example, Abu-Lughod, 1989; Chaudhuri, 1990; Curtin, 1984; Pollock, 1996), in the 'old world' at least, these moments of occupation were redistributions of social relations in already existing cultural ecumene, whose now-lost space–time conceptions and institutions scholars have only begun to reconstruct. This problem is not fixed in Anderson's added chapter on colonial states. When it comes to its own amnesia concerning specifically colonial imaginations and institutions, Anderson's text should seem suddenly very familiar: in this sense what Anderson's text is really reproducing is the story of modernization. The 'three worlds' primitive complex as analysed by Pletsch has been revised by Anderson in two major ways. First, virtually or perhaps actually anticipating the globalization viewpoint, Anderson dumped the segregating out of a 'second' world and downplayed the Cold War. Second, very curiously, he has relocated a community, a kind of community, a *gemeinschaft* of the imagination, not in the prior stage but in the later one. What are communities doing there at the end of evolutionary time?

Of course there are other ways to punctuate a general history of globalization, issues for inquiry that I have not raised. Most important, nothing I have considered addresses the patterns given to space–time by changing forms of money, trade and capital. One could punctuate globalization, and even re-engineer the concept of homogeneous, empty time, in relation not to late eighteenth century political revolutions, but rather in relation to later nineteenth century antiteleology. One could imagine an increasingly purely quantified, highly anxious global time manifold, a world of quantified essences, materialism (especially Darwin's), a globe of uneven, compared rates of sheerly quantitative increase (for instance, increasingly precisely theorized, measured, and regulated rates of interest and return on investment). In this world, still, space and time were not, in all senses, homogenized or empty — nothing as neat, either, as a world system, but a gapped machinery only fixable by flows of capital, goods and people, and more often moved through in lurches creating new instabilities. Still no transverse symmetry there, but definitely, in the primacy of sheer quantity, a homogenizing and emptying force stalking all other meanings.

This iron-cage emptying of utopian possibility is also important; many scholars portray nationalist imagined *gemeinschaft*, in effect, fake community, as a kind of doomed protest against it. But I don't think this gets us wholly to our North Pole. We still don't know what happened to Macaulay's arrogance, his derision of community in favour of a relation to past and future generations, his quest for glory. Prasenjit Duara suggests something important when he emphasizes one of the themes that he thinks Anderson underplays: Duara is less convinced of the revolutionary break to nationalist mentality in the early nineteenth century, than of something significant taking shape in the twentieth: 'What is novel about modern nationalism is not political self-consciousness, but the world *system* of nation-states' (Duara, 1996: 157). When, then, is a 'system' of nation-states instituted? As Bernard Cohn has been saying for years, it is time we all looked more seriously at World War II and its aftermath.

A full account might start earlier, at least with the League of Nations, with attention also to more specifically European treaties, 'concerts', papal bisections, and so on. Specifically in relation to the tempering of glory, however, and thus the ethical revaluation of colonization, one doesn't, in fact, get even a fantasy globe of Anderson's transverse symmetries until the United Nations — and then it gets systematized very quickly. A full account would recall Woodrow Wilson's valorization of 'self-determination', his world that 'must be made safe for democracy', but it is really the United Nations world in which such sentiments clearly rule out colonization, a world in which the formal symmetry of nation-states makes decolonizing the ticket of entry, and promises substantive development at the price only of amnesia about colonial exploitation and in its place, shame at 'backwardness'.

Before the 'world wars', ambitions could be open, from Protector's vows to elbow room, from manifest destiny to race wars (as Dower, 1986 persuasively describes World War II in particular). Nations could have glorious destinies, and their states could have War Departments rather than Defence Departments. Then came the new system. In short, everything happened as if the US, bomb in hand, commanded every nation, in 1946, to henceforth imagine itself only as a community, to abjure all other histories and destinies, with demonization of all resistance from Communism to Islam.

Here, precisely, is when, where and why historic time was homogenized into transverse-symmetric progress stories, and emptied of fuel for political will: so that nations will not aspire to conquer, colonize or occupy each other any more, now that glory is too dangerous. Only corporations, not nations, are free to pursue dreams of domination. Localities can only be quiescent or in crisis. Against this grain, the paths out of locality, the new vents for human ambition, are those of the new, élite diaspora. In relation to these trends, scholarship is arrayed variously. In 1946, aware of the stakes, Benedict self-consciously intervened on the side of Pax Americana, but deliberately to undermine its arrogance. (Just an ethnography? The cover of the first edition of *Chrysanthemum and the Sword* bore a single sentence to depict the book's intent: 'An investigation of the pattern of Japanese culture which suggests a program for new understanding among nations'.) In contrast Anderson's conscious heterodoxy challenged the revolutionary fantasies and dialectical dreams of Marxist intellectuals, with a sense of pathos that it took Benjamin's angel of history to convey. Addressing deep-felt disappointment in actually existing revolutions, rejecting the comforting idea that national-ism was the century's pathology, Anderson argued instead that the strange new communities were the century's culture (cf. his definition 'in an anthropological spirit', 1991: 5). It was not his intention to become the arbiter of American orthodoxy, its leading global historian, to be Harry Truman in Marxist drag, any more than Benedict set out to bolster Japanese chauvinists. Nonetheless, trolling for deeper roots, Anderson has created the fictitious global genealogy of American geopolitics.

Especially now that scholars increasingly frame their research to explore the idea of global–local relations, rather than conceptions and categorizations of self and other, it does not help to aspire to symmetric or reflexive relationships, a simple common ground, between all localities, between all identities, or especially between people who can choose to flow globally and people who cannot. Amelioration, let alone anything approaching redemption, will not come from any general theory of identity or community. It will not come by way of either compassion or rebuke for the 'identity politics' allegedly motivating all local crises. I think we should seek, instead, a clearer understanding of the asymmetries in global flows, including the actual dissemination of homogeneous empty time, and all else that now sets the apparent limits to political possibility.

REFERENCES

Abu-Lughod, Janet (1989) *Before European Hegemony: The World System A.D. 1250–1350.* New York: Oxford University Press.

Anderson, Benedict (1983) *Imagined Communities: Reflections on the Origin and Spread of Nationalism.* London: Verso.

Anderson, Benedict (1991) (rev. edn.) *Imagined Communities: Reflections on the Origin and Spread of Nationalism.* London: Verso.

Asad, Talal (1993) *Genealogies of Religion: Discipline and Reasons of Power in Christianity and Islam.* Baltimore, MD: Johns Hopkins University Press.

Benedict, Ruth (1946) *The Chrysanthemum and the Sword: Patterns of Japanese Culture.* New York: New American Library.

Benjamin, Walter (1968) 'Theses on the Philosophy of History', in *Illuminations*, pp. 253–64. New York: Schocken Books.

Benjamin, Walter (1989) 'N (Re the Theory of Knowledge, Theory of Progress)', in Gary Smith (ed.) *Benjamin: Philosophy, History, Aesthetics*, pp. 43–83. Chicago, IL: University of Chicago Press.

Boon, James (1984) 'Folly, Bali, and Anthropology, or Satire Across Cultures', in E. Bruner (ed.) *Text, Play, and Story*, pp. 156–77. Washington, DC: Proceedings of the American Ethnological Society for 1983.

Buck-Morss, Susan (1989) *The Dialectics of Seeing: Walter Benjamin and the Arcades Project.* Cambridge, MA: The MIT Press.

Chaudhuri, K. N. (1990) *Asia Before Europe: Economy and Civilization of the Indian Ocean from the Rise of Islam to 1750.* Cambridge: Cambridge University Press.

Chow, Rey (1993) *Writing Diaspora: Tactics of Intervention in Contemporary Cultural Studies.* Bloomington, IN: Indiana University Press.

Cohn, Bernard (1983) 'Representing Authority in Victorian India', in Eric Hobsbawm and Terence Ranger (eds) *The Invention of Tradition*, pp. 165–209. Cambridge: Cambridge University Press.

Curtin, Philip (1984) *Cross-cultural Trade in World History.* Cambridge: Cambridge University Press.

Dower, John (1986) *War Without Mercy.* New York: Pantheon Books.

Duara, Prasenjit (1996) 'Historicizing National Identity, or Who Imagines What When', in Geoff Eley and Ronald Grigor Suny (eds) *Becoming National*, pp. 151–77. New York: Oxford University Press.

Fabian, Johannes (1983) *Time and the Other: How Anthropology Makes its Object.* New York: Columbia University Press.

Fardon, Richard (1995) 'Introduction: Counterworks', in Richard Fardon (ed.) *Counterworks: Managing the Diversity of Knowledge*, pp. 1–22. London: Routledge.

Friedman, Thomas L. (1996) 'Big Mac II', *New York Times* 11 December: A27.

Guha, Ranajit (1981) *A Rule of Property for Bengal.* Delhi: Orient Longman.

Hannerz, Ulf (1992) *Cultural Complexity: Studies in the Social Organization of Meaning.* New York: Columbia University Press.

Kaplan, Martha (1995a) 'Panopticon in Poona: An Essay on Foucault and Colonialism', *Cultural Anthropology* 10(1): 85–98.

Kaplan, Martha (1995b) 'Blood on the Grass and Dogs Will Speak: Ritual Politics and the Nation in Independent Fiji', in Robert J. Foster (ed.) *Nation-Making: Emergent Identities in Postcolonial Melanesia*, pp. 95–125. Ann Arbor, MI: University of Michigan Press.

Kaplan, Martha, and John Kelly (1994) 'Rethinking Resistance: Dialogics of "Disaffection" in Colonial Fiji', *American Ethnologist* 21(1): 123–51.

Kaplan, Martha, and John Kelly (forthcoming) *Laws Like Bullets: Imagined Disorder Made Real in British Colonies.* Durham, NC: Duke University Press.

Kelly, John (1988) 'Fiji Indians and Political Discourse in Fiji: From the Pacific Romance to the Coups', *Journal of Historical Sociology* 1: 399–422.

Kelly, John (1991) *A Politics of Virtue: Hinduism, Sexuality, and Countercolonial Discourse in Fiji*. Chicago, IL: University of Chicago Press.

Kelly, John (1995) 'Diaspora and World War, Blood and Nation in Fiji and Hawai'i', *Public Culture* 7(3): 475–97.

Lal, Brij V. (1992) *Broken Waves: A History of the Fiji Islands in the Twentieth Century*. Honolulu, HI: University of Hawaii Press.

Latour, Bruno (1988) *The Pasteurization of France*. Cambridge, MA: Harvard University Press.

LeCarré, John (1994) 'The Shame of the West', *New York Times* 14 December.

Macaulay, Thomas Babington (1860/1829) 'Mill's Essay on Government', in *Essays, Critical and Miscellaneous*, pp. 670–83. New York: D. Appleton and Co. (reprinted from *Edinburgh Review*, March 1829).

Macaulay, Thomas Babington (1910/1833) 'Government of India, A Speech Delivered in the House of Commons on the 10th of July, 1833', in *The Complete Works of Lord Macaulay, vol. 9: Miscellaneous Works*, pp. 146–93. Philadelphia, PA: The University Library Association.

Macaulay, Thomas Babington (1910/1840) 'War With China, A Speech Delivered in the House of Commons on the 7th of April, 1840', in *The Complete Works of Lord Macaulay, vol. 10: Misellaneous Works*, pp. 247–69. Philadelphia, PA: The University Library Association.

Macaulay, Thomas Babington (1972/1835) 'Minute on Indian Education' (originally dated 2 February 1835), in John Clive and Thomas Pinney (ed.) *Thomas Babington Macaulay: Selected Writings*, pp. 237–51. Chicago, IL: University of Chicago Press.

Pletsch, Carl E. (1981) 'The Three Worlds, or the Division of Social Scientific Labor, circa 1950–1975', *Comparative Studies in Society and History* 23(4): 565–90.

Polanyi, Carl (1944) *The Great Transformation*. Boston, MA: Beacon Press.

Pollock, Sheldon (1996) 'The Sanskrit Cosmopolis, 300–1300 CE: Transculturalism, Vernacularization, and the Question of Ideology', in Jan E. M. Houben (ed.) *Ideology and Status of Sanskrit: Contributions to the History of the Sanskrit Language*, pp. 197–247. Leiden: E.J. Brill.

Rabinbach, Anson (1989) 'Introduction', in Gershom Scholem (ed.) *The Correspondence of Walter Benjamin and Gershom Scholem, 1932–1940*, pp. vii–xxxviii. New York: Schocken Books.

Renan, Ernest (1990/1882) 'What is a Nation?', in Homi Bhabha (ed.) *Nation and Narration*, pp. 8–22. London: Routledge. (Also available in Geoff Eley and Ronald Suny (eds) *Becoming National*, pp. 42–55. New York: Oxford University Press.)

Scholem, Gershom (1976) *On Jews and Judaism in Crisis: Selected Essays*. New York: Schocken Books.

Scholem, Gershom (1981) *Walter Benjamin: The Story of a Friendship*. Philadelphia, PA: The Jewish Publication Society of America.

Scholem, Gershom (ed.) (1989) *The Correspondence of Walter Benjamin and Gershom Scholem, 1932–40*. New York: Schocken Books.

Semmel, Bernard (1970) *The Rise of Free Trade Imperialism: Classical Political Economy, the Empire of Free Trade and Imperialism, 1750–1850*. Cambridge: Cambridge University Press.

Singer, Daniel (1996) 'The Real Eurobattle', *The Nation* 23 December: 20–3.

Spivak, Gayatri Chakravorty (1994) 'Can the Subaltern Speak?', in Patrick Williams and Laura Chrisman (eds) *Colonial Discourse and Post-Colonial Theory*, pp. 66–111. New York: Columbia University Press.

Stocking, George W. (1987) *Victorian Anthropology*. New York: The Free Press.

Stoler, Ann Laura (1995) *Race and the Education of Desire: Foucault's History of Sexuality and the Colonial Order of Things*. Durham, NC: Duke University Press.

Tiedemann, Rolf (1988) 'Dialectics at a Standstill: Approaches to the *Passagen-Werk*', in Gary Smith (ed.) *On Walter Benjamin: Critical Essays and Reflections*, pp. 260–91. Cambridge, MA: The MIT Press.

Tiedemann, Rolf (1989) 'Historical Materialism or Political Messianism? An Interpretation of the Theses "On the Concept of History"', in Gary Smith (ed.) *Benjamin: Philosophy, Aesthetics, History*, pp. 175–209. Chicago, IL: University of Chicago Press.

Viswanathan, Gauri (1989) *Masks of Conquest: Literary Study and British Rule in India*. London: Faber and Faber.

Weber, Max (1978) *Economy and Society*. Berkeley, CA: University of California Press.

Witte, Bernd (1991) *Walter Benjamin: An Intellectual Biography*. Detroit, MI: Wayne State University Press.

Wolf, Eric (1982) *Europe and the People Without History*. Berkeley, CA: University of California Press.

Yans-McLaughlin, Virginia (1986) 'Science, Democracy and Ethics: Mobilizing Culture and Personality for World War II', in George W. Stocking, Jr. (ed.) *Malinowski, Rivers, Benedict and Others: Essays on Culture and Personality*, pp. 184–217. History of Anthropology, vol. 4. Madison, WI: The University of Wisconsin Press.

Globalization and Virtuality: Analytical Problems Posed by the Contemporary Transformation of African Societies

Wim van Binsbergen

GLOBALIZATION

Towards the end of the first international conference to be organized by the Dutch national research programme on 'Globalization and the Construction of Communal Identities', Ulf Hannerz stressed the need for further conceptual development, not just within the Dutch programme, but in globalization studies generally. This article is an attempt to take up that challenge. While situated against the background of a rapidly growing social-science literature on globalization,[1] my aim is not to review that literature in its impressive scope and depth; rather more modestly, and perhaps not inappropriately at this stage, I have let myself be inspired by a series of recent discussions and presentations within the programme and within the wider intellectual framework of Dutch anthropology.

This article concentrates on *virtuality*, which I have come to regard as one of the key concepts for a characterization and understanding of the forms of globalization in Africa. The first two sections of the article are taken up defining virtuality and globalization and provisionally indicating their theoretical relationship. The problematic heritage of a locality-obsessed anthropological tradition (as explored in the subsequent section) provides the analytical framework within which virtuality makes an inspiring topic. The transition from theory to empirical case studies is made by examining the problem of meaning in the African urban environment. Finally, by invoking a specific ethnographic situation (urban puberty rites in present day Zambia) the article illustrates particular forms of virtuality as part of the globalization process.

---

1. Cf. Fardon (1995); Featherstone (1990); Forster (1987); Friedman (1995); Hannerz (1992a); and references cited there. Some of the underlying ideas were expressed decades ago, for example by Baudrillard (1972, 1981); see also McLuhan (1966). That the world was becoming a 'global village' was a truism throughout the 1980s, but work by Toynbee (1952: 134–5) and Spengler (1993/1923) can be cited to show that the idea of a global confrontation of cultures, with global cultural coalescence as a possible outcome, has been in the air throughout the twentieth century.

My own field-work career has oscillated between urban and rural African settings.[2] African towns have always been a context for cosmopolitan meaning which does not stem from the villages in the rural regions surrounding the town, but reflects, and is reflected in, the world at large. Yet I have decided to dwell here upon problems of meaning which — under the heading of virtuality — can only be formulated (even if their solution calls for a much broader geographical scope) when we look upon globalization from the vantage point of the African village and its largely internal processes of signification. Seeking to illuminate virtuality as an aspect of globalization requires that we set the scene by taking a closer look at the latter concept.

The Globalization Process

Taken at face value, globalization is primarily a spatial metaphor, the socio-cultural implications of the mathematical properties of the earth's surface, notably the fact that from any point on that surface any other point can be reached, while (provided the journey is continued for long enough in the same direction) the point of departure will also be the ultimate destination: in other words, the entire surface will be covered. Yet it is important to also investigate the temporal dimension of the globalization metaphor: the compressing of time and of time costs[3] in relation to spatial displacement, as well as the meaning and the effects of such displacement. It is the interplay between the temporal and the spatial dimensions which allows us to pinpoint why globalization has taken on a substantially new form in the last few decades. Since the shape of the earth has not noticeably changed over the last few million years, human culture, or cultures, could perhaps be said to have always been subject to globalizing tendencies.[4] Before the invention of the telegraph, the railroad, and the aeroplane, however, the technology of time and space was in most parts of the world so limited that the effective social and cultural life-world tended to be severely bound by geographical propinquity. Most people thus lived in a world where localizing tendencies would greatly outweigh whatever globalization took place or came along. People, ideas, and goods did travel, often across wide distances, as archaeological and historical records demonstrate. If writing and effective imperial organization then created a continuous

---

2. True to the Manchester/Rhodes-Livingstone tradition by which that career was largely fed.
3. Notions on space–time compression in globalization are to be found, for example, in Giddens (1990; cf. 1991: 16ff.) and Harvey (1989). Some of my own recent work (van Binsbergen, 1996b) suggests that we should not jump to the conclusion that such compression is uniquely related to the globalization context. An argument leading through African divination systems and board-games right to the Neolithic suggests that such compression is an essential feature of both games and rituals throughout the last few millennia of human cultural history.
4. For a similar view see Friedman (for example, 1995), who chides anthropology for having relegated other cultures to the status of isolated communities.

and more or less stable orientation across space and time, the conditions would be set for *early* or *proto-globalization*, characteristic of the communication technology of the mounted courier and the sailing boat. Where no such conditions prevailed, movement inevitably meant dissociating from the social setting of origin, and establishing a new local world elsewhere — a world usually no longer connected, through effective social interaction, with the one left behind, initially strongly reminiscent of the latter but decreasingly so — even in the case of nomadic cultures whose persistence in the face of spatial mobility has depended on their comparatively low investment in spatial attachment as an organizing principle.

If today we have the feeling that globalization expresses a real and qualitative change that uniquely characterizes the contemporary condition, it is because of the hegemonic nature of capitalist technology, which has brought about unprecedented levels of mastery of space and time. When messages travel at light speed across the globe using electronic media, when physical displacement is hardly needed for effective communication, yet such displacement can be effected within one or two days from anywhere on the globe to anywhere else, and when the technology of manufacturing and distribution has developed to such levels that the same material environment using the same objects can be created and fitted out anywhere on the globe at will — then we have reduced the fees that time and space impose on the social process to virtually zero. Then we can speak of globalization in the true sense.

Globalization is not about the absence or dissolution of boundaries, but about the dramatically reduced fee imposed by time and space, and thus the opening up of new spaces and new times within new boundaries that were hitherto inconceivable. Globalization as a condition of the social world today revolves around the interplay between unbounded world-wide flow, and the selective framing of such flow within localizing contexts; such framing organizes not only flow (of people, ideas and objects) and individual experience, but also the people involved in them, creating more or less enduring social categories and groups whose collective identity as supported by their members' interaction creates an eddy of particularism, of social localization, within the unbounded global flow.

VIRTUALITY

Virtuality Provisionally Defined

The terms *virtual* and *virtuality* have a well-defined and illuminating history, which in its broad sweep of space and time, its multi-lingual aspect and its repeated changes of meaning and context, reminds us of the very globalization process we seek to illuminate by the use of these terms. Non-existent in classical Latin (although obviously inspired by the word *virtus*, 'there'), these are late-medieval neologisms, whose invention became necessary when, partly via Arabic versions of Aristotle's works, his Greek concept of δύνᾰμις ('potentiality, power, quadrate') had to be translated into Latin (Hoenen, 1947: 326, n.1; Little et al., 1978 s.v. 'virtual'). While the Scholastic/ Aristotelian philosophy, with its emphasis on general potential to be realized in the concrete, gradually retreated from most domains of North Atlantic intellectual life, the terms found refuge in the expanding field of physics, where virtual velocity, virtual moment, virtual work became established concepts around 1800. This was a century after optics had formulated the theory of the 'virtual image': the objects shown in a mirror image do not really exist, but are merely illusory representations, which we apparently observe at the end of the light beams connecting the object, the surface of the mirror, and our eye. In our age of information technology the term 'virtual' has gained a new lease of life,[5] which takes its cue from the meaning given to the term in optics.

In the globalization perspective we frequently refer to products of the electronic industry, and the furtive, intangible projections of texts and images on electronic screens as an obvious example of virtuality. *Virtual reality* has now become a cliché of the postmodern experience: computer games and simulations which — with extreme suggestions of reality — conjure up, for the consumer, vicarious experiences in the form of illusions. As electronic media, like television and video, march on in contemporary Africa, it is also in that continent that we can make out this form of virtuality in the context of the globalization process.

However, the applicability of the concept of 'virtuality' extends further. Drawing on a notion of 'virtual discourse' which, while inspired by Foucault (1966), is in fact equivalent to that of performative discourse in analytical philosophy,[6] Jules-Rosette, in a splendid recent paper, reserves the notion of virtuality for a specific discursive situation: the 'symbolic revindications of modernity's broken promise' (Jules-Rosette, 1996: 5), which play a central role in the construction of postcolonial identity: 'When a virtual discourse becomes a master cultural narrative [e.g. *authenticité, négritude*], individuals must accept it in order to validate themselves as members of a collectivity' (ibid: 6). This allows her to link the specific form of postcolonial political discourse in Zaire (for a strikingly similar example from Nigeria under Babangida, see Apter, 1996) to the macro-economic predicament of Africa today, of which the elusive magic of money then emerges as the central symbol.

Inspiring as this is, it is not necessary to limit the concept of virtuality to that of explicit, verbal discourse, and there is much to be said for a wider application, encompassing implicit beliefs, the images on which the electronically-inspired use of the concept of virtuality would concentrate,

---

5. IBM (1987) lists as many as fifty-six entries starting with 'virtual'.
6. Cf. Austin (1962): statements which cannot be true or false, such as exhortations, or the expression of an ideal.

and object. Here we may allow ourselves to be inspired by a recent paper by Rüdiger Korff (1995) even if our emphasis is to be on the cultural and symbolic rather than — as in Korff's case — on the technological and economic side:

> Globalization is accompanied by virtuality. The financial markets gained autonomy by producing the goods they trade among themselves and thereby developed into speculators' 'Monopoly'. Virtuality is well shown by the information networks in which the hardware determined the possibilities for person to person interaction. This allows an anonymity in direct interaction. All personality features are hidden, and virtual personalities take over the conversation. Even the world of commodities is virtualized. While for Marx a commodity had two aspects, use- and exchange-value, today a 'symbolic' value has to be added. Traditions and cultures are created as virtual realities and states offer imaginations in their search for political subjects. This indicates a new stage in the dialectic of disenchantment and mystification. While capitalism disenchanted morality and substituted it with the magic of commodities and technology (*Verdinglichung*), today commodity fetishism is substituted by postmodern virtual realities. ... Appadurai (1990) mentions in a similar vein ethnoscapes, mediascapes, technoscapes, financescapes and ideoscapes. ... As with commodities, these 'imagined worlds' and virtual realities develop their own dynamics and start to govern their creators for whom it is impossible to distinguish reality from virtuality. Just like Goethe says in the *Magician's Apprentice*: 'Die Geister, die ich rief, die werd ich nicht mehr los'. (Korff, 1995: 5)[7]

Ultimately, virtuality stands for a specific relation of reference as existing between elements of human culture $(A_1, A_2, \ldots, A_n)$. This relation may be defined as follows: once, in some original context C_1, $A_{virtual}$ referred to (that is, derived its meaning from) A_{real}. This relationship of reference is still implied to hold, but in actual fact $A_{virtual}$ has come to function in a context C_2 which is so totally dissimilar to C_1, that $A_{virtual}$ stands on itself; and although still detectable on formal grounds as deriving from A_{real}, has become effectively meaningless in the new context C_2, unless for some new meaning which $A_{virtual}$ may acquire in C_2 in ways totally unrelated to C_1.

Virtuality, then, is about disconnectivity, broken reference, de-contextualization, yet with formal continuity shimmering through.

Non-Locality as Given, Locality as an Actively Constructed Alternative, Virtuality as the Failure of Such Construction

Applying the above abstract definition, we may speak of virtuality when, in cases involving cultural material from a distant provenance in space or time or both, signification is not achieved through tautological, self-contained, reference to the local, so that such material is not incorporated and domesticated within a local cultural construct, and no meaningful contemporary symbolic connection can be established between these alien contents and other aspects of the local society and culture.

---

7. On virtuality and related aspects of today's automated technology, also see Cheater (1995); Rheingold (1991).

That geographical nearness should be considered of key importance to any social structure was already stated by that pioneer of legal anthropology, Maine (1883: 128ff.). Kroeber (1938: 307ff.) reiterated the same point when reviewing the first decades of scientific anthropology. In Radcliffe-Brown's words (1940: xiv):

> Every human society has some sort of territorial structure. ... This territorial structure provides the framework, not only for the political organisation ... but for other forms of social organisation also, such as economic, for example. The system of local aggregation and segregation ... is the basis of all social life.

Before the development of contemporary communication technologies (which include such inventions, already more than a century old, as the telephone and the motor car, and the even older railway) the coincidence between interactive, social space and geographical space could conveniently be taken for granted for practical purposes. If horse-riding and the talking drum represent the paroxysm of technological achievement, the effective social horizon coincides with the visible horizon. It is only the invention of modern technologies which has revealed this time-honoured coincidence as accidental and not inevitable. For complex reasons which indirectly reflect the state of communication technology by the end of the nineteenth century, anthropology in its formative decades concentrated on social contexts outside the industrial North Atlantic, where such technologies were not yet available, so that social space and geographical nearness continued to be two sides of the same coin.

For the geographically near to become the local in the classic anthropological sense, we need to add an appeal to the *systemic nature of local culture*. This refers to the claim (usually highly exaggerated) that the elements of local culture hang together systematically, making it possible to reduce it to a manageable array of elements and informing principles, rather than the astronomical number of separate cultural events that take place, and material cultural objects that exist among the set of people involved, within a fairly limited space and time. Creolization (cf. Hannerz, 1987) then means, not that the systemic nature of local culture has been abandoned by the actors or destroyed by the onslaught of outside influences, but that it accounts for appreciably less than the entire culture: a considerable part falls outside the system. Such creolization can be argued to be merely a specific form of virtuality, as a departure from the systemic nature of local culture. If culture produces reality in the consciousness of the actors, then the reality produced under conditions of such departure is, to the extent to which it is virtual, only ... virtual reality.

This is ground covered by Appadurai in his well-known paper on 'The Production of Locality' (1995). A merging of two notions of locality ('*geographical* space of nearness, neighbourhood' versus '*social* space of identity, home') was an ingredient of earlier versions of Appadurai's argument; fortunately that element was dropped in the final, published version, in favour of a view of locality not only as *social* space regardless of geographical contiguity, but also as problematic, to be actively constructed in the face of the standard situation of non-locality (Appadurai, 1995).

Under modern conditions of both communication technology and the social engineering of self-organization for identity, the socially local is no longer necessarily the geographically near. We need a concept of social, culture and identity space which (especially under conditions of 'zero time-fees', that is, electronic globalization) is carefully distinguished from geographical space — even though the latter is, like that other Kantian category, time, far less self-evident and unchangeable than Kant, and naïve contemporary consumers of secondary school physics, would tend to believe. In the same way as the Euclidean two-dimensional geometry of the flat plane can be demonstrated to be only a special case of the immense variety of n-dimensional geometries which modern mathematics has come to conceive, the insistence on geographical propinquity as a prime determinant of social relations is merely a reflection of the state of communication technology prevailing during much of man's history — in the hunting and herding camps and the farming villages that until only a few millennia ago were the standard human condition. As such it has been built into classic anthropology. Meanwhile, the distinction between social space and geographical space does not mean that the material technologies of geographical space have become irrelevant or non-existent in the face of the social technology of locality construction: a prudent approach to globalization has to take account of both.

As advocated by Appadurai, we have to study in detail the processes through which localization as a social process takes place. The local, in other words, is in itself a problem, not a given, let alone a solution. We need to study the process of the appropriation of globally available objects, images and ideas in local contexts, which more often than not constitutes itself in the very process of such appropriation. Let us take our cue from the history of a major family of divination systems found throughout Africa, under conditions of 'proto-' globalization (with the intermediate technology of seafaring, caravan trade and élite-restricted, pre-printing literacy).

This history is basically that of localization processes involving astrological and numerological interpretational schemes as current in the medieval Arabian culture of North Africa and the Middle East, where they are known under the name of geomancy or *Âilm al-raml* ('the science of sand').[8] This process produced the interpretative catalogues for all African divination systems based on a material apparatus producing 2^n different configurations,

---

8. Even in that Arabian culture such schemes were already highly virtual in that their symbolism and iconography did not derive from the local society of that time and age, but carried (in clearly demonstrable ways, open to the patient scrutiny of scholarship rather than to the brooding fantasies of New Age) distant echoes of Hebrew, pre-Islamic Arabian, Old-Egyptian, Northwest African, Sumerian, Akkadian, Indian, Iranian and Chinese systems of representation.

such as *Fa, Ifa, Sixteen Cowries, Sikidy, Four Tablets*: illiterate African versions so elaborate and so saturated with local African imagery that they would appear to be authentically, autochthonous African. In the same way it can be demonstrated that the actual material apparatuses used in this connection (tablets, divining boards, divining bowls), although ultimately conceived within an African iconography and carving techniques, and clad in awesome African mystery and imputed authenticity, are in fact extreme localizations of the intercontinentally mediated scientific instruments (the sand board, the wax board, the lode compass, and the square wooden simplification of the astrolabe) of Greek, Arabian, and Chinese nautical specialists and scribes. The example has considerable relevance, because here some of the main factors of globalization and universalism (notably literate scholarship, empirical research and long-distance seafaring), have rather ironically ended up as forms of the most entrenched, stereotypical African localization and particularism. The hardest analytical nut to crack is to explain why, and as a result of what ideological, social, economic, and technological mechanisms, such extreme localization seems to be more typical of sub-Saharan Africa than of other parts of the Old World in the second millennium CE. Whatever of the original, distant contexts still clings to these localized African precipitates (the overall format of the apparatus, immutable but locally un-interpretable formal details such as isolated astrological terms and iconographic representations) amounts to virtuality and probably adds much to these systems' charisma (cf. van Binsbergen, 1995b, 1995c, 1996a, 1996c).

Such extreme localization of outside influences, rendering them practically imperceptible and positioning them within the rural environment, although typical for much of Africa's history, is, however, no longer the dominant form which globalization takes in Africa. Present-day virtuality manifests itself through the incomplete systemic incorporation of cultural material which is both alien and recognized by the actors to be so, and which circulates not primarily in remote villages but in cities.

Examples of this form of virtuality are to be found all over Africa today, and in fact (in a way which would render a classic, holistic anthropological analysis nonsensical) they constitute the majority of cultural expressions: from world religions to party politics mediating world-wide models of formal organization, development and democracy;[9] from specialist production of contemporary art, *belles lettres* and philosophy inspired by cosmopolitan models, to the production — no longer self-evidently but self-consciously, as a deliberate performance — of apparently local forms of music and dance during an ethnic festival like Kazanga in western central Zambia

---

9. Cf. van Binsbergen (1995a) where a cultural relativist argument on democracy is presented.

(van Binsbergen, 1992a, 1994); from fashionable lingerie to public bodily prudery demonstrably imposed by Christianity and Islam.

These symbolic processes are accompanied by, in fact carried by, forms of social organization which (through the creation of new categories and groups, the erection of conceptual and interactional boundaries around them, and the positioning of objects and symbols through which both to reinforce and to transgress these boundaries) create the socially local (in terms of identity and home) within the global. Such categories and groups are (in general) no longer spatially localized, in the sense that they no longer create a bounded geographical space which is internally homogeneous in that it is only inhabited by people belonging to the same bounded organization ('village', 'ward', 'neighbourhood'). We have to think of such organizations (whose membership is typically *geographically* dispersed while creating a *social* focus) as ethnic associations, churches, political parties, professional associations, schools, hospitals, and so on. If they are geographically dispersed, this does not mean that their membership is distributed all over the globe. Statistically, they have a fairly limited geographical catchment area commensurate with the available transport technology, but within that catchment area, the vast majority of human inhabitants are non-members — they do not, therefore, constitute contiguous social spaces.

The typical, although not exclusive, abode of such organizations is the town, and it is to African towns that we shall shortly turn for a case study of urban puberty rites, which will add a measure of descriptive and contextual substance to these theoretical exercises. However, virtuality presents itself in the case study in the form of an emulation of the village as a virtual image; so let us first discuss that unfortunate obsession of classic anthropology, the village.

THE VIRTUAL VILLAGE

The classic anthropological image of 'the' African culture as holistic, self-contained, locally anchored, effectively to be subsumed under an ethnic name, was deliberately constructed so as to constitute a local universe of meaning — the opposite of virtuality. Since such a culture was thought to form an integrated unity, all its parts were supposed to refer to that same coherence, which in its entirety gave the satisfactory illusion of localized meaningfulness.

Characterizing African Village Society

It is necessary to dwell on this point, since (as I discovered when presenting an earlier version of this argument) it is capable of producing considerable confusion. Although there are notable exceptions,[10] and although the research programme of which this collection is a first product is prompted by the determination to change that situation, it is true to say that most of the existing literature on globalization was not written by established ethnographers of African rural life. The typical focus for globalization studies is the metropolis, the self-evident access to international lifestyles mediated by electronic media, with a dominant presence of the state and the culture and communication industry. However, people born in African villages are now also being globalized, and an understanding of their experiences requires an analytical and descriptive grip on African rural social formations.

Not infrequently, Marxist studies of the 1970s and 1980s, including my own, are claimed to have demonstrated the deficit of earlier mainstream anthropology. This is largely a spurious claim. Modes-of-production analysis, as the main contribution of Marxism to contemporary anthropology, has done a number of essential things:

- reintroduce an emphasis on material production and appropriation;
- dissolve the assumed unitary nature of the local rural society into a handful of subsystems ('modes of production'), each with their own logic of exploitation and ideological legitimation, and linked together ('articulated') within the 'social formation', in such a way that the reproduction of one mode depends on the exploitation of another mode; and finally,
- provide a theoretical perspective which could account for the persistence and relative autonomy (also as 'logics' of signification and legitimation) of these various modes and their articulations, even under conditions of capitalism and the colonial or post-colonial state.

This revolutionary reformulation of the classic anthropological perspective could therefore accommodate internal contradictions, multiplicity of fields of symbolic reference (notably: as many fields as there were modes of production), while the articulation process itself also generated a field of symbolism of its own (van Binsbergen, 1981), and outside functioning within the world system. However, it did not discard the essentially local nature of the social formation, nor its systemic nature even if the latter was no longer conceived as unitary, holistic integration, but came to be represented as a dialectic composite of contradictions between the few specific 'logics', each informing a specific mode of production. The Marxist approach did not render the notion of local integration obsolete: to the extent to which the articulation of modes of production under the hegemony of one dominant

---

10. See the collections by Comaroff and Comaroff (1993) and Fardon (1995); also De Boeck (in this volume); Geschiere and Fisiy (1995); Meyer (1995); Pels (1993); and perhaps my own recent work.

mode has succeeded, the resulting social formation is effectively integrated by its very contradictions.

So even from a Marxist perspective it appears to be true to say that African historic societies in the present millennium have invariably displayed cleavages in terms of gender, age, class, and political power, while containing only partially integrated elements deriving from and still referring, beyond the local society, to other cultural complexes which were often remote in space and time. Yet they have offered to their members (and largely in order to accommodate those very contradictions) a fairly coherent universe, in which the human body-self, interpersonal relations, the landscape and the supernatural all featured in one composite, comprehensive world-view, whose symbolism and ritual elaboration were to reconcile and conceal, rather than articulate, such internal contradictions as constitute the whole and render it dynamic.

In this context, the *meaning* of an element of the local society and culture (to attempt a definition of a word used too loosely in the argument so far) consists in the network of referential relations at the centre of which such an element is perceived and conceptualized by the participants; through this relational network the element is taken by the actors, explicitly or implicitly, as belonging to that general socio-cultural order, cognitively and emotively linked to many other aspects of that order — a condition which produces a sense of proper placement, connectivity and coherence, recognition, identity as a person and as a group, aesthetics, bodily comfort and even healing.

Yet the Rural African Community is Problematic, or: The Virtual Village

In Africa, village society still forms the context in which many present-day urbanites were born,[11] and where some will retire and die. Until recently, the dichotomy between town and village dominated Africanist anthropology. Now we have to admit that, considering the constant movement of ideas, goods and people between town and village, the dichotomy has lost much of its explanatory value. In terms of social organization,

11. How many? That varies considerably between regions and between countries. The post-independence stagnation of African national economies, the structural adjustment programmes implemented in many African countries, the food insecurity under conditions of civil war and refugeeship, the implementation of rural development programmes — all these conditions have not been able to bring the massive migration to African towns to an end, even if their continued growth must of course be partly accounted for by intra-urban reproduction, so that even in African towns that were colonial creations, many inhabitants are second, third or fourth generation urbanites. Typical figures of village-born, first generation urbanites available to me range from an estimated 15 per cent in Lusaka, Zambia, to as much as 50 per cent in Francistown, Botswana.

economic and productive structures, goals and evaluations, town and village have become complementary, even converging options within the social experience of Africans today; their difference has become gradual, and is no longer absolute. However, while of diminishing value in the hands of analysts, the dichotomy between town and village remains relevant in so far as it informs African actors' conceptualizations of their life-world and social experience. Here the idealized image of the village stands for an imaginary context (no longer to be found in the real villages of today) where production and reproduction are viable and meaningful, pursued by people who — organized along the lines of age and gender divisions, and historic ('traditional') leadership — are turned into an effective community through an un-eroded kinship system, symbolism, ritual and cosmology. Vital in this set-up is that — typically through non-verbal means — ritual manages to construct the bodies of the members of the residential group as charged or inscribed with a shared meaning, a shared identity; while the body moves across time and space this indelible mark is carried to new contexts, yet remains.

Even in the village context the effective construction of community cannot be taken for granted. Central African villages, for instance, have been described (see van Binsbergen, 1992b; Turner, 1968; van Velsen, 1971) as the scene of an uneasy truce between strangers, only temporarily constructed into community — at the expense of kinship rituals which take up an enormous part of available resources and even so barely conceal or negotiate underlying contradictions among the village population. Such rituals of kinship (those attending pregnancy, birth, adolescence, marriage, and death) not only transform biological human individuals into competent social persons with a marked identity founded in the local community (or in the case of death transform such social persons in the face of physical decomposition); such rituals also construct, within that overall community, specific constituent identities, such as those of gender and age. They refer to, and to a considerable extent reproduce and perpetuate, the productive and social organization of the village society. Perhaps the central characteristic of the old (nineteenth-century) village order was that the construction of community was still so effective that in the villagers' consciousness their actual residential group self-evidently appeared as the realization of that ideal.

It is crucial to realize that in the twentieth century, even with reference to rural settings, we are not so much dealing with 'real' communities, but with rural folks' increasingly problematic model of the village community. Perhaps we could say that the village was becoming a virtual village. Rural ideological change in Africa during the twentieth century (van Binsbergen, 1981) can be summed up as a process of people actively confronting the erosion of that model, its becoming irrelevant and impotent in the face of political economic realities. Throughout the twentieth century, rural populations in Africa have struggled, through numerous forms of organizational, ideological and productive innovation combining local practices with outside borrowings, to reconstruct a new sense of community in an attempt to revitalize, complement or replace the collapsing village community in its viable nineteenth century form. In fact the entire ideological history of twentieth century Africa could be written from this perspective. Peasants have been constantly engaged in the construction of new, alternative forms of community on the basis of rather new principles as derived from political, cultic, productive and consumerist ideas introduced from the wider world. Many of these movements have sought to re-formulate the notion of the viable, intact village community in new terms and with new outside inspiration and outside pressure. Ethnicity, healing cults, prophetic cults, anti-sorcery movements, varieties of imported world religions and local transformations thereof, for instance in the form of Independent churches, struggles for political independence, involvement in modern national politics including the recent wave of democratization, involvement in a peripheral-capitalist cash economy with new symbols of status and distinction — these have been some of the strategies by which villagers have sought (often against many odds) to create and bring to life the image of a new world, and a continued sense of meaning and community, when the old village order was felt, or said, to be falling apart. That old village order, and the ethnic cultures under which it was usually subsumed, may in themselves have been largely illusory, strategically underpinned by the ideological claims of elders, chiefs, first-generation local intellectuals, colonial administrators and missionaries, open to the cultural *bricolage* of invented tradition on the part of these vocal actors (Hobsbawm and Ranger, 1983; Vail, 1989).

If the construction of community in the rural context has been problematic, the village still represents one of the few models of viable community among Africans today, including urbanites. It is the only model which is part of a collective idiom pervading all sections of contemporary society. As such it features massively as a nostalgic reference in ethnic identity construction. Whatever alternative models of community are available, they are shallowly rooted and reserved to specific sections of the society: Christians or Muslims (the local religious congregation as a community, and by extension the abstract world-wide collective of co-religionists), cult members (the cultic group as a community), members of a specific ethnic group (where the ethnic group is constructed into a community, but typically constructed by emphatic reference to the village model as a focal point of origin and meaning), the élite (patterns of consumerism which replace the notion of community through interaction with the notion of virtual or vicarious global community through media transmission and the display of appropriate manufactured symbols — status symbols in clothing, transport, housing, and so on).

We are now ready to step into African urban life as an obvious locus of globalization, and explore virtuality there.

THE PROBLEM OF MEANING IN AFRICAN TOWNS TODAY

Globalization theory has stressed the paradoxical phenomenon that the increasing unification of the world in political, economic, cultural and communication terms does not lead to increasing uniformity but, on the contrary, goes hand in hand with a proliferation of local differences. It is as if myriad eddies of particularism (which may take the form of ethnic, linguistic and religious identities, consumerist lifestyles, and so forth) are the inevitable accompaniment of the swelling stream of globalizing universalism. Anthropologists have — in theory, that is — long ceased to define their research object primarily by reference to a more or less demarcated part of the global landscape assumed to be the habitat of a bounded, integrated 'culture' supposedly shared by a people, tribe or ethnic group. While the time-honoured technique of participant observation still favours their focusing on a set of people who are more or less tied together by enduring social relations and forms of organization, such a set need no longer be localized (for modern technology — not just fax machines and E-mail, but also simple telephones and rural buses — enables people to effectively maintain relationships across wide distances: as members of the same ethnic group, as employees of the same multinational corporation, as members of a cult, as traders) nor do the individuals which constitute that set (as a statistical conglomerate, or a social network of dyadic ties) necessarily and as a dominant feature of their social experience construct that set as an ideal community with a name, an identity, moral codes and values. Fragmentation, heterogeneity, alienation and cultural and organizational experiment are characteristic of the global condition, not only in North Atlantic urban society but also, for much the same reasons, in the rapidly growing towns of Africa today.

In essence, the aspect of globalization which we seek to capture by concentrating on virtuality, revolves around issues of African actors' production and sustaining of meaning. It is hoped that the notion of virtuality will equip us for the situation — rather more common than village anthropology prepared us to believe — that meaning is encountered and manipulated in a context far removed, in time and space, from the concrete social context of production and reproduction, where that meaning was originally worked out in a dialectical interplay of articulated modes of production; where, on the contrary, it is no longer local and systemic, but fragmented, ragged, virtual, absurd, maybe even absent. The study of such forms of meaning is of course doubly problematic because anthropology itself is a globalizing project, and one of the first in western intellectual history. African towns, with their usually recent history, heterogeneous migrant population, and full of social, political and economic structures apparently totally at variance with any village conditions in the surrounding countryside, are laboratories of meaning. What can the anthropologist, and particularly the variety of the rurally-orientated anthropologist unfashionably favoured in this article, learn here about virtuality?

To what extent has the contemporary urban environment in Africa managed to produce and nurture symbols which selectively refer to the state and the world economy, yet at the same time negotiate dilemmas of rural-derived identity and of urban-rural relations? It is here that one can begin to look for the stuff that African urbanism is made of. Is it true to say that these towns have engendered collective representations which are strikingly urban, and which offer partial and tentative yet creative solutions to such typically urban problems as incessant personnel flow, ethnic, class and religious heterogeneity, economic and political powerlessness, and the increasing irrelevance, in the urban situation, of historic, rural-derived forms of social organization (kinship, marriage, 'traditional' politics and ritual)? Mitchell's *Kalela Dance* (1956) still offers a classic paradigm, stressing how at the city boundaries elements of rural society and culture (such as a rural-based ethnic identity, a minority language, expressive forms of music and dance, specific ways to organize production and reproduction in localized kin groups) may be selectively admitted onto the urban scene, yet undergo such a dramatic transformation of form, organization and function that their urban manifestations must be understood by reference to the urban situation alone. Or, in Gluckman's (1960: 57) famous words, 'the African townsman is a townsman'. In other words, the African townsman is not a displaced villager or tribesman but, on the contrary, 'detribalized' as soon as he leaves his village. These ideas evidently circulated in African urban studies long before 1960 (see, for example, Gluckman, 1945: 12).

Statements of this nature have helped to free our perception of African urbanites from traditionalist and paternalistic projections; for according to the latter they continued to be viewed as temporarily displaced villagers whose true commitment and identity continued to lie with their rural societies of origin. The stress on the urban nature of African urbanites even amounted to a radical political challenge, in a time when the colonial (and South African) economy was largely based on the over-exploitation of rural communities through circulatory migration of male workers conveniently defined as bachelors while in town (see Meillassoux, 1975; cf. van Binsbergen and Geschiere, 1985; Gerold-Scheepers and van Binsbergen, 1978). We can therefore forgive these authors their one-sidedness, but there is no denying that they failed to address the fundamental problems of meaning which the construction of a town-based culture in the (by and large) new cities of Africa has always posed.[12]

So what happens to meaning in town? It is particularly in the context of meaning that we see African towns as the arena where a migrant's specific, disconnected and fragmented rural-based heritage is confronted with a

---

12. Nor should we over-generalize. Mitchell's seminal *Kalela Dance* should be contrasted with the work of Philip and Ilona Mayer, which was far more subtle, and much better informed, on rural cultural material as introduced into the towns of Southern Africa (see Mayer, 1971, 1980; Mayer and Mayer, 1974).

limited number of 'cosmopolitan' socio-cultural complexes, each generating its own discourse and claiming its own commitment from the people drawn into its orbit in exchange for partial solutions of their problems of meaning. Before discussing these complexes, it is useful to realize that, as a source of meaning, the historic rural background culture of urban migrants is not necessarily as fragmented as the multiplicity of ethnic labels and linguistic practices in the town may suggest. Ethnic groups have a history (Chrétien and Prunier, 1989), and while some ethnic groups can be said to be recent, colonial creations, underlying their unmistakable differences there is in many cases a common substratum of regional cultural similarities and even identities: continuities such as a patrilineal kinship system, emphasis on cattle, similarities in the marital system, the cult of the land and of the ancestors, patterns of divination and of sacrifice, shared ideas about causation including witchcraft beliefs, converging ideas about conflict resolution and morality. The result is that even urban migrants with a different ethnic, linguistic and geographical background may yet find that they possess a cultural lingua franca that allows them to share such historic meanings as have not been mediated through the state and capitalism. Sometimes specific routinized modes of inter-ethnic discourse (such as joking relations) explicitly mediate this joint substratum. Traditional cults and independent Christian churches in town, which tend to be trans-ethnic, derive much of their appeal from the way in which they articulate this historic substratum and thus recapture meanings which can no longer be communicated with through migrants' direct identification with any specific historic rural culture. Moreover, partly on the basis of these rural continuities, urban migrants creatively develop a new common idiom not only for language communication, but also for the patterning of their everyday relationships, their notions of propriety and neighbourliness, the interpretation and settlement of their conflicts, and the evaluation of their statuses.

After this qualification, let us sum up the principal cosmopolitan complexes:

- *The post-colonial state*: a principal actor in the struggle for control of the urban space; a major agent of social control through its law-and-order institutions (the judiciary, police, immigration department); a major mediator of 'cosmopolitan' meaning through the bureaucratically organized services it offers in such fields as education, cosmopolitan medicine, housing, the restructuration of kinship forms through statutory marriage and so on; a major context for the creation of new, politically instrumental meaning in the process of nation-building and élite legitimation; and through its constitutional premises the object (and often hub) of modern political organizations.
- A variety of manifestations of the *capitalist mode of production*, largely structuring the urbanites' economic participation and hence their experience of time, space, causation, personhood and social relations;

involving them in relations of dependence and exploitation whose ideological expression we have learned to interpret in terms of alienation (the destruction of historic meaning); but also, in the process, leading on to modern organizational forms (such as trade unions) meant to counter the powerlessness generated in that process; and finally producing both the manufactured products on which mass consumption as a world-wide economic and cultural expression — in other words, as another, immensely potent form of 'cosmopolitan' meaning — depends, as well as the financial means to participate in mass consumption.

- *World religions*, which pursue organizational forms and ideological orientations rather reminiscent of the post-colonial state and the capitalist mode of production, yet tending to maintain, in time, space and ideological content, sufficient distance from either complex to have their own appeal on the urban population, offering formal socio-ritual contexts in which imported cosmopolitan symbols can be articulated and shared between urbanites, and in which — more than in the former two complexes — rural-based historic symbols can be mediated, particularly through Independent churches.

- *Cosmopolitan consumer culture*, ranging from fast food shops to hire-purchase furniture stores displaying the whole material dream of prospective middle-class lifestyle, and from video outlets and record shops to the retail shops of the international ready-made garment industry, and all the other material objects by which one can encode distinctions in or around one's body and its senses, and create identity not by seclusive group-wise self-organization but by individual communication with globally mediated manufactured symbols.

These four cosmopolitan repertoires of meaning differ considerably from the ideal-typical meaning enshrined in the rural historic universe. While historically related, they are present on the urban African scene as mutually competitive, fragmented, optional, and more or less anomic or even — when viewed from a competitive angle — absurd. Yet together, as more or less élite expressions, they constitute a realm of symbolic discourse that, however internally contradictory, assumes dominance over the rural-orientated, local and historic repertoires of meaning of African migrants and workers.

The ways in which African urbanites, in their interactions and conceptualizations, construct, keep apart, and merge as the case may be, cosmopolitan and rural idioms, are ill understood for several reasons. Those who, as social scientists, are supposed to study these patterns of interaction are, in their personal and professional lives, partisans of cosmopolitan repertoires and are likely to be identified as such by the other actors on the urban scene. Much of the actors' juggling of repertoires is evasive and combines the assumption of rigid subordination with the practice of creative challenge and tacit symbolic resistance in private spheres of urban life where few representatives of the cosmopolitan repertoires have access. Whereas anthropology has developed great expertise in the handling of meaning in one spatio-temporal context (like rural African societies) whose wholeness and integration it has tended to exaggerate, the development of a sensitive approach to a fragmented and incoherent multiplicity of repertoires of meaning, each assaulted and rendered more or less meaningless by the presence of the other, had to wait until the advent of Postmodernism as an attempt to revolutionize, or to explode, anthropology.[13] Our classic predecessors in African urban studies worked on the assumption that the African urban situation was very highly structured — by what they called the 'colonial-industrial complex' imposing rigid segregation and class interests, by voluntary associations, by networks (cf. Epstein, 1958, 1967; Mitchell, 1956, 1969). In the contemporary world, such structure is becoming more and more problematic, and the town, especially the African town, appears as the postmodern social space *par excellence*. My greatest analytical problem here is that as a social space the town lacks the coherent integrated structure which could produce, like the village, a systematic (albeit internally segmented and contradictory) repertoire of meaning ready for monographic processing; but this may not merely be one researcher's analytical problem — it appears to sum up the essence of what the urban experience in Africa today is about, in the lives of a great many urbanites.

Postmodernism is not the only, and deliberately unsystematic, analytical approach to multiplicity of meaning within a social formation consisting of fundamentally different and mutually irreducible sub-formations. As a paradigm that preceded Postmodernism by a decade in the circulation of intellectual fashions, the notion of articulation of modes of production is in principle capable of handling such a situation (see, for example, van Binsbergen, 1981; van Binsbergen and Geschiere, 1985). However, the emphasis, in this approach, on enduring structure and a specific internal logic for each constituent 'mode of production' renders it difficult to accommodate the extreme fragmentation and contradiction of meaning typical of the urban situation. The various cosmopolitan and local historic repertoires of meaning available in the Francistown situation, for instance, cannot convincingly be subsumed under the heading of a limited number of articulated modes of production (see van Binsbergen, 1993a). Yet while deriving inspiration from the postmodern position, my plea here is for rather greater insistence on structure, power and material conditions than would suit the convinced postmodernist.

The work of Ulf Hannerz (1980, 1986, 1989, 1990, 1992a, 1992b) is exemplary for the kind of processes of cultural production, variation and control one would stress when looking at African towns (or towns anywhere else, for that matter) from the perspective of the modern world as a unifying, globalizing whole. However, it is significant that his work, far from

---

13. Cf. Geuijen (1992); Kapferer (1988); Nencel and Pels (1991); Tyler (1987); and references cited therein.

problematizing the concept of meaning as such, takes meaning rather for granted and concentrates on the social circulation of meaning, in other words the management of meaning (Hannerz, 1992a: 17, 273; taking his cue from Cohen and Comaroff, 1976). Hannerz's position here is far from exceptional in anthropology, where we theorize much less about meaning than would be suggested by the large number of anthropological publications with 'meaning', 'significance', 'interpretation' and 'explanation' in their titles. Nor am I doing much better here myself: I did offer, above, a homespun definition of ethnographic meaning, but must leave the necessary theoretical discussion for another paper, or book.

For Hannerz too, the African townsman is truly a townsman, and even the analyst seems to have entirely forgotten that 'many' (see note 11 above) of these urbanites, even now, have been born outside town under conditions of rural, localized meaning evoked today, and that this circumstance is likely to be somehow reflected in their urban patterns of signification. In certain urban situations rural models of interaction and co-residence tend to be more prominent than in others. We need to remind ourselves of the fact that urban does not necessarily mean global. For instance, as a fresh urban immigrant, one can take refuge among former fellow-villagers in an urban setting. The vast evidence on urban immigration in Africa suggests that the rural-orientated refuge in a denial of globalization tends to be partial and largely illusory; in other words towns, precisely in their display of apparently rural-derived elements, tend towards high levels of virtuality/discontinuity/transformation. Even so it remains important to look at meaning in African towns not only from a global perspective but also from the perspective of the home villages of many of the urbanites or their parents and grandparents. Our first case study deals with an urban situation, and should help us to lend empirical and comparative insight in the applicability of the virtuality concept.

THE VIRTUAL VILLAGE IN TOWN: GIRLS' PUBERTY CEREMONIES IN URBAN ZAMBIA[14]

Historic ('Traditional') Village-derived Ritual in African Urban Settings Today, and its Interpretation

When central reproductive institutions of the old village order, including rituals of kinship, are already under great pressure from new and external

---

14. The following section is based on a text which I wrote in 1994 as a statement of intent for the WOTRO Programme on Globalization and the Construction of Communal Identities. Before long, as a result of a PhD conducted within the same programme, we may expect Thera Rasing's more detailed ethnographic and analytical answers to the questions raised in this section: meanwhile, see Rasing (1995). Of the vast literature on puberty initiation in South Central and Southern Africa, see also Corbeil (1982); van Binsbergen (1987, 1992b,

alternatives in the rural environment, one would hardly expect them to survive in urban contexts. For in town, life is obviously structured, economically and in terms of social organization, in ways which would render all symbolic and ritual reference to rural-based cults reproducing the old village order hopelessly obsolete. Who would expect ancestral cults to take place in urban settings in modern Africa? What theory of change and continuity would predict the continued, even increasing practice of ecstatic possession ritual in urban residential areas, often in the trappings of new formally organized cults posing as Christian churches or Islamic brother-hoods, but often also without such emulation of world religions? Why do people pursue apparently rural forms when socially, politically and eco-nomically their lives as urbanites are effectively divorced from the village? The fact is, however, that rural symbolic forms are prominent on the African urban scene; as such they represent a conspicuous element of virtuality, since urban life is no longer informed by the patterns of production and repro-duction that corresponded with these rural symbols in the first place.

Stressing the complementarity between a local community's social, political and economic organization and the attending religious forms, the Durkheimian ·heritage in the social science approach to religion, however dominant, provided no ready answers when applied to the study of historic ('traditional') urban ritual, at least in Africa.[15] For how can there be such continuity when African urbanites stage a rural ritual in the very different urban context? What would be the referent of the symbols circulating in such ritual? The relative paucity of studies on this point stands in amazing contrast with the prevalence and ubiquity of the actual practice on the ground. It is as if the absence of an adequate interpretative framework has caused anthropo-logists to close their eyes to the ethnographic facts staring them in the face. At the same time they have produced in abundance studies of forms of urban ritual in the context of world religions (especially studies on urban Inde-pendent and mainstream Christian churches), which of course do 'feel right' in an urban setting, where (far more directly than in the remote countryside) globalization made its impact on the African continent.

The relatively few researchers (including myself) who have documented urban 'traditional' ritual in modern Africa and sought to interpret it, have

---

1993b); De Boeck (1992); Gluckman (1949); Hoch (1968); Jules-Rosette (1979–80); Maxwell (1983: 52–70); Mayer (1971); Mayer and Mayer (1974); Richards (1982), which includes a 'regional bibliography' on girls' initiation in South Central Africa; Turner (1964, 1967); White (1953).

15. This embarrassment created by the dominant paradigm is probably the main reason why the study of African historic urban ritual is much less developed than the empirical incidence of such ritual would justify. Such studies as do exist have tended to underplay the historic, rural dimension in favour of the modern dimension (Mitchell, 1956; Ranger, 1975), or have drawn from other founts of inspiration than the dominant Durkheimian paradigm (van Binsbergen, 1981; Janzen, 1992).

come up with answers which, while persuasive in the light of the analytical paradigms prevalent at the time, now seem rather partial and unsatisfactory.

- The most classic argument is that couched in terms of *socialization and the inertia of culture*: even if urbanites pursue new forms of social and economic life especially outside their urban homes, in childhood they have been socialized into a particular rural culture which seeks continued acknowledgement in their lives, especially where the more intimate, existential dimensions are concerned; staging a rural kinship ritual in town would be held to restore or perpetuate a cultural orientation which has its focus in the distant village — by which is then meant not in the intangible ideal model of community, but the actual rural residential group on the ground.

- A more sophisticated rephrasing of the preceding argument would be in terms of broad, largely implicit, long-term cultural orientations that may be subsumed under Bourdieu's term *habitus*: girl's initiation deals with the inscribing, into the body and through the body, of a socially constructed and mediated personal identity which implies, as an aspect of habitus, a total cosmology, a system of causation, an eminently self-evident way of positioning one's self in the natural and social world; in a layered conception of the human life-world, it is at the deepest, most implicit layer that such habitus situates itself, largely impervious to the strategic and ephemeral surface adaptations of individuals and groups in the conjuncture of topical social, political and economic conditions prevailing here and now.

- Then there has been the *urban mutual aid argument*: economically insecure recent urban migrants seek to create, in the ritual sphere, a basis for solidarity so that they may appeal to each other in practical crises such as illness, funerals, unemployment, and so on; being from home, the traditional ritual may help to engender such solidarity, but (a remarkably Durkheimian streak again, cf. Durkheim's theory of the arbitrary nature of the sacred) in fact *any* ritual might serve that function, and world religions often provide adequate settings for the construction of alternative, fictive kin solidarity in town.

- The *urban–rural mutual aid argument* is a related argument deriving from modes-of-production analysis, which stresses the urban migrants' continued reliance on rural relationships in the face of their urban insecurity; since rural relationships are largely reproduced through rural ritual, urbanites stage rural-derived ritual (often with rural cultic personnel coming over to town for the occasion) in order to ensure their continued benefit from rural resources: access to land, shelter, healing, historical, political and ritual office.

- Having thus stressed the shared economic and ideological interest between townsmen and villagers, it is only a small step to the argument of *ethnic construction*. This revolves around the active propagation of a specific ethnic identity among urban migrants, which serves to conceptualize an urban–rural community of interests, assigns specific roles to villagers and urbanites in that context (the townsmen would often feature as ethnic brokers *vis-à-vis* the outside world), and effectively re-defines the old localized and homogeneous village community into a de-localized ethnic field spanning both rural and urban structures, confronting ethnic strangers and organizing those of the same ethnic identity for new tasks outside the village, in confrontation with urban ethnic rivals, with the urban economy and with the central state. In this ethnic context, the urban staging of 'traditional' rural ritual would be explained as the self-evident display of ethnically distinctive symbolic production. Again, however, any *bricolage* of old and new, local and global forms of symbolic production might serve the same purpose.

These approaches have various things in common. They assume the urbanites involved in rural kinship ritual to be recent urban migrants still retaining one foot in the village. They do not make the distinction (which, I argued above, emerged as a dominant feature of South Central African symbolic transformations throughout the twentieth century) between the actual rural residential group and the ideal model of the village community, and hence cannot decide between two fundamentally different interpretations of the ritual performance in town: does it seek to recreate a real village and by implication to deny urbanism? or does it seek to create *urban* community, as (in South Central Africa, at least) a new form of social locality, open to world-wide influences and pressures, merely by *reference* to an inspiring village-centred *abstract* model of community?

Finally, these approaches ignore such alternative and rival modes of creating meaning and community, precisely in a context of heterogeneity and choice which is so typical for towns wherever in the modern world. If urbanites stage rural kinship rituals in town it is not because they have no choice. They could tap any of the four complexes of cosmopolitan meaning outlined above, do as Hannerz and the many authors he cites suggest, and completely forget about rural forms. If they do insist on selectively adhering to rural forms in the urban context, further questions can be asked. Do they retain firm boundaries *vis-à-vis* each other and *vis-à-vis* the rural-centred model, or is there rather a mutual interpenetration and blending? How to explain that these globalizing alternatives leave ample room for what would appear to be an obsolete, rural form, the puberty rite? How do these symbolic and ideological dimensions relate to material conditions, and to power and authority: do they reflect or deny material structures of deprivation and domination; do they underpin such power as is based on privileged position in the political economy of town and state, or do they, on the contrary, empower those who would otherwise remain underprivileged; to what strategies do they give rise in the inequalities of age and gender, which are symbolically enacted in the village model of community and in the associated kinship rituals, but which also, albeit in rather different forms, structure urban social life?

Girls' Initiation in the Towns along the Zambian 'Line of Rail'

While the centrally-located farmers' town of Lusaka took over from the town of Livingstone in the extreme south of the country as territorial capital, a series of new towns were created in Zambia (then Northern Rhodesia) at the northern end of the 'Line of Rail' from the late 1920s, in order to accommodate the massive influx of labourers in the copper mining industry. As 'the Copperbelt', this is the most highly urbanized part of the country, and the site of famous and seminal studies in urban ethnicity, politics and religion. While imposed on a rural area where ethnic identity was primarily constructed in terms of the Lamba identity, the Copperbelt attracted migrants from all over South Central Africa but particularly from Northern Zambia; the Bemba identity (in itself undergoing considerable transformation and expansion in the process) became dominant in these towns, and the 'town Bemba' dialect their lingua franca.

If rural kinship rituals may seem out of place in town, they would seem even more so in the context of mainstream urban churches such as the Roman Catholic church. As a major agent of globalization, this world-wide hierarchical organization has sought to vigorously impose its particular conception of cosmology, hierarchy, sanctity and salvation (through the image of a community of believers and of saints), in short its system of meaning, on the African population, and part of its project has been the attempted monopolization of the social organization of human reproduction and human life crisis rituals.

Throughout South Central Africa, the female puberty ritual is one of the dominant kinship rituals (even more so than the male counterpart); its remarkably similar forms have been described in detail in many rural ethnographic contexts from Zaire to Northern Transvaal. For almost a century, female puberty ritual has been banned as pagan and sinful in Roman Catholic circles in Zambia. However, even during my research on urban churches in Zambia's capital Lusaka in the early 1970s, I found women's lay groups within the formal organization of mainstream churches willing to experiment with Christian alternatives to female puberty training. Therefore I was not surprised to learn that by the late 1980s, these experiments had grown into accepted practice. Nor is the phenomenon strictly confined to urban churches; for instance in the area of my main Zambian research, in Kaoma district in the western part of the country, a limited number of women now claim to have been 'matured [the standard expression for puberty initiation in Zambian English] in church' rather than in a family-controlled rural or urban kinship ritual.

The situation in the urban church congregations, as highlighted by Rasing's recent research (1995), is of inspiring complexity. On the one hand there is a proliferation of lay groups, each with their own uniforms and paraphernalia, formal authority structure within the overall church hierarchy, routine of meetings and prayers, and specialized topics of attention: caring for the sick, the battle against alcoholism, and so on. Already in these groups the organizational form and routine, and the social embeddedness this offers to its socially uprooted members, would appear to be an attempt at the construction of social locality. The latter might be of greater interpretative relevance than the specific contents of the religious ideas and practices circulating there; the result is, to use this phrase once more, 'a place to feel at home' — but at the same time a place to engage in formal organization. At first sight such voluntary organizational form would appear to be an aim and a source of satisfaction and meaning in itself; that is how, for instance, I looked at the Independent churches which I first studied in Lusaka in the early 1970s, when my theoretical baggage was still totally inadequate to appreciate them beyond the idea that they were contexts in which to learn about bureaucracy and modernity. However, I am now beginning to realize that it is such formal organizations which create the bedding, and the boundaries, within which the uncontrolled flow of goods, images and ideas as conveyed by globalization, can be turned into identity.

Some of these lay groups specialize in girls' initiation. However, contrary to what might be expected on the basis of comparative evidence from my own field research (Lusaka in the early 1970s, western central Zambia in the 1980s/90s), the lay group's symbolic and cultic repertoire for puberty initiation has incorporated far more than just a minimal selection of the rural ritual, far more than a mere token appendage of isolated traditional elements to a predominantly Christian and foreign rite of passage. On the contrary, the women lay leaders have used the church and their authority as a context within which to perform puberty ritual that, despite inevitable practical adaptations and frequent lapses of ritual knowledge and competence, emulates the historic, well-described Bemba kinship ritual to remarkable detail, and with open support from the church clergy.

Selected analytical and theoretical questions to which this state of affairs gives rise have been outlined above by way of introduction. Meanwhile the complexity of the situation calls for extensive ethnographic research, not only on the Copperbelt but also in present-day rural communities in Northern Zambia; in addition, a thorough study must be made of the ideological position and the exercise of religious authority of the clergy involved, as mediators between a world-wide hierarchically organized world religion (which has been very articulate in the field of human reproduction and gender relations) and the ritual and organizational activities of urban Christian lay women. A secondary research question revolves around the reasons for the senior representatives of the Roman Catholic church to accept, even welcome, a ritual and symbolic repertoire which would appear to challenge the globalizing universalism of this world religion, and which for close to a century has been condemned for doing just that.

The crucial interpretative problem here lies in its *virtuality*: in the fact that the Copperbelt women staging these rituals, as well as their adolescent initiates, do not in the least belong, nor consciously aspire to belong, to the ideal village world which is expounded in the ritual. These rituals belong to a realm of *virtuality*, very far removed from the Durkheimian premise (1912) of a coincidence between religious form and local group. Here we have to assess the various orders of reality, dream, ideal, fantasy and imagery that informs a modern African urban population in the construction of their life-world. For while the kinship ritual emphasizes reproductive roles within marriage, agricultural and domestic productive roles for women, and their respect for authority positions within the rural kinship structure, these urban women are a long way removed from the model of rural womanhood upheld in the initiation, where it is formally taught through songs, through the supervising elders' pantomimes, wall pictures specifically drawn for the purpose, and especially by reference to clay models of human beings, their body parts, and man-made artefacts. Admittedly, many of these women still cherish their urban garden plots, but even if these are not raided by thieves around harvest time, their produce falls far short of feeding the owners and their families through the annual cycle. These women have hardly any effective ties any more with a distant village — those that exist are mainly revived in the case of funerals. In their sexual and reproductive behaviour they operate largely outside the constraints stipulated by the kinship ritual and the associated formal training; as female heads of households, they are often without effective and enduring ties with a male partner; and they do not all even subscribe to the Bemba ethnic identity.

Very clearly this urban puberty ritual is concerned with the construction of meaningful social locality out of the fragmentation of social life in the Copperbelt high-density residential areas, and beyond that with the social construction of female personhood; but why, in this urban context, is the remote and clearly inapplicable dream of the village model yet so dominant and inspiring? Is the puberty ritual a way, for the women involved, to construct themselves as ethnically Bemba? That is not the case, since the church congregations are by nature multi-ethnic and no instances of ethnic juxtaposition to other groups have been noted so far in relation to this urban puberty ritual. Is the communal identity to be constructed through the puberty ritual rather that of a community of women? Then why hark back to a rural-based model of womanhood which, even if part of a meaningful ideal universe, no longer has any practical correspondence with the life of Copperbelt women today — women who do not till the soil; who, in their daily life including its sexual aspects, do not observe the rules of conduct and the taboos to which they were instructed at their initiation; and who in many cases will not contract a formal marriage with their male sexual and reproductive partners. Or is the social construction of womanhood, and personhood in general, perhaps such a subtle and profound process that foreign symbols (as mediated through the Christian church) are in themselves insufficiently powerful to bring about the bodily inscription that produces identity — so that what appears as virtuality, as a lack of connectedness between the urban day-to-day practice of womanhood today and the ideological contents of the initiation, might mark merely the relative unimportance of the details of the women's day-to-day situation (including the fact that this happens to be urban), in the face of an implicit, long-term habitus?

CONCLUSION

Perhaps, after the earlier theoretical explorations, this case study will set some descriptive basis for a further theoretical elaboration of the concept of virtuality in a context of globalization in Africa today. The kinds of problems pinpointed in this article continue to strike me as both relevant and tantalizing, and I realize that my own commitment to the study of globalization is largely fuelled by my hope that somewhere in that sort of perspective those analytical problems which haunt me (cf. van Binsbergen, 1981: Ch. 6) may come closer to a solution. This article makes only a small step towards such a solution, and in the process reveals how difficult it is to capture, in academic discourse whose hallmark is consistency, the contradictions which exist in reality.

This article has concentrated, as forms of virtuality, on phenomena of dislocation and disconnectedness in time and space, and has all but overlooked forms of disembodiment, and of dehumanization of human activity. As Norman Long remarked during a recent conference,[16] under contemporary technological conditions new questions of agency are raised. Agency now is more than ever a matter of man/object communication (instead of primarily man/man communication). This means that the formal organizations stressed here, if based on such agency, are no longer what they used to be. The images of Africa as conveyed in this article are rooted in years of anthropological participation in African contexts, by myself and others, yet the mechanics of the actual production of these images has involved not only human intersubjectivity (both between the researcher and the researched, and between the researcher and his colleagues), but also days of solitary interaction between me and my computer. There is also virtuality for the reader, of the self-reflective kind so much cherished by our postmodernists. Anthropology may be among the more sympathetic globalizing projects of

---

16. WOTRO Programme on Globalization and the Construction of Communal Identities, conference, Bergen, The Netherlands (15–16 February 1996).

the West, but that does not prevent it from being infested with the very phenomena which it tries to study with detachment.

ACKNOWLEDGEMENTS

Earlier versions of this article were presented on the following occasions: at two meetings of the WOTRO (Netherlands Foundation for Tropical Research) Programme on 'Globalization and the construction of communal identities': in the form of an oral presentation at the Bergen (Netherlands) conference (15–16 February 1996), and as a paper at the programme's monthly seminar, Amsterdam (6 May 1996); at the one-day conference on globalization, Free University, Amsterdam (7 June 1996); and at the graduate seminar, Africa Research Centre, Catholic University of Louvain (8 November 1996). For constructive comments and criticism I am indebted to all participants, and especially to (alphabetically) Filip De Boeck, René Devisch, Martin Doornbos, André Droogers, Mike Featherstone, Jonathan Friedman, Peter Geschiere, Ulf Hannerz, Peter Kloos, Birgit Meyer, Peter Pels, Rafael Sanchez, Matthew Schoffeleers, Bonno Thoden van Velzen, Rijk van Dijk, Wilhelmina van Wetering, and Karin Willemse. Most of all I am indebted to the editors of this volume, for their encouragement, advice, and criticism.

REFERENCES

Appadurai, A. (1990) 'Disjuncture and Difference in the Global Cultural Economy', in M. Featherstone (ed.) *Global Culture: Nationalism, Globalization and Modernity*, pp. 295–310. London/Newbury Park: Sage.

Appadurai, A. (1995) 'The Production of Locality', in R. Fardon (ed.) *Counterworks: Managing the Diversity of Knowledge*, ASA decennial conference series 'The Uses of Knowledge: Global and Local Relations', pp. 204–25. London: Routledge.

Apter, A. (1996) 'IBB = 419: Nigerian Democracy and the Politics of Illusion'. Paper presented at the conference 'The struggle for civil society in Africa', University of Chicago (31 May–2 June), and at the 'Panel on hybrid democracies', 1996 Annual Meeting, American Anthropological Association, San Francisco.

Austin, J. L. (1962) *How to do Things with Words*. Oxford: Oxford University Press.

Baudrillard, J. (1972) *Pour une critique de l'économie politique du signe*. Paris: Gallimard.

Baudrillard, J. (1981) *Simulacres et simulation*. Paris: Galilée.

van Binsbergen, W. M. J. (1981) *Religious Change in Zambia: Exploratory Studies*. London/Boston: Kegan Paul International.

van Binsbergen, W. M. J. (1987) 'De Schaduw waar je niet overheen mag stappen: Een westers onderzoeker op het Nkoja meisjesfeest', in W. M. J. van Binsbergen and M. R. Doornbos (eds) *Afrika in Spiegelbeeld*, pp. 139–82. Haarlem: In de Knipscheer.

van Binsbergen, W. M. J. (1992a) 'Kazanga: Etniciteit in Afrika tussen staat en traditie', inaugural lecture. Amsterdam: Free University. (Shortened French version (1993), 'Kazanga: Ethnicité en Afrique entre État et tradition', in W. J. M. van Binsbergen and K. Schilder (eds) *Perspectives on Ethnicity in Africa*, special issue on 'Ethnicity', *Afrika Focus* (1): 9–40; English version with postscript (1994), 'The Kazanga Festival: Ethnicity as Cultural Mediation and Transformation in Central Western Zambia', *African Studies* 53 (2): 92–125.)

van Binsbergen, W. M. J. (1992b) *Tears of Rain: Ethnicity and History in Central Western Zambia*. London/Boston: Kegan Paul International.

van Binsbergen, W. M. J. (1993a) 'Making Sense of Urban Space in Francistown, Botswana', in P. J. M. Nas (ed.) *Urban Symbolism*, pp. 184–228. Studies in Human Societies, volume 8. Leiden: Brill.

van Binsbergen, W. M. J. (1993b) 'Mukanda: Towards a History of Circumcision Rites in Western Zambia, 18th–20th Century', in J.-P. Chrétien et al. (eds) *L'invention religieuse en Afrique: Histoire et religion en Afrique noire*, pp. 49–103. Paris: Agence de Culture et de Coopération Technique/Karthala.

van Binsbergen, W. M. J. (1994) 'Dynamiek van cultuur: Enige dilemma's van hedendaags Afrika in een context van globalisering', *Antropologische Verkenningen* 13(2): 17–33. (English version (1995), 'Popular Culture in Africa: Dynamics of African Cultural and Ethnic Identity in a Context of Globalization', in J. D. M. van der Klei (ed.) *Popular Culture: Africa, Asia and Europe: Beyond Historical Legacy and Political Innocence* (Proceedings Summer School 1994), pp. 7–40. Utrecht: CERES.

van Binsbergen, W. M. J. (1995a) 'Aspects of Democracy and Democratisation in Zambia and Botswana: Exploring Political Culture at the Grassroots', *Journal of Contemporary African Studies* 13(1): 3–33.

van Binsbergen, W. M. J. (1995b) 'Four-tablet Divination as Trans-regional Medical Technology in Southern Africa', *Journal on Religion in Africa* 25(2): 114–40.

van Binsbergen, W. M. J. (1995c) 'Globalization *avant la lettre?* The Case of Islamic Geomancy and its World-wide Spread, ca. 900–1995 CE'. Paper read at the conference on 'The global oikumene and the spread of knowledge', organized by the Department of Social Anthropology, University of Stockholm (9–12 September).

van Binsbergen, W. M. J. (1996a) '*Black Athena* and Africa's contribution to Global Cultural History', *Quest — Philosophical Discussions: An International African Journal of Philosophy* 9/2/10(1): 100–37.

van Binsbergen, W. M. J. (1996b) 'Time, Space and History in African Divination and Board-games', in D. Tiemersma and H. A. F. Oosterling (eds) *Time and Temporality in Intercultural Perspective: Studies presented to Heinz Kimmerle*, pp. 105–25. Amsterdam: Rodopi.

van Binsbergen, W. M. J. (1996c) 'Transregional and Historical Connections of Four-tablet Divination in Southern Africa', *Journal of Religion in Africa* 26(1): 2–29.

van Binsbergen, W. M. J. and P. L. Geschiere (eds) (1985) *Old Modes of Production and Capitalist Encroachment: Anthropological Explorations in Africa*. London/Boston: Kegan Paul International.

De Boeck, F. (1992) 'Of Bushbucks without Horns: Male and Female Initiation among the Aluund of Southwest Zaire', *Journal des Africanistes* 61(1): 37–72.

Cheater, A. P. (1995) 'Globalization and the New Technologies of Knowing: Anthropological Calculus or Chaos', in M. Strathern (ed.) *Shifting Contexts: Transformations in Anthropological Knowledge*, ASA Decennial Conference Series 'The Uses of Knowledge: Global and Local Relations', pp. 117–30. London: Routledge.

Chrétien, J.-P. and G. Prunier (eds) (1989) *Les ethnies ont une histoire*. Paris: Karthala/Agence de Coopération Culturelle et Technique.

Cohen, A. P. and J. L. Comaroff (1976) 'The Management of Meaning: On the Phenomenology of Political Transactions', in B. Kapferer (ed.) *Transaction and Meaning: Directions in the Anthropology of Exchange and Symbolic Behavior*, pp. 87–107. Philadelphia, PA: Institute for the Study of Human Issues.

Comaroff, J. and J. Comaroff (eds) (1993) *Modernity and its Malcontents: Ritual and Power in Postcolonial Africa*. Chicago, IL: University of Chicago Press.

Corbeil, J. J. (1982) *Mbusa: Sacred Emblems of the Bemba*. Mbala (Zambia): Moto-Moto Museum; London: Ethnographica Publishers.

Durkheim, E. (1912) *Les formes élémentaires de la vie religieuse*. Paris: Presses Universities de France.

Epstein, A. L. (1958) *Politics in an Urban African Community*. Manchester: Manchester University Press.

Epstein, A. L. (1967) 'Urbanisation and Social Change in Africa', *Current Anthropology* 8(4): 275–95.

Fardon, R. (ed.) (1995) *Counterworks: Managing the Diversity of Knowledge*, ASA decennial conference series 'The Uses of Knowledge: Global and Local Relations', London: Routledge.

Featherstone, M. (ed.) (1990) *Global Culture: Nationalism, Globalization and Modernity* London/Newbury Park: Sage.

Forster, H. (ed.) (1987) *Post-modern Culture*. London/Sydney: Pluto Press (first published under this title, 1985; earlier published as: Foster, H. (ed.) (1983) *The Anti-Aesthetic: Essays on Post-modern Culture*. Port Townsend, WA: Bay Press.)

Foucault, M. (1966) *Les mots et les choses: Une archéologie des sciences humaines*. Paris: Gallimard.

Friedman, J. (1995) *Cultural Identity and Global Process*. London: Sage (first published 1994).

Gerold-Scheepers, T. J. F. A. and W. M. J. van Binsbergen (1978) 'Marxist and non-Marxist Approaches to Migration in Africa', in W. M. J. van Binsbergen and H. A. Meilink *Migration and the Transformation of Modern African Society*, pp. 21–35. Leiden: African Studies Centre.

Geschiere, P. L. with C. F. Fisiy (1995) *Sorcellerie et politique en Afrique: La viande des autres*. Paris: Karthala (series Les Afriques).

Geuijen, K. (1992) 'Postmodernisme in de antropologie', *Antropologische Verkenningen* 11(1): 17–36.

Giddens, A. (1990) *The Consequences of Modernity*. Cambridge: Polity Press.

Giddens, A. (1991) *Modernity and Self-Identity*. Cambridge: Polity Press.

Gluckman, M. (1945) 'Seven-year Research Plan of the Rhodes-Livingstone Institute of Social Studies in British Central Africa', *Rhodes-Livingstone Journal* 4: 1–32.

Gluckman, M. (1949) 'The Role of the Sexes in Wiko Circumcision Ceremonies', in M. Fortes (ed.) *Social Structure*, pp. 145–67. London: Oxford University Press.

Gluckman, M. (1960) 'Tribalism in Modern British Central Africa', *Cahiers d'Etudes Africaines* 1: 55–70.

Hannerz, U. (1980) *Exploring the City: Inquiries towards an Urban Anthropology*. New York: Columbia University Press.

Hannerz, U. (1986) 'Theory in Anthropology: Small is Beautiful? The Problem of Complex Cultures', *Comparative Studies in Society and History* 28(2): 362–7.

Hannerz, U. (1987) 'The World in Creolisation', *Africa* 57: 546–59.

Hannerz, U. (1989) 'Culture between Center and Periphery: Toward a Macroanthropology', *Ethnos* 54: 200–16.

Hannerz, U. (1990) 'Cosmopolitans and Locals in World Cultures', in M. Featherstone (ed.) *Global Culture: Nationalism, Globalization and Modernity*, pp. 237–51. London/Newbury Park: Sage.

Hannerz, U. (1992a) *Cultural Complexity: Studies in the Social Organisation of Meaning*. New York: Columbia University Press.

Hannerz, U. (1992b) *Culture, Cities and the World*. Amsterdam: Centrum voor Grootstedelijk Onderzoek.

Harvey, D. (1989) *The Condition of Postmodernity*. Oxford: Basil Blackwell.

Hobsbawm, E. and T. O. Ranger (eds) (1983) *The Invention of Tradition*. Cambridge: Cambridge University Press.

Hoch, E. (1968) *Mbusa: A Contribution to the Study of Bemba Initiation Rites and those of Neighbouring Tribes*. Chinsali: Ilondola Language Centre.

Hoenen, P. (1947) *Philosophie der anorganische natuur*. Antwerpen/Nijmegen: Standaard-Boekhandel.

International Business Machines Corporation (IBM) (1987) *Dictionary of Computing Terms*. Poughkeepsie, NY: IBM.

Janzen, J. M. (1992) *Ngoma: Discourses of Healing in Central and Southern Africa*. Los Angeles, CA: University of California Press.

Jules-Rosette, B. (1979–80) 'Changing Aspects of Women's Initiation in Southern Africa: An Explanatory Study', *Canadian Journal of African Studies* 13(3): 389–405.

Jules-Rosette, B. (1996) 'What Money Can't Buy: Zairian Popular Culture and Symbolic Ambivalence toward Modernity'. Paper presented at the international conference on

'L'Argent: feuille morte: L'Afrique Central avant et après le desenchantement de la modernité', Louvain (21–2 June).

Kapferer, B. (1988) 'The Anthropologist as Hero — Three Exponents of Post-modernist Anthropology', *Critique of Anthropology* 8(2): 77–104.

Korff, R. (1995) 'The Urban Revolution: Civilisation in the Concrete Jungle?'. Paper read at the EIDOS (European Interuniversity Development Opportunities Study network) conference on Globalization and Decivilization, Wageningen (14–16 December).

Kroeber, A. B. (1938) 'Basic and Secondary Patterns of Social Structure', *Journal of the Royal Anthropological Institute* 2: 299–309.

Little, W., H. W. Fowler and J. Coulson (eds) (1978) *The Shorter Oxford English Dictionary: On Historical Principles*, revised and edited by C. T. Onions, etymologies revised by G. W. S. Friedrichsen (3rd reset edn), 2 vols. Oxford: Clarendon Press.

Maine, H. S. (1883) *Ancient Law*. London: John Murray (first published 1861).

Maxwell, K. B. (1983) *Bemba Myth and Ritual: The Impact of Literacy on an Oral Culture*. American University Studies, series XI (Anthropology/Sociology), vol. 2. New York/ Frankfurt am Main/Berne: Peter Lang.

Mayer, P. (1971) '"Traditional" Manhood Initiation in an Industrial City: The African View', in E. J. de Jager (ed.) *Man: Anthropological Essays presented to O. F. Raum*, pp. 7–18. Cape Town: Struik.

Mayer, P. (ed.) (1980) *Black Villagers in an Industrial Society: Anthropological Perspectives on Labour Migration in South Africa*. Cape Town: Oxford University Press.

Mayer, P. and I. Mayer (1974) *Townsmen or Tribesmen: Conservatism and the Process of Urbanization in a South African City* (2nd edn). Cape Town: Oxford University Press (first published 1961).

McLuhan, M. (1966) *Understanding Media: The Extensions of Man*. London: McGraw-Hill.

Meillassoux, C. (1975) *Femmes, greniers et capitaux*. Paris: Maspero.

Meyer, B. (1995) 'Translating the Devil: An African Appropriation of Pietist Protestantism: The case of the Peki Ewe in Southeastern Ghana, 1847–1992'. PhD Thesis, University of Amsterdam.

Mitchell, J. C. (1956) *The Kalela Dance: Aspects of Social Relationships among Urban Africans in Northern Rhodesia*. Rhodes-Livingstone Paper No. 27. Manchester: Manchester University Press.

Mitchell, J. C. (ed.) (1969) *Social Networks in Urban Situations*. Manchester: Manchester University Press.

Nencel, L. and P. Pels (eds) (1991) *Constructing Knowledge: Authority and Critique in Social Science*. London: Sage.

Pels, P. (1993) 'Critical Matters: Interactions between Missionaries and Waluguru in Colonial Tanganyika, 1930–1961'. PhD Thesis, University of Amsterdam.

Radcliffe-Brown, A. R. (1940) 'Preface', in M. Fortes and E. E. Evans-Pritchard (eds) *African Political Systems*, pp. xi–xxiii. London: Oxford University Press.

Ranger, T. O. (1975) *Dance and Society in Eastern Africa, 1890–1970*. London: Heinemann.

Rasing, T. (1995) *Passing on the Rites of Passage: Girls' Initiation Rites in the Context of an Urban Roman Catholic Community on the Zambian Copperbelt*. Leiden: African Studies Centre; Aldershot: Avebury.

Rheingold, H. (1991) *Virtual Reality*. London: Secker and Warburg.

Richards, A. I. (1982) *Chisungu: A Girls' Initiation Ceremony among the Bemba of Zambia*. London/New York: Tavistock (Intro Jean La Fontaine; first published 1956).

Spengler, O. (1993) *Der Untergang des Abendlandes: Umrisse einer Morphologie der Weltgeschichte*. München: DTV (first published 1923, München: Beck).

Toynbee, A. J. (1952) *Beschaving in het Geding*. Bussum: Kroonder.

Turner, V. W. (1964) 'Symbols in Ndembu Ritual', in M. Gluckman (ed.) *Closed Systems and Open Minds*, pp. 20–51. Edinburgh: Oliver and Boyd.

Turner, V. W. (1967) 'Mukanda: The Rite of Circumcision', in V. W. Turner *The Forest of Symbols: Aspects of Ndembu Ritual*, pp. 151–279. Ithaca/London: Cornell University Press.

Turner, V. W. (1968) *Schism and Continuity in an African Society: A Study of Ndembu Village Life*. Manchester: Manchester University Press (reprint of 1957 edn).

Tyler, S. (1987) *The Unspeakable: Discourse, Dialogue, and Rhetoric in the Post-modern World*. Madison, WI: University of Wisconsin Press.

Vail, L. (ed.) (1989) *The Creation of Tribalism in Southern Africa*. London: James Currey; Berkeley/Los Angeles, CA: University of California Press.

van Velsen, J. (1971) *The Politics of Kinship: A Study of Social Manipulation Amongst the Lakeside Tonga of Malawi*. Manchester: Manchester University Press (first published 1964).

White, C. M. N. (1953) 'Conservatism and Modern Adaptation in Luvale Female Puberty Ritual', *Africa* 23(1): 15–25.

Dead Certainty: Ethnic Violence in the Era of Globalization

Arjun Appadurai

Under what conditions is group violence between previous social intimates associated with certain forms of uncertainty regarding ethnic identity?[1] In one widely shared perspective, ethnic violence, as a form of collective violence, is partly a product of propaganda, rumour, prejudice, and memory — all forms of knowledge and all usually associated with heightened conviction, conviction capable of producing inhumane degrees of violence. However, there is an alternative approach to ethnic violence, with roots traceable to Durkheim's (1951) work on anomie and Simmel's (1950) ideas about the stranger. This tradition of thinking — which focuses on doubt, uncertainty, and indeterminacy — has surfaced recently in many different ways. It animates the ongoing work of Zygmunt Bauman (1997) on the roles of the stranger, the consumer, the parvenu, and the vagabond as social archetypes of the postmodern world. It appears, too, in the work of Piotr Hoffman (1986, 1989) on doubt, time, and violence. Julia Kristeva's (1991) work on strangers, a philosophical reflection clearly prompted by the renewed fear of xenophobia in France, belongs to this tradition. This line of thought has also been invoked, at least implicitly, in several recent anthropological works on ethnic violence. These works have in common the sound intuition that, given the growing multiplicity, contingency, and apparent fungibility of the identities available to persons in the contemporary world, there is a growing sense of radical social uncertainty about people, situations, events, norms, and even cosmologies.

Some of these works discuss the politics of the body in such a world of uncertainty. In others, there is a recognition that what is new about these uncertainties has something to do with the forces of globalization — weakened states, refugees, economic deregulation, and systematic new forms of pauperization and criminalization. This latter connection is especially suggestively made in Bauman (1997). Yet, to my knowledge, no single work has sought to explore the precise ways in which the ethnic body can be a theatre for the engagement of uncertainty under the special circumstances of globalization. This link is an important preoccupation of the essay that follows.

---

1. In sketching an approach to this question, I build on an argument against primordialism developed in previous work (Appadurai, 1996) and lay the foundations for a larger study of ethnic violence currently in progress.

Significant steps to engage these challenges are found in a growing body of work on ethnic violence by anthropologists (Daniel, 1996; Das, 1990, 1995; Desjarlais and Kleinman, 1994; Devisch, 1995; Hayden, 1996; Herzfeld, 1997; Jeganathan, 1997; Malkki, 1995; Nordstrom, 1997; Tambiah, 1996). Part of what emerges from this work is a consensus that the ethnic labels and categories involved in contemporary ethnic violence are frequently products of recent state policies and techniques, such as censuses, partitions, and constitutions. Labels such as 'Yugoslav', 'Sikh', 'Kurd', and 'Muslim', which appear to be the same as long-standing ethnic names and terms, are frequently transformations of existing names and terms to serve substantially new frameworks of identity, entitlement, and spatial sovereignty.

Given the high-level mobilization of such names and terms, three consequences follow. First, given the increasingly porous borders between nation-states in matters of arms, refugees, trade, and mass media,[2] these ethnic names and terms become highly susceptible to transnational perturbation. Second, where local identities and identifications often were far more important than higher-order names and terms, modern state-level forces tend to generate large-scale identities (such as Latino, Scheduled Caste, and Serb), which become significant imagined affiliations for large numbers of persons, many of whom reside across large social, spatial, and political divides. Third, and by extension, the angers, frustrations, and quarrels of small (face-to-face) communities and larger megaethnic groupings tend to affect each other directly and explosively, so that certain communities, in Robert Hayden's provocative phrase, become unimaginable (1996: 783).

Since the subject of ethnic violence is large and horrifying in its range and variety, this article confines itself to violence involving neighbours, friends, and kinsmen — persons and groups who have some degree of prior social familiarity. Thus the organized violence of police, armed hoodlums, professional torturers and investigators, and paid ethnic militias is not discussed here, except as it directly informs the problem of violence between socially proximate persons.[3] Also, rather than focus on all forms of

---

2. Virtually all borders, however rigidly policed, are porous to some extent. I am not suggesting that all borders are equally porous or that all groups can cross particular borders at will. The image of a borderless world is far from what I wish to evoke. Rather, I wish to suggest that borders are increasingly sites of contestation between states and various kinds of non-state actors and interests and that it is only in respect to some populations, commodities, and ideologies that states succeed in maintaining tight borders. Further, the movement of ethnic populations across national borders, whether in flight or not, is frequently a factor in intranational ethnic conflict.

3. However, I do not wish to imply that these different forms and registers of violence are analytically or empirically insulated from one another. Indeed, Claudio Lomnitz (personal communication) has suggested various ways in which the vivisectionist violence between intimates and the banalized violence of professional torturers (especially in Latin America) may be linked through the politics of identity and the state, and thus of globalization. I hope to pursue these suggestions in future work on this subject.

violent confrontation, the discussion will concentrate on those associated with appalling physical brutality and indignity — involving mutilation, cannibalism, rape, sexual abuse, and violence against civilian spaces and populations. Put simply, the focus here is on bodily brutality perpetrated by ordinary persons against other persons with whom they may have — or could have — previously lived in relative amity.

This focus allows an examination of limiting conditions and extreme cases for testing the idea of uncertainty as a key factor in severe ethnic violence. Focusing on bodily violence between actors with routine — and generally benign — prior knowledge of one another is also a way to illuminate 'threshold' or trigger conditions, where managed or endemic social conflict gives way to runaway violence.

Although transregional contacts and transnational processes have antecedents and anticipations over centuries (Abu-Lughod, 1993; Wallerstein, 1974) in the form of what we refer to as world-systems, there is a widely shared sense that there is something new about these processes and systems in the last few decades. The word globalization (both as a socioeconomic formation and as a term of folk ideology in journalism and in the corporate world) marks a set of transitions in the global political economy since the 1970s, in which multinational forms of capitalist organization began to be replaced by transnational (Rouse, 1995), flexible (Harvey, 1989), and irregular (Lash and Urry, 1987, 1994) forms of organization, as labour, finance, technology, and technological capital began to be assembled in ways that treated national boundaries as mere constraints or fictions. In contrast with the multinational corporations of the middle of the century which sought to transcend national boundaries while working within existing national frameworks of law, commerce, and sovereignty, the transnational corporations of the last three decades have increasingly begun to produce recombinant arrangements of labour, capital, and technical expertise which produce new forms of law, management, and distribution. In both phases global capital and national states have sought to exploit each other, but in the most recent decades it is possible to see a secular decline in the sovereignty of national states in respect to the workings of global capital. These changes — with accompanying changes in law, accounting, patenting, and other administrative technologies — have created 'new markets for loyalty' (Price, 1994) and called existing models of territorial sovereignty into question (Sassen, 1996).

It is not difficult to see that the speed and intensity with which both material and ideological elements now circulate across national boundaries have created a new order of uncertainty in social life. Whatever may characterize this new kind of uncertainty, it does not easily fit the dominant, Weberian prophecy about modernity in which earlier, intimate social forms would dissolve, to be replaced by highly regimented bureaucratic-legal orders, governed by the growth of procedure and predictability. The links between these forms of uncertainty — one diacritic of the era of globalization — and the world-wide intensification in ethnocidal violence inform this essay and are explicitly addressed in its conclusion.[4]

The forms of such uncertainty are certainly various. One kind of uncertainty is a direct reflection of census concerns: how many persons of this or that sort really exist in a given territory? Or, in the context of rapid migration or refugee movement, how many of 'them' are there now among 'us'?[5] Another kind of uncertainty is about what some of these megaidentities really mean: what are the normative characteristics of what the Constitution defines as a member of an OBC (Other Backward Caste) in India? A further uncertainty is about whether a particular person really is what they claim or appear to be or have historically been. Finally, these various forms of uncertainty create intolerable anxiety about the relationship of many individuals to state-provided goods — ranging from housing and health to safety and sanitation — since these entitlements are frequently directly tied to who 'you' are, and thus to who 'they' are. Each kind of uncertainty gains increasing force whenever there are large-scale movements of persons (for whatever reason), when new rewards or risks attach to large-scale ethnic identities, or when existing networks of social knowledge are eroded by rumour, terror, or social movement. Where one or more of these forms of social uncertainty come into play, violence can create a macabre form of certainty and can become a brutal technique (or folk discovery-procedure) about 'them' and, therefore, about 'us'. This conjecture might make special sense in the era of globalization.

The first step toward such an understanding must be the most obvious and striking feature of such violence, which is its site and target — the body. Even a quick scan of the extensive literature suggests that the human body is the site of the most horrifying acts of ethnic violence. It might seem banal to say that the body is the site of the worst possible infliction of pain, terror, indignity, and suffering, in comparison with property or other resources. Yet it is clear that the violence inflicted on the human body in ethnic contexts is

---

4. It is difficult to make plausible quantitative claims about changes in the incidence of ethnic violence over long periods of time. There is some evidence that intrastate conflict (including ethnic violence) is more frequent today than interstate conflict. It appears that there is a secular increase in extreme forms of bodily violence between ethnic groups, even though many societies are remarkable for their striking degree of ethnic harmony and social order generally. There is no doubt that the amplification of our impressions of ethnic violence through the mass media creates the inherent risk of exaggerating the global occurrence of extreme violence.

5. For a suggestive discussion of the widespread uncertainty concerning the identities of persons, social categories, villages, and even about the link between religion and nation-hood during the process of partition in 1947, I am indebted to a draft paper by Gyanendra Pandey, 'Can a Muslim Be an Indian?' delivered at the University of Chicago in April 1997. A similar kind of uncertainty, produced by late colonial and postcolonial politics, is remarked by Quadri Ismail (1995) with respect to Sri Lankan Muslim self-understandings of identity.

never entirely random or lacking in cultural form. Wherever the testimony is sufficiently graphic (Das, 1990; Feldman, 1991; Malkki, 1995; Sutton, 1995), it becomes clear that even the worst acts of degradation — involving faeces, urine, body parts; beheading, impaling, gutting, sawing; raping, burning, hanging, and suffocating — have macabre forms of cultural design and violent predictability.

The single most forceful anthropological account of such design is Liisa Malkki's 1995 description of the memories of Hutu refugees in Tanzania in the 1980s of the genocidal violence perpetrated against them principally in the early 1970s in Burundi. This study, which brings together themes of exile, morality, memory, space, and nationalism in its effort to interpret genocidal violence, has many points of convergence with the principal arguments made here, but just two issues raised by Malkki directly concern me: the forms of bodily violence and the relationship of purity to identity.

Built around partially standardized accounts (mythico-histories) by Hutu refugees in Tanzania of the ethnocidal violence they experienced in Burundi since the 1960s, but especially in the bloodbath of 1972 directed against the Hutu majority, Malkki shows how questions of identification and knowledge of the ethnic body lay at the heart of the atrocious violence of this moment. Discussing a detailed response to her question of 'how it could be possible to know a person's identity with certainty enough to kill', Malkki shows how earlier colonial efforts to reduce the complex social differences among local ethnic groups to a simple taxonomy of racial-physical signs had come to be elaborated in the 1970s and 1980s. These 'necrographic' maps were the basis for detailed, technical recollections of the ways in which death was administered to victims in specific, humiliating, and drawn-out ways. Malkki (following Feldman, 1991) suggests that these maps of bodily difference are themselves delicately poised between acquired knowledge and techniques of detection. These maps 'help construct and imagine ethnic difference', and 'through violence, bodies of individual persons become metamorphosed into specimens of the ethnic category for which they are supposed to stand' (Malkki, 1995: 88). A slightly different approach to the relationship between 'bodies', 'persons', and 'identities' appears in this essay.

In the account that Malkki presents of the mythico-historical presentation of how Tutsi killers used shared maps of physical differences to identify Hutu, it is clear that the process is racked with instability and uncertainty (even in survivors' views of the uncertainty faced by their killers), so that multiple physical tests have to be applied. Malkki offers a bold interpretation of the specific ways in which Hutu men and women were killed (often with sharp bamboo sticks, using the grid of vagina, anus, and head; often removing fetuses from pregnant women intact and forcing the mother to eat the fetus, and so on). She concludes that these recollected practices, played out on the necrographic maps of the Hutu ethnic body 'seem to have operated through certain routinized symbolic schemes of nightmarish cruelty' (ibid: 92).

It remains to draw out the link between the mapped body of the ethnic other and the peculiar and specific brutalities associated with ethnic murder. While much of Malkki's analysis strikes me as deeply persuasive, what is vital for the present argument is the link between indeterminacy and brutality in the negotiations over the ethnic body.[6] Although it is difficult to be sure (especially for an analyst who is one step away from Malkki's firsthand exposure to these narratives), there is enough evidence to suggest that we are looking here at a complex variation of Mary Douglas's classic arguments about 'purity and danger' (1966) and about the body as a symbolic map of the cosmos (1973). In her classic argument about 'matter out of place' (which Malkki also discusses), Mary Douglas made a symbolic-structural link between categorical mixture, the cognitive anxiety it provokes, and the resultant abhorrence of taxonomic hybridity in all sorts of social and moral worlds. In subsequent work on body symbolism, Douglas showed how and why the body works to compress and perform wider cosmological under-standings about social categories and classifications. Several recent analysts of ethnic violence have made useful recourse to Mary Douglas's ideas about purity and category-mixture (Hayden, 1996; Herzfeld, 1992, 1997) in addressing issues of ethnic cleansing in Europe.

The argument here owes a direct debt to Douglas, but some distinctions are worth making. While Douglas takes a cosmology (a system of categorical distinctions) as culturally given, thus leading to taboos against 'matter out of place', ethnic violence introduces contingency into this logic, for the situations discussed here are explicitly about cosmologies in flux, categories under stress, and ideas striving for the logic of self-evidence. What is more, the sort of evidence presented by Malkki (and supported by similar accounts from Ireland, India, and Eastern Europe) suggests an inversion of the logic of indeterminacy, category-mixture, and danger identified by Douglas. In Malkki's evidence, for example, the body is both a source and a target of violence. The categorical uncertainty about Hutu and Tutsi is played out not in the security of the 'body maps' shared by both sides but by the instability of the signs of bodily difference: not all Tutsis are tall; not all Hutu have red

---

6. This is the appropriate point at which to acknowledge the pathbreaking contribution of Allen Feldman's study of ethnoreligious violence in Ireland (1991). Most subsequent anthropological studies of violence, including several that I cite here, are in his debt. His brilliant examination of the logic of space, torture, fear and narrative in Northern Ireland brings a radical Foucauldian perspective to bear on a series of searing ethnographic observations of militarized ethnic terror. The ways in which Feldman's arguments set the stage for my own are many: they include his observations about interrogation as a ceremony of verification (Feldman, 1991: 115), torture as a technique for the production of power out of the body of the victim (ibid), the medicalization involved in interrogation (ibid: 122–3), and the role of the corpse, or 'stiff', to mark the transfer of larger spatial maps onto the map of the enemy body (ibid: 73). My effort is to shift the focus away from state-sponsored violence to its 'ordinary' forms and agents and to elaborate the links between clarification and purification.

gums; not all noses help identify Tutsi, nor do all modes of walking help identify Hutu.

In a word, real bodies in history betray the very cosmologies they are meant to encode. So the ethnic body, both of victim and of killer, is itself potentially deceptive. Far from providing the map for a secure cosmology, a compass from which mixture, indeterminacy, and danger may be discovered, the ethnic body turns out to be itself unstable and deceptive. It is this reversal of Douglas's cosmologic that might best explain macabre patterns of violence directed against the body of the ethnic other. The peculiar formality — the specific preoccupation with particular body parts — is an effort to stabilize the body of the ethnic other; to eliminate the flux introduced by somatic variation, by mixture and intermarriage; and to evict the possibility of further somatic change or slippage. It is difficult to be sure whether such a shift in the role of the body in ethnic violence is a qualitatively new feature either of modernity or of the most recent decades of globalization or simply an intensification of earlier tendencies. I shall return to this interpretive challenge later.

This sort of brutality belongs to the theatre of divination, sorcery, and witchcraft. It literally turns a body inside out and finds the proof of its betrayal, its deceptions, its definitive otherness, in a sort of premortem autopsy (see also Feldman, 1991: 110–15), which, rather than achieving death because of prior uncertainty, achieves categorical certainty through death and dismemberment. In Peter Geschiere's recent and magisterial analysis of witchcraft in West Africa (1997), with special reference to regional variation in Cameroon, we are presented with a powerful reminder that witchcraft and sorcery, far from being static cultural forms, are elastic and highly flexible moral discourses for bringing to 'account' new forms of wealth, inequality, and power. They both feed and are fed by news of national politics, global flows of commodities, and rumours of illegitimate flows of people and goods. Flourishing in an atmosphere of rumour, deception, and uncertainty, these discourses place large-scale political and economic uncertainties onto maps of kinship and its local discourses of equity and morality. Among the Maka of Cameroon, witchcraft is focused on the frightening figure of the *djambe*, a small creature that occupies the body of the victim and drives him or her to sacrifice their kin, to participate in nocturnal anthropophagic banquets, and thus to 'introduce treason into the most reliable space in Maka society' (Geschiere, 1997: 40), the space of kinship and the household. We shall return to the themes of treason, cannibalism, and morality shortly. For the moment, though this is not Geschiere's principal concern, let us note that the many variations on witchcraft and sorcery studied by anthropologists in sub-Saharan Africa, going back to Evans-Pritchard's classic study (1937) of these matters among the Azande, the sources of witchcraft and sorcery often involve forces and creatures embedded inside the body of the victim/perpetrator, and the establishment of guilt and accountability often involve techniques of bodily investigation, whether of other animals or of humans. Finally, Geschiere is able to show that witchcraft links the world of kinship to the world of ethnicity and politics in Cameroon and is held responsible for the new found wealth and potential power of large ethnic groups. This extension of an idiom of intimacy gone awry to large-scale suspicion of adversarial ethnic groups is a matter that will be re-engaged shortly.

For now, it is sufficient to note that the macabre regularities and predictabilities of ethnocidal violence cannot be taken as simple evidence of 'calculation' or as blind reflexes of 'culture'.[7] Rather, they are brutal forms of bodily discovery — forms of vivisection; emergent techniques for exploring, marking, classifying, and storing the bodies of those who may be the 'ethnic' enemy. Naturally, these brutal actions do not create any real or sustainable sense of secure knowledge. Rather, they exacerbate the frustration of the perpetrators. Worse, they create the conditions for pre-emptive violence among those who fear being victims. This cycle of actual violence and the expectation of violence finds its fuel in certain spatial conditions of information flow, human traffic, and state intervention.

Anthropology has long known about the ways in which the body is a theatre for social performances and productions (Bourdieu, 1977; Comaroff, 1985; Douglas, 1966; van Gennep, 1965; Martin, 1992; Mauss, 1973). Combining Malkki's material on ethnic violence in Burundi with Geschiere's study of witchcraft in Cameroon, against the backdrop of Douglas's path-breaking work on category confusion, power, and taboo, allows us to see that the killing, torture, and rape associated with ethnocidal violence is not simply a matter of eliminating the ethnic other. It involves the use of the body to establish the parameters of this otherness, taking the body apart, so to speak, to divine the enemy within. In this sense, the fruitful studies of witchcraft logics in Africa might have much wider interpretive salience.

The role of the body as a site of violent closure in situations of categorical uncertainty is closely allied with a theme that has already been touched upon, the theme of deception. The literature on ethnocidal violence is shot through with the related tropes of deception, treachery, betrayal, imposture, and secrecy. Considerable sustenance for this view of the suspicion, uncertainty, and cognitive paranoia about the identity of the ethnic enemy comes from a variety of sources. Benedict Anderson has shown the salience of the Nazi fear about the 'secret agency' of Jews in Germany, and the desperate deployment

---

7. This may be the place to note the peculiar relationship between spontaneity and calculation in collective ethnic violence. The emphasis in this essay on uncertainty and vivisection may cast new light on this difficult problem. Existing approaches tend to encounter a missing link between the planned (generally politically motivated) forces behind ethnic violence and the undeniable element of spontaneity. The approach taken here suggests that, at least under certain conditions, the vivisectionist response to uncertainty may mimic modern scientific modes of verification just as the planned aspects of ethnic violence may mimic other legitimate modes of politics that stress procedure, technique, and form. There may thus be an inner affinity between spontaneity and calculation in modern ethnic violence which requires further explanation (cf. Tambiah, 1996).

of all sorts of means to smoke out the 'real' Jews, many of whom seemed 'Aryan' and 'German' in every regard (Anderson, 1991). The murder of Jews under Hitler constitutes a large area of research and of ongoing debate that exceeds the scope of this essay, but the importance of Nazi ideas of racial purity (Aryan-Germanness) for the extraordinary genocidal violence directed against Jews seems beyond debate.

The idea of Jews as 'pretenders' — as ethnic quislings, as a cancer within the German social body — draws our attention to a crucial way in which the Nazi handling of the Jewish body far exceeds the logic of scapegoating, stereotyping, and the like. What it shows is how those needs, under certain conditions, evolve into policies for mass extermination of the ethnic other. This brutally modern fact, which is the peculiarly horrifying feature of the Holocaust (associated with its totality, its bureaucratization, its 'banality', its goal of complete ethnonational purification) is certainly complicated by the special history of European anti-Semitism.[8] However, in its drive for purity through ethnocide and its 'medicalization of anti-semitism' (Proctor, 1995: 172) it sets the stage for the ethnic cleansing of, at least, Eastern Europe, Rwanda-Burundi, and Cambodia in the last two decades, the era of globalization. In the case of Nazi racial ideology, the idea of the Jew as secret agent brings together the ambivalence of German Nazis about race, religion, and economy. Jews were the perfect sites for the exploration of Nazi uncertainty about both Christianity and capitalism. Like the Hutu for the Tutsi, the Jews were 'the enemies within', always potential threats to German national-racial purity, secret agents of racial corruption, of international capital (and, paradoxically, of communism).

As Malkki shows, the theme of secrecy and trickery pervaded Hutu ideas about the Tutsi élite that governed Rwanda. Here seen from the vantage point of the victims, their oppressors appear as 'thieves who stole the country from the indigenous Hutu', as innately skilled in the arts of deception (Malkki, 1995: 68). The Hutu were seen as foreigners who hid their origins, as malign tricksters who were 'hiding their true identity' (ibid: 72).

The trope of deception, fake identity, and betrayal finds further support in the context of the violence perpetrated in North India since the 1980s in

---

8. There is a vast literature about the relationship between German nationalism, Jewish identity, and the dynamics of the Holocaust. Some of this literature, including some work produced by the Frankfurt School, recognizes the relationship between modernity, irrationality, and the fear of international cosmopolitanism represented by Nazi anti-Semitism. It is also apparent that the banalization and mechanization of death in Nazi Germany had much to do with the Jewish body as a site of fear about abstract forms of capital and identity. The recent debates surrounding Daniel Goldhagen's study (1996) of the involvement of ordinary Germans in the extermination of Jews in Nazi Germany have reopened many of these questions. The scope of this literature makes it impossible to take it up intensively here. Suffice it to say that Nazi policies toward Jews raise issues about both purity and clarity in ethnonational projects, which are closely connected to the argument of this essay.

struggles between Hindus and Sikhs, articulated eventually in powerful demands for an autonomous Sikh state (Khalistan). In the discourse of Sikh militants in India, Veena Das (1995) has shown the importance of concern with 'counterfeit' claims to Sikh identity, even where such claims pertained to identities that were not the most legitimate forms of Sikhness. In a chapter on Sikh militant discourse, Das shows how, in the key years of the early 1980s, a Sikh militant discourse emerged in the Punjab which identified the state with Hinduism and Hindus with a dangerous effeminacy that threatened the community of Sikhs conceived as male. This discourse selectively identified key events in the Sikh past and present so as to play down the crucial tensions between Sikhs and Muslims in favour of the current opposition between Sikhs and Hindus. Das has much to say about history and memory, speech and violence, gender and the state, but her crucial concern is with the ways in which militant discourse both represents and induces the possibility of violence through its graphic mobilization of sexual, personal, and political images and narratives and exhortations. In many ways, Das shows how the public speeches of Sikh militants, such as Sant Bhindranwale, transform the experience of individuals into the shame of the community, and thus all violence committed in the name of the Sikhs is justified as individual action against collective injustice, as a step toward martyrdom. The many rich details of this analysis of Sikh militant discourse cannot be engaged here, but two phenomena concerning identity addressed by Das are highly relevant.

Especially in the speeches of Bhindranwale, as cited by Das, a recurring theme is the question of who the Sikhs really are. One vital issue in mobilizing the uncertainty surrounding what it means to be Sikh concerns a breakaway group among the Sikhs, called the Nirankaris. Here is what Das has to say about Sikh militant violence against the Nirankaris in the 1970s and 1980s:

> There is a huge mistrust of alternative definitions of the Sikh community. This comes to the fore in the relationship between Sikh militants and communities on the peripheries of Sikhism. One such community is the Nirankaris, who may be considered a sectarian development within Sikhism. Since the followers of this sect worship a living guru, this being contrary to orthodox Sikh teaching, they were declared enemies of the panth in 1973 by the priests of the Golden Temple. In April 1978 some of Bhindranwale's followers clashed violently with the Nirankaris on both sides ... Though it acknowledges that they were a sect with close connections with the Sikhs, their present forms of worship are considered unacceptable; they are declared 'counterfeit Nirankaris' ... The Nirankaris are declared to be agents of the Hindu government, whose only mission is to destroy Sikhs. (Das, 1995: 133–4)

So here is a vivid example of having to bring the killing close to home to clarify who real Sikhs are and what the label Sikh really means. Note the ideas of 'counterfeit Nirankaris' and of 'agents' of the hostile group (Hindus), along with the terrible fury against the 'pure' Sikh. We are back here with the theme of purity, first remarked by Douglas (1966), then elaborated by Malkki (1995), Robert Hayden (1996), and Michael Herzfeld (1997) in various directions. In Malkki's account, this ideology of the pure and the counterfeit explains the paradoxical sense among Hutu living in refugee camps in Tanzania that their very exile was the sign of their purity as 'Hutu' (and anticipates Bauman's [1997] reflections on purity, strangers and otherness). While the Nazi case shows the power of the discourse of purity for the powerful majority (often using the idiom of the minority as a 'cancer' within the social body), the Sikh case shows the domino effect of violent efforts to cleanse, as they ripple through the victim group, creating further efforts to cleanse grey areas and achieve complete clarity and purity. Of course, clarity and purity are not identical concerns, nor do they call forth similar forms of motive and commitment. While clarity is a matter of cognition, purity is a matter of moral coherence. These dimensions seem to converge in the collective heat of ethnocide, where the logic of cleansing seems both dialectical and self-perpetuating, as one act of 'purification' calls forth its counterpart both from and within the ethnic 'other'. Likewise, purification and clarification appear to be in a dialectical and productive relationship.

The terror of purification and the vivisectionist tendencies that emerge in situations of mass violence also blur the lines between ethnicity and politics. Indeed, just as ethnocide is the limiting form of political violence, so certain forms of political hysteria lead to a quasi-ethnic preoccupation with somatic strategies. This somatic rendition of political identities offers another angle on the issue of masks, counterfeits and treachery. A powerful example of this dynamic comes from China, where Donald Sutton (1995) interprets the significance of widespread reports of cannibalism in Guangxi Province in China in 1968, toward the tail end of the violent phase of the Cultural Revolution. Again, this complex essay takes up a large range of fascinating issues involving cannibalism in the cultural history of this region, its reactivation under the violent conditions of the Cultural Revolution, the complex relations between regional politics and the politics of Beijing, and so on.

What is striking for our purposes in Sutton's analysis is the issue of violence among persons who live in considerable social proximity to one another. Consider this chilling description of the general forms of events of what Sutton calls 'political cannibalism'. The forces of law and order, not the revolutionary rebels, were the killers and eaters. Moreover, the forms of cannibalistic consumption varied within a narrow range. People agreed on the best body parts and insisted on them being cooked; and the selection, killing, and consuming of victims were relatively systematized (Sutton, 1995: 142).

By closely examining what were referred to in Wuxuan as 'human flesh banquets' and what were known during this period as 'struggles' (ritualized events involving accusation, confession, and physical abuse of suspected class enemies), Sutton is able to show convincingly that, while these episodes involved ostensible political categories of persons, their logic appears fully compatible with the sorts of violence we would usually call ethnic. In analysing a related case from Mengshan, Sutton shows how the designation of a man as a 'landlord' made him such a convincing villain that a neighbour did not warn him of his impending murder by a local group of militia.

Sutton also shows how political labels took on immense somatic force: an urban youth cited in one of his sources says of the former landlords, 'I felt that deep in their hearts they still wanted to overthrow everything and kill all of us. In movies, they had awful faces. And in the village when I saw them I feared them and thought they were repulsive to look at. I guess ugliness is a psychological thing'. This remarkable quotation offers a brief glimpse of how political labels (such as 'landlord', 'class enemy', and 'counterrevolutionary') become powerful bearers of affect, and of how, in at least some cases, verbal propaganda and mass-mediated images can literally turn ordinary faces into abominations that must be destroyed.[9] In a final, crucial piece of data from Sutton's essay, a former party leader, when expelled from the party in the early 1980s on the grounds of his earlier cannibalism, says with contempt: 'Cannibalism . . .! It was the flesh of a landlord that was eaten, the flesh of a secret agent' (Sutton, 1995: 162).

With this example, we are back again with the problem of identification and uncertainty, the transformation of neighbours and friends into monsters, and the idea that social appearances are literally masks (Fitzpatrick, 1991, 1995), beneath which truer, deeper, more horrible forms of identity may subsist. 'Secret agency' is found in a wide range of sources that deal with ethnic violence, and it is an indicator of the crucial trigger of the sense of betrayal, treachery, and deception that seems to underwrite its most dramatic expressions. This essay about political cannibalism from China casts an eerie light on descriptions from Bosnian concentration camps in which men were made to bite the severed genitals of friends or fellow prisoners and similar hints of forced cannibalism in other contexts.

---

9. The entire issue of dual identities and split subjectivities has been approached in a highly suggestive manner by Slavoj Zizek (1989) in his creative Lacanian revision of Hegel. As part of this reading, Zizek observes the sense in which anxiety about the resemblance between Jews and German is a key part of anti-Semitism. He also notes the peculiar ways in which Stalinist terror demanded that its victims, in political trials, for example, confess their 'treason' precisely because they are, in some sense, also 'good' communists who recognize the needs of the party for purges and exposures. In both cases, the victims endure the suffering of being both 'us' and 'them' in reference to a totalizing ideology.

   Sheila Fitzpatrick first pointed out to me the salience of the Stalinist trials of 'class traitors' to the general logic of my argument. In her own brief essay on autobiographical narratives and political trials in Stalin's Russia, Fitzpatrick shows that the fear of uncertainty about their class histories affected many Soviet citizens at this time, since everyone had some sort of vulnerability: 'Then their Soviet masks would be torn off; they would be exposed as double dealers and hypocrites, enemies who must be cast out of Soviet society. In the blink of an eye, as in a fairy tale, Gaffner the kolkhoz pioneer would become Haffner the Mennonite kulak. A clap of thunder and the face looking back from Ulianova's mirror would be that of Buber the wicked witch, enemy of the Soviet people' (Fitzpatrick, 1995: 232; see also 1991).

Ethnocidal violence evidently mobilizes some sort of ambient rage about the body as a theatre of deception, of betrayal, and of false solidarity. Whenever the charge of categorical treachery is made to appear plausible, secret agents are unmasked, impure ethnicities are exposed, and horribly cancerous identities are imputed to what we may call the inner body, numerous collective forms of vivisection seem possible, with the most ordinary of people as their perpetrators.

In many of these forms of violence, we can see a horrible range of intimacies. It is of course true that the most extreme forms of ethnic violence involve major dramas of power, of degradation, of violation, and of emotional and physical pain. It is also true that some of this is explicable as part of a cycle of memory and countermemory, where one remembered atrocity becomes the basis for another. However, something else is present in at least some of these situations: that is, this violence is a horrible effort to expose, penetrate, and occupy the material form — the body — of the ethnic other. This may well be the key to the many ways in which sexuality is implicated in recent global forms of ethnic violence. Eating the liver or heart of the exposed 'class enemy' is surely a horrible form of intimacy, and one does not have to make recourse to deeper structural theories about 'friendly' cannibalism to see that eating the enemy is one way of securing a macabre intimacy with the enemy who was so recently a friend.[10] Making one prisoner bite off the genitals of another is an even more grotesque way of simultaneously inflicting deep pain, injury, and insult while imposing a brutal sort of intimacy between enemy bodies.

This may be the place to briefly note that rape in such circumstances is not only tied up with special understandings of honour and shame, and a possible effort to abuse the actual organs of sexual (and thus ethnic) reproduction, but is additionally the most violent form of penetration, investigation, and exploration of the body of the enemy. These factors may account for the renewed salience of rape in ethnic violence. Rape, from this point of view, is the counterpart to the examination of males suspected to be Muslim (in places like Bombay) to check whether they are circumcised. Like the wooden stakes driven through the anus of the ethnic enemy and up into his skull (in the case of Hutu–Tutsi ethnocide reported by Malkki) the penis in ethnocidal rape is simultaneously an instrument of degradation, of purification, and of a grotesque form of intimacy with the ethnic other. This is not of course to suggest that the sexual violence directed against men and women — for

---

10. This sort of brutal intimacy could be viewed as a fatal deformation of the sort of 'cultural intimacy' which Herzfeld (1997) defines as that sense of familiarity, proximity, trust, and inside knowledge that is preserved by local communities in the face of state taxonomies, policies, and stereotypes. Given the delicate line between popular essentialisms and state essentialisms that Herzfeld notes in his larger analysis, it may not be far-fetched to suggest that some sort of intimacy — gone terrifyingly awry, to be sure — is a feature of the vivisectionist quality of much ethnic violence today.

example, in recent events in Eastern Europe — is the same either in quantity or quality. It is clear that, in the history of warfare generally and of ethnic violence more recently, women bear the largest burden as victims of sexual violence.[11] Still, it may be worth considering that there is something that links the violence of ethnocidal rape with other forms of bodily violation and disposal.

In the end, when all the horrible descriptions are read and all the large-scale political, social and economic factors are taken into account, the body remains the site of intimacy, and in the many different forms that bodily violence takes in different contexts, there is a common thread of intimacy gone berserk.[12] Looking at the question of uncertainty and vivisection in the context of intimacy returns one to the question of number and abstraction — and thus of globalization — discussed earlier in this essay.

To repeat, one of the key features of the new ethnic categories is their large-scale, officialized quality. In no case of ethnocide of which we have knowledge can it be shown that these categories are innocent of state practices (usually through the census and often involving crucial forms of welfare or potential punishment). The question is, how can forms of identity and identification of such scope — ethnic labels that are abstract containers for the identities of thousands, often millions, of persons — become transformed into instruments of the most brutally intimate forms of violence? One clue to the way in which these large numerical abstractions inspire grotesque forms of bodily violence is that these forms of violence — forms that I have called vivisectionist — offer temporary ways to render these abstractions graspable, to make these large numbers sensuous, to make labels that are potentially overwhelming, for a moment, personal.[13]

---

11. Several colleagues have suggested to me that in the United States and in the advanced industrial societies of Western Europe many of the features that I see in global ethnic violence are strikingly present in domestic abuse directed against women. This comparative insight opens up the wider question of the links between ethnic and sexual violence and of the structural relation between these forms of violence in more and less wealthy societies. In the current context, this link is a reminder that large-scale violence in the context of intimacy is not restricted to the non-European or less-developed countries of the world.

12. This point resonates with the provocative analysis of power and obscenity in the postcolony by Achille Mbembe, where he discusses the dynamics of 'the intimacy of tyranny' (1992: 22). Here the body appears as the site of greed, excess, and phallocentric power among the ruling élites and thus as the object of scatological intimacy in popular discourse. The relation between this sort of political obscenity and the logic of vivisection which I explore here must await another occasion (see also Mbembe and Roitman, 1995).

13. Of course, not all forms of abstraction in social life conduce to violence, nor have such potentially violent forms of abstraction as the map, the census, and models of economic development always led to coercion or conflict. Here, as elsewhere, one needs to examine the multiple vectors of modernity and the particular ways in which they converge and diverge in the era of globalization. In this most recent epoch of globalization, these instruments of abstraction combine with other forces, such as migration, mediation, and secession to create conditions of heightened uncertainty, but that is not an inherent quantitative or structural property of these abstractions.

To put it in a sanitized manner, the most horrible forms of ethnocidal violence are mechanisms for producing persons out of what are otherwise diffuse, large-scale labels that have effects but no locations.[14] This is why the worst kinds of ethnic violence appear to call for the word 'ritual' or 'ritualized' from their analysts. What is involved here is not just the properties of symbolic specificity, sequence, convention, and even tradition in particular forms of violence but something even more deep about rituals of the body: they are always about the production, growth, and maintenance of persons. This 'life-cycle' aspect of bodily rituals (remarked upon by Arnold van Gennep and many distinguished successors in anthropology) finds its most monstrous inversion in what we may call the 'death-cycle' rituals of mass ethnocide. These horrible counterperformances retain one deep element in common with their life-enhancing counterparts: they are instruments for making persons out of bodies.[15] It may seem odd to speak of the production of persons out of bodies in an argument that rests on the presumption of prior social intimacy (or its possibility) between agents and victims. However, it is precisely in situations where endemic doubts and pressures become intolerable that ordinary people begin to see masks instead of faces. In this perspective, extreme bodily violence may be seen as a degenerate technology for the reproduction of intimacy where it is seen to have been violated by secrecy and treachery.

Through this ritualized mode of concretization we can see how the bodily violence of ethnocide is an instrument for the production of persons in the context of large-scale ethnic identities that have, for whatever reason, turned mutually hostile. It may seem frivolous to suggest that such violence produces persons, in the face of the fact that so much of it is not only degrading and deadly but also literally appears to deconstruct bodies (through various forms of mutilation and butchery). This macabre technique for the production of persons is, of course, special. Nevertheless, in the intimacy and intricacy of preoccupation with body parts and wholes, with penetration and with consumption, with exit and with access, these forms of violence are methods of assuring that some bodies are — without doubt —

---

14. Here and elsewhere in the paper I have preferred the use of person over subject, although the Hegelian idea of subjectivity, as well as its Foucauldian version in respect to violence and agency, is deeply relevant to my analysis. While the idea of the subject is more immediately and explicitly tied to the dialectics of modernity, there is no easy bridge between it and the category of the person that continues to be central to the anthropology of the body and of ritual. I hope to engage more fully with the discursive implications of these key terms in future work on this topic. For now, I can only suggest that my use of the term person is not intended to foreclose the sorts of readings that for some may more comfortably flow from the substitution in such contexts of the idea of the subject.

15. This part of the analysis resonates with many aspects of Feldman's interpretation (1991) of the ceremonial — indeed, sacrificial — overtones of the interrogation and incarceration of political prisoners by state functionaries in Northern Ireland, as well as his account of the transformations of these eschatological procedures by the victims.

real persons. The horrible negativity of this technology is that the production of 'real' persons out of the bodies of traitors, secret agents, and despised group enemies seems to require their vivisection. Here, too, is the link between intimacy and uncertainty. Where fear about ethnic body snatching and secret agency becomes plausible, then producing 'real' ethnic enemies out of the uncertainty posed by thousands of possible secret agents seems to call forth a special order of rage, brutality, and systematicity, all at once. The problem of fake identities seems to demand the brutal creation of real persons through violence. This is the modification I propose to the suggestion of Allen Feldman (1991), echoed by Malkki (1995), that ethnic violence produces abstract tokens of ethnicity out of the bodies of real persons.

Such examples can be multiplied. They testify to one important fact: as large populations occupy complex social spaces and as primary cultural features (clothing, speech styles, residential patterns) are recognized to be poor indicators of ethnicity, there tends to be a steady growth in the search for 'inner' or 'concealed' signs of a person's 'real' identity. The maiming and mutilation of ethnicized bodies is a desperate effort to restore the validity of somatic markers of 'otherness' in the face of the uncertainties posed by census labels, demographic shifts, and linguistic changes, all of which make ethnic affiliations less somatic and bodily, more social and elective. Mixed marriages, of the sort that have long taken place in many cosmopolitan regions and cities, are the biggest obstacles to simple tests of ethnic 'otherness' (Hayden, 1996). It is such facts that set the stage for the body as a site for resolving uncertainty through brutal forms of violation, investigation, deconstruction, and disposal.

This proposal — linking categorical uncertainty to the bodily brutalities of ethnocide — builds on other components of a general theory of ethnic violence, many of which are already in place: the classificatory policies of many colonial states; the large involuntary migrations created by such powerful states as Stalin's USSR; the confusions created by policies of affirmative action applied by democratic constitutions to quasi-ethnic classifications, such as the 'Scheduled' Castes created by the Indian Constitution; the stimuli of arms, money, and political support involved in diasporic populations, creating what Benedict Anderson (1994) has called 'long-distance' nationalism; the velocity of image circulation created by Cable News Network, the World Wide Web, faxes, phones, and other media in exposing populations in one place to the goriest details of violence in another; the major social upheavals since 1989 in Eastern Europe and elsewhere that have created dramatic fears about winners and losers in the new open market, thus creating new forms of scapegoating, as with Jews and Gypsies in Romania (Verdery, 1990).

These larger forces — global mass mediation, increased migration, both forced and voluntary, sharp transformations in national economies, severed links between territory, citizenship, and ethnic affiliation — return us to the theme of globalization, within which the argument was earlier framed. It is not hard to see the general ways in which transnational forces impinge on local ethnic instabilities. Hayden's (1996) discussion of national populations, censuses, and constitutions in the former Yugoslavia, and the resultant drive to eliminate the 'unimaginable' in new national formations, is one clear demonstration of the steps that lead from global and European politics (and history) to imperial breakup and ethnic meltdown, especially in those zones characterized by the greatest degree of ethnic mixture through intermarriage. However, the road from constitutional mandates to bodily brutality cannot wholly be handled at the level of categorical contradiction. The peculiar and ghastly forms of vivisection that have characterized recent ethnocidal violence (both in Eastern Europe and elsewhere) carry a surplus of rage that calls for an additional interpretive frame, in which uncertainty, purity, treachery, and bodily violence can be linked. This surplus or excess makes sense of the hyperrationalities — noted throughout this essay — that accompany what seems to be the hysteria of these events: the quasi-ritual order, the attention to detail, the specificity of bodily violation, the systematicity of the forms of degradation.

Yet globalization does not produce just one road to uncertainty, terror, or violence. In this essay I have identified a logic for the production of 'real persons' which links uncertainty, purity, treachery, and vivisection. There are surely other 'ethnocidal imaginaries'[16] in which the forces of global capital, the relative power of states, varying histories of race and class and differences in the status of mass mediation, produce different kinds of uncertainty and different scenarios for ethnocide. The examples I have relied on here — the People's Republic of China in the late 1960s, Central Africa in the 1970s, North India in the early 1980s, and Central Europe in the late 1980s and early 1990s — do not have either the same spatial or temporal relationship to the process of globalization. In each case, the degree of openness to global capital, the legitimacy of the state, the internal and external flow of ethnic populations, and the variety of political struggles over group entitlement were clearly not the same. Though the vivisectionist hypothesis put forward here may not thus apply uniformly in these cases, its critical elements — purity, clarity, treachery, and agency — may well provide key ingredients that might be recombined fruitfully to cast some degree of light on them.

In an earlier effort to analyse the link between large-scale identities, the abstraction of large numbers, and the theatre of the body, I suggested that global forces are best seen as 'imploding' into localities, deforming their normative climate, recasting their politics, and representing their contingent characters and plots as instances of larger narratives of betrayal and loyalty (Appadurai, 1996: 149–57). In the present context, the idea of implosion might account for actions at the most local of globalized sites — the

---

16. I am grateful to Dipesh Chakrabarty (personal communication) for this striking phrase and for alerting me to the dangers of moving from global questions to globalizing answers.

ethnicized body, which, in already confused and contradictory circumstances, can become the most natural, the most intimate, and thus the most horrifying site for tracking the somatic signs of the enemy within. In ethnocidal violence, what is sought is just that somatic stabilization that globalization — in a variety of ways — inherently makes impossible. In a twisted version of Popperian norms for verification in science, paranoid conjectures produce dismembered refutations.[17]

The view advanced here of ethnocidal violence between social intimates is not only about uncertainty about the 'other'. Obviously, these actions indicate a deep and dramatic uncertainty about the ethnic self. They arise in circumstances where the lived experience of large labels becomes unstable, indeterminate, and socially volatile, so that violent action can become one means of satisfying one's sense of one's categorical self. Of course the violent epistemology of bodily violence, the 'theatre of the body' on which this violence is performed, is never truly cathartic, satisfying, or terminal. It only leads to a deepening of social wounds, an epidemic of shame, a collusion of silence, and a violent need for forgetting. All these effects add fresh underground fuel for new episodes of violence. This is also partly a matter of the pre-emptive quality of such violence: let me kill you before you kill me. Uncertainty about identification and violence can lead to actions, reactions, complicities, and anticipations that multiply the pre-existing uncertainty about labels. Together, these forms of uncertainty call for the worst kind of certainty: dead certainty.

ACKNOWLEDGEMENTS

Earlier versions of this essay were presented before audiences in Amsterdam, Cambridge (MA), Chicago, Paris, and Rio de Janeiro. The valuable criticisms and suggestions offered to me on these occasions were too numerous to fully engage in this revision. Many persons who raised valuable questions at these sessions cannot be named here, for the list would be too long. However, I must note the encouragement, queries, and suggestions of the following persons: Anthony Appiah, Fredrik Barth, Jean-François Bayart, Jacqueline Bhabha, Dipesh Chakrabarty, Sheila Fitzpatrick, Susan Gal, Manu Goswami, Michael Herzfeld, Marilyn Ivy, Beatrice Jaguaribe, Pradeep Jeganathan, Rashid Khalidi, David Laitin, Ben Lee, Claudio Lomnitz, Achille Mbembe, Candido Mendes, Birgit Meyer, Federico Neiburg, Peter Pels, Enrique Rodrigues, Janet Roitman, Roger Rouse, Livio Sansone, Doris Sommer, George Steinmetz, Mary Steedly, Ron Suny, Stanley Tambiah, Xiaobing Tang, Katie Trumpener, Peter van der Veer, and Unni Wikan. Special thanks are due to Carol Breckenridge and Peter Geschiere, friendly critics and patient creditors, who urged me to pay equal attention to deadlines and to deliberation.

---

17. The issues alluded to in these concluding remarks will be pursued more fully in the larger work of which this essay is a preview. Close attention will be paid to the question of what distinguishes situations that share a large number of features with other situations of globalized stress but do not produce ethnocidal violence. Likewise, the complex epidemiology that relates various forms of knowledge (including propaganda, rumour, and memory) to various forms of uncertainty will be explored more fully.

REFERENCES

Abu-Lughod, Janet L. (1993) *The World System in the Thirteenth Century: Dead-End or Precursor?* Washington, DC: American Historical Association.

Anderson, Benedict R. (1991) *Imagined Communities: Reflections on the Origin and Spread of Nationalism.* London: Verso.

Anderson, Benedict R. (1994) 'Exodus', *Critical Inquiry* 20(2): 314–27.

Appadurai, Arjun (1996) *Modernity at Large: Cultural Dimensions of Globalization.* Minneapolis, MN: University of Minnesota Press.

Bauman, Zygmunt (1997) *Postmodernity and Its Discontents.* Cambridge: Polity Press.

Bourdieu, Pierre (1977) *Outline of a Theory of Practice.* Cambridge: Cambridge University Press.

Comaroff, Jean (1985) *Body of Power, Spirit and Resistance: The Culture and History of a South African People.* Chicago, IL: University of Chicago Press.

Daniel, Valentine E. (1996) *Charred Lullabies: Chapters in an Anthropology of Violence.* Princeton, NJ: Princeton University Press.

Das, Veena (1990) *Mirrors of Violence: Communities, Riots and Survivors in South Asia.* Delhi: Oxford University Press.

Das, Veena (1995) *Critical Events: An Anthropological Perspective on Contemporary India.* Delhi: Oxford University Press.

Desjarlais, Robert and A. Kleinman (1994) 'Violence and Demoralization in the New World Disorder', *Anthropology Today* 10(5): 9–12.

Devisch, Rene (1995) 'Frenzy, Violence and Ethical Renewal in Kinshasa', *Public Culture* 7(3): 593–629.

Douglas, Mary (1966) *Purity and Danger: An Analysis of Concepts of Purity and Taboo.* London: Routledge and Kegan Paul.

Douglas, Mary (1973) *Natural Symbols: Explorations in Cosmology.* London: Routledge.

Durkheim, Emile (1951) *Suicide: A Study in Sociology.* Glencoe, IL: Free Press.

Evans-Pritchard, Edward E. (1937) *Witchcraft, Oracles and Magic among the Azande.* Oxford: Clarendon Press.

Feldman, Allen (1991) *Formations of Violence: The Narrative of the Body and Political Terror in Northern Ireland.* Chicago, IL: University of Chicago Press.

Fitzpatrick, Sheila (1991) 'The Problem of Class Identity in Nep Society', in Sheila Fitzpatrick, Alexander Rabinowitch and Richard Stites (eds) *Russia in the Era of the Nep: Explorations in Soviet Society and Culture*, pp. 12–33. Bloomington, IN: Indiana University Press.

Fitzpatrick, Sheila (1995) 'Lives under Fire: Autobiographical Narratives and Their Challenges in Stalin's Russia', in Martine Godet (ed.) *De Russie et d'ailleurs*, pp. 225–32. Paris: Institut d'Études Slaves.

van Gennep, Arnold (1965) *The Rites of Passage.* London: Kegan Paul.

Geschiere, Peter (1997) *The Modernity of Witchcraft: Politics and the Occult in Postcolonial Africa.* Charlottesville, VA: University Press of Virginia.

Goldhagen, Daniel (1996) *Hitler's Willing Executioners: Ordinary Germans and the Holocaust.* New York: Knopf.

Harvey, David (1989) *The Condition of Postmodernity: An Enquiry into the Origins of Cultural Change.* Oxford: Blackwell.

Hayden, Robert (1996) 'Imagined Communities and Real Victims: Self-Determination and Ethnic Cleansing in Yugoslavia', *American Ethnologist* 23(4): 783–801.

Herzfeld, Michael (1992) *The Social Production of Indifference: Exploring the Symbolic Roots of Western Bureaucracy.* Chicago, IL: University of Chicago Press.

Herzfeld, Michael (1997) *Cultural Intimacy: Social Poetics in the Nation-State.* New York: Routledge.

Hoffman, Piotr (1986) *Doubt, Time, Violence.* Chicago, IL: University of Chicago Press.

Hoffman, Piotr (1989) *Violence in Modern Philosophy*. Chicago, IL: University of Chicago Press.

Ismail, Qadri (1995) 'Unmooring Identity: The Antinomies of Elite Muslim Self-representation in Modern Sri Lanka', in Pradeep Jeganathan and Qadri Ismail (eds) *Unmaking the Nation: The Politics of Identity and History in Modern Sri Lanka*, pp. 55–105. Colombo, Sri Lanka: Social Scientists' Association.

Jeganathan, Pradeep (1997) 'After a Riot: Anthropological Locations of Violence in an Urban Sri Lankan Community'. PhD Thesis. Department of Anthropology, University of Chicago.

Kristeva, Julia (1991) *Strangers to Ourselves*. New York: Columbia University Press.

Lash, Scott and John Urry (1987) *The End of Organized Capitalism*. Madison, WI: University of Wisconsin Press.

Lash, Scott and John Urry (1994) *Economies of Signs and Space*. London: Sage.

Malkki, Liisa H. (1995) *Purity and Exile: Violence, Memory, and National Cosmology among Hutu Refugees in Tanzania*. Chicago, IL: University of Chicago Press.

Martin, Emily (1992) 'The End of the Body?', *American Ethnologist* 19(1): 121–40.

Mauss, Marcel (1973) 'Techniques of the Body', *Economy and Society* 2(1): 70–85.

Mbembe, Achille (1992) 'The Banality of Power and the Aesthetics of Vulgarity in the Postcolony' (Janet Roitman, trans.), *Public Culture* 4(2): 1–30.

Mbembe, Achille and J. Roitman (1995) 'Figures of the Subject in Times of Crisis', *Public Culture* 7(2): 323–52.

Nordstrom, Carolyn (1997) *A Different Kind of War Story*. Philadelphia, PA: University of Pennsylvania Press.

Pandey, Gyanendra (1997) 'Can a Muslim Be an Indian?' Unpublished ms.

Price, Monroe E. (1994) 'The Market for Loyalties: Electronic Media and the Global Competition for Allegiances', *Yale Law Journal* 104(3): 667–705.

Proctor, Robert N. (1995) 'The Destruction of "Lives Not Worth Living" ', in Jennifer Terry and Jacqueline Urla (eds) *Deviant Bodies*, pp. 170–96. Bloomington, IN: Indiana University Press.

Rouse, Roger (1995) 'Thinking through Transnationalism: Notes on the Cultural Politics of Class Relations in the Contemporary United States', *Public Culture* 7(2): 353–402.

Sassen, Saskia (1996) *Losing Control: Sovereignty in an Age of Globalization*. New York: Columbia University Press.

Simmel, Georg (1950) 'The Stranger', in Kurt H. Wolff (trans. and ed.) *The Sociology of Georg Simmel*, pp. 402–8. Glencoe, IL: Free Press.

Sutton, Donald S. (1995) 'Consuming Counterrevolution: The Ritual and Culture of Cannibalism in Wuxuan, Guangxi, China, May to July 1968', *Comparative Studies in Society and History* 37(1): 136–72.

Tambiah, Stanley J. (1996) *Leveling Crowds: Ethnonationalist Conflicts and Collective Violence in South Asia*. Berkeley, CA: University of California Press.

Verdery, Katherine (1990) *National Ideology under Socialism: Identity and Cultural Politics in Ceausescu's Romania*. Berkeley, CA: University of California Press.

Wallerstein, Immanuel (1974) *The Modern World-System*. San Diego, CA: Academic Press.

Zizek, Slavoj (1989) *The Sublime Object of Ideology*. London: Verso.

Epilogue: On Some Reports from a Free Space

Ulf Hannerz

In his very interesting article on contemporary African witchcraft and East Asian spirit cults, Peter Geschiere notes that both involve a kind of 'free space' for an exuberant production of meaning (and perhaps a tough struggle for interpretative control as well). Reflecting on the broad range of materials and analytical emphases presented in his and other contributions to this volume, one may be tempted to think of 'globalization' itself as a somewhat similar cult in the human sciences at the end of the twentieth century. The recognition of global and transnational interconnectedness, in several disciplines but not least in anthropology, has had an emancipatory effect as scholars have allowed themselves to take a more conscious, critical view of the local and 'national' (state) frames within which they have had a habit of placing their research.[1] And so the 'free space' of globalization, for some time anyway, serves as an attractive intellectual habitat in which a great many interests can be cultivated. If only a couple of decades ago 'globalization' was barely a keyword in our vocabulary, perhaps ten years from now these interests will again belong in a range of different compartments. It is hardly likely that globalization itself will have gone away, but more probable that it will have become so normalized that it may frequently be understood rather more as a context than as a focus of many research interests.

At this point, however, it is not surprising that it can bring together the variety of topics represented here — diasporas, border crossings, ritualized violence, civilizational ideology, citizenship laws, consumption, popular culture — and a great many more. The editors have provided an elegant overview of the contributions in their Introduction. I can therefore limit myself to some brief comments on a handful of issues raised in these reports from a free, but certainly no longer empty, space.

To begin with, we might note, as the editors also point out, that several of the articles support the critical stance many of us have by now developed toward assumptions and catchwords which, despite everything, still remain part of (to use Janet Abu-Lughod's 1991 term) the global-babble of our times. Globalization does not mean global homogenization; witchcraft is alive and well in Africa, although changing with new circumstances. This is

---

1. Perhaps I take a rosier view of this emancipation here than the editors, who begin their Introduction by referring to 'problems and uneasy feelings'. I should also note that it is possible to assemble a rather fragmented, discontinuous but not entirely useless past for transnational anthropology (cf. Hannerz, 1997).

not a 'borderless world'; the point is rather that borders are not absolute barriers, but that they become significant social, cultural, political, economic and legal facts in the way they are crossed — in the Caucasus, between Mexico and the United States, between Angola and what was until recently Zaire, within the European Union. To deal with globalization is to deal with diversity under increasing interconnectedness.

A theme which is recurrent in this collection might be labelled 'imagined worlds'. In an earlier publication, Appadurai (1991: 197ff.) drew attention to the fact that globalization has altered the balance between actual and possible, imaginable lives. Whoever or wherever you are, you are less likely to be dependent on your everyday mundane experience for ideas about what is and what could be — not only the dream factories of Hollywood or Bombay, but imported consumer goods, and alien newcomers in your neigh-bourhood, may suggest alternative materials for your fantasy.

Van Binsbergen turns the idea around, in his intriguing elaboration of a notion of virtuality where he perhaps straddles the line between what Robertson (1992: 146) has distinguished as 'nostalgic theory' and 'the theory of nostalgia'. Here African townspeople are seen, figuratively, to transport themselves back, in selected contexts, to an imagined village.[2] The more outward looking kind of imagination becomes evident, for example, in De Boeck's lively frontier zone between (what was) Zaire and Angola, as well as in the same author's retrospective view of earlier Zairean urban youth subcultures, where the culture heroes of 'Billism' were Buffalo Bill and Pecos Bill. Here the widened horizons may include models for an improved, more interesting and fashionable you.[3] Yet as Appadurai (1991) points out, the observation that the sources of fantasy have changed is not necessarily a cheerful one. Globalization entails not only new and better opportunities (when it does so at all) but also new risks, greater uncertainty; perhaps more suspicions. In his article in this volume, on recent horrors of ethnic violence, Appadurai turns to the darkest corners of what he sees as global implosion. In Geschiere's interpretation of the postcolonial reconfiguration of African witchcraft, too, we learn that witchcraft discourses go well with the open imaginary landscapes of globalization. Geschiere and Appadurai both recognize the parallels between their arguments.

As I have noted elsewhere, one almost expects any mention of global-ization nowadays to be accompanied by either booing or cheering; but taken as a whole, it is really too complicated and diverse to be either applauded or condemned. Nevertheless, we must be aware that there are people in many

---

2. At this point, let me note that I do not accept van Binsbergen's argument that I have disregarded the fact that many African urbanites are born outside town, and that this might be reflected in their 'urban patterns of signification'. In my book *Exploring the City* (1980: Ch.4–5), I draw attention to contexts of rural-urban cultural continuity in a number of places.
3. I have discussed similar West African materials elsewhere (Hannerz, 1984).

places who are worried by too much openness, by borders seen as too easily crossed. Geschiere's and Appadurai's discussions here of contemporary witchcraft and ethnic violence also remind me of current varieties of 'cultural fundamentalism' in Europe, as described by Verena Stolcke (1995). According to the assumptions of cultural fundamentalism, human beings are by nature culture bearers; cultures are distinct and incommensurable; relations between bearers of different cultures are intrinsically conflictive; and it is human nature to be xenophobic. Such cultural fundamentalism, Stolcke points out, differs from traditional racism in that it does not necessarily carry with it assumptions of hierarchy. It may well proclaim a sort of cultural relativism, but then each culture should stay in its place. As they are incommensurable, they must be spatially segregated. Cultural fundamentalism thus now serves, not least in Europe, as an alternative doctrine of exclusion. It is a nativist reaction against transnational migration, against the presence of strangers. Probably at times, its tenets also have some part in resistance to European integration, that 'ever closer union among the peoples of Europe'. In virulent forms, it has led to physical attacks and fire bombings. At higher levels and in more sophisticated forms, as Jacqueline Bhabha notes in her article, it may also find some expression in the treatment of 'third country nationals' within the legal framework of the European Union.

The notion of 'identity politics' may sometimes have seemed to be something characteristically North American. In the form of cultural fundamentalism, however, it is clearly a more widespread phenomenon. Moreover, it occurs at varied levels. Recently, Samuel Huntington's thesis about 'the clash of civilizations' has indeed suggested a globalization of identity politics — with the worst scenario setting the West against the Muslims and the Confucians: 'We know who we are only when we know who we are not and often only when we know whom we are against' (Huntington, 1996: 21).

I am again reminded of Huntington's argument as I read Prasenjit Duara's account of Asian redemptive transnationalisms in earlier periods of the twentieth century. Here, too, the message was one of Asia against the West. Yet in Duara's treatment, this becomes less of an enduring civilizational fact and more a complex of ideas with which different actors maneuver, in shifting historical contexts. Towards the end of his article, Duara points to ways in which, as the century draws to a close, such ideas once more have to seek an intellectual and ideological niche within a new set of circumstances. It seems to be along such lines — bringing people back in, seeing civilizations as internally diverse entities with blurred boundaries, and attending to their changing internal cultural debates (often with external sources of inspiration) — that historians and anthropologists can contribute to an understanding of contemporary civilization(s) substantially different from Huntington's. And, indeed, one finds such contributions elsewhere in this collection as well.

Finally, some comments on identity, and on diffusion. I will admit to belonging to those who are a little sceptical of the prominence that 'identity' has achieved in the current vocabulary of the human sciences, and not least in anthropology.[4] Certainly it occurs with much greater frequency now than it did, say, a few decades ago (when the senior contributors to this volume began their research careers). Why do we need it now in a way that we did not seem to need it then? Perhaps we have become wiser, and more sensitive. Or perhaps it is because the world has really changed, so that whereas before people would go about their 'identity work' without noticing it much (embedded as it could be in daily routines), they now face uncertainties — brought not least by globalization itself — which are also uncertainties about self and other. Some of the papers here surely suggest that this is part of the answer. Issues of identity would thus grow more or less spontaneously out of varied local contexts.

On the other hand, there has also no doubt been a tendency for the terms of identityspeak to become intellectual export goods, in a trade where academics have played a part alongside media, movements and a number of other cultural brokers. There may have been some reluctance to admit this, not least among anthropologists, and I believe the editors are right when they suggest in their Introduction that the preoccupation with identity is in part related to a lingering (or even renewed) professional celebration of the local. Even as we reject the conception of globalization as global homogenization, however, I believe we also need to take seriously, and try to develop our analytical grasp of, the occurrence of transnational diffusion — of various kinds, through many channels, and frequently involving simultaneous processes of reinterpretation and changes of form. The intercontinental spread of identity discourse and identity politics during the last third of the twentieth century seems to me to be an intriguing question in contemporary world cultural history.

No doubt it would be naive to try to identify a single source, an 'Ancient Egypt' of identity ideas from which everything would flow; yet it seems to me that the late 1960s turn of African-Americans from more assimilationist/ integrationist strategies toward more dramatic self-affirmation had some special significance here, nationally in the United States as well as globally, not least due to media attention.[5]

This argument that we should also try to develop our understandings of diffusion — as part of our attempt to 'grasp the flux' — also relates to points raised by John Kelly at the end of his complex critique of Benedict Anderson, where (acknowledging Bernard Cohn) he emphasizes the need to look seriously at the aftermath of World War II. A part of that accelerating dynamic of constructing a formal symmetry among the 'nation-states' of the world has clearly involved major organized processes of diffusion, in

---

4. I find Roger Rouse's (1995) critical discussion, in the context of his work on Mexican migration to the United States, very illuminating here.
5. Possibly, however, I am inclined to attach such importance to that historical shift because I was close to it in my first field study.

considerable part managed by international organizations and agencies (not least within the 'United Nations family'). The work on such processes by John Meyer and his collaborators (for example, Meyer et al., 1997) should be interesting, even provocative, to many anthropologists concerned with the present overall ordering of globalization. While anthropologists are still habitually rejecting 'diffusionism', it appears, sociologists have been quietly reconstructing it.

REFERENCES

Abu-Lughod, Janet (1991) 'Going Beyond Global Babble', in Anthony D. King (ed.) *Culture, Globalization and the World-System*. Binghamton, NY: MRTS.

Appadurai, Arjun (1991) 'Global Ethnoscapes: Notes and Queries for a Transnational Anthropology', in Richard G. Fox (ed.) *Recapturing Anthropology*. Santa Fe, NM: School of American Research Press.

Hannerz, Ulf (1980) *Exploring the City*. New York: Columbia University Press.

Hannerz, Ulf (1984) 'Tools of Identity and Imagination', in Anita Jacobson-Widding (ed.) *Identity: Personal and Socio-Cultural*. Stockholm: Almqvist & Wiksell International.

Hannerz, Ulf (1997) 'Fluxos, fronteiras, híbridos: palavras-chave da antropologia transnacional', *Mana* (Rio de Janeiro) 3(1): 7–39.

Huntington, Samuel P. (1996) *The Clash of Civilizations and the Remaking of World Order*. New York: Simon & Schuster.

Meyer, John W., John Boli, George M. Thomas and Francisco O. Ramirez (1997) 'World Society and the Nation-State', *American Journal of Sociology* 103: 144–81.

Robertson, Roland (1992) *Globalization*. London: Sage.

Rouse, Roger (1995) 'Questions of Identity: Personhood and Collectivity in Transnational Migration to the United States', *Critique of Anthropology* 15: 351–80.

Stolcke, Verena (1995) 'Talking Culture: New Boundaries, New Rhetorics of Exclusion in Europe', *Current Anthropology* 36: 1–13.

Notes on Contributors

Arjun Appadurai is Samuel N. Harper Professor of Anthropology at the University of Chicago, where he is also Director of the Globalization Project. The author of many books and journal articles, his most recent book is *Modernity at Large: Cultural Dimensions of Globalization* (1996).

Jacqueline Bhabha, formerly a practising human rights lawyer in London specializing in immigration and refugee law, is now Director of the Human Rights programme at the University of Chicago. She is the author/co-author of several books, including *Women's Movement: Women under Immigration, Nationality and Refugee Law* (1994), and of articles on globalization, human rights and European law. She is currently conducting research on children's rights, European asylum and immigration law, and citizenship in Europe.

Wim van Binsbergen is chair of the theme group 'Globalization and Sociocultural Transformations' at the African Studies Centre, Leiden. He has been Professor of Ethnic Studies at the Free University Amsterdam since 1990, and has recently been appointed to the chair of Foundations of Intercultural Philosophy, Erasmus University Rotterdam. His latest book, *Sub-Saharan Africa, Ancient Egypt and the World: Beyond the Black Athena Thesis* is currently at press. Besides his many scholarly works, he has also published extensively as a poet and novelist. His globalized symbolic production includes a practice as a Botswana-licensed traditional healer.

Filip De Boeck received his PhD in medical anthropology from the University of Leuven and is currently Assistant Professor at the Leuven Department of Anthropology. He has conducted long-term field research in southwestern Congo (formerly Zaire). His main theoretical interests include processes of state collapse, crisis analysis, local politics and ritual processes in the postcolony. His research has produced numerous articles in various academic journals and books, and he also co-edited the volume *Alimentations, traditions et développements en Afrique intertropicale* (1995). He is currently preparing a book about the impact of diamond trading on rural and urban life in Congo.

Mamadou Diouf is Professor of Modern and Contemporary History at the Cheikh Anta Diop University (Dakar). At present, he is Director of the Research and Documentation Programme of CODESRIA (Council for the Development of Social Sciences in Africa), in Senegal. He has published extensively on the history and the politics of Senegal and Africa in general. He is currently preparing a book on 'urban inventions' in nineteenth and twentieth century Senegal.

Prasenjit Duara was born in Assam, India, and was educated in Delhi and Harvard Universities. He is Professor of History at the University of Chicago, and is the author of many books and articles, including *Culture, Power and the State: Rural North China, 1900–1942* (1988, 1991) *Rescuing History from the Nation: Questioning Narratives of Modern China* (1995, 1996), and 'Historicizing National Identity, or Who Imagines What and When', in Geoff Eley and Ronald G. Suny (eds) *Becoming National — A Reader* (1996). His books have been translated into both Chinese and Japanese and he has recently had a Guggenheim fellowship to work on a manuscript tentatively entitled, 'World Culture and the Frontiers of the East Asian Modern'.

Peter Geschiere is Professor of African Anthropology at the University of Leiden. His main field-work has been conducted in various parts of Cameroon. His recent publications include *The Modernity of Witchcraft, Politics and the Occult in Postcolonial Africa* (1997); and, together with Josef Gugler, *The Rural-Urban Connection, Changing Issues of Belonging and Identification in Postcolonial Africa*, a special issue of *Africa* (1998).

Ulf Hannerz is Professor of Social Antropology at Stockholm University, Sweden. His current research is on transnational cultural processes, including a project on news media foreign correspondents. His most recent books are *Cultural Complexity* (1992) and *Transnational Connections* (1996). He is the Antropology editor for the forthcoming *International Encyclopedia of the Social and Behavioural Sciences*.

John D. Kelly is an Associate Professor in the Department of Anthropology at the University of Chicago. His publications include *A Politics of Virtue: Hinduism, Sexuality, and Counter-Colonial Discourse in Fiji* (1991), and more recently, 'Aspiring to Minority and Other Tactics Against Violence in Fiji', in Dru Gladney (ed.) *Making Majorities* (1998), and 'Gaze and Grasp: Plantations, Desires, and Colonial Law in Fiji', in Margaret Jolly and Lenore Manderson (eds) *Sites of Desire/Economies of Pleasure: Sexualities in Asia and the Pacific* (1997). Jointly with Martha Kaplan, he is currently working on two book projects that connect issues in globalization to colonial history, *Laws Like Bullets: Imagined Disorder Made Real in British Colonies* and *Nation and Decolonization*.

Norman Long is Professor and Head of Development Sociology at Wageningen Agricultural University. He has also held chairs at the Universities of Durham and Bath (UK). He is currently directing field research on globalization, migration and changing livelihoods in Mexico and the Highlands of Peru. His recent publications include: *Battlefields of Knowledge* (1992), 'Globalization and Localization: New Challenges to Rural Research', in H. Moore (ed.) *The Future of Anthropological Knowledge* (1996); *Images* *and Realities of Rural Life*, co-edited with Henk de Haan (1997), and *Myths, Monsters and Modernity: An Anthropological Perspective on Development*, with A. Arce (forthcoming in 1999).

Birgit Meyer is a lecturer at the Research Centre 'Religion and Society' at the University of Amsterdam. She has conducted extensive historical and ethnographic research on the emergence of local appropriations of Christianity among the Ewe in southeastern Ghana. This study has resulted in a number of articles and her book *Translating the Devil. Religion and Modernity Among the Ewe in Ghana* (forthcoming in 1999). She is currently carrying out research on globalization and popular culture in Accra.

Seteney Shami is a Jordanian anthropologist who obtained ber degrees from the American University of Beirut and the University of California, Berkeley. From 1982 to 1995 she taught at Yarmouk University in Jordan, and was the founding chair of the Anthropology Department. She has been a visiting professor at the University of California, Berkeley, Georgetown University, the University of Chicago and Stockholm University. She is currently director of MEAwards, a regional research programme in population and the social sciences based in Cairo. Her research interests include ethnicity and nationalism, urban politics and population displacement in the Arab countries, Turkey and the North Caucasus.

Magdalena Villarreal is Senior Researcher at CIESAS Occidente (Centre for Research and Advanced Studies in Social Anthropology in Guadalajara, Mexico), where she is co-ordinator of the MSc programme. Her recent publications include: 'The Poverty of Practice', in N. Long and A. Long (eds) *Battlefields of Knowledge* (1992), 'Secretos de poder: el estado y la mujer campesina', in *Nueva Anthropología* (1996), 'Las hijos de vecino ante la crisis en el agro', in Valencia (ed.), *A Dos Anos. Bienestar par La Familia* (1997), and 'Power and identity in the forging of a project', in Melhuus and Stølen (eds), *Machos, Mistresses and Madonnas: The power of Latin American gender imagery* (1996).

INDEX

Africa (*see also* Cameroon; Ghana; Senegal; Zaire; Zambia), 9, 10; village society, 200–1, 281–5; witchcraft in, 211, 200–30, 231, 237

Ahmut v. The Netherlands, 117, 118

Algeria, Islam in, 87, 88

allochronism, 260–4

Anderson, B., 19, 241, 312–13; *Imagined Communities*, 243–8, 249, 253, 255, 256, 265–6, 268

Angola, diamond trade with Zaire, 180–4

Appadurai, A., 3, 126, 216, 278–9

Ardener, E., 223

Aron, R., 110

Asad, T., 263, 264

Asian cultures, 56, 58–9, 67

assimilation, 24, 75–6; law and, 85–93; religion and, 79–85

Austen, R., 231n

Badie, B., 42

Balibar, E., 116

bana Lunda, 179, 187–8, 195–6, 201, 202, 205–6

Baohuanghui (Society to Protect the Emperor), 64–5

Battaglia, D., 201

Bauman, Z., 305

Bayart, J-F., 10

Benedict, R., 251–2, 260–2, 268

Bengal, Permanent Settlement in, 253–4

Benjamin, W., 241, 245, 249, 250, 265; Anderson and, 246–8

Bhindranwale, S., 314

Bhopal, 102–3

Binsbergen, W. van, 326

Bittremieux, L., 185

Bloch, E., 260n, 262

body, as site of ethnic violence, 308–12, 317–19, 321–2

Boilat, Father David, 79–80, 81, 82, 83–4

Bou El Moghdad Seck, 84

Buddhism, 54–5

California, consumption practices, 136–42

Cameroon, witchcraft in, 220–30, 233, 311–12

Caucasus, 23, 25–6; journey of Circassians to, 27–38, 39–42

Chatterjee, P., 9

Chechnya, 31

Chen Lifu, 55

China: cannibalism in, 315–16; nationalism in, 47; transnationalism in, 50–68

Christianity (*see also* pentecostalism; Roman Catholic Church), 153–5

chronopolitics, 259–64

Circassians, 23; identity of, 24–5, 26, 27–31; migrations of, 23–4, 28; returns to homeland, 27–38, 39–42

citizenship, 39, 48–9, 77, 83, 93-4; European, 107–12; Macaulay and, 257

civic nationalism, 21, 48–9

civil law, and Islamic law, 85–93

Clifford, J., 43

colonialism, 55–7, 62–4, 254–5; in Senegal, 72–94

Comaroff, Jean, 5n, 211, 213, 214–15

Comaroff, John, 211

commodities, 12, 151, 152, 169–70; networks of, 125–6, 130–6; origins of, 167–8

consumption: and appropriation, 167–8, 170–2; pentecostalism and, 164–8, 172–3; wealth and, 192–3

Convention on the Elimination of All Forms of Discrimination against Women, 103

Convention on the Rights of the Child, 103

Convention of the Status of Refugees, 104, 120

Copet-Rougier, E., 226

creolization, 252, 253, 278

cultural identity, globalization of food and, 130, 136–42, 146–8

culture, 1–2, 3–4, 79, 92

Dai Jitao, 57

Das, V., 314

Debre, J-L., 116

Debrunner, H.W., 164

Deleuze, G., 203

Deng Xiaoping, 48

Diagne, Blaise, 93

diamond trade, 12–13, 177–8, 179–84, 197; and territorialization, 199–203

diamonds, 187–9, 192–3

diasporas, 17–18, 38–44, 249–51

Douglas, M., 310

Duara, P., 267, 327

Dublin Convention, 105

Eighteen Lords temple, 217–18

El Hadj Onmar Tell, 89

Eni, Emmanuel, 165

ethnic identity, 18, 19, 21, 22, 28; nationalism and, 19–21, 38; in USSR, 26